VALE OF HUMILITY

VALE OF HUMILITY

Plain Folk in Contemporary North Carolina Fiction

An Approach to the Works of

DORIS BETTS

REYNOLDS PRICE

FRED CHAPPELL

LEE SMITH

CLYDE EDGERTON

RANDALL KENAN

GEORGE HOVIS

The University of South Carolina Press

© 2007 University of South Carolina

Published by the University of South Carolina Press
Columbia, South Carolina 29208

www.sc.edu/uscpress

Manufactured in the United States of America

16 15 14 13 12 11 10 09 08 07   10 9 8 7 6 5 4 3 2 1

Library of Congress Cataloging-in-Publication Data

Hovis, George.
    Vale of humility : plain folk in contemporary North Carolina fiction / George Hovis.
    p. cm.
    Includes bibliographical references and index.
    ISBN-13: 978-1-57003-696-5 (alk. paper)
    ISBN-10: 1-57003-696-9 (alk. paper)
    1. American fiction—North Carolina—History and criticism. 2. American fiction—20th century—History and criticism. 3. Characters and characteristics in literature. 4. North Carolina in literature. I. Title.
    PS266.N8H68 2007
    813'.540932756—dc22

                                                                                    2007007322

Grateful acknowledgment is made to the following for permission to reprint previously published material: Excerpts from *Walking on Water*, by Randall Kenan, © 1999 by Randall Kenan, used by permission of Alfred A. Knopf, a division of Random House, Inc. Excerpts from *The Floatplane Notebooks*, by Clyde Edgerton, © 1988 by Clyde Edgerton, reprinted by permission of Algonquin Books of Chapel Hill. Excerpts from *In Memory of Junior*, by Clyde Edgerton, © 1992 by Clyde Edgerton, reprinted by permission of Algonquin Books of Chapel Hill. Excerpts from *Raney*, by Clyde Edgerton, © 1985 by Clyde Edgerton, reprinted by permission of Algonquin Books of Chapel Hill. Excerpts from *Fair and Tender Ladies*, by Lee Smith, © 1988 by Lee Smith, used by permission of G. P. Putnam's Sons, a division of Penguin Group (USA) Inc. Excerpts from *Oral History*, by Lee Smith, © 1983 by Lee Smith, used by permission of G. P. Putnam's Sons, a division of Penguin Group (USA) Inc. Excerpts from *A Visitation of Spirits*, by Randall Kenan, © 1989 by Randall Kenan, used by permission of Grove/Atlantic, Inc. Excerpts from "Assuming the Mantle of Storyteller: Fred Chappell and Frontier Humor," by George Hovis, reprinted by permission of Louisiana State University Press from *The Enduring Legacy of Old Southwest Humor*, edited by Ed Piacentino, © 2006 by Louisiana State University Press. Excerpts from "Darker Vices and Nearly Incomprehensible Sins: The Fate of Poe in Fred Chappell's Early Novels," by George Hovis, reprinted by permission of Louisiana State University Press from *More Lights Than One: On the Fiction of Fred Chappell*, edited by Patrick Bizzaro, © 2004 by Louisiana State University Press. Excerpts from *Midquest: A Poem*, by Fred Chappell, reprinted by permission of Louisiana State University Press, © 1981 by Fred Chappell. Excerpts from "'When You Got True Dirt You Got Everything You Need': Forging an Appalachian Arcadia in Fred Chappell's *Midquest*," by George Hovis. Originally published in *Mississippi Quarterly* 53 (Summer 2000), reprinted with permission. Excerpts from *Clear Pictures*, by Reynolds Price, reprinted with the permission of Scribner, an imprint of Simon & Schuster Adult Publishing Group, © 1988, 1989 by Reynolds Price. Excerpts from *The Surface of Earth*, by Reynolds Price, reprinted with the permission of Scribner, an imprint of Simon & Schuster Adult Publishing Group, © 1973, 1974, 1975 by Reynolds Price. Excerpts and adaptations from "'I Contain Multitudes': Randall Kenan's *Walking on Water* as Collective Autobiography," by George Hovis, © 2004 by the *Southern Literary Journal* and the University of North Carolina at Chapel Hill Department of English, reprinted with permission. Excerpts from "The Legacy of Thomas Wolfe in Contemporary North Carolina Fiction," by George Hovis, originally published in the *Thomas Wolfe Review* 29 (2005), reprinted with permission.

This book was printed on Glatfelter Natures, a recycled paper with 50 percent postconsumer waste content.

For my parents, Ray Wilbur Hovis and Rebecca Rowena Rhyne Hovis

CONTENTS

PREFACE

In the past several decades, historians have provided a wealth of information about the previously ignored figure of the yeoman farmer and about other plain folk of the South. Treatments of the yeoman in southern literature have been significantly less forthcoming. This study hopes to fill that gap by focusing on the prevalence of plain folk in contemporary North Carolina fiction, with special emphasis given to the yeoman as a cultural icon. Six representative writers from the state's three geographic regions are treated. They include, in order of first major publications, Doris Betts, Reynolds Price, Fred Chappell, Lee Smith, Clyde Edgerton, and Randall Kenan. Their work is investigated within relevant literary traditions with particular focus on the ways that these North Carolina writers have revised such southern modes as pastoral, family saga, and frontier humor in order to portray their own specific regional experience.

I would like to acknowledge the assistance and support of those people who helped to make this book possible. Fred Hobson at the University of North Carolina at Chapel Hill provided guidance from the project's inception. Joseph M. Flora, Julius Rowan Raper, Townsend Ludington, and Kimball King helped to shape my vision of the project, as did Harry L. Watson and the Southern Research Circle at Chapel Hill, as well as the members of the Dead Mule Gang: Farrell O'Gorman, Douglas Mitchell, and Collin Messer. Peter Murphy provided critical advice during the project's later stage. Thanks to Robert Anthony, Alice Cotten, and the other staff of the North Carolina Collection at Wilson Library at the University of North Carolina. I am grateful to Doris Betts, Fred Chappell, Clyde Edgerton, Randall Kenan, Dale Ray Phillips, Reynolds Price, Louis D. Rubin, Jr., and Lee Smith for graciously granting interviews and otherwise responding to my queries about their work. My research was facilitated by grants and fellowships from the Center for the Study of the American South and the Department of English at the University of North Carolina, the Thomas Wolfe Society, the College of Humanities and Fine Arts at Murray State University, and the Office of the Provost at the State University of New York at Oneonta. Thanks, finally, go to my wife, Kim Jastremski, who read multiple drafts of the manuscript, assisted with the preparation of endnotes, bibliography, and index, and lent sustained emotional support.

INTRODUCTION

Plain Folk and the Yeoman Ideal in
Contemporary North Carolina Fiction

Early in the twentieth century an expression entered the language of North Carolinians that came to characterize what many Tar Heels felt to be a fundamental distinction between themselves and their aristocratic neighbors in surrounding southern states. By comparing their own humble origins to the blue-blooded families in Virginia and South Carolina, North Carolinians thought of themselves as inhabiting "a vale of humility between two mountains of conceit." This phrase echoes the same antipathy for aristocratic privilege and pretense found in the state's motto adopted by the 1893 General Assembly: *esse quam videri*, "to be rather than to seem." North Carolina's history helps to explain this self-assessment. Compared to Virginia and South Carolina, as well as most of the Deep South and southern states along the eastern seaboard, North Carolina failed—largely as the result of unfavorable geography—to produce an antebellum economy based upon large plantations. Especially in the central and western portions of the state, North Carolina's planters were vastly outnumbered by yeoman farmers or small landowners, who remained, well into the twentieth century, the most populous group in the state. Together with landless farmers and nonagricultural wage earners, the yeomen constituted the "plain folk."

Not surprisingly, such a class identity informed North Carolina's literature very early on. In fact, William Powell finds that the image of the state as a "vale of humility" originated in an address entitled "The Native Literature of North Carolina" delivered to the Mecklenburg Historical Society on March 6, 1900, by Mrs. Mary Oates Spratt Van Landingham. Mrs. Van Landingham declared, "Where there are mountains of conceit, there are apt to be valleys of humility."[1] Her statement gains increasing resonance when the date of its first utterance is considered. At the turn of the twentieth century, southern letters were dominated by the genteel tradition of moonlight and magnolias. Southerners—especially southern planters—were still suffering from the economic devastation of the Civil War, but, at the same time, writers such as Virginia's Thomas Nelson Page were busy spinning out nostalgic myths of a grand Old South, peopled by noble planters and their loyal servants.

Whereas this cavalier myth had decades earlier superseded the Jeffersonian ideal of a yeoman republic throughout most regions of the interior South,[2] in North Carolina Jefferson's ideal of independent yeomen working small farms remained the reality or the goal for the vast majority of North Carolinians into the twentieth century—even though, during the latter half of the nineteenth century, capitalization of agriculture had made deep inroads into farm ownership, increasing the rate of tenancy and giving rise to the rapidly expanding industries that would soon overtake farming as the base of the economy throughout the Piedmont. During the twentieth century the state's economy underwent increasingly rapid change, until most small farms were superseded: in the Piedmont, first by textiles, tobacco, and furniture and then by banking and a variety of light and technology-driven industries; down east, by corporate farming; and in the mountains, by the exploitation of timber and mineral resources, followed by a boom in tourism. In the latter half of the twentieth century, North Carolina climbed from forty-seventh of forty-eight states in per capita income to thirty-first of fifty, and in the 1990s was ranked by *Fortune Magazine* as first in probusiness climate, while Raleigh-Durham was listed by *Money Magazine* as having the highest quality of life in the South.[3] In half a century, North Carolina transformed itself from a "vale of humility" into the buckle of the Sun Belt. Many of the state's writers who emerged during this period have responded to the cultural transformations that have accompanied economic progress. The state's current burgeoning literary activity derives from a pastoral impulse, from an interest—on behalf of both writers and readers—in preserving the yeoman's culture in collective memory.

If during the spring of 1998 there was anyone unaware of the literary renaissance taking place in North Carolina, they certainly would have been enlightened at the state's first semiannual literary festival, held on the campus of the University of North Carolina at Chapel Hill. Over the course of that weekend, thousands of readers swarmed the quads and packed into classrooms and auditoriums to hear dozens of writers, most of them hailing from the Tar Heel state. Although North Carolina writers had reached a national audience throughout the twentieth century, never had they done so in such numbers as during the period beginning around the early 1980s. Since that time, the state's writers have won nearly every major literary award available, including (to name a few) the National Book Award, the National Book Critics Circle Award, the Bollingen Prize in Poetry, the Sue Kaufman Prize, numerous listings among the *New York Times* Notable Books, and frequent inclusion in annual anthologies such as *Best American Short Stories* and *New Stories from the South*. In addition to such critical acclaim, North Carolina writers have enjoyed a great degree of popular success, with several novels adopted by Oprah Winfrey's Book Club and numerous novels adapted to motion picture and television. Within the past two decades, North Carolina has been home to more writers of national stature than perhaps any other southern state, with the possible exception of Mississippi.

Recognition of this Tar Heel literary renaissance has also been forthcoming from within the state. In the past ten years, the University of North Carolina Press published two anthologies of stories by forty-seven contemporary Tar Heel writers—*The Rough Road Home* (1992), edited by Robert Gingher, and *This Is Where We Live* (2001), edited by Michael McFee—as well as an anthology of work by fifteen contemporary North Carolina poets, *The Language They Speak Is Things To Eat* (1995), also edited by McFee. Major literary festivals have appeared throughout the state, and in 1993 the North Carolina legislature established funding for the state's Literary Hall of Fame, with its first members inducted in 1996.[4] Numerous practical factors have helped foster North Carolina's current literary renaissance: the presence of several prestigious university creative-writing programs, numerous fine literary journals and several new publishing houses, state-level awards and events recognizing literary achievement, the establishment of a thriving writers' network in 1985, and supportive communities of writers in centers such as Hillsborough / Chapel Hill, Greensboro, Asheville, and Wilmington.[5] Perhaps the single-most important event was Louis D. Rubin's establishment, in 1983, of Algonquin Books of Chapel Hill. Algonquin has launched the careers of North Carolina writers such as Clyde Edgerton, Kaye Gibbons, and Jill McCorkle, promoted the careers of other established writers, including Robert Morgan and Lee Smith, and brought increased attention to Chapel Hill and the surrounding region as a haven of literary activity.

Rather than offering a survey of the many talented contemporary writers from North Carolina,[6] this study thoroughly examines the work of six representative writers: Doris Betts, Reynolds Price, Fred Chappell, Lee Smith, Clyde Edgerton, and Randall Kenan. These writers are contemporary in that they are all currently producing important work, even though Betts's first book-length publication came in 1954, while her student Randall Kenan's first novel appeared as recently as 1989. With the exception of Lee Smith, each of these writers is a native of the state. Smith's "nonnative" status has been overlooked, because she has made North Carolina home for most of her writing and teaching career (since 1974) and because of her interest in the experience of plain folk in the Virginia mountains, a region that culturally resembles Appalachian North Carolina in many ways. Although the emphasis of this study is upon contemporary fiction, several works of nonfiction and poetry are discussed, given the extent to which they provide a more complete understanding of their respective authors' engagement of the plain folk.

The work of these six writers is examined within the broader southern literary tradition, with attention to how they have revised such modes as pastoral, family saga, and frontier humor, in order to portray their own specific regional experience. More specifically, these six writers address the class experience of most North Carolinians throughout the past three centuries. This class experience, based in an identification of the small farm, rather than the plantation, as an ideal life, distinguished North Carolinians from many people throughout the South and, not surprisingly, has been a distinguishing feature of North Carolina literature.

Though yeoman farmers, in fact, predominated throughout most regions of the Old South,[7] the cotton boom of the early nineteenth century gave rise to a new prominent planter elite throughout the interior South, an elite to which yeomen aspired. Ritchie Devon Watson has written insightfully about the ways that this newfound economic prosperity was accompanied by the emergence of a cavalier mythology. Even though these farmers were "one or two generations removed from the frontier," southerners for whom a "unifying cultural icon might have been the yeoman, celebrated earlier in the century," Watson argues that "a profound mythic shift" took place "in the interior South during the opening decades of the nineteenth century."[8] As they sought to identify themselves culturally with the older plantation states of the eastern seaboard, most notably Virginia, the ideal of the aristocrat "became the dream of most southern farmers."[9] According to Watson, this mythic shift constituted a shift away from the democratic republicanism inherent in the yeoman ideal to an aristocratic ideal, "with its fundamental assumption of the inequality of man reflected in the inequality of social condition."[10] Arguably, many contemporary plain-folk writers from the Deep South have inherited this same mythology, a mythology they often self-consciously repudiate and sometimes, through their grotesque depictions of poor whites, unconsciously promulgate.

Because a planter elite was significantly less prominent and wealthy in North Carolina than in the Deep South—a difference most pronounced when considering North Carolina's Piedmont and mountains—the plain folk did not develop a class identity based as deeply in relation to elite planters. Paul D. Escott convincingly argues that, although North Carolina's gentry possessed considerably less wealth and cultural refinement than planters in the large Tidewater regions of neighboring Virginia and South Carolina, they nevertheless composed a decidedly elite class, which successfully promoted its own economic interests in state and local politics for two centuries. North Carolina, Escott claims, was both "humble *and* aristocratic."[11] Contrary to Frank Owsley's view of yeomen and planters sharing a common culture and social world, Escott, like Bill Cecil-Fronsman, identifies clear class distinctions between

North Carolina planters and the yeomen and landless whites who comprised the vast majority of the white population. Furthermore, instead of deferring to the paternalistic leadership of the planter class, both scholars study the ways that common whites challenged planter hegemony. In stark contrast to Faulkner's vision in *Absalom, Absalom!* of the poor white Thomas Sutpen, whose impoverished vision of himself and his poor white class eventuates his attempt to make himself over in the image of the wealthy Virginia planter, Escott and Cecil-Fronsman discover proud and independent populations of common whites. Escott notes, for example, that North Carolina's yeomen were "a self-directed, stubborn, and independent group. . . . The yeomen were not bent on dominance over others, but they proved to be always ready to defend themselves."[12]

Cecil-Fronsman focuses primarily on North Carolina's landless whites, who, like the yeomen, he concludes, "fought for equal political rights" and "objected to the planter class's presumed social superiority."[13] In support of his argument that yeomen and landless whites should be grouped together in a common class, which he terms "common whites," Cecil-Fronsman concludes, "However different in character poor white trash and prosperous yeomen may have been, they (along with the other nonelite groups) had enough in common that it seems reasonable to use a single term to describe them."[14] Scholars of North Carolina history—including Escott, Cecil-Fronsman, and Robert Kenzer—disagree about the extent of class consciousness among the state's plain whites, just as they disagree about where class boundaries should be drawn and what terminology ought to be used to apply to the various groups. Nevertheless, these scholars are in agreement that North Carolina's plain whites developed their own independent, proud communities, which, though economically threatened by an elite class, consistently challenged the aristocratic basis of that group's privilege.

Another point on which most scholars agree is the pervasiveness of racism among whites of all classes in the state—a racism that resembled not only that of white southerners but also white Americans of the period.[15] North Carolina's African Americans have a long history of struggling against oppression and pursuing their own freedom and equality. During the late eighteenth and early nineteenth centuries, slave uprisings were frequent throughout the eastern portion of the state. Some of the most important literature of the abolitionist movement was produced by former slaves from North Carolina. During the latter nineteenth century, blacks sought political representation and resisted oppression in the form of disenfranchisement and the rise of the Ku Klux Klan. Black North Carolinians were involved in seminal efforts of the civil rights movement; 1960 saw two major events: the Greensboro sit-ins that sparked similar activism elsewhere in the South and the formation in Raleigh of the Student Nonviolent Coordinating Committee (SNCC), which became a major advocate for civil rights throughout the region.[16] The black farmer played a major role in fostering the desire and capacity for autonomy among North Carolina blacks. John Hope Franklin reports that free blacks in North Carolina during the antebellum period more than doubled the number of free blacks in any state farther south and that, unlike free blacks elsewhere in the South, in North Carolina they lived not in cities but in rural areas as agriculturalists.[17] After emancipation, most blacks, like most whites, identified ownership of a small farm as an ideal, and for many of them it became an achievable goal. Although the rate of tenancy was higher among black farmers than whites, in the final decades of the nineteenth century tenancy was actually decreasing among blacks while it was increasing among whites.[18]

In addition to North Carolina's lack of a cultivated, prominent gentry—relative to other southern states—the absence of an enduring gentrified literary tradition has left its mark on the state's contemporary writers. Unlike the self-identified *poor white* writers of the Deep South—writers such as Rick Bragg, Harry Crews, Dorothy Allison, and Larry Brown—who are perhaps consciously reacting to a long tradition of gentrification not only in southern society, but also in southern belles lettres, and therefore wear their lower-class status as a badge of honor, in North Carolina no tradition of gentrified letters exists for contemporary writers to supersede. Instead, nearly all of the major writers in the state's literary history are representatives of the plain folk, and often they were staunch partisans.

The most obvious example of this tendency is Thomas Wolfe, the writer whom North Carolinians most celebrate. Robert Morgan, a contemporary poet and fiction writer from western North Carolina, has said, "I am often asked why there are so many important writers from North Carolina. . . . My short answer is: Thomas Wolfe. Once Wolfe achieved such great fame in the 1930s, other young North Carolinians got the idea that writing was an opportunity, a real possibility. The same is probably true of Faulkner and Mississippi."[19] Morgan's comparison of Wolfe with Faulkner is instructive, especially as it relates to the image of a writer that subsequent generations of would-be writers in North Carolina and Mississippi have, respectively, inherited. Although the Nobel Laureate from the Deep South wrote accurately and insightfully about the various social classes present in northern Mississippi, including the yeomen, he has himself most often been associated with the fading aristocrats of his fiction: the Compsons, Sartorises, and McCaslins. By contrast, Wolfe is closely identified with his highly autobiographical protagonist, Eugene Gant. Like Eugene's parents, Wolfe's father was a stonecutter and his mother operated the boarding house where Tom grew up. The contrast between Wolfe's Old Kentucky Home and Faulkner's pillared Rowan Oak is itself telling, as is the contrast between the fictional version of Wolfe's home, Dixieland, and the numerous grand mansions that haunt Faulkner's novels.

This contrast between Wolfe and Faulkner as plain folk and genteel writer can be extended to a comparison of Wolfe and southern writers, in general, during the first half of the twentieth century. In a 1982 essay, Louis D. Rubin, Jr., points out that, because of his class identity, Wolfe did not "appear to belong to the club" of southern writers. Most of the prominent southern writers from the 1920s through the 1940s, Rubin observes, "were of the gentry, or perhaps the upper middle class would be a better way of describing it; in any event, 'of good family' as the expression went (which as I think Ellen Glasgow once pointed out was to say something very different from they were 'of good people'—i.e., of the rural working or lower middle class, the so-called 'yeomanry')."[20] Rubin makes clear that southern writers were not true blue-blooded aristocrats who "grew up in stately Tidewater mansions."[21] Nevertheless, he asserts that "the 'Big House' and the southern gentlemen were involved in the southern ideal, and almost every one of the twentieth-century southern writers has at one point in his or her work (often at frequent points) presented, with more than a little approval, characters who look down disdainfully upon the 'trash' and the 'riff-raff' without 'family'—i.e., without approved social connections."[22] Not only did Thomas Wolfe hail from a working-class family and grow up in a boarding house, but he also made a point of his yeoman background, in both his fiction and his interactions with other writers, to whom he liked to boast "that because of his origins he was honest and open and democratic and genuine, while those who weren't from similar origins were snobbish and defensive and aristocratic and full of pretense."[23] Many of the best writers of the Southern Renascence wrote convincingly *about* the yeomanry—especially Faulkner, Eudora Welty, Flannery O'Connor, John Crowe Ransom, and Ellen Glasgow, though none of them identified *themselves* as closely with the yeomanry as did Wolfe.

Before turning to fiction and publishing the phenomenally successful *Look Homeward Angel* (1929), Wolfe aspired to a career as a playwright, a dream that was fostered by his participation in the newly formed Carolina Playmakers at the University of North Carolina. Frederick Koch founded the group in 1918 after developing similar efforts in folk drama in North Dakota. Of the plays written and performed by his students, Koch observed, "They are pioneer plays of North Carolina life. The stories and characters are drawn by the writers from their own tradition, and from their observation of the lives of their own people."[24] This early training among the Carolina Playmakers, observing the lives of North Carolina plain folk, was no doubt formative for Wolfe, as it was for his friend Paul Green, by far the most successful dramatist to emerge from the group.

Like Wolfe, Green was born into a yeoman family, though in Harnett County, which lies along the dividing line between Piedmont and coastal plain. He is best known for *In Abraham's Bosom* (1926), winner of the Pulitzer Prize, his dramatic adaptation of Richard Wright's *Native Son* (1941), and his numerous outdoor "symphonic dramas," which chronicle episodes in the region's history and are patriotic in spirit. The first and most successful of these, *The Lost Colony*, is still produced every summer on Roanoke Island. It tells the story of Sir Walter Raleigh's failed attempt to establish a British colony along what is now the North Carolina shore. As Laurence Avery notes, however, unlike his historical counterpart, the Raleigh of Green's play "is motivated by the dream of founding a democratic society."[25] In contrast to the rigid social castes of the Old World—and its counterpart in the plantation South—Green imagines in *The Lost Colony* a republican spirit taking shape among those early settlers, who serve to anticipate the egalitarian spirit of the yeomen that would successfully colonize the Tar Heel state in the following centuries. Green's plays reflect his avid interest in the folklore of North Carolina plain folk—both white and black—as does his *Wordbook* (1990), in which he spent a lifetime cataloguing folk expressions and cultural practices.

According to Vincent Kenny, during the late 1920s Green was ranked "second only to O'Neill among American playwrights."[26] Despite international acclaim, like Wolfe, Green did not quite belong to the club of southern literati comprised of genteel writers. For example, according to Thomas Underwood's recent biography of Allen Tate—the Fugitive/Agrarian from Nashville, who might be characterized as the dean of southern letters during the 1930s—Tate referred to Green condescendingly as "a good Carliny country boy"[27] and, worse, as "North Carolina poor white trash."[28] Even Andrew Lytle, whose contribution to the Agrarian manifesto idealizes life on the subsistence farm, said of Green, "He looks like the kind of man that would burn your barn."[29] By associating Green's yeoman background with his home state, Tate betrays a genteel prejudice toward North Carolina. Furthermore, he demonstrates a tendency to conflate *plain* whites with "poor white trash," an oversight not uncommon among gentility.

Looking back to North Carolina's literature during the nineteenth century, the work of most lasting significance was produced by African American writers, who, either as former slaves or the descendants of slaves, championed freedom and democracy for all people and articulated an impassioned critique of the economic system that supported the planter class. At the age of eight, Charles Chesnutt moved with his family from Cleveland, Ohio, to Fayetteville,

North Carolina, where they had deep ancestral ties.[30] His most celebrated work, *The Conjure Woman* (1899), is a novel in stories, which parodies the genteel local-color tales of the Virginia aristocrat Thomas Nelson Page. With *The Hope of Liberty* (1829), George Moses Horton, the "black bard" from Northampton County, became the first southern black to publish a book of poems. A number of African American writers from North Carolina were significant figures in the abolitionist movement, including David Walker, born free in Wilmington around 1796. William Andrews identifies Walker's *Appeal to the Colored Citizens of the World* (1829) as "the most influential African American pamphlet of the antebellum era."[31] Walker's *Appeal*—along with the groundbreaking slave narratives of Moses Roper, Lunsford Lane, Moses Grandy, and Thomas H. Jones—helped propel the abolitionist movement and bring the horrors of slavery to national and international audiences. The best-known slave narrative from North Carolina was Harriet Jacobs's *Incidents in the Life of a Slave Girl* (1861), which fully dramatizes the psychological horrors of the female slave's sexual exploitation in a way that slave narratives by male writers can only suggest.

One of the most historically significant antebellum publications by a white North Carolinian also took the form of an attack on the institution of slavery, although its objective was not the emancipation of slaves but the economic betterment of white yeomen throughout the South. In 1857, Hinton Rowan Helper, from the western Piedmont, published *The Impending Crisis of the South*, in which he blames slavery (and, thus, the aristocracy) for all of the South's economic shortcomings. The book was relatively ignored until 1860, when the antislavery Republican Party adopted an emended version of the book for its national campaign, resulting in Helper's effective banishment from his home state and from the rest of the South. Helper would later earn the unusual distinction of being both an abolitionist and a racist, when in a series of virulently racist publications he turned his scorn from southern slaveholders toward the descendants of slaves, since, as Fred Hobson points out, he then believed that it was "the freedmen who most threatened the poor white."[32] Although Helper was denounced, even during his time, as a "madman," "unbalanced and unfit,"[33] his ideas about race and class were not atypical among southern plain whites, demonstrated not only by the rise of race-bating demagogues who championed plain and poor whites, but also by the sensational popular success of racist publications. One of the most notorious and most successful of such publications was *The Clansman* (1905), by another writer from the North Carolina Piedmont, Thomas Dixon, of Cleveland County. *The Clansman* depicts freed blacks as lustful, villainous beasts and members of the Ku Klux Klan as the valiant heroes of a nation newly reunited after the Civil

War. D. W. Griffith's film adaptation, *The Birth of a Nation*, became a nation-wide sensation and held attendance records for twenty-five years, until the re-lease of *Gone with the Wind* in 1939.[34]

To counter the savage South of *The Clansman*, Dixon's contemporary and fellow Watauga Club member, Walter Hines Page, of Cary, North Carolina, was a progressive journalist who labeled as "Mummies" those southerners who stood in the way of education reforms necessary to elevate the New South out of its cultural and economic stagnation. Page anticipated the Tar Heel social reform-ers of the 1920s and 1930s, a group of journalists, sociologists, and writers, many of them associated with the University of North Carolina at Chapel Hill, who were not afraid to study honestly and objectively the problems in con-temporary southern society, rather than glorifying the myth of a genteel past. Prominent among this group were Gerald Johnson, whom H. L. Mencken praised as "the best editorial writer in the South,"[35] and Howard Odum, who came to Chapel Hill to chair the university's first Department of Sociology and found the Institute for Research in Social Science and the *Journal of Social Forces*.

The social critic from North Carolina to make the most profound and lasting statement about the South, especially his own Piedmont South, was Wilbur Joseph Cash, who grew up in Thomas Dixon's Cleveland County and, like Dixon, attended the Baptist institution Wake Forest College. However, rather than serving as an apologist for the South, Cash became one of its harsh-est and most insightful critics. In *The Mind of the South* (1941), Cash undercut the myth of the Old South by convincingly portraying antebellum southern gentlemen as nouveau riche yeoman farmers, rather than a true blood aristoc-racy. Far from serving as an apologist for the yeoman, Cash echoed the criti-cism of Mencken, castigating his society as culturally and intellectually barren. Cash attributed this cultural sterility to a "savage ideal," or an epidemic resis-tance to free thought and expression, a problem that he traced to the South's defense of slavery and its continuing racism.

In the tradition of the state's best writers, contemporary North Carolina writers are not uncritical of pervasive social problems, both current and his-torical. Among the issues they investigate are slavery and its legacy of racism, patriarchy and gender inequality, narrow-minded religiosity, materialism, and cultural insularity, which is often seen to produce family and community rela-tions that stifle personal independence. The tension between independence and interdependence inherent in yeoman farm life receives ample attention from most of these writers. Despite the importance of social criticism to most of their work, however, some identification of positive cultural values must underlie their critiques. By comparison many scholars have observed how

Faulkner's critique of a degenerating aristocracy and a rapacious rising lower class of Snopeses was based upon values he associated (if not exclusively so) with the noblesse oblige that had characterized earlier generations of gentry. Although these values may often be difficult to discern in his darker work, he articulated them clearly in his Nobel Prize address as "love and honor and pity and pride and compassion and sacrifice."[36] Similarly North Carolina writers tend to identify—if only implicitly so, and very often explicitly—a set of values associated with the plain folk, and primarily with the yeoman farmer.

This study of the state's contemporary fiction includes a consideration of the various groups that have comprised North Carolina's plain folk—including tenant farmers and sharecroppers (often referred to collectively as "tenant farmers"), as well as mill hands. The yeoman farmer, however, occupies a central place, just as he did throughout most of the state's history. Well into the twentieth century the yeoman was by far the most populous group in the state. Even when the rate of tenancy increased beyond 40 percent of the agricultural population in the early twentieth century, ownership of a small farm remained the goal for most North Carolinians, including many mill workers who aspired to earn sufficient capital to purchase their own farms and return to an agrarian life. And, even after extensive cultivation of cash crops severely reduced the viability of the yeoman farm, there was a pervasive awareness throughout the state of the need of farmers to replace their dependence on the market economy with a return to subsistence farming, as exemplified by the "Live-at-Home" movement of the 1920s and 1930s.[37] Just as these early twentieth-century farmers sought to emulate the economic independence and simple lifestyle of the subsistence farmer, who had predominated from the state's colonial period until at least the Civil War, contemporary writers have likewise looked back to the yeoman farmer and his community as a source of values that have been eroded by modernity.

A systematic articulation of "yeoman values" is problematized by the lack of primary sources. In contrast to planters, yeomen tended not to leave diaries, collections of letters, or other personal records of their lives. In 1996, after twenty years of searching, Paul Escott admits finding a total of only six diaries by antebellum yeomen.[38] In his 1949 landmark study, *Plain Folk of the Old South*, Frank Owsley compares to "archaeology" the task of cultural recovery of the plain folk and declares that his study might have been entitled "The Forgotten Man of the Old South."[39] More is known even about the experience of slaves, thanks to the wealth of nineteenth-century autobiographies and twentieth-century WPA interviews. Most of what we do know about plain folk of the nineteenth century is made available through a quantitative analysis of census records, tax reports, marriage certificates, wills, and other legal documents. In the absence of their own testimonies, we must rely heavily on what has been said *about* them—by their contemporary observes, recent historians, and by their descendants who have chronicled their lives in the form of belles lettres. Although the yeomen and other southern plain folk have increasingly received attention from historians during the past several decades, relatively little scholarly attention has been given to the figure of the yeoman in southern literature.[40] This study hopes to help remedy that silence by a comparison of historical and contemporary literary treatments of North Carolina's plain folk.

The earliest information on North Carolina's plain folk comes from frequently disparaging accounts made by outside observers. For example, in his histories of the Dividing Line Expedition of 1728, the aristocratic Virginian William Byrd II provided an insulting account of the unrefined and socially backward North Carolina "lubbers," whom he consistently depicts as lacking any instinct for self-improvement. More than a century later, Frederick Law Olmsted, born into a patrician family in Hartford, Connecticut, offered a similarly scathing account. In *A Journey in the Seaboard Slave States* (1856), he observes that "North Carolina has a proverbial reputation for the ignorance and torpidity of her people," traits that Olmsted attributes to the state's poor soil, inadequate transportation, the isolation of its farms, and the lack of education.[41] In a work that launches consistently unrestrained attacks on southerners, Olmsted's indictment of North Carolinians stands out.

More recent historians have also depicted North Carolina as lagging behind other southern states socially and economically from colonial times until the twentieth century. David Bertelson describes colonial North Carolina as a land almost totally lacking social organization beyond the level of the individual family farm. "In contrast to the other southern colonies," he notes, "North Carolina represented not so much the disintegration and failure of a sense of community and of social vision as the almost total absence of both. . . . The colony for many years had essentially an isolated small farm economy although there were some plantations."[42] According to historian William Powell, post-Revolutionary North Carolina had not changed much from its colonial days and, as a result, was nicknamed "Rip Van Winkle," "a state asleep," cut off from the outside world, indifferent to progress, resistant to improvements in education and infrastructure that would be imposed by a meddlesome state government.[43] An 1860 census shows that 97.5 percent of the population was rural.[44] There were 85,000 farmers in the state, and less than a third of them owned slaves. In the Piedmont, of the slave-owning minority of farmers, one in fifty was considered a "planter," owning twenty or more slaves. Down east there were larger farms, larger slave holdings, commerce, and political power. Here, one in twenty slaveowners was a planter, though, of the 300 southern planters who owned 300 or more slaves and were thus considered millionaires, only four lived in North Carolina.[45]

The lack of a flourishing plantation system in North Carolina was largely owing to an accident in geography—treacherous coastal waters and the lack of navigable rivers, as well as unfavorable soils and climate throughout the extensive Piedmont.[46] Historians disagree about the trajectory slavery might have taken in North Carolina had the South not seceded.[47] In 1861, however, North Carolina was sufficiently ambivalent about allegiance with the Confederacy that it was the last state of the Confederacy to secede, remaining in the Union until secession seemed inevitable. According to William C. Harris, North Carolinians were openly bitter about South Carolina's disruption of the Union, seeing its act of secession—as most northerners likely did—as the rash and arrogant act of a state controlled by aristocratic interests.[48] When North Carolina finally did secede, it did so not "because of any real sense of southern nationalism" but because it felt its security "endangered by a tyrannical northern regime."[49]

Why nonslaveholding farmers supported the planters' cause throughout the South by joining the war effort is a question that still preoccupies scholars. Among others, both George M. Frederickson and W. J. Cash have argued that nonslaveowners supported slavery as a way of demonstrating the racial inferiority of blacks and thereby demonstrating the racially based superiority of *all* whites, independent of social class. Both Harry Watson and Eugene Genovese find this explanation incomplete and argue that one of the most important factors promoting the uneasy alliance between yeomen and planters was their mutual opposition to outside forces that would impose unwanted capital development and corresponding taxation. Genovese notes that, despite the upcountry yeomen's hatred for "the pretensions of the black-belt planters," the small farmers nevertheless "benefited from and reinforced the slaveholders' commitment to state rights—or rather to opposition to the centralization of political power."[50]

Because yeoman farms were characterized by diversified crops intended primarily for subsistence, with labor performed by the family and perhaps a few slaves, yeomen stood less to gain from thorough integration into a market economy than did planters, who produced primarily staples crops, such as cotton, tobacco, rice, and sugar.[51] Aware of the vicissitudes of the market, yeomen tended to avoid the financial risk of dependence on staple crops, pursuing a course of "safety first."[52] "They owned their own capital," says Harry Watson, "owed very little money, and supported themselves by their own labor. Subjection to others could only present itself as a profound threat to personal well-being, so a passionate commitment to 'liberty' was a crucial product of the yeoman experience."[53] Watson finds in the southern yeoman's isolation from the market economy a point of contrast with the northern yeoman, whom "the free labor economy offered innumerable opportunities" when he "wearied of self-sufficiency."[54] Investigating the participation of yeomen women in both domestic and market economies, Stephanie McCurry observes that "none of the products of yeoman households was definitively a subsistence or a market crop," since produce, dairy products, grain, and even cotton—which could be converted to finished products for domestic use—might be consumed by the farming family or sold as surplus.[55]

Relative exclusion from a market economy produced interdependence among small farmers, both within families and throughout communities. Steven Hahn has investigated the development of networks of mutual obligations within rural communities that depended upon a barter system, rather than cash exchange.[56] Owsley has also written about the pervasiveness throughout the South of "swapping work." As Owsley explains, when a farmer had "fully hoed and plowed all his fields, and had several days of idleness in prospect, he and his sons—and his slaves if he had a few—would ofttimes go into a neighbor's fields and 'catch him up with his work' as the phrase went. Later, when needed, this work would be repaid. This was putting not money, but work in the bank to be drawn on when it was required."[57] In his introduction to the diary of North Carolina yeoman Basil Armstrong Thomasson, Escott notes how the diary "makes clear that he lived in a practically cashless economy."[58] The absence of cash did not mean that farmers were oblivious to cash; in fact, as this North Carolina yeoman's diary demonstrates, farmers who swapped resources of goods or labor often did so by attributing to each exchange of goods and services a cash value in the form of a note, which they frequently also repaid and collected in goods and services of a commensurate cash value. This form of barter was more flexible in terms and schedule of repayment than was typically available from banks and merchants. By allowing them to remain relatively independent from creditors, such neighborhood barter systems involved farmers in networks of interdependence with their rural neighbors.

In addition to their involvement in cooperative networks of goods and services with neighbors, small farmers were typically even more deeply interdependent with such networks within their own families. Thomasson's diary shows how extensively his own economic life (as well as his emotional life) was intertwined with that of his parents—long after he had established his own farm. Escott observes that the Thomasson family economy "functioned almost as a unit across two generations" and that the farms of Basil Thomasson and his father were "two parts of one connected enterprise. . . . Together the Thomasson men slaughtered hogs, hauled rails, mended fences, sheared sheep, washed wool, and sometimes helped one another in planting and cultivating their crops. The son also borrowed tools, draft animals, and pasture land from his father, compensating him with his own labor."[59] Owsley attributes not only the economic interdependence of an extended family but its emotional inter-dependence to the "rural environment of the Old South," which contributed to the relative isolation of kinship groups. These extended families "worked together, hunted together, went to church and parties together, and expected to be buried together and to come to judgment together on the Last Day."[60]

Ever since the settlement of frontier America, historians and contemporary observers have speculated about the values derived from the yeoman farming life. Despite his status as a wealthy planter, Thomas Jefferson so thoroughly idealized the yeoman that he based his model of the republic upon him. In particular, he praised the yeoman's freedom from market pressures that ensnared both planters and industrialists. In his *Notes on the State of Virginia* (1787), he asserts that the corruption of morals is "the mark set on those, who not looking up to heaven, to their own soil and industry, as does the husbandman, for their subsistence, depend for it on the casualties and caprice of customers. Dependence begets subservience and venality, suffocates the germ of virtue, and prepares fit tools for the designs of ambition."[61] This passage makes clear Jefferson's celebration of the yeoman's self-sufficiency, lack of ambition for social status, and virtue based on industry in the form of tilling of the soil. Indeed, Jefferson's deism leads him to wax rhapsodic on this latter point. "Those who labour in the earth," he maintains, "are the chosen people of God, if ever he had a chosen people, whose breasts he has made his peculiar deposit for substantial and genuine virtue."[62]

In *Letters from an American Farmer* (1782), J. Hector St. John de Crève-coeur based his promotion of American settlement upon the freedom, democracy, and autonomy of the yeoman farmer, whose relative absence he observed in his contemporary Europe. In contrast to European society, where he notes "hardly any other distinctions but lords and tenants," he praises America as a "fair country . . . settled by freeholders, the possessors of the soil they cultivate, members of the government they obey, and the framers of their own laws, by means of their representatives." Crèvecoeur was careful to distinguish the free-hold farmer from the first group of trappers, hunters, herders, and squatters who settled the frontier. In contrast to these first "vicious" frontiersmen, who "felled the first trees," he praises the yeomen as "the true American freeholders; the most respectable set of people in this part of the world: respectable for their industry, their happy independence, the great share of freedom they possess, the good regulation of their families and for extending the trade and the dominion of our mother country."[63]

Many contemporary scholars have continued to see the yeoman by similar lights—praising his industry, freedom, and self-sufficiency, and doing so in contrast to some other class of society. In *Success in America: The Yeoman Dream and the Industrial Revolution*, Rex Burns argues that the "yeoman dream" prevailed throughout America until the mid–nineteenth century, when the yeoman was superseded by the "self-made man" as a national cultural icon.[64] In contrast to the self-made man, whose success depended upon the acquisition of material wealth and fame, the yeoman achieved success by attaining "a competence, independence, and morality," which Burns defines as "wealth somewhat beyond one's basic needs, freedom from economic or statutory subservience, and the respect of the society for fruitful, honest industry."[65] Like Burns's dichotomy of the yeoman versus the self-made man of the Horatio Alger myth, Escott finds a similar distinction between the values of yeomen and those of planters. Escott observes that North Carolina yeoman Basil Thomasson "was not attracted by slaveholding society's love of wealth and aristocratic display"; instead he "was drawn . . . to ideals of progress, democracy, and Jeffersonian agrarianism."[66] This is consistent with Ritchie Devon Watson's distinction, finding accumulated wealth and social eminence to be of significantly greater importance to the planter's sense of self than to the yeoman's. Frank Owsley also asserts that "relatively few of the plain folk . . . seem to have had a desire to become wealthy. Their ambition was to acquire land and other property sufficient to give them and their children a sense of security and well-being, to be 'good livers' and 'have something saved for a rainy day' as they would have put it."[67] Owsley also frequently echoes Jefferson in lauding their connection to the soil. The southern plain folk's European forebears, Owsley points out, "had been yeomen and peasant farmers since before the dawn of recorded history. To them the land was, with God's blessings, the direct source of all the necessities of life and of all material riches."[68]

These representative sources reference the most common characteristics attributed to the yeoman: economic self-sufficiency and social autonomy based in subsistence agriculture; an independent spirit and love of liberty; industry and frugality aimed at securing this liberty; a connection to the earth through farm labor; an interdependence with family and community through cooperative labor; an economic system reliant upon swapping, borrowing, and bartering; egalitarianism, a humble lifestyle, and democratic rejection of social hierarchy based upon wealth; and, frequently, religious piety. Also frequently noted is the virtuous life associated with tilling the soil; as Jefferson asserts, this virtue is largely a product of the yeoman's innocence of the deleterious effects on character that accompany ownership of slaves and participation in market capitalism. Of course, the reality of yeoman participation—to varying extents—in market capitalism and the slave economy calls into question Jefferson's idealism. For many scholars—as for the contemporary writers treated in this study—of great interest are the contradictions between the ideals and realities of yeomanry. For example, these six writers address the ways that the independent rural farm sometimes produced an unhealthy cultural insularity; the extent to which egalitarianism among white yeomen did not extend to blacks; the degree to which patriarchal family structure restricted the freedom of women; the frequency with which yeomen and their descendants willingly abandoned subsistence farming in favor of the greater material wealth potentially available through participation in a market economy; and the ways that the interdependent family threatened personal independence.

Despite the shared identification of the yeoman as a cultural icon, the work of the six fiction writers examined in this volume offers differing perspectives on the plain folk of North Carolina, perspectives that are largely conditioned by their respective genders and ethnic identities. Class background also exerts an influence, because the families that appear in these writers' genealogies and fiction variously contain tenant farmers, mill hands and other nonagriculturalists, planters, and slaves—as well as yeomen, who are prominent in each case. Furthermore, these six writers hail from three distinct geographic regions: the mountains, the Piedmont, and the coastal plain, demonstrating how, even within the state, such geographic differences provide ample divergences of experience. Each of the writers considered in this study chronicles family histories that extend backward into the nineteenth century, and each writer meditates extensively on the positive and negative influences of inherited folkways, values, types of family relationships, and relationships between whites and blacks and between yeomen and members of other classes. These writers tend to make use of family history, however, to understand the present, rather than reversing the process. In that same spirit, the foregoing investigation of the yeoman's history should be considered not so much for its own sake but as a context that will allow a better understanding of North Carolina's contemporary literature.

Like her fellow Piedmont writer Clyde Edgerton, Doris Betts has inherited the spirit of sociological inquiry from the journalists and writers of the 1920s, 1930s, and 1940s, most notably from W. J. Cash, to whom Betts says her first novel was too thoroughly indebted.[69] Betts's *The River to Pickle Beach* (1972) and Edgerton's *Raney* (1985) critique the racism typical among whites of the Carolina Piedmont during the civil rights era. Both writers investigate the inherent contradiction between such pervasive racism and the spirit of egalitarianism they associate with yeoman heritage. Betts also combines the tradition of social criticism with its antithetical southern tradition of Christian literature. Like Flannery O'Connor and Walker Percy, she sees the modern consumer culture pervading the twentieth-century urban South as a threat to spiritual health and, like them, ultimately finds social critique alone insufficient to produce positive cultural change. Betts distinguishes herself from these Catholic writers of the lower South, however, in that she positively identifies the Christian values of her people with values derived from their yeoman heritage. In particular she views the spirit of egalitarianism integral to both, remarking that "Christianity taught democracy about equality of souls."[70] Although her Presbyterian theology is far from Jefferson's deism, like him she associates the agrarian lifestyle of the small farm with spiritual health and virtue.

Beyond the northeastern edge of the Piedmont, in Reynolds Price's Warren County, the landscape has not been as radically altered as it has been in Betts's mill towns or Edgerton's Durham County, now overwhelmed by the Research Triangle Park. Change has been slower to come, as well, to relations between the races in eastern North Carolina. Despite their candid treatment of racism in the Piedmont, neither Betts nor Edgerton sheds much light on the relations that once obtained in their region between slaves and their owners. This historical blindness is largely because of the relative economic success of African Americans in the Piedmont—at least when compared to the lives of blacks in eastern North Carolina. During the twentieth century, numerous urban black communities grew and thrived throughout the industrialized Piedmont, fulfilling, to varying degrees, Booker T. Washington's dream of a socially segregated black population free to pursue its own separate prosperity. By contrast, throughout the eastern part of the state, where large plantations—and slaves— were once much more numerous, agriculture remained the primary industry and Old South labor relations continued to prevail, with blacks primarily filling the same types of jobs as house servants and agricultural dependents that they occupied during the antebellum period.

Although there is considerable debate about whether small slaveowners can be called "yeomen,"[71] this study will treat them as such, because many non-slaveowning farmers became small slaveholders while they continued to work their own farms and to be integrated into the same communities. Price's memoir and novels indicate how in the twentieth century even wealthy planters, like his uncle Macon Thornton, often pursued extremely frugal and unostentatious lifestyles, further suggesting the pervasiveness of yeoman values throughout the state. The prominence of yeoman values was advanced following the Civil War when former planters were frequently forced to sell large portions of their estates[72] and they and their descendants were often thereby reduced to the state of yeoman farmers and plain-folk artisans struggling for subsistence, even when they continued to employ "black help," as was the case with members of Price's family and families in his fiction. Much more than any other white writer in this study, Price focuses on the enduring problematic relations between white plain folk and their dependent blacks. Not only are his black characters more numerous and more fully developed, but evolving long-term relationships between black and white individuals are consistently among the most important in his fiction.

When Price's depiction of Warren County is compared with Fred Chappell's and Lee Smith's portraits of Appalachia, the first thing the reader likely notices about the latter two—beyond the mountains themselves—is the absence of blacks.[73] In Chappell's fiction class tensions appear prominently, instead, between yeomen and their *white* tenants. Throughout his career Chappell has investigated the negative impact of capitalized agriculture and industry on the lives of Appalachian farmers—including both dependent tenants and yeomen struggling for a competency. Also of intense interest to Chappell is the insularity of the mountain farm, which produces the much touted independence of the mountaineer. In his early novels Chappell launches a steady critique against the insularity of the mountain farm, which for the protagonists of these works produces not positive independence but, rather, alienation and self-loathing. During the 1970s, Chappell began incorporating into his fiction and poetry elements of frontier humor and pastoral, finding in these modes a new, more positive approach to the figure of the yeoman farmer and discovering a means of mitigating the inherent tension between the yeoman values of independence and interdependence. In the book-length poem *Midquest* and the following Kirkman tetralogy of novels, Chappell portrays the mountain farm not as a prison to be escaped but, rather, as an Arcadia to be preserved in memory.

As in Chappell's later work, Smith's fiction demonstrates a strong pastoral impulse, identifiable by the frequent tension between an isolated, rural, yeoman past and a present-day Appalachia overcome by consumerism and exploited by technologies imported from the mainstream society outside Appalachia. Smith's pastorals are problematized, however, in that the binary opposition of an idyllic past and a corrupted present does not remain a stable one. Her critique of Appalachian pastoral is driven by a feminist exploration of the many ways the present social order merely reinscribes the male chauvinism of the frontier past, in which women isolated on yeoman farms were deprived of emotional and political support networks. As in Chappell's early darker novels, Smith's farmers are themselves often characterized by an intense taciturnity and emotional paralysis, revealing the downside of yeoman independence. Throughout Smith's fiction, the mountains serve as a metaphor for cultural entrapment that women must escape in order to find personal wholeness. Many of her narratives thus involve a quest theme, in which memory and imagination compete in the creation of identity.

If the women in Lee Smith's fiction suffer deprivations associated with the isolation of farm life and the lack of community, the men and women in the fiction of Clyde Edgerton experience the mixed blessing of *too much* community. The fictionalized small towns of Edgerton's Piedmont are populated by an embattled yeomanry attenuated by the forces of encroaching civilization. Very unlike the loosely organized frontier patriarchy of Smith's Appalachia, in Edgerton's novels a rising matriarchy rules by promoting collectivism and undermining—often unwittingly—the values of independence and autonomy at the heart of the yeoman ideal. If the yeoman values of independence and interdependence always imply an inherent tension, in Edgerton's fiction the balance tips unhealthily toward interdependence. Edgerton's matriarchs tend to control kinship, as well as the influence of the church, thereby locating community power decidedly with the women.

In contrast to Doris Betts, who laments the passing of a genuine religious spirit she associates with plain-folk culture in North Carolina, in Edgerton's novels religion is all too alive and well. Furthermore he associates religious zealotry with the sort of ethnic and regional insularity responsible for the racism, conformity, and narrow-mindedness typified by Cash's savage ideal. Whereas Betts seeks to reclaim plain-folk egalitarianism in the form of authentic religious worship practiced by earlier generations, Edgerton seeks similar values by penetrating the veneer of civilization's orthodoxies, religious or otherwise. Like Twain and other frontier humorists, Edgerton associates masculinity with the liberty of frontier life, and femininity with the conformist pressures of civilization. Edgerton's novels celebrate an obsolescent ideal of masculine independence associated with the yeoman frontier while very consciously problematizing that ideal.

Whereas other writers considered in this study often treat the yeoman experience as defined by geographic and economic circumstances seemingly a part of the North Carolina landscape, the autonomous community of black farmers examined by Randall Kenan is anything but a given. Kenan fictionalizes the unincorporated black township of Chinquapin, North Carolina (Duplin County), as Tims Creek; in his debut novel, *A Visitation of Spirits* (1989), and the story collection *Let the Dead Bury Their Dead* (1992), Kenan recreates the town's past, exploring how legendary leaders fought white oppression in order to create a space in which disenfranchised blacks could earn their own free and autonomous life from soil to which their ancestors had been enslaved. Like other contemporary writers from North Carolina, Kenan mourns the cultural changes that have accompanied the disappearance of the yeoman farmer and his community. Whereas the state's white writers typically celebrate the fruits of racial integration as perhaps the single-most-positive change to have taken place during the twentieth century, Kenan is never unambivalent about those fruits, which he sees as being largely responsible for the dissolution of autonomous black communities, communities that were built by the legendary ex-slaves and other black yeomen he celebrates. In his travelogue, *Walking on Water: Black American Lives at the Turn of the Twenty-First Century* (1999), Kenan takes with him his concern for an autonomous black culture as he travels across North America exploring the present realities of African American communities, as well as their histories of resistance to white oppression. By contrasting the fragmentation of contemporary urban black communities with the history of farming villages he discovers in small towns and rural areas across the country, he looks to the past of the yeoman farmer for the ideals that will allow black Americans to recreate themselves. In the yeoman values of collective independence, as well as community interdependence, he finds the antidote to the problems facing contemporary black America.

In his introduction to *This Is Where We Live: Stories by 25 Contemporary North Carolina Writers*, Michael McFee declares, "Where we live now, in turn-of-the-century and turn-of-the-millennium North Carolina, is not where we lived before, as citizens or writers: it's a profoundly changed and changing world."[74] Quite possibly, this rapid change is one of the most important causes of North Carolina's current literary renaissance. Just as writers of the Southern Renascence (roughly 1920–50) were characterized by a "backward glance" to a passing culture, today's writers in North Carolina often critique or seek to understand a present-day society by comparing it to what they see as a long-gone or quickly disappearing yeoman past. A survey of the most prominent contemporary writers from North Carolina will likely not yield the equivalent of neo-Agrarian Wendell Berry, someone who actually proposes the possibility of the region's returning to an agricultural economy comprised of subsistence farmers. Instead these writers hope to help preserve in cultural memory the yeoman's values while simultaneously interrogating those values and the various ways they have been embodied, as a means of better understanding and critiquing the evolving communities within their state and region. North Carolina resisted the shift from a yeoman to a cavalier mythology, but it has led the states of the old Confederacy in a shift to the new myth of Sun Belt prosperity. In their exploration of that shift (and its attendant markers of class identity), contemporary North Carolina writers revise and refigure the yeoman ideal of a past era as they strive to orient their vision in a new age.

DORIS BETTS

Plain Folk in Mill Town

Why begin a study of contemporary North Carolina literature with Doris Betts?—in part because her Piedmont offers the most representative case study of the plain folk in the state during the twentieth century. The changes in economic structure that were evolving in mill towns like Betts's Statesville at the beginning of the century have, to varying degrees, caught up with virtually all regions of the state and are largely responsible for the urgency many North Carolina writers feel to record both a contemporary culture in flux and the earlier culture it has replaced. Growing up in Statesville during the 1930s and 1940s, Betts was born into a region already in the throes of industrialization. Farmers flocked to the textile mills made possible in the western Piedmont by the region's swift rivers. These same rivers that powered mechanical looms during the nineteenth century were, by the early twentieth century, used to generate electricity for electrically powered mills, effectively anchoring the textile industry in the Piedmont. In 1939, the triumvirate of textiles, tobacco, and furniture dominated manufacturing in the state, with two thirds of manufacturing laborers working in textile mills, most of them located within the Piedmont.[1] Betts's novels and stories chronicle the urbanization of her Piedmont and the class and racial divisions that accompanied that transition.

Read together, Betts's novels offer the broadest perspective on the lives of plain folk in North Carolina—from her depiction in *The Scarlet Thread* (1964) of the rise of the textile industry during the early twentieth century, to her depiction in *The Sharp Teeth of Love* (1997) of Chapel Hill during the final decade of the century as a town peopled by immigrants from outside the state, from outside the South. As she explores the changes that have come to her state, sorting through gains and losses, Betts's attention invariably turns to the Protestant faith of her farming ancestors in an attempt to find permanence; in this, too, she represents the experience of many plain folk in North Carolina.

A still more obvious reason to begin with Betts is that, of the six writers under consideration, she was the first—by nearly a decade—to publish a book. Though Reynolds Price was the first of this group to establish a national reputation, Betts anticipated the current North Carolina renaissance with the publication of her story collection *The Gentle Insurrection* (1954), which she wrote while still an undergraduate at the University of North Carolina at Greensboro (then named "Woman's College"). After publishing another col-lection of stories and two novels that were regionally praised, Betts finally began to reach a national audience with her third novel, *The River to Pickle Beach* (1972), which the *National Observer* listed as one of the year's best twenty novels. The following year, Betts's story collection *Beasts of the Southern Wild* (1973) was nominated for the 1974 National Book Award, and in 1981 her fourth novel, *Heading West*, became a Book-of-the-Month Club pick. The *New York Times* listed *Souls Raised from the Dead* as one of the best twenty books of 1994, and her latest novel, *The Sharp Teeth of Love* (1997), has also been widely praised and the subject of considerable critical study. In addition to bringing attention to literature in North Carolina through her writing, Betts has had a direct impact on the growth of writing in the state by serving as a teacher of creative writing for three and a half decades. Together with Max Steele and Louis Rubin, Jr., Betts built a nationally recognized creative-writing program at Chapel Hill. After beginning as a part-time lecturer in 1966 (without complet-ing a college degree), she became director of freshman composition (1972–78), assistant dean of the honors program (1978–81), Alumni Distinguished Profes-sor of English (1980–2001), and the first woman chair of the faculty (1982–85).[2] Upon Betts's retirement in 2001, the university recognized her decades of ser-vice by creating an endowed professorship of creative writing in her honor.

The Gentle Insurrection: We Were the Snopeses

On June 4, 1932, Doris June Waugh was born in her grandmother's farm house in Statesville, North Carolina, and spent her early years in a concrete block house near the cotton mill where her father worked long hours during the Depression. They later moved to an apartment, where they lived until Doris was fourteen and her parents were able finally to buy a house.[3] Before moving to the mill town to enter "public works," both of her parents had grown up on nearby farms—her mother the child of yeomen, and her father the adopted child of sharecroppers.[4]

To understand the conditions that might have prompted not only Betts's sharecropping father but also her yeoman mother to leave the farm and become mill hands, it is instructive to take a brief look at changes in North Carolina's farm economy as well as its laws regarding yeomen and land owner-ship that were enacted during the latter half of the nineteenth century. Most anyone with the slightest interest in southern history has some basic knowledge of the postbellum history of freed slaves and their former masters: the political upheavals of Reconstruction, the enfranchisement and disenfranchisement of freedmen, the loss of wealth and influence experienced by planters, and the transformation of a plantation economy based on slave labor into a plantation economy based on the labor of former slaves and their descendants now under the bondage of an entrenched system of sharecropping. By comparison, the postbellum history of the Piedmont South and the majority population of plain whites there is less widely known.

With the devastation of the Civil War, many yeomen found it necessary or desirable to take liens on their harvests, thereby indebting themselves to increasingly prominent furnishing merchants. The burden of debt made it necessary for these yeomen to expand beyond subsistence farming to the cultivation of cash crops such as cotton and tobacco. When cotton and tobacco prices dropped in the 1870s and 1880s and then plummeted in the 1890s, many yeomen found themselves dispossessed of their lands and forced into tenant farming. Even yeomen who were wary of commercial agriculture found themselves victim to its pressures. New fence laws and property taxes, designed to promote commercial agriculture and the construction of new roads and railroads that would provide access to regional and national markets, had deleterious effects on the independence of subsistence farmers. "Farmers found themselves between a rock and a hard place," writes Jacquelyn Dowd Hall and her coauthors. They could "either refuse to grow cash crops and risk losing their land because they could not pay the new taxes, or they could enter the treacherous commercial farm economy."[5] The rise of tenancy rates in North Carolina corresponds with the rise of commercial agriculture between 1860 and 1900; during that period cotton production tripled and tobacco production increased four-fold, while a third more tenant farmers appeared in the Carolina Piedmont.[6] Of the early twentieth century William Powell notes, "Just as the small farmer had characterized North Carolina in the colonial period, now the tenant farmer seemed to outside observers to represent the typical North Carolinian."[7]

Of the transition to a market economy I. A. Newby writes, "Subsistence farming had been growing obsolescent, and farmers found themselves nudged into the money economy whether they wanted to be or not. . . . Traditional self-sufficiency and the skills that sustained it were giving way to cheap consumer goods, and cash income was increasingly necessary even for subsistence. The folk were being pulled into the consumer society, and many offered little resistance. Their values were evolving."[8] One of the fundamental changes among poor whites in the Carolina Piedmont during the latter nineteenth century was their awareness of the larger world. According to Newby, with improved transportation isolated farmers became increasingly aware of their poverty.[9] Furthermore, the rise in tenancy exacerbated the problem of rootlessness among tenants. As the market was glutted with cheap labor, tenants wandered from farm to farm on an annual basis, searching in vain for improved conditions. In his study of tenancy in North Carolina from 1900 to 1925, Samuel Hobbs finds that roughly 40 percent of tenants changed farms every year. "This wandering mass of humanity has no abiding interest in any community," says Hobbs, "because the tenants have no stake in the land. They are strangers, sojourners, pilgrims, forever on the move, and always discontented."[10] These sociological and economic pressures made very attractive the possibility of employment in the textile mills that began to proliferate during the 1880s and 1890s and then became increasingly numerous during the early decades of the twentieth century.

Tenant farmers frequently took on mill work with the hope of obtaining the cash necessary to purchase their own farms. Many farmers worked in the mills on a seasonal basis. It was not uncommon for Piedmonters to move back and forth between mill town and rural farm on an ongoing basis. Members of a farming family (more often than not, young women and girls) commonly would be sent to the mills to augment the income of a farming family. An economic profile of the state published in 1963 reveals that in 1959 more than 25 percent of North Carolina farmers spent at least 100 days a year working away from the farm and a third of farming families depended on nonfarm labor for over half their family income. These trends were most prominent in the Piedmont and mountains.[11] In most cases mill workers still had strong ties to the countryside. To attract labor, many mill owners sought to make the transition from farm to factory less overwhelming not only by providing homes for their workers but by supplying land for livestock and for some minor level of cultivation. For example, in a 1920 newsletter, the High Shoals Cotton Mill Company boasts of the farming opportunities available to its villagers. The people of the village are "noted for their fine hogs and good cattle. The company has a large pasture along the river for the benefit of employees who keep stock. Good gardens and lots of chickens are to be seen, too, around all the cottages."[12]

Even during the 1930s and 1940s, most mill families had farming kin that kept them connected to an agrarian past. During Doris Betts's childhood, Statesville was still a fairly small, rural town, closely connected to the surrounding farmland. Betts remembers the many summers she spent on the farms of her grandparents, where life had

not much changed from that of the nineteenth century. No electricity, no indoor plumbing, no farm machinery. In her sunbonnet, my grandmother milked cows, dug whitewash for the hearth, waved the flymop she had made from a split stick with attached shredded paper over bowls of vegetables, dried apples; in his straw hat, my grandfather plowed with mules.

Neighbors pitched in to help one another thresh, kill hogs, boil molasses. Butter was churned by womanpower and stored in thick milk crocks in the cellar. My grandfather had dug that cellar—and the well—himself, had built the unpainted house and outbuildings. . . . Both families only went to town on occasional Saturdays for staples and every Sunday to church.[13]

In this same essay, Betts celebrates the "use-it-up, wear-it-out, make-it-do essence" of her people,[14] thereby finding in the material hardships of farm life not deprivation, but rather the source of their strength and values. Furthermore, Betts remembers no feelings of material impoverishment. As she recalls, everyone she knew in the mill town was poor, and she was surrounded by a supportive extended family.[15] In many respects life in the mill village did provide continuity with the community-mindedness often absent from the lives of itinerant tenant farmers but common to yeoman society, in which neighboring farmers routinely gathered for such labor rituals as wheat threshing, corn shuckings, hog killings, and barn raisings.

The stories in her first book, The Gentle Insurrection (1954), offer a moving portrait of dispossessed yeomen struggling to adjust to changing times. "Child So Fair" and "The Gentle Insurrection" feature aging matriarchs who have lost their husbands in part as a result of the changing economic structure of their region. In the former story, Big Woman (so named by her grandchild) remembers the loss of her husband. "My man died when he was fifty-odd," she laments. "That was just after the sawmill come to the village, and nobody was used to its ways yet. I told him he had hands for dirt and growing, but he went off from the patch and down the hill to the village because of the rich wage."[16] The farmer dies on his second day at the mill when the "belt threw back a slab of wood that drove his head in" (228). The sawmill, which represented the first intrusion of industry into the Piedmont, well before the textile boom years, is associated with the long-term devastation of this family.

A similar disruption occurs in the lives of the Barnes family of "The Gentle Insurrection" as a result of the commercialization of agriculture. The father of the Barnes family has fled the exhausting labor and diminishing returns of cultivating cotton on a tenant farm. In his absence, his wife and two children attempt to make ends meet, although the son, Theo, shouldering the work his father abandoned, complains, "Mama, I work harder than a man ought to have to work. . . . Hell, we don't get it anyway. That man [Mr. Chambers, the landlord], he gets it. Hell, he gets it all" (170). The level of their impoverishment is suggested by their diet, which seems limited to beans, and the mother dreams of subsistence farming primarily for dietary reasons. She pleads with her son to approach the landlord, saying, "Maybe he'd give us enough money to set out some vegetables, Theo. Why don't you ask him pleasant?" (171). She placates her children with the fantasy of escaping tenancy. "After this season we'll make enough cotton to get ahead," she tries to reassure them. "We'll buy us a place of our own and we won't work hard any more" (179). The story ends, however, with a reiteration that the only escape from tenancy is a literal escape from the farm.

"A Mark of Distinction," another story from this early collection, chronicles the lives of those who have fled the farm and settled in the mill village, just as Betts's parents did. In this story Betts focuses on the new social pressures of industrial life that created class identity among the mill hands and, as John A. Salmond points out, challenged the "sustaining qualities of egalitarianism and individualism" common to the "rural culture that mill villagers had left behind."[17] Whereas I. A. Newby argues that the majority of farmers who made the transition to mill work were landless,[18] Paul D. Escott points out that these landless farmers shared with yeomen "attitudes of rural individualism"[19] and a readiness to challenge the presumptions of the upper classes. "However poor they were," these landless whites "remained proud and believed, in accordance with Jacksonian politics and Christian faith, that they were as good as anybody."[20] Henry Orlon, the protagonist of "A Mark of Distinction," exemplifies this sort of assertive individualism. A common textile laborer and middle-aged father of three daughters, Orlon is the self-appointed leader of the mill hands whenever they have grievances with management. Orlon is a "hero" (25) among his peers, and indeed Betts has created something of a folk hero, a man who does his appointed work "quietly and well" (25) but who adamantly refuses to compromise his personal dignity or to accept a position of lesser manhood in relation to management. The mill is owned by the Kyles family and managed by the comically ineffectual Charlie Kyles, a plump, forty-year-old bachelor who has "once taken a college course on personnel relations" and has "never gotten over it" (25). Kyles, who is certain that "all the men adored him" (32), is constantly mimicked and ridiculed by the mill hands but openly challenged only by Orlon, who has made passive aggression a fine art. Whenever Kyles, who regularly makes a point of being seen on the factory floor, stops at Orlon's station to impose his authority, Orlon shuts off his machine to show Kyles that he is "a troublesome fellow who [is] always holding up production in his own plant by disturbing his efficient workers" (27). When Kyles makes a patronizing remark and pats Orlon on the shoulder, Orlon switches on the machine again nearly ensnaring the manager's hand (28).

The power struggle between Orlon and Kyles comes to a head when Orlon decides to build a fence around the house his family rents in the mill village, thereby breaking company policy and forcing Kyles implicitly to threaten

Orlon with eviction and termination. The stakes are raised when the entire community of mill hands—normally afraid to confront management openly—join Orlon in the construction of the fence. The class struggle ends with a triumphant collective assertion of individual autonomy and community interdependence, notably values at the heart of the yeoman ideal, values that have been challenged by the sharecropping system and even more so by the new urban industrial Piedmont, where mill hands sell their labor for wages. Orlon's resistance to the imposition of management demonstrates that even in the world of capitalized industry the individual can leverage some control of his own labor and that, in fact, the proximity of so many workers sharing a common work space and mill village makes collectivism more possible. The gathering of the community to erect Orlon's fence might be compared to the community labor rituals of corn shuckings and barn raisings common among earlier generations of farmers—with the added element of class struggle.

To protest unfair wage reductions, increased work load, and unsanitary living conditions, mill workers throughout the Carolina Piedmont occasionally challenged the hegemony of mill owners and supervisors by striking. Around the turn of the twentieth century, and again in 1921 and 1929, mill strikes spread throughout the region. In the early phase of transition from farm to factory, mill workers typically confronted their supervisors on an individual basis, as Henry Orlon does in Betts's story. As Salmond explains, such direct confrontation was made possible until World War I because of local investment and ownership of the mills and because of the high demand for mill labor. After the industry's depression of the 1920s, many small mills were purchased by larger conglomerates, often by absentee owners in the Northeast. These factors along with the postwar glut of labor in the 1920s made individual challenge to authority less viable.[21] Although "A Mark of Distinction" is set sometime after 1939,[22] it seems to chronicle an earlier phase of mill life, a time when the worker still had personal access to management and could assert his individualism in a meaningful way.

Although Betts celebrates in "A Mark of Distinction" the efforts of textile laborers to balance the agrarian values of independence and interdependence in a new urban environment, this story demonstrates the limits of this possibility. Whereas independence is a natural condition of yeoman society, created geographically by the relative isolation and economic autonomy of each farming family, in a crowded mill town like Henry Orlon's independence must be asserted and its very assertion necessarily implies some rejection of interdependence. Orlon wants a fence to commemorate what he considers his special place among his peers—as their spokesperson to management. He is depressed not merely by the meagerness and plainness of the mill town but also by its severe uniformity, which he views as a personal affront to his independence and distinction: "all the grayish houses on both sides of Millwood Street were exactly alike—just so many identical, dingy boxes lined up at exact intervals all up and down the street, with exactly the same number of windows showing the same green window shades, and exactly the same four porch posts and the eight green steps that went up from every dusty walkway" (23). Before arriving at the plan of a fence, Orlon becomes so desperate to assert his difference from his neighbors that he even considers knocking down the front porch of his house. Upon crawling under the porch, however, he discovers that "every board was nailed to every other board" and that if he took a single brick out of the foundation, the ceiling would likely fall in (24). While Orlon's wife, Sarah, whom he repeatedly describes as being "long on common sense" (24), is not surprised by this discovery, Orlon himself is deeply troubled by it and by the obvious comparison to the interdependence of his community.

Ironically Henry Orlon, the champion of the mill hands' egalitarianism and class solidarity, is himself such an individualist that he finds the community worthwhile not for its own sake but only to the extent that it furthers his own ascendancy above it. Orlon is not surprised by the support for his projected fence among his fellow workers, who he believes "immediately accepted it as his right and privilege, just as in an older age they would have accepted without question the chieftain's having a more durable tent" (32). Convinced of his own special bravery and capacity for leadership, Orlon believes that he was "misborn" into the wrong time and place; when thinking of how he is "stuck incongruously in Lincolnton, S.C., at 209 Millwood Street, along with four placid women in a house that was just like every other house and for eight hours daily running a machine that was like eighteen other machines," he concludes that it would have "dampened the soul of King Arthur; it would have bored Thomas Paine to tears" (26). Not unlike his boss, Charlie Kyle, Orlon, too, is a consummate egotist—the individualist and hedonist and romantic that W. J. Cash points to as the typical southern type. In fact, Orlon more closely resembles the ambitious, self-assertive yeoman, whom Cash labels "the man at the center" of southern society, than the "poor white," whom Newby characterizes by his lack of "acquisitive values" or "the desire to save and possess and get ahead."[23]

In light of her own Presbyterianism and the doctrines of original sin and mankind's resulting total depravity inherited from the Presbyterians' Calvinist and Puritan forebears, Betts would likely not view Orlon purely as a product of the mill town. Viewed from the Calvinist perspective, Orlon's egotism is not socially constructed but rather is an inherent human trait that would have been equally present on the farm. What differs, however, is the particular opportunity for the fostering of his egotism found in the southern textile village, an opportunity that would have been less available in the preindustrial South and even less so in the antebellum Piedmont before the capitalization of agriculture, in an age when subsistence farming predominated. Orlon does not represent the model yeoman or tenant farmer transplanted to the mill village; rather, he represents, if not the antiyeoman, then at least the yeoman's alter ego, the yeoman taken to the extremes of his tendency toward autonomy and assertive individualism. His desire to erect a fence between himself and his neighbors represents the mindset of the independent farmer who aspires through the cultivation of cash crops to surround himself with sufficient acreage that he might reign as the undisputed patriarch of his own private Eden and that perhaps soon he might even own men and their progeny to work his fields for him; ideologically at least, Henry Orlon exemplifies as much as Charlie Kyles what Cash refers to as "the man at the center."

The Kyles family intuits that Orlon's brand of revolution poses no significant threat of solidarity, because Orlon does not appeal to the mill hands' feelings of community as much as to their collective fantasies of individual autonomy or—taken to its extreme—distinction. Among the mill owners, Orlon is "respected as a shrewd but restrained leader of the mill's employees, and the Kyles family [feels] that if he should be cast down, some less civilized rabble-rouser with communist leanings would spring up to take his place" (29). As further evidence that he harbors no true feelings of responsibility or loyalty to his mill community, Orlon frequently mutters at home, "I wish we could move up town," to which his practical wife, Sarah, always responds, "Away from your work and at three times as much rent?" (26).

Sarah represents what Betts shows to be the nobler heritage of plain-folk farmers: she values what is necessary and useful to sustain their family; she does not despise her husband's aspirations as much as she simply cannot fathom them—they are utterly alien to her. She opposes the construction of the fence as a frivolous expense. Even though Charlie Kyles fears that Orlon's fence would spark a movement of fence building throughout the village (33), no such collective resistance to management takes place; Orlon's fence merely serves the community as a reminder of their one shining moment. For Sarah Orlon, the fence remains simply a nuisance: "She said it took half her time putting down packages to unlatch the gate" (37). This early story demonstrates Betts's mastery of economy and awareness of the need for narrative meaning to be mirrored by narrative form: that Sarah Orlon appears in relatively few lines of the story only reinforces the poignancy of her humble asides, which offer an alternative vision to her husband's avarice and pride. This is a subtly feminist story. Although women workers occupied a substantial portion of the textile labor force from the industry's beginnings in the South throughout its development, they were consistently denied the positions of prestige and higher pay, which were reserved for men.[24] And, yet, Betts suggests that the women were responsible for maintaining their farming heritage in the face of the eroding forces of modernity.

The degree to which Henry Orlon subscribes to the capitalist values of the "New South" is reflected in his habitual quotation of statistics (the vast majority of which he simply invents) to support his agenda at work or at home. Whenever, for example, he contradicts the mill manager's authority, Orlon relies upon statistics, understanding that this is the language of progress and industry. From Orlon's "reverent tone of voice, Statistics was conjured up as being an infallible, rather ill-tempered old man—a kind of second lieutenant to God—who had been let in on the secrets of the universe. Charlie Kyles had a vast and growing respect for statistics, which had been carefully fostered during his acquaintance with Mr. Orlon" (28). That God or any religious sensibility is superfluous to Orlon—who like Kyles has become the devotee of statistics and progress—is suggested by Orlon's comic revision of "The Battle Hymn of the Republic." Immediately after first deciding to build the fence, Orlon omnipotently enters his home to greet his waiting family, belting out, "I am trampling out the vintage where the grapes of wrath are stored, / I have loosed the fateful lightning . . ." (29 [emphasis added]). Orlon is characterized by the hubris of which the Nashville Agrarians accused eastern industrialists and sociologists, whose embrace of materialistic progress the Agrarians believed to foretell the erosion of the traditional agrarian culture of southerners. Like the Agrarians, Betts fears that the religious and agrarian values organic to her culture have been eroded by industrialism, as illustrated in "A Mark of Distinction" by the concluding image of the "glory of the fence" that encloses a barren yard in which "not even morning-glories would take root" (37).

Plain Folk by Virtue of Original Sin

Betts's allegiance to the plain-folk values of her culture is most consistently expressed in her engagement with the Protestant faith of her Piedmont. Throughout her fiction, she depicts the capitalist faith in industrial progress that transformed her region as appealing to the baser, individualistic, instincts of yeomen. Faith in progress, she finds, is antagonistic to faith in God. Her stories and novels depict a world in which descendents of farmers, having abandoned a subsistence lifestyle, succumb to the temptations for material advancement at the expense of spiritual advancement.

In her practice of faith, Betts is something of an anomaly among contemporary writers, even among contemporary southern writers. Unlike those who have felt it necessary to distance themselves from the orthodox faiths of their youth (either by leaving the church or by moving from more mainstream or fundamentalist churches to upper-class Episcopal or Unitarian churches), Betts has continued to be active in the Presbyterian church in which she was reared. She writes that during her college years she "flung away [her] faith and chose intellect, believing it to be a forced either/or choice."[25] With maturity she found this early assessment to be far from valid, as her own writing so thoroughly demonstrates. Although Betts has moved away from the small, primitive sect of her girlhood—the Associate Reformed Presbyterian Church, or ARP, which she grew up hearing her mother refer to as "All Right People"[26]—her renewed commitment to the mainstream Presbyterian church has provided her with a means of reforging a connection to the culture of her childhood. She is very involved in the life of Pittsboro Presbyterian, having served as an elder, a Sunday school teacher, and a part-time organist.[27]

Of Pittsboro Presbyterian she says, "There's maybe one other person in the church who has anything to do with the university. Most of these people are farmers or people who do public work or work in factories or are school teachers."[28] These are the sort of people she writes about, so her regular contact with them as a fellow congregation member proves invaluable to her writing. Most significantly, this regular interaction prevents her from condescending to her characters, of succumbing to the pitfalls of local colorists who depict their characters as quaint stereotypes. "The stereotypes annoy me," she says, "so I resist all that."[29] One of Betts's greatest achievements is to write realistically about the struggles of average, working-class people, while simultaneously engaging the timeless philosophical questions of Western culture. Betts is easily one of the most allusive of southern writers. Her latest novel, *The Sharp Teeth of Love*, for example, abounds in literary and philosophical subtexts, including Blake, Luther, Thoreau, Aquinas, Nietzsche, Kafka, Jung, Merton, and Mann.

Although she has often been compared to Flannery O'Connor and, like O'Connor, has been called a gothic writer, Betts resists the "gothic" label, as she resists all labels—including "Christian," "feminist," and "southern"—finding any such label too limiting.[30] Nevertheless a comparison to O'Connor is helpful in delineating Betts's Christian perspective. David M. Holman finds that, like O'Connor's, Betts's fiction is "enigmatic; it involves the interior stories of characters who are desperately trying to make sense out of a modern world which consistently thwarts their understanding."[31] When compared to O'Connor's, however, Holman argues that Betts's fictional world "is more modern, more complexly confused. The questions, the mysteries of faith and iniquity may be the same, but in Betts's fictional world the unanswerable questions are perhaps harder to articulate, and the absence of answers even harder to take on faith."[32] Betts's own comparisons of her writing with O'Connor's corroborate Holman's assessment; she remarks in an interview with Susan Ketchin that O'Connor "wrote about incarnation, or immanence, in a whole different way. She would have the red sun seem to be God peeping over the pines. I don't go that far. I don't trust God as magic. It's not something I see every day."[33] Betts tends to see evidence of God more in the lives of people, and, although she believes in the presence of evil—demonstrated by the abundance of villains in her fiction—she defines "original sin" as a biologically programmed selfishness that humans can at least provisionally overcome by teaching one another to recognize this "centering on self."[34]

Betts attributes the contrast between her social emphasis and O'Connor's mysticism to her own Protestantism and O'Connor's Catholicism.[35] To illustrate this difference, Betts recalls O'Connor's story "The River," in which a boy drowns during his baptism and "presumably passes through. [O'Connor] sees that moment of passing out of this life into the next as the achievement, the promotion. I'm a little less confident; therefore, my inclination is to pull that boy out of the river and go give him a haircut and something to eat. Live as well as you can and leave the rest to the Father."[36] In contrast to O'Connor's often nearly allegorical stories, in which the actions of characters function within some overarching structure of symbolic meaning, Betts demonstrates a higher degree of empathy with her characters. She notes that, whereas O'Connor "draws these dark, stylized lines around people . . . I really prefer ordinary people who are muddling through. They're the only kind I know anything about."[37] Although O'Connor writes insightfully about the dislocations of modernity in the South, her ultimate purpose for exploring social problems—such as poverty and racism—is to illuminate man's inherent depravity and need for grace. Betts, on the other hand, calls attention to the need for religion in *correcting* social problems associated with modernity. Even while acknowledging the ubiquitous presence of evil and imperfection in humanity, Betts affirms the scriptural promise of "life in all its abundance."[38] Unlike O'Connor's characters, who are capable of finding grace only in the most violent, often fatal, events, Betts's characters undergo gradual conversions; her stories and novels typically depict pilgrims whose journeys remain far from complete. Similarly, she characterizes her own faith as one of slow and steady growth, the product of years of questioning and hard work.[39] Her linking of spiritual growth to hard work, a key component of the Protestant ethic of her plain-folk forebears, signifies her belief in human potential.

Despite her Protestant roots, however, Betts has shown an interest in Catholicism, frequently creating Catholic characters and admiring Catholic writers such as O'Connor, Walker Percy, and Graham Greene. Betts explains that she admires the "symbols and rituals" of Catholicism, which have been purged from the Protestant church. "These things," she says, "seem to me a way of making the body do what the heart is inclined to do."[40] She has even gone so far as to state, "I'd probably convert to the Catholic Church if not for the fact that my mother would perish on the spot since she still thinks the Pope is the Antichrist; and I'm just not up to dealing with that."[41] Ultimately Betts finds in both the Catholic and Protestant traditions the same essential values—a body of believers united by a common spirit and a common thirst for truth and connection to God. Participation in either religious tradition promises an antidote to the forces of modernity that Betts identifies as conducive to the growth of a divisive individualism, a characteristic at odds with the plain-folk spirit of interdependence.

Some historians would disagree with Betts's assessment that southern Protestantism does indeed promote a spirit of interdependence. On the contrary, Christie Anne Farnham argues that support of slavery evolved a form of revivalism in the antebellum South that was fundamentally different from its northern counterpart. Whereas northern revivalism "spurred social reform," she notes that southern evangelicals "focused on personal vices" and that, furthermore, this "privatized, individualistic religious outlook became a central aspect of southern culture and remains so today."[42] Bill Cecil-Fronsman pursues a more balanced view of revivalism among "common whites" in antebellum North Carolina, stating that, although it "made *personal* piety the meaningful measure of the *individual*" [emphasis added], this emphasis on piety, as opposed to wealth, "transformed the hierarchical religious culture of the eighteenth century," promoted egalitarianism, and diminished the importance of secular status among individuals.[43] Betts's perspective is consistent with Cecil-Fronsman's, and, indeed, she identifies the greatest problems of modernity to be the extent to which secular measures of worth infiltrate the domain of religion and challenge its hegemony. In an interview with Dale Brown, Betts comments on the decline of the church in America, which she typifies by recalling a minister friend who had been influenced by "a mixture of various California religions." "After a while," she remarks, "I can't sit through any more about my child within, or about my anima and animus. . . . That is not what I come to church for. I come to church to learn whether this thing is really true and what difference it really makes to me. . . . so I agree that we have lost something in losing people who are committed to something. We've tried to be all things to all people so that anybody can come in. Just believe any little ol' thing, you just come right in and smile, have a little sunshine."[44] Betts finds that by abandoning traditional forms of religion Americans have replaced a search for truth with the tendency to project individual fantasies of wish-fulfillment onto the world. She traces the decline of religion to the rise of a fragmented, pleasure-driven commercial culture, one in which we have "a support group for every ailment, a political committee for every cause, a childish public life demanding all rights, no obligations; in a culture which has selected for aristocracy its athletes and entertainers. Sometimes our American individualism has moved so far from our American sense of community that the secret national ethic seems to be 'Every man for himself.' Or every woman for hers."[45]

This critique of American culture sounds remarkably similar to the book-length critique of southern culture penned by another Piedmont Carolinian; in *The Mind of the South* (1941), W. J. Cash argues that the perennial ills of southern society were owing to a deeply ingrained individualism, resulting from a frontier society where pioneers lived egotistically without the claims of civic responsibility typical in northern towns. According to Cash, the rise of a plantation system only further solidified this tendency, and when towns eventually did emerge in the South—largely as a result of the textile industry that emerged toward the end of the nineteenth century—the plantation system was merely transplanted to the mill and the town, with the mill barons owning the houses, schools, and churches occupied by the laborers.[46] The mill barons, like the parvenu planters before them (and like the "athletes and entertainers" whom Betts identifies as the contemporary American "aristocracy"), constituted no true aristocracy, but, rather, they represented the common, even the basest, elements in southern society. They typically had no genuine sense of noblesse oblige; rather, they rose from the most individualistic, "hard, pushing, horse-trading type of man."[47] Even though Cash argues that the "Virginia aristocrat," who hailed from an authentic aristocratic lineage, occupied only a nominal place in southern history, he does make a distinction between the "finer pioneer type" of yeoman and the "generally coarser kind" of backwoods man, whom first the plantation system (made possible by capitalized agriculture) and then industry promoted "steadily to the front" of society.[48] Betts makes a similar distinction; class struggle in her fiction often takes the form of family dissension, with the more materialistic, ego-driven members of a family seeking to rise above their class and thereby separating themselves from any authentic humanitarian tradition.

Betts's second novel, *The Scarlet Thread,* is a book that one reviewer finds to have been "too much sieved through other books;"[49] Betts acknowledges the truth of this assessment, adding that the "main screen it passed through" was *The Mind of the South*.[50] Set around the turn of the twentieth century in Greenway and Stone County (her fictional versions of Statesville and Iredell County), the book tells the story of the Allen family's Snopes-like rise to power as mill barons. The patriarch Sam Allen swindles his way from the rank of general store manager to major stockholder in the textile mill that gradually changes the economic and social structures of the small rural town of Greenway. In the wake of change, we see the rise of the Klan and the formation of social classes where before there had been none. Sam's wife Mildred, for example, forbids her children to play with the mill kids. If Sam Allen and his ruthless son Thomas represent what Cash saw as the "coarser kind" of backwoods individualist who came to prominence with the rise of industry, Thomas's brother, David, represents the "finer pioneer type" of yeoman. David possesses humility and concern for his fellow man, as well as an artistic sensibility, though he lacks the assertiveness or interest necessary to fight his way to power. Instead of working with his dishonest father and brother in the mill's management, David renounces his birthright—like Faulkner's Ike McCaslin—and goes to live with and apprentice himself to the crippled stonecutter, Bungo Mayfield. Thomas and David's sister, Esther, renounces both her family and her town, finding that whereas individualism may be rewarded in men, it is punished and restrained in women. After leaving home at fifteen and marrying well in the North, she returns home incognito twenty-two years later for a daylong visit to her hometown, though she cannot make herself visit the surviving members of her family.

In *The Mind of the South*, Cash argues that the industrial progress of the early twentieth century produced among common whites "a mighty confirmation and revivification of the individualistic outlook—a revivification quite as great as that in the upper classes."[51] This "revivification" of individualism was possible among common mill hands, Cash explains, because they did not identify barriers of caste between themselves and the mill owners or supervisors and because the issue of class was vastly superseded by the issue of race, by the racist myth of the "proto-Dorian bond," the belief that all whites—rich, common, and poor—occupied the same higher link in the evolutionary chain above blacks. Beyond "providing sanctuary for the common whites"[52] from economic competition with blacks as sharecroppers, employment in mills and mill towns, Cash argues, led common whites to believe, at least during the early years of southern industrialization, that they were connected to capital and progress. This connection bred the Horatio Alger myth that they, too, could access the new wealth. The stories that proliferated throughout the New South involved a "farm boy who began his career as a hired hand and crowned it with the mastery of a township."[53] Cash offers real-life accounts of rags to riches, telling of the "barefoot" Dukes, the Cannons, the Reynoldses, and the bastard barons of Gastonia, stories repeated among common laborers throughout the Piedmont.

In her essay on the North Carolina Piedmont "We Were the Snopeses" (1999), Betts repeats these same stories: "Few families in my area declined when the Snopeses moved in; we *were* the Snopeses. Patriarch R. J. Reynolds did not learn to read and write until after he was a rich man and built his hundred-room house. Though Washington Duke and his daughter hawked his first bags of smoking tobacco from a wagon that criss-crossed Orange County, he wound up advertising the Durham Bull on signs actually stuck on the pyramids of Egypt."[54] Contrary to the cavalier myth of the Deep South, Betts demonstrates the plain-folk myth of her Piedmont and corroborates Cash's thesis: there never had been a true aristocracy; in her part of the South, at least according to the myth, success was available to anyone with the industry and pluck to reach for it. In this quite apologetic essay, Betts does not share Cash's criticism of her region. In fact, she deliberately distances herself from the book that, she claims, had so heavily influenced her second novel. "To reread Cash now," she says, "makes clear how different our Piedmonts were, though his Cleveland County lies not far south of my Iredell."[55] Instead of revisiting the racism, poverty, and narrow-mindedness of the early twentieth century, at least in this essay, she focuses on the progress Piedmonters have made in the areas of both economics and civil rights. She describes her people as "'scrub oak people,' lacking the grandeur of sequoias, perhaps, but capable of holding the world together."[56] Although Betts emphasizes the commonalties among all ranks of Piedmonters in "We Were the Snopeses," in her fiction she typically finds more significance in class distinctions, identifying the impulse to rise socially and materially as an unfortunate renunciation of one's better nature and the egali-tarian traditions of the plain folk. Just as she criticizes this impulse in the mill-baron Allens of *The Scarlet Thread,* she criticizes the same "individualist" and materialist impulse among the mill-hand Fetners of her following novel, *The River to Pickle Beach.*

The River to Pickle Beach: Mill Town "Savage Ideal"

Like the previous two books, much of *Pickle Beach* takes place in the mill town of Greenway and surrounding Stone County—although the setting is contem-porary to the novel's composition, the summer of 1968. Although the Fetners occupy a lower socioeconomic level, the sibling relationships among Bebe and her two older brothers, Earl and Troy, resemble those of the Allen children. And, like Esther Allen, who leaves home only to return twenty-two years later to find it irrevocably altered, Bebe leaves home and returns to view the changes in her family and community from an outsider's perspective. The principal setting of *Pickle Beach* is the North Carolina coast, where Bebe and her hus-band Jack Sellars (another Greenway native) have recently moved to serve as caretakers for rental properties owned by one of Jack's army buddies, George Bennett. Greenway holds painful memories for both Bebe and Jack, and, in

returning home, Bebe seeks to confront her past and to regain a sense of wholeness she finds missing from her current life. However, like the rest of the
country, which is reeling from the civil rights movement and the recent assassinations of Martin Luther King, Jr., and Robert Kennedy, Greenway is under-
going its own racial conflicts, which serve to further divide Bebe's already
fragmented family.

Although Bebe is relatively content with her childless marriage and enjoys
their new life at the beach, a rare postcard from her mother provokes a sudden
emptiness and a need to visit the hometown she has not seen in three years.
She attempts to express her inchoate longing to her husband: "'There is this
big . . .' she'd say and stop, shaking her head. Or she'd slide her fingers between
each other and hook them the way kids play church-and-steeple, look at interlocked knuckles, try again. 'Things go together more than . . .' and then give
up that sentence, too."[57] Her making of the "church-and-steeple" with her
hands recalls the childhood rhyme that accompanies the gesture—"This is the
church, this is the steeple, open the doors and see all the people"—with the
people represented by fingers dangling from "interlocked" knuckles. This simple gesture speaks volumes about Bebe's longing for the interconnectedness she
knew in childhood. Not only do her memories of a vital extended family make
her own barrenness more painful, but the traditions of her family, organic to
the place and people of Stone County, also contrast starkly with the resort
community of Pickle Beach, where no one has roots or traditions beyond those
of their own making and where Bebe and her neighbors spend more time
indoors *pickling* their minds in front of the TV than outdoors enjoying the natural scenery of the seashore.

When Bebe unexpectedly returns home, her mother begins calling kinfolk
and puts together an impromptu family reunion and grave cleaning, a family
ritual they periodically hold out in the country at the Old Hebron Church, one
of the community's oldest monuments to its past. When they arrive, Bebe's
point of view merges with an omniscient perspective, demonstrating the power
of this place to evoke for her not only personal memories but also the collective memories of her community:

> Years before on surrounding farms, Morrison children and Fetner children
> and Alley Bost's children (and, if you went far enough back, Allen and
> Grimes children) grew up and played together, and on Sundays sat neatly
> in this church, males on the left side, females the right. Some of them
> married each other and moved into town but could not feel at home in
> the brick and stained glass of First Church, or Second Church, whose
> names even sounded impersonal; so mostly they gave up church except

for holidays, and then they drove back to Hebron. Their children—Earl's
age and Bebe's—often had no real church at all except for the summer
revivals. But they admired the look of this one, so much like a toy, like
a copy from history books or off Christmas cards. (201)

As this passage demonstrates, the loss of a common church in Betts's fiction
represents much more than the disappearance of a congregation; it implies a
move from rural roots to an urban, rootless life, accompanied by the emergence
of a class system that divides a population. Before they became mill barons,
even the Allen children played with the ancestors of men and women who
later worked for the Allen family in the Greenway mill. Contrary to the common urban segregation of church congregations according to class, the Old
Hebron Church united all people of the region into one essentially classless
congregation.

Betts's depiction of the church's democratizing influence evokes the early
history of Protestantism throughout the South. The rise of evangelicalism with
the second Great Awakening (1795–1835) infused an aggressive egalitarianism
within southern religion, which was consistent with the republicanism of the
American Revolution and even more so with the political revolution of Jacksonian democracy. Not surprisingly, religious worship created an opportunity
for class conflict. Christie Anne Farnham observes that the southern gentry
"initially resisted the evangelicals, using armed bands to break up services,
for they posed a threat to planter culture and authority. Evangelical leaders
attacked the planters' lifestyle by opposing dancing, gambling, drinking, rac-
ing, whoring, and cockfighting."[58] Farnham further notes that evangelical
ministers "organized their churches more democratically" and preached that
"all—even women and slaves—are equal in the sight of God," giving rise to
the "first large-scale conversion of slaves to Christianity."[59] Paul Escott likewise
reports that southern evangelicalism did "breach racial barriers and involve black
and white together in worship."[60] The narrative of the Reverend Thomas H.
Jones, who had been a slave near Wilmington, North Carolina, offers moving
accounts of poor whites and black slaves worshipping together, meetings that
were condoned by Jones's owner, even though the meetings were opposed by
other whites in the community. With the emancipation and Reconstruction,
Protestant churches, like everything else in southern society, divided along
racial lines. Even earlier in the century, Farnham points out that the formerly
radical evangelical congregations had become "defenders of the status quo," as
Baptist and Methodist congregations became "numerically dominant and inclusive of all classes—even planters."[61] W. J. Cash goes even further to demonstrate how southern churches were primary engines for the "savage ideal," or

silencing of dissent, created by the southern unanimity against abolitionism.[62] Betts likewise admits the Protestant church's resistance to the civil rights movement of the 1950s and 1960s; she laments that the church "didn't take leadership in the biggest moral issue of this century for Americans."[63] Although the southern Protestant church has historically reflected the degree to which whites of all classes have limited their ideas about social equality to members of the white race, most scholars observe democratizing elements of evangelicalism. For example, Escott notes that the "thrust of evangelicalism was to democratize religion and make salvation available to all, not just a few elect."[64] This egalitarian tendency "moderated the aristocratic tendencies in the social order. To the extent that it reached people at all levels of society, it tended to blur the line between aristocracy and democracy, hierarchy and equality."[65] Even though evangelicalism was not successful in obliterating class distinctions, and while the "social order remained highly divergent and stratified,"[66] evangelicalism, nevertheless, served to strengthen democratic values throughout society.

In an interview with Susan Ketchin, Betts directly addresses what she perceives as the unifying and democratizing purpose of religion: "Christianity taught democracy about equality of souls, that despite worldly condition, nobody is more or less innately worthwhile."[67] In the same interview, she sounds a Jeffersonian note by connecting the religion of a people to their folkways and their physical connection to the earth:

> In a rural state we live close to nature, and natural images, which again are biblical. We are still open to them though we're losing that rapidly to malls and highways and suburbs. . . . Landscape makes a difference. In the southern landscape where we can be outdoors and nearer to animals, we can feel there is a rhythm which we do not create and do not control, and that affects what we think in a way that if all your milk comes from the dairy, you're not affected like the man who bred the cow to freshen her. . . . Most consumers don't have to kill anything. They don't have to have any mixed emotions. Part of the decline of religion may be just that simple. A whole way of life has changed. The peasantry is disappearing.[68]

Like Fred Chappell, who feels that the peasant or yeoman practice of planting by the signs is another essentially religious practice that "connect[s] the order of the earth to the order of the stars,"[69] Betts doubts the durability of religion in a modern, urban world, where people are cut off from agrarian traditions. Because religion, for Betts, represents the only reliable means of perceiving reality —of understanding one's proper relation to others, to the Deity, and to the universe—a world without religion presents an insurmountable epistemological

crisis. *Pickle Beach* is full of characters who have been cut off from any authentic traditions and are thereby lost to wander through mazes of private fantasy
that lead them ever further from any meaningful contact with the real.

In Greenway or Pickle Beach, this loss of contact with the real is depicted
as the product of upward mobility. Bebe's older brother Earl, for example, has
escaped their family's humble origins by opening a used car lot, which has
allowed him to build a Gold Medallion home replete with new vinyl furniture,
fake marble tile, fake wood paneling, adjustable lighting, a plasterboard eagle
with a plastic eye over the fireplace (which suggests the superficiality of his
own patriotic vision of himself as a new leader in the community and upstart
politician), and air conditioning he runs full blast while burning an artificial
fire in the fireplace for effect. The bar he has stocked with sodas and bonded
whiskeys of every variety merely completes the artificiality of the environment,
in which all parts combine to produce intoxication, to allow the individual
to live in a space that most nearly matches his personal fantasies of wish-
fulfillment. Troy observes of his brother, "If Earl lived within his income now,
he wouldn't even think he was living" (159). The degree to which such an artificial environment has compromised Earl's ability to make contact with a world
that includes experiences beyond his own becomes plain when the Fetners
arrive at the Old Hebron Church for their reunion and grave cleaning, and
Earl's wife, Tweet, "the world's best housecleaner" (196), remarks, "This place
doesn't seem real does it?" (201). To a generation accustomed to fabricating
and maintaining their own private worlds (or to accepting as normative the
enclosed space of the textile mill with its deafening racket and polluted air),
this church and its graveyard, which represented for prior generations the most
concrete expression of a common reality, becomes merely a "toy," or a pastoral
image known only from "Christmas cards" (201).

Without the touchstones of church and genuine community, Earl and
Tweet become what Cash identifies as the typical southern type (which Betts
sees as the typical American type): the "romantic" and the "hedonist,"[70] who
has little "capacity for the real"[71] but, rather, prefers "the extravagant, the
flashing, and the brightly colored."[72] Earl's car lot, which he has placed in the
historic district of Greenway, is covered in neon lights, "whirling red propellers
on a high cable," a sign that flashes night and day, "Earl's Pearls" (157), and
tacky signs covered with banal slogans written by Earl's brother, Troy: *"Become
a Rich Pedestrian! Sell Us Your Car!" "Owned by High School Boy—Used Mostly
for Parking"* (158). Instead of dividing the lot by make of vehicle, Earl has
arranged the cars at Earl's Pearls by color: rubies, emeralds, and sapphires. The
trucks are parked together under a sign that reads *"Diamonds in the Rough"*
(158). Upon first viewing the lot, Bebe winces and thinks to herself, "It seemed

like a sacrilege . . . that one of the Fetners had made it to this side of town after all, in just this way" (157).

If Earl's reduced "capacity for the real" seems at first harmless, it becomes less so when he begins to reveal his political views. Earl has become the Stone County manager for the American Party, promoting George Wallace's presidential campaign and vocally opposing school integration, a position popular with many whites in the area and one that furthers his business interests. Earl's racism reflects that of many North Carolinians of his period, as represented by Wallace's widespread support in the state during his 1968 presidential bid. Wallace placed second in North Carolina, behind Nixon but besting the Democratic candidate, Hubert Humphrey, even though 75 percent of the state's voters were registered Democrats.[73] When Bebe calls Wallace "common," Earl retorts, "Common *sense*, you mean. . . . You've got to admit Wallace is a man will say what he thinks, Bebe. . . . He says what everybody knows at heart" (198–200). Earl's egotistical tendency to believe that what he holds true—namely, blacks are inferior to whites and should be kept socially segregated—equals "what everybody knows at heart" leads him to vilify anyone who does not agree, including his brother, Troy, whom he accuses of "getting mixed up with the wrong people. . . . People that didn't grow up here and think they know it all" (199). Earl neatly fits Cash's paradigm of the common white who employs the "savage ideal," or ideological conformity, out of fear of dissenting views that might inauthenticate his own private fantasy of social superiority.

If Earl represents what Cash views as the "hard, pushing, horse-trading type of man," the basest, most common sort who tended to advance in southern society, his brother, Troy, represents the "finer pioneer type," whom Betts presents as the bearer of the plain folk's nobler tradition: the individual capable of respecting the dignity and individuality of each person without feeling the need—out of a deep-seated insecurity—to seek material and social advancement by sowing division. This difference between the brothers becomes most apparent in their reactions to the recent activism of the black Wilkie family, friends of the Fetners for generations. When the Wilkies integrate the schools and lobby for jobs at the Allen textile mill, they are threatened by whites, who later pour kerosene into the Wilkies' well. While Earl protects the identity of the perpetrators—and may have himself been involved—Troy meets with Otis and Blake Wilkie in an effort to discover the culprits and turn them over to the law. Troy tells his sister, Bebe, "Someday you try to figure out how Earl is modern and hates the blacks, and I'm old-fashioned and don't" (205). This apparent paradox lies at the heart of the novel's vision of social entropy in America, and particularly in the South. While Earl parlays his racism into economic and political capital, Troy becomes ostracized from his family and community, even though the Fetners have been friends with the Wilkies for generations and have convinced themselves of their tolerance and belief in equality.

Troy puts the family's vision of itself to the test by joining the Wilkies in their struggle for social and economic equality. Unlike his politically outspoken and socially prominent brother, however, Troy retires from civic leadership, preferring the solitude of his run-down house in the country and the solace of whiskey. His second wife, Mary Ruth, complains, "He'd be happier if he could live on some island, miles at sea, and never have to work" (246). After working part time in the Allen mill for a while, Troy's present labor consists of writing slogans and jingles for his brother's advertising campaign. Disconnected from the farming tradition of his forebears, Troy is misplaced, and he squanders his talent for traditional bluegrass music on banal lyrics for Earl's Pearls autos, in effect squandering his own soul, or "pearl of great price," to survive in the modern world. As with Thomas and David Allen from *The Scarlet Thread*, the juxtaposition of Earl Fetner's success and Troy's withdrawal from society emphasizes the continuing cultural erosion Greenway (and, by inference, America) suffers as a result of industrialization and commercialization. Like Cash, Betts suggests that these forces of modernity have promoted the baser elements of frontier society, the exaggerated individualism and ambition for prominence by means of accumulated wealth, which characterized Cash's "man at the center" of southern society.

Historical studies of North Carolina yeomen provide numerous examples of the bifurcated responses to modernity that we find in the Fetner brothers. This difference is especially noticeable when considering the ways that yeomen responded to the rise of commercial agriculture.[74] Although numerous yeomen resisted the temptation to participate in the market economy, others willingly abandoned diversified subsistence agriculture for the prospect of wealth available through cultivation of cash crops and the possibility during the antebellum period of rising, through the acquisition of slave labor, to the position of planter. In the late-nineteenth and early twentieth centuries, the road to prosperity often involved an abandonment of agriculture for industrial entrepreneurship, and even in the antebellum period industrialization represented a viable alternative to increased wealth. Escott distinguishes wealthy farmers in North Carolina by noting that they were "entrepreneurs rather than seigneurs. Planters moved into commerce and industry while others traveled the reverse direction, all united in the search for profit."[75] For Escott this desire for profit so distinguishes the economically ambitious yeomen, especially those who acquired slaves, that he places them in a "middle class," more closely aligned with the planter elite, a class separate from yeomen who continued in a traditional subsistence-style agriculture.[76]

Hinton Rowan Helper, the notorious racist-abolitionist from Rowan County (which borders Betts's Iredell County to the east), provides a curious example of the southern yeoman who renounces subsistence agriculture for the promise of wealth and status available through participation in the market economy. After Helper's failed attempt to strike it rich in the California gold rush, chronicled in *The Land of Gold* (1855), he published his most important work, *The Impending Crisis of the South* (1857). *The Impending Crisis* promotes the interests of nonslaveholders in the South and attacks the institution of slavery and the hegemony of southern planters as opposed to those interests, demonstrating how small farmers in the free soil states of the North were much more prosperous than their southern counterparts. This disparity he attributes primarily to the fact that slaveholders tied up the majority of available capital in the South, thereby stymieing the development of a diversified and industrial economy that would have benefited the great majority of whites in the middle and lower classes. Although Helper purports to speak for the small farmer, his more genuine interest lies with commerce and industrialization. "Our theme is a city," he says, "a great Southern importing, exporting, and manufacturing city,"[77] and, elsewhere, "In this age of the world, commerce is an indispensable element of national greatness. Without commerce we can have no great cities, and without great cities we can have no reliable tenure of distinct nationality. Commerce is the forerunner of wealth and population; and it is mainly these that make invincible the power of undying States."[78] As George M. Frederickson convincingly argues in his 1968 introduction to *The Impending Crisis*, Helper's "real social ideal was the successful capitalist, rather than the moderately prosperous independent yeoman."[79] Contrary to Jeffersonian agrarianism, exemplified by the tradition of yeoman farmers pursuing lives relatively independent of a market economy in a region unspoiled by industrialization and urbanization, Frederickson identifies Helper as a "precursor of Henry W. Grady and the postwar advocates of 'a New South,'" rather than "the Populists and agrarian radicals who opposed them."[80]

Like Hinton Helper, Earl Fetner, the successful auto salesman of *Pickle Beach*, proposes a form of New South prosperity that promotes the interests of his class and race. Just as Helper advocates the removal of all blacks back to Africa, Earl supports Wallace and vehemently opposes the integration of schools and the work force in his community. When Troy Fetner associates his brother's modernity with his racism, Betts seems to be likewise suggesting this connection, identifying the degree to which the possibility for racial tolerance that might have developed among agrarians was overwhelmed by "progressive" capitalists. Modernization results in the loss of native tolerance and promotes the confluence of racism pervasive throughout American society with a version deeply rooted in plain white society of North Carolina. This connection between local and national cultures is emphasized by the frequent references to the recent assassinations of Martin Luther King, Jr., and Robert Kennedy. Like millions of other Americans, Bebe watches hours of television news coverage of Kennedy's assassination.

The novel's structure also suggests such an extrapolation of local crises to national. Although Bebe's visit with her family in Greenway, near the Katesaw River, occupies the middle third of the novel, this major subplot is framed by her life at the North Carolina coast, where she becomes embroiled in a private controversy very similar to the one besetting her family back home. After settling in at their new home and in their new positions as caretakers, Jack and Bebe learn from the landlord, George Bennett, his hidden motives for hiring them: in addition to conducting business with the regular tenants who come to Pickle Beach in the summer, they are to watch over George's handicapped in-laws, whom he and his wife have hidden from their friends and even from their own children. Because the institution that cares for George's sister-in-law Rosie and her son releases its staff every July for vacation, George and his wife, Laverne, must make alternative arrangements: they pay a nurse to live with them at the beach every July. In exchange for Jack and Bebe's silence on the matter, George agrees to give them a lifetime deed to the beach house, in addition to the salary he pays them. Although the exact nature of Rosie and her son's handicap is never explicitly understood by any of the characters involved, they seem likely to have Down syndrome: George describes Rosie as always happy and "Big-headed. Had a face like a Chinese" (99). He admits in confidence to Jack and Bebe that his wife has always feared passing on the same genes and that her father had always washed his hands after handling Rosie (99, 104). If the Bennetts' fear of difference seems absurd by contemporary standards, Betts suggests how common such fears were in the South in 1968. Even Bebe's intelligent and self-educated husband, Jack, is unnerved by the arrival of the "Pinheads." And George and Jack's army buddy, Mickey McCane, exceeds even George in his paranoia.

Mickey, from Angier, North Carolina, rents one of the beach cottages on weekends to get away from his wife, to shoot his guns down on the strand, and to pursue his infatuation with Bebe. Mickey epitomizes the southerner whom Cash describes as the "child-man," whose innate tendency is to "expand his ego, his senses, his emotions," and to "accept what pleases him and reject what does not" (Cash, 45). Even more so than Earl Fetner, Mickey vocally blames all of America's problems on "niggers," "queers," "Pinheads," and anyone who demonstrates the least difference from himself. For a writer who says that she dislikes "stereotypes," Betts's Mickey fits most of the stereotypes of the southern chauvinist: he views women as sexual objects, loves guns, hunts just to kill things for the fun of it, looks nostalgically back at his army days when he enjoyed the unchecked freedom to destroy, and constantly passes gas. For all of his bravado, he is impotent; Bebe thinks of Mickey as "a rapist that can't do the rape and blames [her] for it" (131). Reminiscent of Faulkner's Popeye and Temple Drake, Mickey threatens to corrupt Bebe, whose head is so filled with Hollywood-inspired rape fantasies that she half-longs to be violated by Mickey.

She is ostensibly saved from his influence by her trip back to Greenwood, which, to an extent, replaces her Hollywood fantasies with a vision of life that is grounded in agrarian traditions of her plain-folk forebears. Her rejection of Mickey, however, pushes him further into his own self-pitying dementia and childhood memories of a neglectful mother. Mickey's self-absorption culminates in his brutal murder of the "Pinheads," which he views as an act of divine justice. "People like that," he concludes, "the government ought to put them to sleep" (349). The novel ends with Mickey fleeing the law and Jack and Bebe Sellars reaffirming their commitment to each other. This juxtaposition emphasizes the contrast between the nearly cartoon villain and the couple, who are described as being "typical" southerners (348). Betts has remarked that, although she generally finds them annoying, stereotypes can prove useful to a writer, by giving her "something solid to push against, attack, overturn."[81] In a novel that focuses on the attempts of characters to see their world more clearly, Betts's use of a stereotype appears almost metafictional, tempting the reader to mistake him as authentic and forcing us to look more closely at the more nuanced thoughts and behaviors of the protagonists. Although they are themselves not entirely free of the prejudices common to their region, Jack and Bebe are willing and able to change, as evidenced by their eventual acceptance of the handicapped couple who have come to their beach and by Bebe's gradual confrontation of her own racial prejudice. If Mickey represents an exaggeration of the yeoman's tendency toward self aggrandizement and isolation resulting in a rejection of the claims of society, Jack and Bebe offer a healthier image of the "typical" southerner, or, considering their heritage, the typical yeoman, capable of balancing independence with interdependence.

The theme of cultural erosion that predominates *The River to Pickle Beach* reappears in Betts's next book. *Beasts of the Southern Wild* contains numerous stories depicting descendants of North Carolina yeomen now modernized and cut off from their heritage or, instead, suffering the excesses of its worst elements. Pregnant Gwen, in "Still Life with Fruit," considers herself a "well-adjusted modern who has accepted her womanhood" and has "decided not to try natural childbirth, mainly because the doctor who advocated it was male."[82] In "Burning the Bed" middle-aged Isabel returns from New York City to wait with her ancient father as he lies dying in the old farm house of her childhood. As a lesbian, Isabel's estrangement from the community of her past is exacerbated by her sexual orientation, which she is certain no one in her conservative hometown could understand. In the title story, a schoolteacher named Carol finds the only way to rebel against her chauvinistic and racist husband (and the society he represents) to be in her libidinous dream life; nightly she dreams of a world where blacks have imprisoned white Americans and Carol is chosen among the ranks of women prisoners to be the mistress of one of the new society's intelligentsia, Sam Porter, provost at New Africa University, which she had attended "under its old name" (70). Sam becomes for her an ideal lover: strong, passionate, and a lover of poetry. One night after being "raped" by her husband, Carol sinks into a retributive dream in which she has Sam hunt down and kill him.

In "The Ugliest Pilgrim," which has been widely anthologized and adapted to both Broadway stage and film, teenager Violet Karl suffers, like Carol and Isabel, from her culture's narrow ideas about femininity. Her face disfigured in a girlhood accident, Violet takes a bus across the country to Tulsa, where she hopes a television faith healer will provide a miracle cure. Not surprisingly, this commercialized form of religion fails in any way to enlighten the girl, who inevitably learns to look beyond her disfigurement and appreciate her own inner beauty. A recurrent theme throughout this collection is the need for individuals to assert their own inherent dignity and by doing so to critique and revise the corrupt norms of their society, norms that impose artificial hierarchies of status. These stories consistently promote the egalitarianism of the plain folk.

As in her celebration of the plain folk's egalitarianism and community orientation, the feminist perspective so pervasive in Beasts is grounded in the same opposition to modernity. Even if the farmer's world was not free of the effects of male chauvinism, the world of commerce and industry that superseded it produced an even greater marginalization of women's rights and values, including the value of women's work. Bill Cecil-Fronsman reports how women in antebellum "common white" families typically produced goods, such as textile and dairy products, for domestic use and sale. With the appearance of low-cost manufactured textiles from the North—and later from the South—the value of these women's homemade goods, and thus their labor, was cheapened to the point that they were excluded from participating in their local and regional markets. Or, rather, in order to compete, these women had to sell their labor to the textile factories that began to proliferate throughout their own region. By 1860, "there were nearly three female cotton-goods workers for every male in the industry. Most of these male workers, moreover, were

probably boys."[83] "What was beginning to take place," Cecil-Fronsman concludes, "was probably less the abolition of opportunities for women to make
money than the mechanization of women's labor within an industrial-capitalist
system."[84]

Jacquelyn Dowd Hall and coauthors find that, even prior to significant
industrialization of the Carolina Piedmont, commercial agriculture had "tipped
the household balance of power in favor of men, who linked the family to the
marketplace."[85] Stephanie McCurry similarly finds that the male heads of yeoman households sought to reproduce their economic and social independence
only in their male heirs, who were initiated into the various political and economic exchanges with neighbors from which women in the household were
excluded. By studying the domestic economy of James F. Sloan's yeoman farm
in the South Carolina Piedmont, as recorded in the farmer's journal (1854–61),
McCurry demonstrates how the sizable contribution of women's work—which
included regular field labor—went unrecognized and uncompensated. Sloan's
journal provides a fairly extensive record of the ways that his son, Seth, was
"initiated into the culture of freemen" through inheritance of property and the
assumption of his father's role as a representative of the family farm to the community. Seth also became his "father's surrogate in the household, command-
ing dependents in his absence." By contrast, Sloan's daughter, Barbara, receives
only "a brief note of her marriage."[86] The great crime that McCurry identifies
in this behavior is the silence maintained in regard to women's domestic labor,
which "was the stuff of which independence—and manhood—was made."[87]
Yeoman farmers could "aspire to self-sufficiency," McCurry maintains, "in large
measure because, in addition to grain, virtually everything else their families
ate was grown or raised, preserved, and cooked by women, and virtually everything they wore was spun and woven, dyed and sewed by women. What little
milk and butter yeomen had their wives or daughters produced. . . . The value
of women's work was clear. By their industry wives and daughters ensured that
nothing was purchased that could be produced at home, whatever the cost in
labor and sweat."[88] The degree to which the yeoman farm economy was incorporated into a market economy, therefore, largely determined the degree
to which both women's work and a subsistence lifestyle were undervalued.
McCurry argues that this silence about the role of women's labor in yeoman
households—especially field work—came as a result of the yeoman's comparison of himself and his economic situation to that of planters, whose women
were not required to bear the burden of farm labor. Thus, to the extent that
yeomen adopted ideas of femininity and masculinity based on the model of the
planter, they undermined the values of egalitarianism and self-sufficiency at
the core of their own culture and valued their women not for their substantial

domestic labor but for the extent to which they contributed to the yeoman's status in the community.

That Betts places great value on the domestic labor of farm women is demonstrated in much of her fiction. Easily her most grounded characters are farm matriarchs, such as Big Woman of "Child So Fair" and Mama Bower of "The Old Are Very Beautiful" (both stories from *Gentle Insurrection*), and Erika Cowan of *The Sharp Teeth of Love*. Furthermore, as in "The Ugliest Pilgrim," she frequently critiques the commoditization of women, which she views as a product of modern, commercial culture, one antithetical to that of the subsistence farm. This theme pervades her two most recent novels.

Souls Raised from the Dead: Plain Folk and The Problem of Evil

Violet Karl of "The Ugliest Pilgrim" in many ways resembles Mary Grace Thompson, the thirteen-year-old protagonist of *Souls Raised from the Dead* (1994), possibly Betts's finest novel. Mary's physical disfigurement, however, is much more serious than Violet's. Mary is diagnosed with an incurable kidney disease that ultimately takes her life. In the meantime, she, like Violet, is forced to confront how this physical difference will result in her exile in a youth culture so obsessed with physical perfection. Both shrewd and articulate, Mary clearly understands her situation: "She had enough brains to notch her way upward, and knew it; she shared with surgeons' daughters the lingo of horses and showrings; she was going to be just pretty enough that the popular girls could have taken her into their group and felt democratic about it."[89] Mary understands (perhaps too well) how the same stratification along the lines of education, wealth, and beauty that she finds in her middle school manifests itself in her larger society. Whereas Betts's earlier novels were set in the fictional mill town of Greenway, in *Souls* she brings her plain-folk sensibility to bear upon the elitism she has observed in Chapel Hill, where she taught creative writing for more than thirty years. She investigates the town-gown division common to university towns, in this case with the upper-class academics in Chapel Hill literally separated by railroad tracks from their blue-collar neighbors in what was originally a textile mill town, Carrboro. Mary understands her exile in terms of this landscape; she "knew the invisible railroad tracks had thrust themselves like a sudden eroding flood surge of the Mississippi. She, like a sandbar, had been cut off, left after all on the Carrboro side to be sorted neatly with her own kind of people—the kind who had hay fever or fits or rode in wheelchairs" (193). By resigning herself to her lot, Mary avoids the petty rituals of self-effacement necessary for social advancement, and likewise she avoids the shallow egotism of the self-appointed elite—illustrated by Earl Fetner of *Pickle Beach*, and even more garishly so by Mary's estranged mother, Christine, a cosmetics saleswoman, who has her own radio show, *Trina's Arena*. Christine seeks to convert not only her radio audience, but also her daughter, to the belief that self worth depends utterly on the perceptions of others and on one's place within a hierarchy constituted not so much by wealth or birth as by differences of physical beauty.

Like most North Carolina writers, Betts understands the subtle distinctions of class that obtain in most parts of her state. She depicts a fluid class system, in which members of the lower class are either busy clawing their way upward or resigned to their place at the bottom. Such is the case with the Broomes, Mary's mother's family. While Christine Broome Thompson identifies cosmetics and physical beauty as her ticket out of poor town, her parents Virgil and Georgia are content to remain. Mary's father, Frank, notes, for example, that his father-in-law had probably "never paid a dime in income tax" and was content to live off of disability checks, social security, and food stamps (236). Frank's social climbing mother, Tacey Thompson, adds, "Wasn't it just like Virgil Broome to hire out to fix houses while living in [an] unpainted wreck, and to cut door keys even if his own door was tied shut with a string!" (41). Though Betts satirizes both the Thompsons' pretensions and the Broomes' sloth, the humor in this novel is gentle. With the exception of Mary's self-absorbed mother (who refuses to donate her kidney to her child because of cosmetic concerns), Betts portrays the anguish and awkwardness each of these family members feels as they attempt to care for the sick child and come to terms with her progressing illness.

Betts calls *Souls* "a religious novel," in the sense that she is "exploring those old questions—if there is a benevolent God, why is there so much evil and suffering in the world? Why does God allow the innocent to suffer? Of course," she concludes, "I don't give anything but my usual ambiguous answers at the end."[90] Because she refuses to provide clear answers omnisciently, the individual characters' quests for meaning become all the more poignant. Each of the characters arrives at a different provisional answer; in facing death, each moves closer to confronting an essential reality from which their modern lifestyles have shielded them. The book's epigraph, an excerpt from a poem by Czeslaw Milosz, foreshadows the characters' journeys in its dual focus on the sorrow and incomprehension surrounding the death of a child and the joy and comfort to be found in faith in future resurrection.

Like Flannery O'Connor and Walker Percy, Betts is critical of Western culture's abandonment of religion in favor of scientific and sociological solutions to "those old questions." In *Pickle Beach*, a Catholic nun serves as Betts's mouthpiece, when she advises Bebe, "Deny metaphysics and the trivial will prevail" (55). Betts clearly states her frustration with contemporary culture, remarking in an interview, "Americans as a rule think everything can be fixed, but I don't think that. . . . They have a childlike faith that everything can be cured by science or technology."[91] In *Souls*, Christine exemplifies this childlike faith in material cures for spiritual dilemmas. She glibly reassures her worried daughter, "Oh, they'll solve it. They'll fix cancer next. Even in my business, Mary, everything depends on science. I'm thinking of putting out a face cream myself once I get the formula right" (140). As in Reynolds Price's memoir *A Whole New Life*, the nurses in *Souls* appear genuinely involved in caring for the patient as well as treating the illness, while the doctors generally are depicted as cold and clinical, speaking through masks (291) and emotionally distancing themselves from their patients and their grieving families by resorting to technical explanations that, in effect, divide the body from the spirit of the sufferer. Furthermore, in their fixation on preserving life, they manifest frigidity and discomfort in dealing with the reality of death, which Betts acknowledges as a fundamental problem of the medical establishment and the culture at large. "We've moved death," she says, "into a mechanistic setting—out of sight."[92]

Betts dramatizes the degree to which our scientific and technological culture has marginalized religion in her depiction of the hospital's "All Faith Chapel," where Tacey and Dandy Thompson go to pray while they await news of their granddaughter's condition. Even the non-church-going Dandy is offended by the anesthetized, politically correct environment. "'They've built this chapel all wrong,' he mutters to his wife, 'Less is not more.' He peered through his fingers to examine the churchy but anonymous room where 'All Faith' meant first no faith in particular and then no faith at all. . . . 'You need to put everything into a room like this. The Virgin Mary. And the Star of David and a crucifix or two and an Indian thunderbird and—who's the ugly female? Kali? The place ought to be jam-packed with statues and candles. . . . Ain't it silly to keep this room so bare when even the doctors wear that snake and staff? Isn't that from Moses?'" (96).

In this passage, Dandy offers a penetrating critique of how the modern American scientific and legal communities have colluded in the deracination of a populace, stripping them of their traditional modes of coping with physical and spiritual suffering and thereby denying them agency in their own lives, denying them access to the moments when they are challenged to confront life's most essential realities. In denying people their forms of religious expression, and reserving only for themselves the arcane symbols of power, the doctors have interposed themselves as the high priests of life and death, with their new technical rituals and Latinate liturgies that relegate their patients to a position of powerlessness. In this very class-conscious novel, nowhere is class more present than in the corridors of the hospital.

The social structure imposed by the hospital on its own staff and on its patients and their families is one that militates against plain-folk values of self-sufficiency and egalitarianism. Nevertheless, despite the hospital's clinical treatment of Mary's physical decline, her death shatters the medical establishment's illusion of power, and the Broomes and Thompsons are forced to confront their helplessness, which ironically serves to re-establish what Betts views as the foundation of a Christian (and what might be viewed as a plain-folk) worldview. All of the class distinctions that had been so important to Tacey and Dandy Thompson dissolve and they are able tentatively to reach out to the lower-class Broomes and mutually grieve the death of their granddaughter. Tacey's hypocritical, social Christianity, which had ossified into mechanical rituals, becomes a vital faith only when she experiences this new desperate need. Even Mary's mother, Christine, confronts the depths of her denial and self-absorption, and when, in the middle of the night, sobbing, she calls her ex-husband, Frank, he listens and commiserates, instead of judging, as he has formerly been too quick to do.

Betts finds such a recognition of our common depravity, or "original sin," to be absolutely necessary to a healthy society. This old Calvinist doctrine served as the "bedrock" of the plain-folk culture in which she grew up, and she finds it sadly lacking in a contemporary culture obsessed with "perfection." She argues that the "route of brotherhood" lies not in pursuit of "perfectibility" but in a common admission of fallibility, in the recognition that "nobody was better than anybody else. One view leads to pride, the other to humility."[93] In describing original sin as a "biologically . . . programmed" "centering on self,"[94] Betts provides a religious diagnosis of her society's ills that curiously resembles the sociological diagnosis of southern "individualism" put forth by the nonreligious W. J. Cash. Although their prescriptions for a cure may diverge significantly—especially because Cash, like his mentor, H. L. Mencken, was critical of religion and was, furthermore, less interested in proposing a cure than in diagnosing the illness—Betts and Cash do share the similar emphasis of calling attention to the class- and race-related problems that frustrate the formation of community.

The Sharp Teeth of Love: Beyond Regionalism—Social Protest on the Road

The Sharp Teeth of Love (1997) portrays an even more thoroughly deracinated modern America. Like *Souls,* this novel begins in Chapel Hill, but, as in "The Ugliest Pilgrim" and *Heading West,* her protagonists travel westward across the continent, demonstrating that Betts is not content to write "regional" literature and that the cultural erosion she finds in North Carolina is national, even international, in nature. Addressing the Americanization of Dixie, Betts writes,

"In every way, the region is now closer to national norms than it used to be. The satellite dish stands where the outhouse used to lean; after the tobacco curing barn gave way to the sharecropper's cabin, that was replaced by a rusting trailer, and now by an elaborate furnished mobile home that cost $35,000. In North or South, the following look much alike: airports, malls, hotel chains, fast food restaurants, television programs, most suburbs, highways, billboards, and city outskirts. The drive from New Jersey to Atlanta offers few surprises."[95] Betts believes that the next generation of southern writers will "explore the internationalism that has moved into the South along with world manufacturing for world markets. It is a safe prediction that there will be a broadening of scale."[96] Elsewhere, she has similarly remarked about the need to understand local dramas globally, stating that "the next great novelists will be international in scope. The move—in religion, art, and politics—is all toward international."[97] In Betts's fiction, this move "toward international" is characterized as an unfortunate one, which produces a homogenized, fragmented culture. Whereas *Souls* concerns itself more with blue-collar residents of Carrboro, *Sharp Teeth* begins on the other side of the railroad tracks, with two students at the University of North Carolina: Luna, an undergraduate art major struggling with anorexia, and her fiancé, Steven, who has just earned his Ph.D. in botany. None of the major characters in the novel is from Chapel Hill, or from the South, and the only character to speak in a southern accent is Luna's father, Major Stone, who, in retiring to Virginia, has affected a genteel drawl. Luna is an "army brat" who has spent her entire life rootless; as the novel begins, she again is in the process of uprooting herself to travel across the continent with Steven. Their plan, formulated by Steven, is to have a quick and easy marriage in Reno, Nevada—America's capital of kitsch and commercialism—then travel on to California, where he will begin a teaching career.

Along the way, however, their personal differences become gradually more apparent. Steven is perhaps too easy a villain; his interests in Luna are ephemeral and selfishly motivated: she supports him financially, provides sketches of plants for his dissertation, serves as an object of his sexual passion (rather than a partner in intimacy), and, as his future wife, she promises to help him rise more quickly through the "ranks" of academia (30), just as her mother helped her father rise through the ranks of the military before being discarded for a younger wife. Luna realizes that she desires roots and a sense of permanence that Steven cannot provide her and so leaves him in Reno and heads for the Sierra Nevada, where she will camp and hike in Donner Lake Park near the location where the fated Donner party spent the winter of 1846–47 snowbound and surviving by eating the dead members of the party.

In the Sierra Nevada wilderness, Luna makes contact with an authentic place in a way she failed to do when taking the interstate across the country. During her road trip with Steven she frequently complains that modern landscapes offer mere simulacra of the real. "Maybe a century ago," she says, "I think travelers left home to see what else was out there in the world and that's what I wanted to see. . . . But now we don't visit what already exists, like the Alps; we're on a trip into somebody's mind, some effect that's been thought up and prepared especially for tourists before they come. Something unnatural. Invented. They've set traps for the eyes of tourists" (46). This artificiality is nowhere more apparent than in Reno, where Steven and Luna are planning to celebrate their union in marriage; not surprisingly, Luna flees the city. The novel's structure—divided between the mountain wilderness and the urban environments of Reno, Chapel Hill, and interstate hotel rooms—emphasizes the pastoral rejection of urban life. Although there are no major southern characters, the novel's protagonists share the southern unease with abstraction. Just as she finds her American journey to lead merely "into somebody else's mind," into "traps" for her eyes, she finds herself confronted by such traps in nearly every aspect of her life, including art, work, and sex. Her art professors (all abstractionists) denigrate her realistic drawings as "naïveté to be out-grown" (15). Steven belittles her objections to American commercialism, explaining that "everything's man-made now. The highest paying guys in the country are playing a game with a ball and a hoop that somebody thought up. The rest of us move paper back and forth to earn a living. Nobody's hunting tigers or anything" (65). In a nondescript hotel room they watch a pornographic movie in which "artificial," "interchangeable" "peach-colored" body-parts come together: even the gender of the actors "seemed a temporary assignment, with extra breasts and cocks waiting offstage until blond players made their costume change" (11). The modern world produces an epistemological crisis for Luna that she can resolve only by escaping that world of abstractions and fleeing to the wilderness, where she hopes to make contact with the concrete world of nature.

The novel's other main point-of-view character similarly escapes to the wilderness. Paul Cowan is a farm boy from Wisconsin and ex-seminary student who traveled to California seeking freedom in a variety of New Age philosophies, until a construction accident damaged his hearing and left him nearly deaf. Paul flees urban California for meditation in the Donner Lake wilderness after deciding that New Age freedom led only to moral drift. Upon leaving the city, he discovers that he hears much better—without all the background noise and sensory overload. Paul's sojourn near Donner Lake invites comparisons to both Thoreau and biblical prophets, though it is Luna whose wilderness experience becomes mystically transcendental. She is visited by a series of visions and dreams in which she witnesses the spirit of Tamsen Donner, who wasted away somewhere near the park a century and half earlier (just as Luna nearly wasted away from anorexia a year prior to this trip into the wilderness). Whether these visions result from a genuine spiritual visitation or merely from psychic projection, Luna is transfigured by them and becomes capable of affirming her own interior experience as real.

For Betts, however, a personal religious experience or a trip to the wilderness are not goals in and of themselves as much as a preparation for the individual better to serve within a community. Paul tells Luna that both religion and sex "carry us outside ourselves" (170), though, according to his mother, religion has often been for him merely another form of abstraction. He remembers her saying, "Paul, if you came to two road signs and one said TO HEAVEN and one said TO A DISCUSSION ABOUT HEAVEN, I know which way you'd go" (245). Through the friendship, conversation, and sexual intimacy they share near Donner Lake, Luna and Paul begin to reach beyond themselves, and, when they become involved with a young, quiet Hispanic boy they call Uncle Sam, they form an incipient community. When they reenter Reno together, however, their circle is broken by the very modern forces all three of them fled to the wilderness to escape. Sam has been exploited by a child pornography ring. His recapture by these outlaws results in a long chase scene followed by Sam's eventual liberation and then, ironically, his entrapment by well-intentioned social workers at St. Mary's hospital, who, not unlike the pornographers, fail to see the boy as a human being. Sam is reduced to a statistic as "a swarm of Social Services bureaucrats [have] clustered around [the hospital's] admissions office on behalf of the rescued boy. Sam was an orphan, a kidnappee, a juvenile, an indigent, a victim of child abuse, a potential prosecution witness, a member of an ethnic minority. He had been lost and then injured in different park jurisdictions, kidnapped within the city limits, and perhaps had residency in two states. So the hospital's hall filled up with staffers from competing agencies, carrying clipboards and snapping their ballpoint pens, in a crowd that included news reporters and one gray-haired priest" (247–48).

The name symbolism of "Uncle Sam" is as heavy-handed as that found in O'Connor; however, in this novel interested in uncanny patterns and coincidences, it is completely natural that the boy represents the collective masses dispossessed of identity by all the various modern forces that collude to turn them into abstractions of "somebody else's mind."

In her agrarian opposition to such abstraction, Betts echoes the Nashville Agrarians' criticism of Howard Odum and other Chapel Hill sociologists, who, in the early decades of the twentieth century, sought to study the South as a sociological problem, which could be solved only by first compiling the data necessary to understand the region. The Agrarians blamed the Chapel Hill progressives, as well as the eastern capitalists who financed the industrialization of the South, for ushering in a century in which the South would "surrender its moral, social, and economic autonomy."[98] Not least among the values superseded by the "victorious principle"[99] of northern industrialism was religion, which, the Agrarians argued, depended upon a life led in close contact with the soil. "Religion," they maintained, "can hardly expect to flourish in an industrial society. Religion is our submission to the general intention of a nature that is fairly inscrutable; it is the sense of our role as creatures within it. But nature industrialized, transformed into cities and artificial habitations, manufactured into commodities, is no longer nature but a highly simplified picture of nature. . . . The God of nature under these conditions is merely an amiable expression, a superfluity. . . ."[100] Although Ransom, Tate, and others among the Agrarians frequently demonstrate a gentrified elitism antithetical to Betts's vision so consistently grounded in the experience of the plain folk, she shares with them an opposition to modern industrialism and commercialism that militate against the natural flourishing of religious sensibility and the healthy sense of community that she finds dependent upon religion. Although her ideas about southern class structure and racism are generally more akin to those of Cash, she, unlike Cash, appreciates the cultural traditions of the common farmer and finds in those indigenous traditions the salvation of a region in a condition of accelerating flux.

The Sharp Teeth of Love ends with just such a reaffirmation of the values rooted in the farming life. Just as the novel's conclusion appears to move inexorably toward tragedy—with Uncle Sam surrounded by social workers and administrators—the boy is again kidnapped, though this time not by pornographers but by Paul Cowan's mother, a loving farm woman from Wisconsin. With the swiftness of a deus ex machina, she penetrates the phalanxes of bureaucracy to take the boy from his hospital bed and spirit him away to her midwestern farm. Aided by the newly engaged Paul and Luna, Erika Cowan will heal the boy's body *and* spirit; living in a sanctuary removed from the degrading and abstracting processes of modern society, these four characters begin building their own small community.

Perhaps Erika Cowan's identity as a midwesterner merely facilitates Betts's plan to write an expansive, American novel, rather than one limited to the South; however, the portrait of the South that Betts provides—the urban melting pots of Chapel Hill and Virginia Beach and such tourist traps as Thomas Wolfe's home and Graceland—offers an unavoidable contrast with Erika

Cowan's Midwest, which appears to be the more authentic region, one where small farms are still viable. In the Sun Belt South of *Sharp Teeth*, occupied by rootless new southerners, familial and regional histories are not even available as a corrective to the moral drift that accompanies urbanization; instead, Luna must look outside the South to the Midwest for a vision of a life ordered by agrarian and religious values. If we recall the frequent jibes against the eastern, urban Midwest—most notably Ohio—in novels by southern writers such as Walker Percy and Josephine Humphreys, Betts's identification of the rural Midwest as a more authentic place than the upper South becomes a bitter pill, indeed. Like Percy's, her novels function as jeremiads, critiquing the contemporary urban South in an effort to restore for her readers healthier values to be found in her region's agrarian past. The same statement she makes about the religious content in her novels might be made about the plain-folk farming culture to which traditional Christian faith was such an integral and organic part: "If there is something worth saving, there is an urgency to save it."[101]

REYNOLDS PRICE
Plain Folk in the Tobacco Belt

2

At the beginning of the twenty-first century, a drive from Doris Betts's Iredell County eastward through the Piedmont to Reynolds Price's Warren County will still reveal persistent contrasts in landscape, economics, and demographics. As the steeply rolling hills flatten out into what Price's character Hutch Mayfield describes as a "nearly invisible rolling"[1] and red clay darkens into the fertile soil of the coastal plain, industry gives way to tobacco fields, black faces become more numerous, and suburban sprawl is replaced by old towns filled with houses preserved from another era. Although corporate interests have recently gained increasingly greater control over farming in eastern North Carolina, this change is not readily apparent to the casual traveler, who might feel as though he has left the modern age and entered a well-preserved agrarian past. These geographical differences—which would have been even more pronounced during the 1940s and 1950s, the formative years of both Price and Betts—might account for the writers' vastly different engagements of their respective regional pasts. Betts typically sets her fictions in the rapidly changing present, whereas Price more often sets his novels in a seemingly unchanging past. Betts appears desperate to record the vestiges of a disappearing yeoman culture; Price, like Faulkner, examines how the past continually reemerges throughout successive generations, calling to mind Hutch Mayfield's description of the landscape.

This feeling of a recurring past yields two distinct engagements of the plain folk in Price's work, which are most clearly demonstrated by a comparison of representative novels from his Mustian trilogy and his Mayfield trilogy. In the first novel of the Mustian trilogy, *A Long and Happy Life*, lower-middle-class farmers are idealized within the traditions of classical pastoral and southwestern humor. Their farming community is depicted as an Arcadia, sealed off from the flow of history that comes to the outside world, thus preserving an ideal way of life. Even relations between the Mustians and their black neighbors are idealized and free of the moral complications that characterize race relations in the Mayfield trilogy. The Mayfields are plain folk, but genteel by comparison to the Mustians; drawn largely from Price's family history, the Mayfields are more realistically rendered, as is the intricate web of relationships between whites and blacks. Furthermore, whereas the idealized pastoral of the Mustian novel *A Long and Happy Life* requires cultural stasis, such stability becomes an obstacle to social progress for the Mayfields, especially with respect to Price's most compelling concern—the possibility of healing between black and white races.

Both trilogies, as well as Price's memoir *Clear Pictures,* provide extended treatments of race relations. In contrast to the segregated Piedmont chronicled by Betts and Edgerton, Price observes a society in which whites and blacks have lived in much closer contact, which suggests a greater continuity with relations between master and slave during the antebellum period. Price's fiction therefore provides much greater access to the history of slavery in North Carolina than does the work of writers from the Piedmont and mountains. Furthermore, his characterizations of small farmers and their communities during the twentieth century blur many of the distinctions often made between planters and yeomen, which suggests that both groups have contributed to the shared values of eastern North Carolina plain folk.

"No Pillared Mansions": Life in Warren County

Focusing on the signs of cultural erosion found in the proliferation of strip malls, fast food franchises, and satellite television dishes, Doris Betts has remarked that the South is "in every way . . . now closer to national norms than it used to be."[2] Price, by contrast, has judged that "the Old South is still very much present. . . . I think we can still say that for all the influx of IBM and Telecom employees, you can go in Kroger's or you can go in the Record Bar and know in 10 seconds if you're at all sensitive that you're not in New Jersey or Michigan. The old culture isn't going to vanish any time soon."[3] Price observes that, during his childhood in eastern North Carolina, the "intellectual and emotional atmosphere" was "in no serious way different from 1865."[4] When asked to compare eastern North Carolina to the Piedmont, Price has said of his people, "They're very Tidewater. Farmers. You have to remember that. And 70 percent black in my childhood. Warrenton was a real architectural gem, along with Edenton and New Bern."[5] Although much farther west than Edenton or New Bern, and geographically situated along the easternmost edge of the Piedmont, Price locates Warrenton culturally and economically within the Tidewater, a claim that is supported by the county's deep roots in plantation agriculture. In 1790, Warren County was one of only three counties in the state where slaves constituted more than 50 percent of the total population.[6] Contrary to the rapid industrialization that has taken place throughout the western and central Piedmont along the Interstate 85 corridor from Charlotte

to Raleigh, Warren County remains principally agrarian and resistant to industrialization. "Warren County has always had this official policy of wanting to
industrialize," Price explains, "but as soon as someone comes in and builds a little underwear factory, the people take a sort of unofficial line against it and the
factory packs up and leaves five years later. I remember once standing with my
aunt out on Main St. Warrenton on a Saturday and three or four strangers rode
by in cars and a friend of my aunt's looked at us and said: 'Look at all these
strangers in here, just wearing our streets out.'"[7] Such staunch regional insularity and agrarianism are qualities that many of Betts's Piedmonters have lost.
Like W. J. Cash, Betts observes among many Piedmonters the instinct for social
upward mobility to be much more primary than an agrarian sentiment—
though, unlike Cash, Betts proves herself to be an agrarian in her lament of
such an instinct. Similarly, Price asserts that "living in cities" is a "primary
error . . . which it seems human beings really weren't ever intended to do—not
if they were ever going to remain human."[8] With his fictional vision focused
on rural Warren County, Price has found it much easier than Betts simply to
ignore the urbanization of the South.

The geographical differences between the family homes of Betts and Price
are compounded by differences of class. Whereas the cultural survival of Betts's
family suffered as a result of regional economic change—her parents left the
farms of humble yeomen and sharecroppers to seek greater stability in mill
work—Price describes his family as "very socially secure people" who had
"solid, respected places in their community, in their church, the power structure of Warren County, and had since the eighteenth century at least."[9]
Although his parents struggled financially during the Depression years of
Price's childhood, their connection to a "socially secure" family provided continuity of class identity. This class security, combined with the continuity of an
agricultural economic base in Warren County, might help explain Price's dis-
regard for social forces, which hardly seem to affect the lives of most of his
characters. In her review of *The Surface of Earth*, a novel that spans the period
of 1903–1944, Anne Hobson Freeman notes, for example, the absence of attention to "the two World Wars and the Depression . . . which must have touched
even families as remote and self-absorbed as these in rural North Carolina and
Virginia."[10] The final section of *Surface* coincides with the Allied forces' inva-
sion of Normandy, but these global events provide only a distant backdrop to
the family drama in the foreground. Whereas Betts's stories involve the reactions of her characters to an accelerating flux of social and economic forces—
which creates opportunities of "upward mobility" and a simultaneous loss of
cultural traditions—Price chronicles a static order with limited evidence of
class fluidity and only gradual cultural change over time.

Significantly no Snopes trilogy appears in Price's oeuvre. Unlike Faulkner's poor whites, Price's lower-class yeomen, the Mustians, pose no threat to the social or economic security of a declining aristocracy. First of all, no true aristocracy, declining or otherwise, appears in Price's fiction. The closest approximates—Mr. Isaac in *A Long and Happy Life*, Fob Foster in *Kate Vaiden*, and the Mayfields of *A Great Circle*—are, as Price says of his own family, "not preening themselves on their aristocratic origins."[11] More important, as Betts makes clear in "We *Were* the Snopeses," in North Carolina the Snopeses were Piedmonters, because throughout the twentieth century that is where opportunities for social and economic advancement arose by means of industrialization and capital investment. By contrast, the economic stasis that characterized the agricultural coastal plain and that variously affected both whites and blacks created little opportunity for social mobility. Planters from eastern North Carolina who survived the Civil War and Reconstruction with capital still intact very often began to transfer their agricultural investments to business ventures throughout the Piedmont. William Powell notes that, contrary to the proliferation of rags-to-riches stories about such figures as Washington Duke or George Alexander Gray, the majority of business development was produced by the upper and middle classes, "most of which came from the planter stratum."[12] Many planters made the transition to an industrial economy less successfully, which is the case with Price's family. Steven Hahn explains how, in contrast to postemancipation societies elsewhere in the Western world, reduced wealth devastated the national political influence of southern planters, leaving the balance of power decidedly with the industrial Northeast.[13] Powell demonstrates how in North Carolina there resulted a similar shift of power toward the emerging urban and industrial centers of the Piedmont.[14] Despite this national and regional loss of power, Price asserts that within their own communities descendants of planters did not so easily yield their social standing.

Although Price says that his people were "definitely not wealthy" or self-conscious of their aristocratic origins,[15] the very fact of those origins signifies a different conception of class than that appearing among the descendants of common yeomen in the Piedmont of Betts—or in the Appalachia of Fred Chappell. In "Welcome to High Culture," a tribute to his friend and mentor and a recollection of their undergraduate years together at Duke University, Chappell recalls Price's early literary accomplishments, as well as his genteel poise. Fresh off his mountain farm, Chappell entered Duke during Price's senior year. After hearing rumors about the upperclassman's stellar accomplishments, Chappell and fellow freshman James Applewhite decided to find out if the rumors were true. They would introduce themselves to the "wizard," the editor of Duke's literary magazine, the *Archive*, but only after finding courage

in an "unwise quantity of beer and cooking sherry." Chappell remembers his
first impression:

> We returned to campus and stumbled up the narrow stairs. We
> pounded, lurching, on his door and Reynolds let us in.
>
> Into, it seemed, an entirely different universe. Our rooms in the fresh-
> man dormitories suddenly seemed a thousand miles away, those rooms with
> the mimeograph-paper green walls and bare, pocked linoleum-tile floors
> and for decoration only the naked, inscrutable smiles of Hugh Hefner's
> pinup girls. Reynolds's room was another kind of place. It was agreeably
> lit with lamps, not with those bald overhead lights found in dormitories
> and police stations. There was a rug on the floor; it wasn't large or expen-
> sive-looking, but it meant that we didn't feel we were hiking a chopblock
> when we crossed the room. On the walls were *framed* reproductions of
> Botticelli and Blake and Matisse, on his desk a miniature of a classical
> torso. A record was playing—Elisabeth Schwarzkopf, I think. . . .
>
> "Hello, jerks. Welcome to High Culture," Reynolds said.
>
> —No, he didn't. He couldn't say those words, or think them in an eon
> of trying. Yet I had the fleeting but certain conviction that he was entitled
> to say them.[16]

Chappell exaggerates, for comic purposes, the contrast between his own
hayseed innocence and Price's cultivated gentility, but this sketch suggests certain personal differences that might be attributed, at least in part, to differences
of geography and class. (For example, Price's father traveled throughout the
eastern Piedmont as a salesman of electrical appliances for Carolina Power and
Light, whereas Chappell's father worked for a time as a lineman for the same
company in Appalachia.) After expressing appreciation for the upperclassman's patient guidance, Chappell admits wonder that, even while they were
undergraduates at Duke, Price's style did not much influence his own. "But
maybe it was already clear to me," he says, "that Reynolds and I were headed
in different directions. There seemed to be a tacit agreement that I was to be
intense and wild and experimental, while he was to be traditional, Olympian,
and successful."[17]

Indeed Price experienced literary success very early. While still a student,
he published several mature stories in the *Archive*, and 1958 saw the appearance in *Encounter* of one of his finest and most anthologized stories to date, "A
Chain of Love," in which he introduced Rosacoke Mustian and her rural family. Rosacoke reappears as the protagonist of Price's first novel, *A Long and
Happy Life* (1962), published shortly after Price returned from three years of
study as a Rhodes Scholar at Oxford University to begin his four decades of

distinguished service at his alma mater. While he was still in his twenties, this first novel established Price as a new major voice in American fiction; in addition to winning the William Faulkner Award for a notable first novel, it attracted unqualified praise on both sides of the Atlantic from such luminaries as Eudora Welty and Stephen Spender and was occasioned by a photo review in *Time* and a cover photo on the *Saturday Review*.

Since then Price has published more than thirty books—including novels, memoirs, poetry, short stories, essays, plays, and translations of the biblical gospels—making Price unmatched by any major North Carolina writer for pure prolificness. Among his accolades are the National Book Critics Circle Award for Fiction (*Kate Vaiden*, 1986) and membership in the American Academy of Arts and Letters. He is James B. Duke Professor of English at Duke University, and his books have been translated into sixteen languages. He is best known for his novels, which might be grouped into three categories: the Mustian trilogy, *A Long and Happy Life* (1962), *A Generous Man* (1966), and *Good Hearts* (1988); the Mayfield trilogy, collectively entitled *A Great Circle*, which includes *The Surface of Earth* (1975), *The Source of Light* (1981), and *The Promise of Rest* (1995); and a cluster of novels—beginning with *Kate Vaiden* (1986)—currently being promoted as Price's *life studies*. These later novels feature first-person narrators who speak in a recognizably southern idiom and are generally more widely accessible than the earlier novels, which tend to be more experimental and frequently include narrative voices that James Schiff describes as "biblical or oracular."[18] Price's memoirs have also received considerable attention: *Clear Pictures: First Loves, First Guides* (1989) chronicles his formative first eighteen years and offers invaluable information about his part of the South; in *A Whole New Life: An Illness and a Healing* (1994), Price recounts his battle with spinal cancer in the mid-1980s, an ordeal to which he lost the use of his legs but after which he gained a redoubled energy for writing.

A Long and Happy Life: Plain-Folk Pastoral

Ever since Price's debut novel won the William Faulkner Award, he has endured more than his share of comparisons to Faulkner, many of them unfair and disparaging. For example, in "Mantle of Faulkner?" a review of Price's second novel, *A Generous Man*, John Wain writes that he feels "a vague disquiet at the book's closeness to Faulkner, whose irritating mannerisms are so much more imitable than his moral and imaginative largeness."[19] Nearly two decades later, in "A Minor Faulkner," Benjamin DeMott offers a similar review of a very different book, *The Source of Light*. "The overall impression left," says DeMott, "is that of a fictional world rendered indistinct by the spreading shade of the great Faulkner Tree."[20] Price objects to all such comparisons. "Everyone thinks that everybody born in the South is created by Faulkner," he complains. "I never even liked Faulkner very much and still don't. I'm far more influenced by baroque poetry, especially Milton. Baroque poetry and baroque music."[21] In *The Promise of Rest,* Price's most important autobiographical character, the poet and scholar Hutch Mayfield, offers a still deeper cut to Faulkner: in response to one of his Milton seminar students, who claims that Faulkner has exhausted the subject of southern race relations, Hutch remarks, "I will admit that I don't think William Faulkner is a genius compared to, say, Tolstoy or Dostoevsky. . . . all Faulkner exhausted was runaway English; country show-off prose" (10–11).

Perhaps the most consistent similarity between Price and Faulkner might be described as a classical detachment. In his Nobel acceptance speech, Faulkner criticizes the post–World War II protest fiction, which he identifies as deriving from a materialist impulse and from a culture of fear, rather than the proper subject of art, "the problems of the human heart in conflict with itself."[22] Unlike the fiction of social protest popular during his era, the authorial voice in Faulkner's fiction appears much more reserved and detached. Louis D. Rubin, Jr., has attributed such narrative characteristics as typical of the genteel southern writer. Quoting Allen Tate, who contended that poetry demanded "a serenity of view and a settled temper of mind," Rubin argues that these same virtues were typically identified with the southern gentleman: "the same sense of restraint, of classical wholeness, of unified personality that characterizes the gentleman of the Old South is used to characterize the writing of poetry."[23]

Although Price himself points to much earlier writers as his primary role models—Milton, other baroque poets, and Tolstoy—it is difficult not to recall Rubin's generalizations about the genteel writers of the Southern Renascence when considering Price, who describes himself as someone whose "basic temperament" is a "calmly watchful attitude," rather than someone who easily gets "angry about social injustice."[24] Arguably, while not being overly inspired by writers of the Southern Renascence, Price has dipped into the same well of classical literary virtues that was visited by an earlier generation of genteel southern writers. Like Faulkner, who distanced himself from writers of social protest, Price is more fascinated than outraged by social problems. He has frequently compared himself to a "spy" collecting evidence. "I've just gone on trying to watch the way my world works," he remarked in a 1987 interview, "the way my world is constructed, and to try to offer in my fiction and in my poetry the clearest reports on that that I can give. Not that I see that as the primary thing that I'm doing. I don't think of myself first and foremost as a social analyst. What I do think is that if someone were interested in trying to understand the structure of the Upper South, say from 1900 to 1987, then my novels could offer him a good deal of quite reliable social information; social, cultural, religious, linguistic, you name it."[25] Price's resistance to an overt engagement with the politics of class, gender, and race distinguishes him from Betts, whose fiction consistently concerns itself overtly with social justice. Betts is heir to a southern tradition of social protest, beginning with a wellspring of activity in North Carolina during the 1920s—which included such figures as Howard Odum, Gerald Johnson, Paul Green, and W. J. Cash. Instead of pursuing such a direct engagement of "the problem South," Price shares the detachment of genteel writers from the Southern Renascence, and like some of them (the Nashville Agrarians, for example), Price frequently flirts with the role of southern apologist.

Price's detachment is best demonstrated by his interest in the legacy of slavery in the South. While acknowledging the evils of slavery and the sharecropping system that replaced it, he sounds remarkably similar to Ransom and Tate in 1930 when he argues that the planters themselves were people of "enormous culture, kindness, generosity, goodness."[26] Or at times even sounding like John Calhoun and other antebellum apologists for slavery, who compared southern culture to the classical cultures of Greece and Rome, Price goes so far as to suggest that the cultural attainments of southern planters—and their descendants—were ironically made possible by slavery, a social structure that similarly made possible the contributions of "Sophocles, Euripides, Homer, Plato, Socrates, everyone who wrote in Rome, everyone who lived in the world up until about the 1820s when the notion of emancipation really got going. No one likes the idea of slavery—well, a few slaveowners do—but the fact is that it has existed for most of the history of the human race and has been, like it or not, an important factor in the sorts of cultures that have produced works of art, leisure cultures."[27] While frequently lamenting the inequities associated with slavery's legacy, throughout most of his career Price has sought more often to understand rather than overtly criticize it. An avid fan of *Gone with the Wind*, a movie he reports having watched forty times,[28] Price might even be suspected of the tendency to aestheticize the history of white-black relations in his region of the South. Like James Agee and Walker Evans's *Let Us Now Praise Famous Men* (1941), much of Price's best work raises the question: Is it possible to turn an experience filled with misery into art without falsifying it? If his Mayfield trilogy serves as Price's defense against such a charge, we might be inclined to judge favorably on his behalf, especially because the trilogy's final novel itself raises this same question so relentlessly.

In his first novel, however, Price seems much less anxious about the dangers of aestheticizing his subjects, less concerned with history, and more exclusively concerned with fully appreciating the pathos at the heart of an isolated yeoman community, even when this requires idealizing that commuity. If *A Long and Happy Life* lacks the scope and the realism of the Mayfield novels, it may be Price's most lyrically beautiful novel. Its beauty may very well derive from the lack of these other qualities—in the same sense that Poe, in "The Poetic Principle," argues that truth "has no sympathy with the myrtles."[29] *A Long and Happy Life* is arguably Price's most stylized novel, and its characters the most idealized, reminiscent of the glorification of the peasants in Tolstoy. Price has admitted that the Mustians and their neighbors have largely been invented rather than remembered, that he never even entered one of the houses of the rural families near Asheboro on whom he based the Mustians, because the children were "working members of families bent on making the crop that was food-or-famine." As a result of such limited access to his subject, he explains, "in all the fiction I've set in their midst, unrealistic as it means to be . . . I've used the faces they showed me in school and have guessed the remainder, the nighttime half."[30] Although Price based the Mustians on farming families near Asheboro (in the central Piedmont), where he spent three years of his childhood, in his fiction he locates their community of Afton in the vicinity of his family's tobacco-belt hometown, Warrenton.

The Mustians and nearly everyone in their small, rural community occupy a lower social class of yeomen than the Mayfields (or Price's extended family upon whom the Mayfields are based). Unlike the Mayfields, the Mustians do not employee a retinue of black help and sharecroppers. Unlike the impressively articulate Mayfields (*The Surface of Earth* is largely composed of beautifully expressive family letters), the Mustians express themselves within a recognizably regional idiom and understand their world in terms of a parochial worldview. Their parochialism and folksy innocence—which have resulted from their extreme cultural insularity—appeared as defining attributes when the Mustians made their first appearance in "A Chain of Love" (1958), Price's first major publication. This story takes the form of a visit by the rural plain folk to the big city, and the confrontation of rural and urban cultures produces much of the story's abundant humor.

Teenaged Rosacoke and Rato Mustian accompany their grandfather, "Papa," to the Raleigh hospital and camp out there with him for several days, waiting to be relieved by their mother, who is obliged to finish her duties preparing for the upcoming children's day at the church back home. The institutional atmosphere of the hospital serves to cast the Mustians' hayseed manners and values in bold relief. For example, Rosa thinks of the Saturday night date she is missing with her boyfriend, Wesley: a trip to Warrenton to view the traveling exhibit of the Florida state electric chair (sponsored by the Lions Club). Rosa wears the robe she made and for which she won honorable mention in the "4-H Fall Dress Review in the Warren County Armory."[31] She is overly worried about her honor, about her decorum, and demonstrates the hayseed's conservative overcompensation in an effort not to be thought a "hussy" (493). Then there is Baby Sister, who is known to cure a sore throat by breathing on it. The story's most outrageously comic figure is Papa; when Rosacoke buttons up his pajamas to his neck because she finds indecent the exposure of his hairy chest, Papa's reaction suggests a combination of Eudora Welty's beard-obsessed Papa-Daddy and cross-dressing Uncle Rondo. Papa protests to being so buttoned up, declaring that he is "hot as a mink in Africa and that his chest [has] been that hairy ever since he shaved it to be Maid of Honor in the womanless wedding Delight Church put on when he was seventeen years old" (491).

This story's considerable power arises from the juxtaposition of the comic with the tragic and sublime—as when Papa stoically confronts his own aging, meditating on how he knows "so many more dead men than live ones" and realizing that there is not "a soul left who could call him by his first name" (512). A deeper pathos arises from Rosacoke's developing concern for a dying man and his family in the room across the corridor. After the man fails to recover from surgery, Rosacoke watches as the family gathers around him, and, standing outside the darkened room where the Latin phrases of extreme unction are being chanted, she realizes with terrible sadness what it must be like to die so far away from home. As in "A Chain of Love," throughout A Long and Happy Life, Price juxtaposes the comic and tragic, the exuberant local color of life in Afton with a very sober and frequent consideration of death. Combining a funeral with a motorcycle, the novel's opening scene vividly illustrates this technique. Rosacoke has enlisted her boyfriend, Wesley, to take her to the funeral of her black childhood friend Mildred Sutton, but she no doubt did not expect to ride with him on the back of his motorcycle while he raced the funeral procession to the church, weaving in and out of the line of cars, "switching coon tails" in their faces.[32] The combination of pathos and comedy continues as Rosacoke sits in the back of the church listening to the preacher while Wesley, oblivious, revs the motorcycle's engine in the parking lot and roars up and down the road.

Price may well have learned the technique of juxtaposing comedy and tragedy from Twain, who employs it to great effect in Adventures of Huckleberry Finn. Moreover, a 1955 journal entry, in which Price writes, "There is nothing finer in our [American] literature than Huck,"[33] suggests the extent to which Price may have borrowed a way of seeing plain folk from Twain—and the tradition of southwestern humor that Twain adapted for higher artistic purposes. Just as the unrefined and uncivilized manners of the frontiersman are emphasized by the genteel, educated narrator in southwestern humor, the genteel voice of Price's omniscient narrator contrasts with the rural idiom of the characters' plain-folk dialogue, thereby emphasizing their innocence and ignorance of a larger world beyond their insular farming community. The other lens through which Price views plain folk in his first novel is the pastoral tradition in English literature, which he studied while a Rhodes scholar at Oxford while conceiving *A Long and Happy Life*. Indeed, a case might be made for southwestern humor as a kind of pastoral, providing bawdy idealizations of frontiersmen in harmony with nature.

Even on the level of plot, *A Long and Happy Life* revolves around the pastoral theme of innocence and its loss, as it follows the courtship of two young lovers from Afton—Rosacoke Mustian and Wesley Beavers—and anticipates their initiation into an adult relationship. In a fictional verse conversation with Price, Fred Chappell has characterized this courtship as a modern version of classical pastoral myth: "What is it but the ancient tale / Of Cupid and muddled Psyche? All / That's added is the motorcycle."[34] Schiff cites a reference in Price's notebook that points to another classical source for the novel, Longus's third-century pastoral romance of "Daphnis and Chloe."[35] As in most classical pastoral—and in the subsequent pastoral tradition in English verse—the courtship of Rosacoke and Wesley takes place completely within an enclosed Arcadia or earthly paradise. Constance Rooke notes that the "repetition of Afton locales and the attention paid to routes and modes of conveyance gradually yield a sense of intimately known space, as well of restriction."[36] Through memory Rosacoke repeatedly visits the same local settings, which become sexually charged, because she associates them with Wesley: the limbs of a pecan tree where she first met him spread-eagled shaking down the nuts; the grounds of the Delight Baptist church, where they have a date at the church picnic; and the secret broomstraw field where they consummate their relationship—though not sufficiently to bind Wesley, who is newly discharged from the navy and restless with youthful freedom. Even Rosa's frequent solitary walks along the dirt road away from her house recall the novel's first image of her clinging "for dear life" to Wesley as they speed along on his motorcycle.

If the repetition of images associated with specific landmarks creates the impression of an Arcadia, sealed off from the outside world, the frequent community rituals complete the impression of a pastoral environment in harmony with the seasons. The novel begins with a funeral and a church picnic in July and concludes with a church Christmas pageant. This church-centered community is exactly the sort Betts imagines to have once gathered around the abandoned Hebron Church in *The River to Pickle Beach*. The lives of these characters are clearly circumscribed and conditioned by shared values and a shared sense of time and place. Theirs is not a world free of suffering; life and death are shown to be inextricably bound, as evidenced by the two deaths recorded in the novel, associated with childbirth (a theme found throughout Price's work). The novel ends with a third pairing of birth and death: the Delight Church Christmas pageant, which celebrates the birth of Christ, is understood by all members of the congregation to prefigure the crucifixion, which they will collectively commemorate in April.

However, as in both the Christian and the pastoral pagan calendars, *A Long and Happy Life* emphasizes the circularity and renewal of life. The novel is the story of Rosacoke's initiation into that natural and cyclical process of life and death. Roughly twenty years old, Rosacoke has willfully resisted knowledge of sexuality, as well as the self-sacrifice required in child rearing, despite having grown up in a home with her "Baby Sister," who is a decade younger than Rosacoke. In light of the emotional deprivations of her own childhood, not to mention the frequent deaths associated with childbirth in her community, Rosacoke's frigidity is easily understood. After conceiving a child with Wesley Beavers, Rosacoke begins divesting herself of innocence, a frightening process that she knows could eventually lead to her own death but that will also fully integrate her into the renewing cycle of death and life found in nature and in her agrarian community. Rooke makes an interesting case for the tripartite structure of the novel as one of temptation, sin, and redemption (15–16). Price nevertheless never judges Wesley's or Rosa's sexual behavior within a Christian paradigm. To the contrary, Schiff calls Wesley and Rosa natural "creatures" and convincingly argues that "Wesley is natural man, responding to the same impulses and stimuli that affect other animals: hunger, sexuality, recognition of danger."[37] Rather than Christian, Price portrays Wesley more from a classical perspective; the abundant erotic images of his male figure appear as healthy and natural. This normalization of sexuality—including forms of sexuality that might be considered aberrant—is one of the prevailing concerns throughout Price's oeuvre. His classical treatment of sex becomes all the more apparent if compared to the dualistic treatment of sexuality found in Betts's novels—which so often feature sexual villains (such as Mickey McCane in *Pickle Beach* and the child pornographers in *The Sharp Teeth of Love*). This differing treatment of human sexuality exemplifies a more fundamental difference in their writing—how Betts is principally concerned with social and moral justice, whereas Price more often concerns himself with aesthetic pleasure.

The extent to which even race relations are idealized within the pastoral vision of this first novel becomes apparent early on, when Rosacoke attends the funeral of Mildred Sutton. The deferential treatment shown to Rosacoke throughout the funeral service by members of the black congregation clearly establishes the paternalistic relationship between whites and blacks in Afton, even between blacks and lower-middle-class whites such as the Mustians. This paternalism is in no way crticized, either explicitly or implicitly. The black characters provide relatively little evidence of resenting their situation, and their humble willingness to be of service establishes a behavior that the whites typically emulate, producing seeming reciprocity between the two groups. For example, Mildred's mother, Mary Sutton, serves as a midwife to the community —including the Mustians—and the Mustians freely give baby clothes to Mildred's surviving baby, Sledge. Though not free of racism, the Mustians are relatively innocent of the kind of historical domination of blacks—both economic and sexual—that characterizes the Mayfields. The very presence of significant friendships between white and black children within the community distinguishes Price's vision of race relations in eastern North Carolina from that of Piedmont writers, whose characters are typically much more fearful of and socially segregated from blacks.

The most vivid image to clarify the dynamics of race and class in Afton occurs when Rosacoke attends a Sunday service at the Delight Church, the community's white Baptist church. Although the congregation is composed primarily of a homogeneous group of plain whites, subsistence farmers and their descendants—such as the Mustians, the Guptons, and the Aycocks—the presence of two other people changes the group's structure into a hierarchy that is readily apparent and equally desired by all members of the congregation. When the aging and ill head deacon, Mr. Isaac, and his lifelong black servant, Sammy, enter the sanctuary, the congregation breaths a collective sigh. After anxiously awaiting their arrival, the preacher "stood up and called for the hymn, and while the hymnals were rustling, the side door opened by the choir, and Mr. Isaac's Sammy walked in with the black leather chair. He nodded to the people in general, and they nodded back in relief, and he set the chair where it belonged by the front of the Amen Corner, half to the preacher, half to the people. Then he went out and everybody waited, not standing, till he came again—Mr. Isaac in his arms like a baby" (74). A wealthy land-owner, Mr. Isaac is the community patriarch, who practices charity to all members of the community, hiring blacks as tenant farmers, giving Rosacoke's family fifty dollars when her alcoholic father walks out into oncoming traffic and is killed, and freely allowing all to enjoy the miles and miles of virginal woodlands he owns. In fact, the most significant moments of Wesley and Rosacoke's courtship take place in Mr. Isaac's woods. In return, they all show him a kind of worship, placing him at the front of the church, ritually bringing him gifts of horehound candy at Christmas.

W. J. Cash would critique the behavior of the whites as symptomatic of a "proto-Dorian" bond, or white racism, noting that the less wealthy whites use

Mr. Isaac as a mirror into which they project their own fantasies of white supremacy; his presence among them is necessary to remind them that because they are white like him they too are superior to blacks. And, even though most of them may not be able to afford black servants—Cash would argue—they generalize Sammy's role as servant to Mr. Isaac as black servitude to all whites. Price, however, seems not at all to share Cash's skepticism about white-black relations. Rather than debasing him, Sammy's servitude empowers and ennobles him and models for all members of the congregation the sort of patient, grateful service they consistently seek to give their patriarch. Furthermore, rather than Sammy being dependent upon Mr. Isaac, the situation is clearly reversed. After suffering multiple strokes, aged Mr. Isaac, who never married, lives alone with his sister, in a state of infantile helplessness, "the only thing that loved him being Sammy his man who had grown from the lean black boy that drove him on the land in a truck to the man who carried him now in his arms" (75). The idealization of the relationship between Mr. Isaac and Sammy is further suggested by the fact that it is modeled upon the relationship between Price's elder cousin Mac Thornton—whom Price idolized—and his black driver, Joe.

Just as Price's vision of white-black relations in eastern North Carolina differs significantly from that of Piedmonter W. J. Cash, so does his vision of the relationship between lower- and upper-class whites. Cash views this relationship as an essentially hostile and exploitive one that ought to provoke class consciousness and rebellion on the part of the poorer whites. For Cash, solidarity among poorer whites fails to materialize because of their own racism and greed, because they dream of one day advancing socially to the same level as their economic betters. To the contrary, in A Long and Happy Life, Mr. Isaac appears to be essentially generous, and the plain whites of the community, rather than demonstrating a desire to diminish the difference between themselves and Mr. Isaac, seek to preserve that difference through a variety of rituals in which they humble themselves before him. Despite his prominence within their community, however, Mr. Isaac, like Price's cousin Mac Thornton, does not willfully separate himself from his lower-class community members. In stark contrast, for example, to William Alexander Percy's 1941 assessment of his Mississippi Delta as composed of "three dissimilar threads and only three"[38]—gentility, poor whites, and blacks—with the upper- and lower-class whites occupying completely separate social worlds, Price's gentleman planter, Mr. Isaac, happily lives within the same social world as his lower-class peers. He attends the Baptist church instead of driving to Warrenton in search of an Episcopal congregation. Except for wealth, which he does not conspicuously display or use to separate himself culturally or socially, Mr. Isaac appears to

hold the same values and participate in the same community rituals and institutions as his less wealthy neighbors.

   If Price's depiction of relations between gentility and poorer whites differs
from Percy's, Price does share with the Mississippian—at least in *A Long and
Happy Life*—a belief in the essentially positive and necessary role of social hierarchy, which distinguishes him from most North Carolina writers of his generation, for whom such hierarchy threatens the Jeffersonian republicanism upon
which the yeoman's society is founded. Whereas most contemporary North
Carolina writers, especially those from the Piedmont and mountains, criticize
the multiple possibilities for exploitation that result from such social hierarchy,
Price finds that these differences between members of a community create the
necessity for them to reach out beyond the limits of their respective groups,
and thus beyond the limits of the isolated self, in order to form a community.
Through the journey of her pregnancy, Rosacoke Mustian comes to understand
how her life is not solitary but bound up with all of the individual lives, regardless of race or class, within her farming village. Reflecting on his own youth in
the memoir *Clear Pictures: First Loves, First Guides,* Price reaches very similar
conclusions.

Clear Pictures: Plain Folk as Planters

Reminiscent of *Lanterns on the Levee*, William Alexander Percy's 1941 memoir
of genteel life in the Mississippi Delta, Price's account of his first eighteen years
focuses on representative figures from his community—parents, other relatives,
"black help," and numerous teachers—who were essential to his maturation
as an artist and as a man. In the process, he offers a thorough exploration of
the mores and values of his culture. Compared to the harrowing tales of childhood from many southerners, especially the increasingly popular autobiographies from the lower or lower middle class—fine books by the likes of Rick
Bragg, Tim McLaurin, Dorothy Allison, and Harry Crews—Price's recollections appear tame. Price himself admits that "as the meat of narrative, most of
my days were tepid broth" (5). What most distinguishes Price's story from other
twentieth-century southern memoirs is the remarkable lack of ambivalence he
feels for his people and their early lessons. With the exception of his criticism
of their racism—which he heavily qualifies to the point of exoneration—he
recalls his childhood with extreme gratitude and acceptance. "I've tried to
honor the family morals and have worked to be honest" (15), he writes, and
elsewhere, "I've never been forced to hate my homeplace, as many of my writing friends came to do" (220). Price explains that, except for the years he spent
as a Rhodes Scholar at Oxford, he never lived outside North Carolina. "Unlike

a number of Southern writers in my generation," he says, "I never felt driven out of my region, whatever its wrongs" (117).

In this celebration of the various members of his family and community who nurtured him as a man and artist, Price also celebrates the values that they collectively represent, values rooted in the specific cultural ideology and folk-ways of Warren County. Like other contemporary writers from North Carolina, Price celebrates the plain folk and identifies with their connection to the earth, their humble, rural lifestyles, and their lack of aristocratic pretense. In contrast to the other writers in this study, however, Price traces his lineage to aristocratic forebears and identifies the southern planter's sense of noblesse oblige as central to his model of a healthy, interdependent community. Because he identifies so thoroughly and unambivalently with his own family's genteel heritage, neither he nor his characters display the hostility to aristocracy or to plantation economy often attributed to yeomen. On the contrary, he views planters as occupying a positively paternalistic and economically sustaining role in a community of dignified but impoverished dependents. Furthermore, Price emphasizes the cultural intermingling of all classes within his society. Planters and their tenants and servants (both white and black) learn from each other the need for interdependent service. This cultural blending produces in both Price's fiction and his memoir what might be called a "plain-folk planter."

Price's identification of the planter and his society as plain folk reflects the postbellum history of many planters and their families throughout the South. Edward Ayers explains that, with the postbellum collapse of plantation economy, most southern planters entered the merchant class,[39] and such is the case with Price's family. Far removed from any real or imagined genteel past, Price's recent ancestors held middle-class jobs as clerks, traveling salesmen, railroad station masters, and carriage makers. Price points out that, with a "single exception," there were no farmers among the prior two generations of his father's and mother's families (86). Likewise, the Mayfields, who are loosely based on Price's family, own farm land that they lease to tenants, while they themselves pursue other, middle- and lower-middle-class, professions and remain what Allen Tate would call "spectator farmers."[40]

Regardless of their recent economic status, Price frequently calls attention to his family's noble past, which was distinguished by positions of community leadership extending back to "the eighteenth century at least."[41] The prominent figures he finds among his family ancestry include Sir Francis Drake (81), Nathaniel Macon (speaker of the house under Thomas Jefferson; 20, 125), John Egerton (who commissioned Milton's Comus for the occasion of Egerton's "elevation" from earl of Bridgewater to the lord presidency of Wales; 19), and

James Agee, whom Price says he and his family share with their "Tennessee cousin, the writer James Agee" (21). He even traces his family blood to the Indian princess Pocahontas (157) and suggests noble African blood for his family's long-term gardener and handyman Grant Terry, whose face he calls "a perfect twin to the face of the pharaoh Akhnaton" (100). Price makes clear that his family was not obsessed or often even aware of their lineage, declaring that, while "the memory of such a standing was retained by a few of the deep-country farmers my Egertons had become, after two centuries in slaveholding Virginia and North Carolina, they seldom bragged on their blood" (19). Price himself appears therefore somewhat uncommon among his kin in his interest in a noble lineage. As evidence of this heritage, he recalls a framed land grant signed by the English Earl Granville to his family's Egerton forebears, which hung in the hallway of the one home other than his parents' that "affected [him] most powerfully" (123), the Thornton homeplace in Macon.

In the town of Macon, his mother's birthplace (and his own), and five miles away in the small county seat of Warrenton, his father's birthplace (and Nathaniel Macon's), Price finds the clearest image of how he imagines his family's agrarian past to have been. Before the Civil War, Price says, Warrenton was a "social and political center of the state. . . . the home of wealthy slave-holding planters, many of whose elegant houses have lately been refurbished" (20). Price's farming relatives, the Thorntons, represented for him a link to his family's past. Price's nuclear family led a nomadic existence, moving eleven times during his first twelve years (71), because of the demands of his father's career as a traveling salesman, first of life insurance and later of electrical appliances. They lived mostly in towns and small cities around the eastern Piedmont, in places such as Raleigh, Roxboro, Henderson, Asheboro, Macon, and Warrenton. Despite their wandering, the Warren County homes of relatives—mostly on his mother's side—remained for Price a spiritual anchor and provided the settings for most of his fiction.

One of the most significant models for living that Price found was his grand-fatherly older cousin Macon Thornton, whom Price and everyone else called Mac (pronounced *Make*). A lifelong bachelor and the manager of a family farm that extended over thousands of acres, Mac became a major benefactor of the young Price. At the age of ten, Reynolds was taken by his cousin Mac out to the tobacco field and told to pick out a row. In the fall of that year the old farmer sent the boy the fifty dollars profit from his row of tobacco, and in subsequent years the amount steadily increased. On his deathbed Mac gave Reynolds a sealed envelope containing three thousand dollars to further his education, which to the college sophomore at Duke in 1951 was an "almost unimaginable" sum (145). More important than the regular financial assistance,

Price identifies the model of a country gentleman that his wealthy, though unassuming, rural cousin set for him. Price idealizes Mac as the ideal blend of planter and plain folk, having the capacity of the planter to serve not only as employer but as paternalistic benefactor to his farm community, and having the lack of pretense and the humility associated with the yeoman.

Just as Price observes "no pillared mansions" (18) in the town of Macon, he qualifies the image of the ostentatiously wealthy southern planter with the figure of Mac Thornton, whom he describes as a "clean" and "neat, if not stylish, country-gentleman dresser" (125). According to family stories, Mac had once attended "a year or so" at Trinity College, later named Duke University, even though he never spoke of books with his young cousin, except constantly to encourage Reynolds in his schooling. Price recalls, "[Mac's] last words to me as I left each summer was 'Be smart, Ren. Any damned fool can fail. Look at me, dumb as dirt. You be some count, hear?'" (132). Price clearly finds in Mac's advice both a recognition by family of the positive value of education and an innate humility, which he sought to emulate. This humility and lack of ostentation appears most notably in Mac's attitude toward the profits from his farms. If Mac's economic relations with his tenants identifies him as a planter, his attitude toward capital more resembles that of yeomen and contrasts sharply with the ostentatious displays of wealth associated with planter culture. Price observes of Mac that "despite his being one of the largest landowners in the county, you'd never have guessed the extent of his holdings. And he'd never have told you. . . . like any self-respecting country squire, Mac's taste forebade the mention of personal finances" (125).

That Mac Thornton might serve as an example of the wealthy planter in North Carolina suggests the extent to which the yeoman and not the planter has served as a cultural icon throughout the state. If some wealthy planters like Mac chose not to indulge in conspicuous consumption but rather practiced extreme frugality and habitually horded their profits by investing in land, they were practicing yeoman attitudes toward capital. Many historians have debated whether ownership of even a few slaves disqualified a farmer as a yeoman.[42] In his study of kinship patterns in antebellum Orange County, North Carolina, Robert Kenzer makes a convincing case for including nonslaveowners and small slaveowners (and even some wealthy planters) within the same social groups, since extended families typically included members of both groups and intermarriage between them was frequent.[43] Those scholars who oppose designation of small slaveholders as yeomen often argue that census data reveal how even farmers who owned one or two slaves moved away from diversification and subsistence farming toward greater cultivation of cash crops and involvement in a market economy. If the designation of *yeoman* or even *plain folk* is based primarily upon economic considerations, not only the modes of production but the modes of consumption should be investigated.

Adam Cloninger and David Golightly Harris, two Piedmont farmers, provide examples of how the small slaveowner's consumption patterns resembled those of the typical yeoman in his region. Cloninger emigrated from Germany during the eighteenth century and settled in what was then Lincoln County, North Carolina, as a small farmer. By the time of his death in 1818 he had acquired three slaves and a "plantation" consisting of 256 acres, which he left to his oldest son. Despite the additional wealth the slaves may have provided, Cloninger's will and estate sale records reveal virtually no investment in the material luxuries that might be expected to be found in a planter home, such as fine china, silver, elaborate furnishings, or musical instruments. Of the 208 lots sold at auction, the vast majority list livestock, tools, and farm products and supplies, such as wool, leather, and barrels. Also telling are the numerous items associated with a self-sufficient farm, such as smith's tools, a loom and spinning wheel, a box of shoemaking tools, and eleven barrels of salt (presumably for preserving meat). These tools likely were used to augment farm income, as well. The three slaves sold at auction constituted 70 percent of the total sales. The lack of luxury items suggests not only the limits of capital available to the small slaveholder but also a frugal, self-sufficient lifestyle and principal investment in land and slaves, aimed at coordinating the capacity of land and labor to maximize production.[44]

The farm of David Golightly Harris was located approximately fifty miles to the southwest of Cloninger's, near Spartanburg Village, South Carolina. Though the son of a wealthy planter, Harris began his farming career in 1845 as the owner of about fifty acres, given to him by his father.[45] By 1860 he owned ten slaves and spent most of his labor in managing the farm. With Reconstruction, he was forced back into cultivating his own fields and even occasionally selling a piece of land to pay his taxes.[46] By the time of his death in 1875 he owned more than a thousand acres, though his total "personal property" amounted to only $1,836.97.[47] In his introduction to Harris's journals, Philip N. Racine identifies this Piedmont farmer's patterns of reinvestment in land as typical. "It was characteristic of Southern farmers," says Racine, "to buy as much land as possible, whether they could use it or not, in most cases in the vain hope of someday being able to cultivate it."[48] Even though Harris was significantly wealthier than the average farmer of his era, and even though, as Racine points out, his journals demonstrate that he "could and, perhaps, should have spent his discretionary income on improved creature comforts for his family," he chose not to. Instead, like the typical farmer of his time, he consistently "looked to the distant future, to the establishment of a financially secure and permanently comfortable lifestyle, rather than to the enjoyment of a materially improved but perhaps transitory present."[49]

A consideration of Harris's social life is relevant to his patterns of consumption. Although he was driven by ambition to amass a fortune, and enjoyed a "wide acquaintance with the powerful people of the district," Harris's journals show that "the vast majority of the time the Harris family devoted to socializing was spent with neighbors" and that he did the majority of his traveling within four miles of his home.[50] His spending habits were, therefore, likely more heavily conditioned by the habits of his closest rural neighbors than by the elites whom he saw less frequently. Contrary, then, to the assumption that social values always flow downward from the social elite to the middle classes, Harris offers an example of a farmer whose values, as embodied in his patterns of consumption, were more consistent with the nonslaveholding yeomen than with the planters above his class. Despite his even more significant wealth, Price's uncle, Mac Thornton, practiced the same plain-folk virtues of industry and frugality exemplified by David Golightly Harris and by the nonslaveholding yeoman Basil Thomasson, who in his diary celebrates the study of these virtues in *Franklin's Life and Essays*.[51] Mac's connection to the society of rural plain folk is typical of many rural planters, such as David Golightly Harris and William Barbee of Orange County, North Carolina, who in 1850 owned forty-one slaves, while continuing to attend the Mount Moriah Baptist church, along with the rest of his kin, who tended to own either no slaves or only a few.[52] Kenzer notes a marked distinction between the social habits of antebellum planters who were descended from small farmers in the region and those who moved to the area without ancestral ties.[53]

While Mac's disinterest in the social advantages associated with wealth resembles the attitudes of some wealthy planters from the antebellum period who were integrated into plain-folk communities by kinship, his adoption of plain-folk attitudes toward wealth was possibly further motivated by the financial distress experienced by small farmers and planters alike in his region from the Civil War well into the twentieth century. This period was characterized by an economic transition that accompanied the decline of planters and the rise of yeomanry and tenancy down east. Following the Civil War and their substantial loss of slave property, many planters left the farm and began investing in industrial and business ventures located in the central and western parts of the state. Wealth and influence flowed westward as well. Throughout the state, Powell finds that, as "plantations and larger farms were divided (land was often sold out of the family that had long owned it), the number of farms in the state increased and the average number of acres per farm correspondingly declined."[54] He notes not only the rise of tenancy but of yeomanry as well,[55] indicating that the "creation of numerous small farms was one of the most obvious legacies of the Civil War."[56] Census data from 1860 and 1900 show that the number of farms nearly tripled, rising from 75,203 to 225,000, while farm ownership also rose, but at a less dramatic rate, increasing only from 104,877 in 1860 to 132,000 in 1900. This disparity points to an obvious rise in tenancy, which was most pronounced statewide in the two decades before 1900, when the percentage of North Carolina farms occupied by tenants increased from 33.5 percent to 41.4 percent.

These rates were significantly higher in regions such as Price's Warren County, where urban centers and industrial jobs were few and farms were more exclusively devoted to cultivation of one or both of the state's two main cash crops: tobacco and cotton.[57] Whereas the Piedmont began to feel a lifting of the yoke of tenancy as sharecroppers fled to textile mills throughout the first half of the twentieth century, down east tenancy continued to worsen and re-mained a significant economic factor well into the 1960s.[58] In 1930, Samuel H. Hobbs, Jr., declared, "It is safe to say that no other region in America has increased its farm tenants as rapidly since 1910 as eastern North Carolina."[59] Throughout the late-nineteenth and early twentieth centuries, the crop-lien system became more thoroughly entrenched and agricultural prices continued to stagnate or fall; the fortunes of farmers of all classes, simultaneously, contin-ued to languish. Although Warren County led the state in tobacco production in 1860, by 1890 it did not even appear in the top ten counties for production of North Carolina's most profitable cash crop.[60] In such an economic climate, the values of the small farmer would have made a significant impact on the agrarian culture of Warren County, even while they coexisted with values derived from a long-standing plantation economy, with its bifurcated classes of farm owners and dependent tenants. In Price's family and his fiction, we find the presence of social hierarchy and noblesse oblige associated with planter culture, along with humble lifestyles and lack of conspicuous consumption associated with plain folk.

Price's family did not depend upon accumulation of wealth for social status or family identity. "For all their faults," he writes, "none of my grown kin were in love with money. Though again, I was born in the pit of the Great Depres-sion, I never heard within my family a whole conversation on the subject of money. There'd be little snatches of worry about a bill, little dry quick laughs at the specter of loss; but money was neither their goal nor theme" (130). Just like Mac Thornton, who "barely used the money" he made from his vast har-vests of tobacco (102), the fictional characters Price has obviously based upon Mac, including Mr. Isaac in A Long and Happy Life, are free from ostentation and aristocratic pretensions. The character most closely identified with Mac is

Kate Vaiden's Fob Foster, Kate's "distant cousin," a wealthy bachelor farmer in his early fifties.[61] Just as Price describes Mac's unostentatious life, Kate notes of Fob that, "though he owned great stretches of land and woods and must have been rich from tobacco and pulpwood, he dressed and lived as simply as a saint" (38). When Kate describes Fob's passion for foxhunting, she is careful to distinguish the event from its aristocratic tradition. The local tradition, she observes, "bore no resemblance to the ones I'd read about—red suits, jumping horses, and a merry chase" (40). Instead of making the event an opportunity for display of groomed blood horses and finely tailored suits, these plain-folk hunters sit around a fire, drinking too much coffee and listening for the baying of the hounds—in much the same way that the Appalachian farmers are described hunting coons in Chappell's *Brighten the Corner Where You Are*.[62]

As individuals Price's family and fictional characters very much resemble the plain folk of the Piedmont and western North Carolina—in their simple folkways and lack of conspicuous consumption. Price's world is distinguished, however, by the social structure in which these individuals find their places. What most distinguishes social structure in Price's world from that of the other writers considered in this study is the acceptance among his characters of a hierarchy in social and labor relations as normative and positive. By comparison, Chappell and Betts present relations between tenant farmers and their landlords as tense, exploitive, and in violation of a yeoman ideal that requires individual farm ownership, social independence, and an egalitarian society free of hierarchy. For example, in Chappell's *Brighten the Corner Where You Are*, both yeoman farmer Joe Robert Kirkman and his tenant Hob Farnum "hated and passionately despised the system of tenant farming." Joe Robert observes that the system keeps the tenant "poor forever and it breaks his pride. Turns him mean sometimes" (103–4). As described by Price, no such tension appears between Mac and his tenants. Price recalls how as a boy he would accompany Mac and his black driver, Joe, on their rounds to the various tenant farmers, with whom Mac humbly accepted his paternal role. Incidentally, Price remembers visiting only white tenants. On these many visits, Price recalls that he never saw his cousin Mac "engaged in harder work than saddling a horse or stepping off the dimensions of a field, but that's not to say he was lazy. He kept the standard farmer's day, sunup to past dark and then early sleep. On an average day he'd visit two farms, overseeing and guiding, encouraging and curbing. To one he'd haul a load of fertilizer; to another, lime and chicken-feed and maybe a case of Carnation milk for the bottle-fed baby that seemed to be failing. He'd listen and watch, laugh and console. It was all the business he'd made for himself but also a steady brand of meditation" (130). Mac's work involves daily practices of noblesse oblige as a kind of "meditation." He fulfills the planter

ideal of the paternal provider attending to the needs of his economic dependents. This work relationship contrasts sharply with the cooperative labor of
yeomen, who, careful not to be "beholden," typically "swapped work" of comparative nature or participated in communal enterprises, such as house raisings
or corn shuckings, with the understanding that such effort would be repaid in
the future in like manner.

Just as Mac's epitaph reads "Write me as one that loves his fellow-men"
(148), Price's entire family is consumed by its members' respective roles as servants to others, whether as parent, friend, or employer. Although the tension
inherent in yeoman society (and in so much of the fiction about yeomen)
between independence and interdependence is certainly prominent in Price's
family sagas, a positive resolution in each of his novels consistently depends
upon a strong reaffirmation of interdependence, with the individual accepting
his place within a hierarchical social structure that demands the observance of
reciprocal duties. Among the words that most frequently appear in his memoir,
as in his fiction, are *gift, care,* and *promise.* In contrast to the stolid independence frequently attributed to the yeoman, Price's vision of community involves
a network of interdependency in which the individual must learn how selflessly
to give and graciously to accept gifts. This mutual dependency characterizes
young Reynolds's relationship with his parents, with his mentally unstable Aunt
Ida, and later with his cousin Mac and his father as they both depend upon the
young man's care during their final days in the hospital. As in these filial bonds,
Price shows how a similar interdependency obtains in the relationships between white employers and their black servants, suggesting a racial paternalism consistent with that of the foregoing plantation system. Although Price
acknowledges the brutal inequity of such a system, he pays at least equal attention to what he finds to be the more benign side of the arrangement.

Of Macon, his mother's hometown, Price observes, "Almost every white
family employed one or more black women, men and children as farm hands,
house servants, yardmen, gardeners and drivers" (18–19). Furthermore Price
claims that such an arrangement was typical for the middle-class white family
of eastern North Carolina throughout his childhood and youth, from the
early 1930s until the early 1960s (83). According to the 1930 census, Warren
County's black population stood at 63.5 percent,[63] and so an abundance of
available black labor made it possible for a family of even modest means to hire
a cook for about "five dollars [per six-day week] and edible leftovers" from the
three meals a day they prepared (85). Despite the low pay and the inequitable
conditions in which blacks lived, Price maintains that the various servants
employed by his extended family were well treated. Of his Aunt Ida's cook, he
claims, "Given the time and the mind of the whole white country, Mary Lee

could not have got better and she knew it; all my kin would have told you the same. They were right" (75). To demonstrate his family's good breeding, as well as their respect and affection for their black servants, Price offers that no one in his family used the derogatory term *nigger*, preferring instead *colored* or *Negro*, pronounced "*Nigra*" (85).

Price states that his family always "quickly recoiled from any news of racial violence" and that his paternal grandfather even once prevented a lynching (86). He further describes his parents as being more relaxed about the codes governing interracial interaction. When, for example, they unexpectedly returned home to find their black housekeeper in their bathtub, it was an occasion for mirth rather than hysteria (90). Far from the stereotype of the belle, who would expect deference and formality from black men, Price's mother engaged black men in the community in a casual repartee that verged on sexual innuendo. He remembers repeated instances when he would accompany his mother into Edwin Russell's store in Macon and an "old black man would turn from the counter with his next dark plug of chewing tobacco. He'd see Elizabeth, study her slowly till he found her old nickname and a smile broke loose, 'Jimmy, Lord God, didn't know you at first—you stoutening up so good I didn't *know* you!' . . . for local black people, human fat was a beauty aid. But she ran a losing battle with weight and would lob him as good a shot as he gave, 'Hey Ben, I see you been nibbling too. Those overalls would fit a damn bull.' Then joint laughter" (101). Price says of his parents that they demonstrated a greater progressiveness than most of their peers, and yet, in an age before the civil rights movement brought to their attention all of the injustices of a system they were passively and unconsciously helping to perpetuate, they too saw no need for change. The "gulf" between the life of blacks and whites in Warren County, Price writes, "was not only silent. To most white eyes in eastern Carolina by the 1920s, it was simply invisible—as unnoticed a part of the landscape as pinetrees" (75). Price recalls that when his aging mother watched Martin Luther King's march on Washington, she fully supported his cause, though "much earlier" she would have responded differently to charges of racial injustice, taking "refuge in the common defense, heard often then—if colored people have been this miserable all these years, why haven't they told us sooner?" (87). The civil rights movement challenged the illusion of innocence perpetuated by Price's family and community.

Despite their purported aristocratic heritage, Price's people demonstrate a blindness to their own participation in slavery. As a child Price knew black servants who "were almost certainly freed slaves" (77). Nevertheless, by the time of his childhood, he observes that neither of his families "preserved actual memories of their own slaveholding past," because "the stench of de facto slavery paralyzed their moral imagination and that of all the rural white South till toward the end of the Second World War" (77). In a full chapter devoted to the development of his own personal spirituality, Price examines his early frustration with the white Protestant church, which only reinforced the racist codes of his culture. While giving credit to the courage of Bishop Waters, who integrated the Catholic churches and schools of the Raleigh diocese before the Supreme Court decision of 1954, he heavily criticizes the white Protestant churches, observing that "almost all the churches I knew in childhood are white to this day" (261) and declaring that "to the undying shame of the churches of my race, it [the civil rights movement] didn't begin with us. It began in Alabama," with Rosa Parks (260).

The basic question he asks about his people regarding race is the same one that Betts and Edgerton ask—"how were so many otherwise intelligent, morally sensitive, watchful and generous people trapped in the running of a brute and tragic machine?" (77). The respective solutions these writers provide to this problem, however, vary considerably. Betts has remarked that, for her people, race was typically a blind spot: "There's just a hole in many southerners. There's just a hole. You can walk right up to it and fall in. It's like the San Andreas fault."[64] Edgerton similarly views the racial consciousness of his people as a nullity, as worthy only of scorn in the form of black humor. Both suggest that a healthy racial consciousness must be created ex nihilo, either imagined out of whole cloth, as in Betts's "Beasts," or imported from without the culture, as in Edgerton's *Raney*, in which a rural Piedmonter begins to learn racial toler-ance from her more liberal husband from Atlanta. By contrast, Price suggests that, within his culture, even in its most brutal manifestations, are to be found the raw materials for racial healing. Ultimately, he believes that the history of regular contact between whites and blacks in eastern North Carolina provides its own palpable challenge to the racist ideology of the region. In the interper-sonal relationships between individuals, and in the South's history of sexual contact between the races, he finds the seeds of reconciliation.

A Great Circle: Plain Folk and the Legacy of Slavery in
Eastern North Carolina

If Price's memoir is relatively devoid of ambivalence for his family and heri-tage, his Mayfield novels frequently demonstrate considerable ambivalence —not the sort that characterizes social critique, but rather that of family drama. Price notes that family drama was the central preoccupation not only for his own family but also for most Americans during the "first half of the twentieth century," before urbanization and social mobility and TV became the norms. "The whole unending, theatrical event of family life," he says, "had a tremendous amount of heartbreak in it, as well as an awful lot of gratification."[65] Unlike A Long and Happy Life, in which Price works in a thoroughly pastoral mode to create stylized characters in an idealized community (one based upon his relatively brief interaction with the poor farming families near Asheboro, North Carolina), his depiction of the Mayfields and the Kendals of A Great Circle borrows heavily from his own family's history and engages his ambivalence for that history.

The first volume of the Mayfield trilogy, The Surface of Earth (1975), is Price's most expansive novel, covering forty-one years (1903–44) and chronicling the lives of four generations. The novel is divided into three novel-length parts, which focus on three successive generations of Mayfield men: Forrest, Rob, and Hutch. Each part involves the son's struggle to connect with an absent father, as well as an exploration of the tension created between the competing demands of family and the individual's need to make his own way in the world, a theme that reaches its fullest expression in the third part, devoted to the poet Hutch Mayfield, who becomes the central consciousness in the subsequent two novels of the Mayfield trilogy, The Source of Light (1981) and The Promise of Rest (1995). This conflict between the demands of family and the independent self are at least in part a result of the genetic and cultural confluence of two families: the Kendals, who have established deep roots in Fontaine, North Carolina, and the geographically rootless Mayfields. As three generations of Mayfield men come to understand their own lives at least in part as an expression of choices made by their Kendal and Mayfield forebears, they each, in turn, confront not only the often conflicting natures of these two families, but also how each family's history is intertwined with the lives of African American servants, neighbors, and kin.

In contrast to the classical worldview that informs A Long and Happy Life, in Surface Price invokes a Christian paradigm to deal more honestly with the legacy of slavery. Doris Betts notes Price's conviction that "blacks survived slavery . . . by believing they were 'moral tutors, the consciences of whites.'"[66] In Surface, they certainly function in such a role. For example, Hutch repeats the words of one of the Mayfield family's servants, Grainger Walters, who declares that "God's plan" for African Americans is one of guardianship over whites, as ministering "angels" or "spirits bringing word."[67] Word of what exactly, Grainger leaves unsaid. Salvation? The need for change and justice? Like Sammy in A Long and Happy Life, Grainger models the role of sacrifice and service, which the white Mayfields recognize they are meant to emulate; Forrest Mayfield calls Grainger "purer than Christ" (257), a role that is reiterated at Rob Mayfield's wedding, when Grainger pours drinks "as carefully as if he had transmuted water itself for these guests" (248). Price has argued elsewhere that the "blood and agony of a victim" is necessary for spiritual growth, just as Christians worship a triumphant victim and are thereby "commanded to revere and serve all other true victims."[68] In *Surface,* successive generations of May-fields are confronted with the ongoing victimization of blacks who live among them, at least in one case as an unacknowledged member of their family. Only through full acknowledgment of this victimization and of their spiritual and lit-eral kinship, they gradually discover, is redemption and healing available.

In a spring 2000 lecture addressed to the Millennial Gathering of Southern Writers in Nashville (published in the *Southern Review* as "An Awful Gift and a Blindness"), Price argues that the coexistence of blacks and whites is the only true southern theme—one that has been scandalously ignored or insufficiently understood. He goes so far as to inaugurate the new millennium by declaring a "benign competition" in which all southern writers should turn their full atten-tion to this theme or otherwise forfeit the label "southern."[69] Whereas other North Carolina writers have addressed the importance of race relations in their state, no white contemporary writer has done so with the same consistent emphasis given by Price—who does so from a perspective thoroughly condi-tioned by life in eastern North Carolina. Of life in the mountains, Price claims that "an absence of black-white melding is a vital and ongoing shaping force, as it was often the motive of mountain settlement."[70] Arguably, the much smaller black population and, thus, the relative lack of contact with blacks in western North Carolina would have produced among whites a greater fear and ignorance of African Americans and their culture. By comparison, the portrait that Price paints of Warren County—the relative ease that blacks and whites appear to feel around each other—seems seductively preferable.

Nevertheless the sit-ins that helped to spark a national civil rights move-ment began in the western Piedmont, in Greensboro, not in the tobacco belt. It is no accident that the four college freshmen who began the 1960 sit-ins were enrolled at a Piedmont university, North Carolina A & T, nor that the Student Nonviolent Coordinating Committee (SNCC), which would help coordinate subsequent sit-ins and become a major advocate for civil rights throughout the South, was founded that same year at Raleigh's Shaw Uni-versity. In fact, the majority of the state's black universities—including North Carolina Central in Durham, Shaw in Raleigh, North Carolina A & T in Greensboro, and Johnson C. Smith in Charlotte—are located in the Piedmont, as are the state's most prominent and politically powerful black churches. These institutions, in large measure the products of black economic growth in the Piedmont, have enabled blacks to organize politically to a degree beyond what became possible down east, even though blacks constituted a substan-tially lower percentage of the population in the Piedmont. Piedmont cities have also led the state in integrating politics. By 1983, black mayors had been elected in at least four major Piedmont cities: Howard Lee in Chapel Hill, Clarence Lightner in Raleigh, T. Jeffers in Gastonia, and in 1983 Harvey Gantt in Charlotte, even though the city's population was 70 percent white.[71] Gantt later entered national politics as the North Carolina Democratic senatorial candidate. The first African American to become a major party contender for the U.S. presidency, Jesse Jackson, was also born in the Carolina Piedmont, in Greenville, South Carolina.

Richard Maschal attributes the success of the national civil rights movement of the 1960s to three factors: (1) the initiative and determination of African Americans, (2) a committed federal government, and (3) national economic prosperity.[72] Although all three of these factors were present in the North Carolina Piedmont, the third was absent throughout the coastal plain, which might account for the emergence of greater black political action in the Piedmont. Booker T. Washington's dream of autonomous black communities and businesses, as described in his 1895 Atlanta Exposition address, became a greater reality throughout the segregated Piedmont, ostensibly because of the region's economic growth during the twentieth century. Just as slavery was less widespread throughout the Piedmont, a system of tenancy remained less thoroughly entrenched than it did down east.[73] In his study of the period between 1876 and 1894, Frenise A. Logan reports a major difference—by region—in attitudes of white landlords toward their black tenants. In contrast to the eastern counties, where there were large black populations, in the Piedmont counties with smaller black populations he finds a greater support of black tenant farmers and their acquisition of property.[74] Furthermore, as Sun Belt prosperity began to take root during the 1960s, Piedmont blacks began to make their way into the industrial work force. Although, as W. J. Cash explains, the grassroots movement to build the textile industry in the Carolina Piedmont during the early twentieth century had been largely motivated by a desire on behalf of poor whites to remove themselves from direct competition with black tenant farmers, during the 1960s blacks entered the textile industry in large numbers. Between 1960 and 1970, black textile workers increased from 3.8 percent to 14 percent of the total work force.[75] Although the economic and political accomplishments of Piedmont blacks are cause for celebration, the various forms of segregation that characterized the Piedmont throughout the twentieth century makes difficult an exploration of the very different relations between blacks and whites that most certainly pervaded the region in an earlier era. By contrast the economic stasis of eastern North Carolina lets Price observe race relations that more closely resemble those of planters and their tenants and house servants in the agricultural economy into which slavery evolved.

By investigating these relationships, *The Surface of Earth* indicts the enduring legacy of slavery while simultaneously finding therein the germ of racial
healing. Although the Kendals have been plain folk for generations—and
though, like Price's own family, they divulge no memories of a slaveholding
past—the family continues to employ black help around the house and retains
a black tenant family in the old family homeplace, a fitting image of planters
in decline. The lower-class Mayfields have married into faded aristocracy—the
Goodwins of Bracey, Virginia—though any trace of aristocratic tradition has
been lost in the marriage of Anna Goodwin to the Snopes-like Robinson Mayfield. Because Anna died before the time frame of the novel, we only learn of
the Goodwins through her surviving husband, who had left her after ten years
of marriage over a disagreement about his sexual proclivities, which he refers
to as "niggering around" (111). In conversation with his son, Forrest, Robinson remembers his wife's family after their circumstances had been drastically
reduced. "They had been good people," he recalls, "a moneyed family; but
the nigger war had knocked em down—killed their father, your Grandfather
Goodwin, and eat up their money and (before I got to town) their land. And
old Mrs. Goodwin was cooking for trash. Like me, as she never missed a chance
to let me know. Hell, what did I care? I was scum and I knew it (scum is what
rises)" (108). This story is told by old Robinson Mayfield, now dying of cancer,
to his thirty-four-year-old son Forrest, from whom Robinson has been estranged
for twenty-nine years.

Forrest's rediscovery of his father coincides with his discovery that old
Robinson's "niggering around" produced at least one child of mixed race. Forrest seeks to make reparations for his father's negligence by virtually (but not
legally) adopting Robinson's twelve-year-old black grandson, Grainger Walters,
but after one year his adoption of Grainger miscarries because of Forrest's lack
of emotional commitment. Although Robinson and Forrest fail Grainger, the
following generations take up the responsibility (reminiscent of Ike McCaslin's
efforts in *Go Down, Moses*), and Grainger plays a significant role in the lives of
Rob, Hutch, and Wade, just as they remain a significant presence throughout
Grainger's long life. In the Mayfield trilogy's final novel, *The Promise of Rest*,
Hutch serves as a mouthpiece for Price on the topic of miscegenation, telling his
Milton seminar at Duke University that "no other writer, since Faulkner drank
himself out of sane action by the age of fifty, has really dived deep into that huge
maelstrom called miscegenation on Southern ground—the feeding of white on
black, black on white—though the problem has gone much further toward
both solution and utter insolubility than Marse Will Faulkner ever dreamed
possible" (11). Obviously Price sees himself as filling the void left by Faulkner
and revising what he feels to be the historical limitations of Faulkner's vision.

In general Price is much more hopeful than Faulkner about human possibility, human sexuality, and the continuing relationship between black and white Americans. In the quotation just given, Hutch considers the sexual "feeding" of blacks and whites to be much more mutual than Faulkner understood it to be. The deeper difference between Price and Faulkner may have less to do with race than with sex. A broad overview of Faulkner's characters reveals roughly two categories: on the one hand, rapists and sexual exploiters (Carothers McCaslin, Popeye, Joe Christmas, Thomas Sutpen) and, on the other hand, sexual innocents (Ike McCaslin, Quentin Compson, Henry Sutpen). Rarely do Faulkner's novels depict a healthy sexual relationship. Price, by contrast, seeks to celebrate and explore human sexuality in all of its manifestations; he is hardly fazed by the taboos that so disturb Faulkner's characters: miscegenation, homosexuality, and incest. Whereas homosexuality appears latent in so many of Faulkner's frustrated men—Quentin Compson, Henry Sutpen, Ike McCaslin, and Ike's Uncle Buck and Uncle Buddy—several decades later Price is able to write openly about homosexual love. Of incest, Price notes that brothers and sisters in his community during his youth frequently lived together, and "it was nobody else's damned business, especially what happened when the shades were down, if anything but sleep" (Clear, 122). James Schiff also notes the frequent erotic content of father-son relationships throughout the Mayfield trilogy.[76]

Of miscegenation, Price remarks that despite the frequent sexual exploitation of African Americans' bodies by white masters, "the most paradoxical of all their gifts to the South was sexual health" (Clear, 107). Although he acknowledges the exception of what he calls the "narrow torrent of fundamentalist Protestantism," Price argues that the example set by black southerners and the sexual contact between blacks and whites enabled white southerners to avoid the "sexual dreads of a decadent Puritanism that blighted, and continues to blight, many other regional cultures" (Clear, 108). The strong currents of Puritanism in Faulkner's work alone suggest that Price's observation of sexual freedom in the South may be overstated. Nevertheless, Price's large contribution lies in his willingness to imagine a wide range of hopeful possibilities for sexual health, racial harmony—and for uses of the past.

In a 1988 interview, he explicitly eschews the tragic worldview so characteristic of southern writers, especially of Faulkner's generation. "I think," he says, "as a Southerner, you're supposed to have a kind of gene for suffering—moaning and regretting the old order, and that we lost the war, and the house was burned by the Yankees. I just don't like to hurt. So I really lack that kind of masochistic equipment that seems to go with being both a Southerner and especially being a Southern writer. . . . I love fun. I love to laugh."[77] Whereas

Faulkner's protagonists are often so overwhelmed by both the glory and the crimes of their forebears that they are paralyzed and ultimately ineffectual in dealing with the challenges of the present, Price's characters are much less crippled by their familial pasts. In fact they tend to find encouragement through association with their forebears, even after witnessing their flaws. Rob Mayfield often thinks of his philandering namesake, his grandfather Robinson, not so much to rationalize as to understand his own desire for black women, to give it an explanatory context. Furthermore, the ancestral crimes in Price are treated with greater sympathy and with less gothic grandiosity than they are in Faulkner. Compared to Faulkner's exploitive plantation owner, Carothers McCaslin (who raped a slave girl and later raped the offspring of that crime), in *Surface* old Robinson Mayfield's "niggering around" is portrayed as consensual. Long after he has been estranged from his two legitimate white children, Robinson keeps in contact with his "nigger kin" (108). He explains his abandonment of his legitimate white family by referring to his sexual need for black women. When telling his son, Forrest, of his mother's reaction, Robinson defends himself, saying, "Imagine being . . . run from your home and children for that. Hell, every good boy with a pecker that worked was niggering round me—you could hardly walk on a weekday night (not to mention Saturday) without stepping smack on a bare white ass pumping joy on black" (111).

Although his sexually innocent son recognizes his father's rationalization (112), Robinson's freedom of expression and romantic vision of his youth are at times seductive, in later years even to his son, who thinks back upon his father more as a charming philanderer than as a criminal. When Robinson recalls his own youth as a railroad fireman in search of "good fresh air" (110) and willing women, his rhetoric even rings Whitmanesque. Devoid of pretension or any sort of conventional restraint, he views his sexual exploits as less exploitive than generous. "I was not only trash," he says, "but also a tramp, my true vocation. I always had—back then, I mean—a lot more life stored up in me than any one woman or house could use; so I spent it on the wind, spreading happiness where your mama couldn't see it to worry over" (110). Robinson's case is made more convincing by his reliance upon the same core vocabulary used by other more sympathetic characters—and by the omniscient narrator—when describing his sexual past. He uses the terms "food" and "need" to evoke the naturalness of sex, and he speaks of his sexual advances as a "gift"—the most common metaphor in the novel. Robinson's use of a language common to other characters humanizes him, bringing him into the fold of common sympathy and making his sexual past seem less criminal and more natural. In *The Promise of Rest*, Robinson's great-great-grandson will make a statement that echoes the sentiments of his forebear: "Don't hoard your body"

(196), says Wade, who in 1993 is dying of AIDS. According to Wade, stinginess with the gifts of the body is "as mean a failing as anything else but strangling children" (196).

In light of his generally positive treatment of sexuality, Price might be expected to affirm Wade's statement, and yet the autobiographical Hutch Mayfield becomes something of a hermit sexually, as has his grandfather Forrest before him. Within the Mayfield patrilineage of Robinson, Forrest, Rob, Hutch, and Wade, personality types skip generations, with Robinson, Rob, and Wade being more sexually adventurous than Forrest or Hutch. This repetition of types suggests an inability to move forward personally or culturally, a problem that becomes especially evident with respect to their sexual involvement with African Americans. The sexual intimacies with blacks enjoyed by Robinson and Rob represent only temporary engagements that are quickly abandoned, often causing lasting trauma that Forrest and Hutch, in turn, attempt to heal. A thorough healing, however, will begin only in the final novel of the Mayfield trilogy, set in the 1990s.

Although generational progress in race relations occurs in *Surface*, this progress comes very gradually and involves a complex pattern of advances and setbacks, a pattern nowhere more evident than in the waiting of Grainger Walters (Robinson Mayfield's black grandson) for the Mayfield men fully to acknowledge his kinship. After failing to follow through on his "adoption" of his younger cousin, Forrest identifies his "greatest mistake" (254) as telling Grainger about his paternity, after which Grainger looks to him as a father, a role that the emotionally detached scholar is not equipped to handle. Forrest is something of a tragicomic paternalist, spending his life teaching black school children and black adults at the James Institute in Richmond, but teaching them mostly classical poetry, which, arguably, can have only limited relevance to their lives. Blacks and whites alike laugh at this cultural whitewashing of his students. As a youth, Grainger studiously applies himself to Forrest's books, which later provokes the resentment of his wife, Gracie. As explanation of her abandonment of her husband, she tells Rob, "But once I showed him every trick I knew [in bed]—he didn't know *nothing*—he figured he'd got to the dead-end of Gracie; so he struck up, you know, to *staring at the wind:* hoping two suits of white skin would blow in the door and him and me be real kin to your dead daddy. Or *one* suit of skin; it was him he dreamed for, dreamed Gracie right on out of his life. You thought I was running; I was looking for home—some warm dry place with a black nigger in it that could use my butt when he come home tired from a hard day's hauling, not gazing at wind like the wind would blow in because you were pretty and bank blessings on you" (434).

Gracie identifies Grainger's problem as "not enough white blood" (434), not enough to pass for white. At Rob's wedding in Goshen, Forrest publicly acknowledges Grainger as "one of my people" (249), but his words are little more than an empty gesture and Grainger is still expected to fulfill the role of the servant. Even though he and the other black cooks are invited to join in a toast, their glasses are filled only with three-quarters of an inch of brandy (250), a courtesy more insulting than altogether refusing them drink. Furthermore, a meaningful union between Forrest and Grainger is blocked by the requirement that Grainger must make himself over in the image of the great white father figure Forrest, who among all the Mayfield men is the "whitest," a classically trained scholar, whose energies are devoted to Latin translations and the perpetuation of classical European culture in the minds of African Americans.

Forrest's son, Rob, who resembles his grandfather Robinson much more than his father, is a more likely candidate for suitable kinship with Grainger, if only because his role is more nearly equal, less that of paternalist than of brother. Furthermore, with maturity, and after suffering disappointment in Forrest, Grainger gains some critical perspective on his own past passivity and begins to consider the criticism of black family and friends, especially his wife, who accuses him of being an Uncle Tom, or, in her words, "Old Misery" (410). At one point, Grainger even refers to himself as a "burdensome pet" (313). In a lecture to Rob in which he criticizes his white cousin for his years of depravity, Grainger speaks with harsh directness. "Mercy all I had for nineteen years," he says, "mercy all my life. Now I mean to *cut* some. Listen here what I done. I watched your mess through all this time and cleaned it behind you. I let your daddy treat me worse than a dog when I was a child he promised to raise" (359). These are words that Grainger would never have been able to say to Forrest, and Rob is able to hear and acknowledge them, in part, because Grainger has become such an integral part of the Mayfield and Kendal families; Rob understands that Grainger's warning is meant to protect Hutch, whom Grainger has now taken upon himself to help raise, in Rob's absence. Thus Rob's behavior carries the double burden of a responsible model for his son and honoring his family's ever increasing debt to Grainger.

Gracie recognizes Rob's responsibility toward Grainger when she tells Rob that Grainger is waiting on the "whole adoption, to be your whole brother. Rob, you all he waiting on. You the one that can do the trick" (434). The sexual connotation of "trick," explicit elsewhere in Gracie's comments about her marriage to Grainger, points to one of the primary modes that Rob pursues to realize his bond with Grainger—and with his black neighbors, in general. If, as Gracie observes, Grainger is waiting to become white, Rob is equally seduced by black sexuality and black culture. On the night of his high school graduation, he enjoys his first sexual experience in the home of the Kendals' housekeeper, Sylvie, in bed with Sylvie's cousin, Flora, who not incidentally shares her name with the actual housekeeper in the Price household where Reynolds made his way through puberty. The biographical Flora was six years older than young Reynolds, who refers to her as "my bridge, my vivid guide" to mature sexual health (*Clear*, 107). Price recalls the constant but never consummated flirtation between them, which closely resembles the sexual nature of the relationship between Rob and Sylvie in *Surface*.

Rob's most significant black lover is another servant, Della, who works for Rob's fiancée's family in Goshen, Virginia. Although their relationship brings mutual pleasure, it is far from equal, and throughout his youth Rob's motives are principally selfish. The fact that he avoids kissing while having sex with Della certainly makes his involvement with her seem little advanced beyond Old Robinson's habit of "niggering around" two generations earlier. Over the course of the following two decades, however, Rob matures and becomes more capable of respecting the needs and feelings of others, white or black, as evidenced in the novel's final chapters, when he returns to Goshen to find Della. Although she is two decades older and far from well preserved, Rob nevertheless experiences a powerful desire to become intimate with her—both sexually and by asking her to tell him about her life. Earlier, Rob has told Hutch, "It has always helped me to sit down with Negroes and smell their strangeness, let them bleed me with questions" (398); with maturity Rob has also learned to sit quietly and allow others to reveal themselves through their own stories.

Sex creates a vital, and in many ways healthy, channel between blacks and whites, but Grainger warns Rob of its potential destructiveness. One night prior to Rob's wedding in Goshen, when Grainger catches Rob sneaking away from Della's room in the servants' quarters, Rob explains that he has been "rubbing on black" (217), perhaps expecting to turn black figuratively himself. In response, Grainger circles Rob's wrist with his hand, rubs and says, "You look at that good; see did dark rub off. Did—it come off Grainger. Grainger give you your wish" (218). As good-naturedly as possible, Grainger is warning Rob of the harm he might do to Della, as well as his future wife, and suggesting (as Price argues in *Clear Pictures*) that the more healthy and enduring mode of black and white intercourse is through friendship, especially friendship between black and white men. In fact, Rob and Grainger's relationship may well be modeled upon the lifelong friendship between Price's father, Will, and his gardener, Grant Terry, a friendship that Price describes as powerfully homosocial, comparing it to a "marriage in its fifth decade" (*Clear*, 100). *Surface* ends hopefully with a similar image of "marriage" between men, complete with the ritual of passing a wedding ring. The Mayfield family wedding band, taken from the hand of Forrest's mother's corpse, has had a long and complicated journey, spending much of its time in the possession of Grainger and his wife, Gracie. As the novel concludes, Gracie returns the ring, by way of Rob, to her husband, as a final act of separation. In the novel's concluding scene, Grainger accepts the ring from Rob then passes it on to Hutch, signifying the bond that binds the three men together and that binds the black and white descendants of Robinson Mayfield well into the future.

Despite its hopeful ending, *Surface* is not without its darker undercurrent of doubt regarding race relations. The role of expressing these repressed doubts is principally assumed by black women, as for example at Rob's wedding in Goshen. After being acknowledged by Forrest as "one of [his] people," Grainger praises the virtues of patient optimism. "I knew this was coming," he announces. "I knew you people would end up happy and doing me right. . . . Mr. Forrest, I told you long years ago it would end up like this if you be patient" (250). Gracie offers her terse response to her husband's optimistic speech in an aside to Della: "Nothing finished, is it, Della?" (250). Similarly, Grainger's great-great grandmother Veenie doubts the ability of white Mayfields or any other whites to keep their promises. When Forrest first offers to take care of twelve-year-old Grainger, assuring Veenie, "You know my people keep their word," she makes a "snorting sound" and retorts, "I ain't studying that—your people's word; I know your people some sixty years before you born" (78). That Forrest breaks his oath to Veenie not to reveal Grainger's paternity to the boy serves further to validate her judgment.

The difference between the naive trust of black men and the wiser doubt of black women derives from their relative roles in relation to their white employers and to their own families. The black men, like the white men in the novel, enjoy a much greater freedom of movement, allowing them to preserve relatively innocent hopes for the future, less encumbered by the lessons of history. Like Grainger, who attaches himself, throughout the trilogy, to four generations of Mayfield men, in each case reviving his original hopes for parity, Bankey Patterson, an eighty-year-old ex-slave, who has been on a quest to find his mother, summarily abandons his search and offers to devote himself to Forrest (70). Bowles Parker, Flora's son, likewise is seen in transit, hitchhiking, on his way to serve in the war. In contrast to Grainger, whose primary relationships are with white men—attachments that frequently uproot him—the women are found rooted to a place, and their vision of racial injustice is informed by their greater involvement with their own families.

Della offers a vivid example of how black women preserve a historical sense through such familial connections; after slaving in the kitchen throughout the day and night of Rob's wedding, Della dreams of her mother, Lucy, returning from the dead to help cook and feed all the wedding guests. In her dream, Della and her mother, both of them exhausted from the endless preparations, sit to rest, only to find the bride's father leading a "pale naked baby" into the kitchen and announcing, "This thing has got to be fed." The infant climbs into Lucy's lap and begins sucking at her nipple. He grows stronger, while Lucy "slowly shrank and was gone" (274–75). The language used to describe the source of Della's dream further suggests the repressed anger that promises eventually to express itself: "Della made this dream from the trapped reservoirs of her mind, heart, body, and not only watched it in sleep like a hemorrhage streaming up from her but wished it on all the sleepers around her in quarters and house, a permanent hurt" (273–74). The description of her servitude as a form of bodily damage that manifests itself as a "permanent hurt" echoes the language Toni Morrison uses to describe the legacy of slavery in *Beloved*—in the form of "rememory," ghosts, and bodily scars. Della's "hemorrhage streaming up" also anticipates Hutch's acknowledgment in *The Promise of Rest* of his family's and his nation's crimes as "the unstemmable progress of the spreading stain of human chattel on his home country through nearly four centuries and its outward seepage now through the nation and the world beyond" (*Promise*, 158).

In *The Surface of Earth*, the repressed complaints of black servants surface only in the form of dreams or barbed innuendoes or whispers of discontent. In *The Promise of Rest*, the Mayfield trilogy's final novel, set in 1993 (a year after the Los Angeles riots), we find what appears to be the return of the repressed. For the first time, members of the Mayfield family fully confront their own complacency in postponing the acknowledgment of equal citizenship on the part of their black relatives and black fellow Americans. In the passage quoted above, Hutch expresses a prophetic vision of the potential apocalypse in America, not unlike the vision of Thomas Jefferson two centuries earlier. He comes to this realization about his family's past—and present—as a result of his son's long-term homosexual relationship with Wyatt Bondurant, a truth-telling black militant, who accuses the Mayfields of at least tacitly perpetuating the unjust legacy of slavery.

While Wade Mayfield precipitously enters the final stages of AIDS in a nearby hospital, Hutch spends several hours searching a box containing his son's journals and letters, hoping to find a clue that will help explain the silence between them over the last nine years. He finds such a clue in a letter—dated nine years earlier—in which Wyatt expressed to Wade his outrage after visiting Wade's family in North Carolina for the first and last time. Among other offenses, Wyatt accuses them of opposing his relationship with Wade and of doing so because of their racial difference. Wyatt recalls their trip out to the Mayfield homestead, where Grainger Walters, then in his nineties, lived in

cottage away from the main house; Wyatt indicts them with the crime of turning their cousin Grainger into "*a tame crippled monkey in a dry little shed you
threw up around him, a shed that's really nothing but his last cage in a century of
cages*" (157). Wyatt saves his most pointed criticism for Hutch and Ann. "*I can
see your mother and father have never done a deed they'd call impolite,*" writes
Wyatt, "*not to mention cruel. I can see what's lovable and likable about them. . . . I
can imagine they sit down Sundays in some well-furnished church—Episcopal, I
bet—and come out thinking they stand a fair chance of eternal life near God in
Glory, a dignified Paradise with no voice raised and loyal colored washerwomen for
the white satin robes. . . . But I bet you all of my life's possessions that, come Judgment Day—if Judgment comes— . . . your two progenitors are rushed up against a
concrete wall by blazing archangels and mowed to a pulp with whatever brand of
automatic weapon the angels are issued for simple justice*" (157). Although Wyatt's
criticism may at times become hyperbolic, it shocks Hutch into an awareness
of his own and his family's complacency. His "whole life," Hutch realizes, "then
amounted to long years of quiet assent to the most colossal act of theft and
murder in human history—assent by Hutch and, again, all he'd loved except
maybe Wade. But in sixty-three years of Hutch's life no one but Wyatt had
pointed toward that lasting assent and called its name, an unstopped crime"
(159). Ironically, Hutch's epiphany produces a sort of cathartic joy, at being
"found out, in one of the vital cores of his life for the first full time" (158).

This acknowledgment of "crime" is followed by the recognition of "another
giant failure" (160), Hutch's inability forty years earlier to commit to a life with
his homosexual lover, Strawson Stuart; instead he married Ann, which resulted
in nearly forty years of misery for both of them. Wade, in choosing a life with
Wyatt Bondurant, boldly seizes a life his father was too timid to choose for
himself. That Wyatt forces Wade to choose either his family or his lover further emphasizes the distance between the paths that Hutch and his son have
taken. Hutch comes to view his son's illness as a form of "vengeance" (158) for
Hutch's own complacency, and, after reconciling himself to his son's death,
Hutch accepts and even celebrates with a poem the genetic absorption of the
white Mayfield line into the black Bondurant family (Wade had sired a son by
Wyatt's sister, Ivory). As the novel ends with Hutch walking hand in hand
toward the sun with his black grandson, Raven Bondurant, he is able to affirm
their "first steps" into a radically different and hopefully redemptive future.

Promise marks a dramatic break from the tone of the earlier two Mayfield
novels. Whereas *Surface* imagines the evolution of racial equality as a gradual
process, *Promise* openly criticizes that position as a paternalistic fantasy. And
while both *Surface* and *The Source of Light* seek to normalize homosexual behavior as a common and natural variant of sexual experience, one that does

not provoke the censure of mainstream society, in *Promise* the battle lines are drawn between those who are willing to live openly gay lives and those who retreat to the closet. In terms of both racial and sexual consciousness, *Promise* appears to be a novel Price could only have written twenty years after the publication of *Surface*, after African Americans and gay men and lesbians had already spoken out to claim their own civil rights. With the character of Hutch, Price even critiques his own distance as a chronicler of race relations in his region of the South, his determination to serve as a "spy" on his family and culture, a detached observer, rather than a militant proponent for radical and immediate change. In *Promise,* Price comes as close as he ever has to writing the sort of socially critical fiction characteristic of Betts, though *Promise* still lacks the kind of dualistic vision found in Betts's work. Price's primary interest is still to understand and explore, even if that exploration involves the evolving consciousness of the aging paternalist, Hutch Mayfield, as he confronts and adapts to the radically changed environment of the late twentieth century.

In *Promise*, Price acknowledges, through the character of Hutch, the peril of employing a pastoral vision when exploring race relations at the turn of the millennium. With the conclusion of the Mayfield trilogy, he has discovered the same difficulty that Betts has encountered in her more recent fiction—that the yeoman farmer no longer provides a viable mode for considering the exigencies of a contemporary world, except as a touchstone. Though for different reasons, in both cases the yeoman has become virtually obsolete. Whereas Betts laments his obsolescence as a product of those immitigable forces of the twentieth century that have transformed his landscape from one of small rural collectives into urban centers, Price focuses more intently on the racial aspects of the yeoman's history. Price apparently shares Hutch's conviction that race and the legacy of slavery are "the central theme of American life, its history and literature for nearly four centuries with no sign of flagging" (159). Considering that this conviction has grown stronger with age for both Hutch and Price, they have both found it increasingly difficult to celebrate the values of agrarianism without constantly acknowledging the pain of slavery and its legacy. Price's ambivalence has evidently reached the point where pastoral is no longer viable, since pastoral—as in *A Long and Happy Life* or even *The Surface of Earth*—depends upon a backward glance intent on cultural preservation. Not surprisingly, as the discussion of Fred Chappell will reveal, pastoral finds more suitable soil in rural Appalachia, where the specter of slavery was less prominent.

Price's clear-sighted depiction of contemporary race relations in *Promise*—so radically altered from those of Hutch's, or of Price's, youth—raises the unavoidable question, What value may be found in the dated vision of Price's earlier writing, especially the critically praised *Surface of Earth*? Might we label *Surface* —as Richard Gilman does in his now notorious 1975 review—a "mastodon" of a novel,[78] one that should be consigned to another, less-enlightened, era? Doesn't *The Promise of Rest*, in fact, so thoroughly challenge and qualify the racial vision of the earlier generations of Mayfields as to make it painfully obsolete? How is it possible to celebrate the lives of white plain folk from eastern North Carolina who throughout the twentieth century continued to exploit the descendants of their forebears' slaves? The solution found by most white North Carolinians, especially those in the western half of the state, is to forget, ignore, or deny that history. Most versions of the yeoman experience in the Tar Heel state downplay a history of slavery, and most of the state's contemporary communities, as elsewhere in America, are sufficiently segregated to make such cultural amnesia possible. In *Clear Pictures* Price informs us that even as early as the 1930s in his family and region, where the black population exceeded 60 percent, a memory of their slaveholding past had been lost. One of the most valuable contributions made by Price's Mayfield trilogy, and by his oeuvre in general, is its unwillingness to let us forget the less tidy aspects of our past. At the same time, it reminds us—in this politically correct era—that, among those white yeomen and planters of eastern North Carolina who employed black servants or sharecroppers, it was possible to strive to live humanely, however limited they may have been by the racist ideas of their age. Spanning nearly all of the twentieth century, the Mayfield trilogy avoids nostalgia by connecting the past to the present and future. Like Hutch, Price has engaged the debate about racial equality as it has progressed throughout the latter twentieth century, and his writing reflects an evolving consciousness, charting a *great circle* that, in its totality, neither ignores the yeoman's past nor enshrines it.

FRED CHAPPELL'S PRISON/ARCADIA
Plain Folk in Appalachia

3

In a 1999 interview, I asked Fred Chappell whether he more considered him-self to be a "southern" or an "Appalachian" writer. He quickly responded:

> Appalachian. That's easy. To me "southern" means Deep South, a region that I really don't know very much about. And I haven't had very much experience with it. The problem of race relations was never an important part of my early experience. I really only got involved with it when I was in graduate school at Duke. I was a member of CORE for a little while. But where I was from, there was such little contact, at least on my part, with black people that it just didn't seem that this great topic that ought to exer-cise the South was much of a force among us. Other things—large land holdings, southern aristocracy, cotton—these things were not a part of my experience. My experience was small land holdings, *no* aristocracy—we're all white trash together, I guess, in the mountains. Little wealth. And ab-sence of any kind of a historical perspective on family that they seem to have in the Deep South. We didn't talk about our family histories, hardly at all. Well, we talked about members of the family, but not in the terms of "Our family's been here for generations and we did such and such." You hear that in the Deep South. You don't hear it where I'm from.[1]

Chappell's identification of Appalachia as a place apart from the rest of the South resembles the plain-folk bravado of Thomas Wolfe. Chappell's state-ment provides a clear articulation of yeoman values: egalitarianism, indepen-dence, and an identification of the small family farm as the basic social unit. Missing from this overview of his Appalachian experience—what for Chappell is perhaps the "elephant in the living room"—is the pervasiveness of an intru-sive lumber and pulpwood industry, which around the turn of the twentieth century led the way to modernization of the region, producing devastating environmental and economic changes that made the yeoman freehold farm increasingly less viable.

In *Miners, Millhands, and Mountaineers*, Ronald D. Eller describes the rapid rise of industrialization throughout southern Appalachia during the years 1880–1930. While coal mining made much less of an impact in western North Carolina than elsewhere in the region, the timber industry irrevocably changed the mountains of North Carolina and the lives of its people. This process began in 1880 with the arrival, after twenty-five years of intermittent construction, of the Western North Carolina Railroad in Asheville. By 1890 the rail line had passed through Haywood County and the future site of Canton, Chappell's hometown. The railroad brought a tourist boom to Asheville, which grew from a population of 2,000 in 1880 to 10,000 by 1890. It also brought to the region speculators and lumbermen who bought up vast tracts of mountain land. By 1900, lumber and timber manufacturing had become the second leading industry in North Carolina, and most of this manufacturing was located in the western portion of the state. By the industry's peak in 1909, southern Appalachia was providing almost 40 percent of the nation's timber production. By the eve of World War I, however, timber production in southern Appalachia experienced a rapid decline as the industry moved to the Pacific Northwest, leaving behind unemployed mountaineers and a devastated natural environment. The clear-cut mountains suffered extensive erosion, and the bottom lands experienced frequent flooding, which made them largely unfit for agriculture.[2]

One timber company that established a sustainable business in western North Carolina was the Champion Paper and Fiber Company, with its primary regional manufacturing site located in Haywood County. In 1905, the company's owner, Peter G. Thompson, from Hamilton, Ohio, "secured" roughly 300,000 acres of timberland throughout Haywood County and began building a pulp mill and a company town which came to be named Canton, after Canton, Ohio. According to Eller, "No other lumber company had as great or as lasting an impact upon the Blue Ridge and the Smokes."[3] In *Birth of Forestry in America*, Carl Alwin Schenck observes of the Champion operation, "The whole scheme was the most gigantic enterprise which western North Carolina had seen."[4] By the beginning of World War I, the company had expanded further throughout Haywood County and into Swain County and eastern Tennessee, producing 200 tons of wood pulp per day, most of which was being shipped to Ohio for conversion to paper. By 1930, six years before Fred Chappell's birth, the Canton operation had developed the capacity to produce postcard paper and had "grown into the largest paper and pulp mill in the nation."[5]

The impact of industrialization on Appalachian yeoman farmers can be measured by the decline in the size of the average farm and total land under cultivation, as well as the declining number of farmers relative to the region's total population. As extractive industries appropriated larger portions of the region's available land—and then later left former farmland unusable—the size of the average farm decreased from 187 acres in the 1880s to 76 acres in 1930. Even though the total number of farmers increased, the available farmland declined by 20 percent, and, although the region's urban population quadrupled and the rural nonagricultural population doubled, the agricultural population increased only by 5 percent.[6] Furthermore, family farms were increasingly integrated into (and threatened by) an expanding market economy.

The industrialization of Haywood County and of western North Carolina, in general, along with the tenuous position of the yeoman farmer produced by this industrialization, affected Chappell's family directly and, not surprisingly, has exerted a powerful shaping force on his fiction. Born in 1936, at a time when the Champion Company was converting pulp into paper more rapidly than any paper mill in the country and pouring its waste into the Pigeon River, Chappell grew up on his mother's family's small farm two miles outside of Canton. The Champion factory, thinly disguised as the Challenger mill, appears as a target of scorn in much of his work. His father struggled to make a small dairy farm financially viable and discovered, like many small Appalachian farmers,[7] that the family's subsistence depended upon his entering public work. In fact, both of Chappell's parents supplemented the family's income by teaching school, and his father also worked for a time as a lineman with Carolina Power & Light. Eventually, they closed the farm and opened a retail furniture business. Much of Chappell's poetry and his later fiction provides fairly autobiographical treatments of his family's struggle to keep their farm in operation. Moreover, at stake in this struggle is the larger effort to retain the preindustrial values and folkways of the yeoman, which are threatened by encroaching capitalism and industrialization.

Such a privileging of an agrarian past has long manifested itself in southern literature in forms that have been associated with a pastoral tradition extending back to classical pastoralists such as Virgil and Theocritus. As Lucinda MacKethan notes, however, southern pastoralists have traditionally chronicled the experience of the planter rather than that of the yeoman. In *The Dream of Arcady*, MacKethan surveys southern pastoral from the antebellum period to the early twentieth century, including writers such as John Pendleton Kennedy, William Gilmore Simms, Thomas Nelson Page, and William Faulkner. Of the major southern pastoralists she examines, all but one represent the plantation tradition—or the antiplantation tradition. MacKethan identifies only Sidney Lanier as writing about the yeoman experience, stating that his "version of the pastoral reflects, for southern literature, the road not taken."[8] Were she to extend her study into the late twentieth century, MacKethan would find a radically different scenario. Recent novels by Chappell—as well as by Robert

Morgan, Charles Frazier, Tony Earley, and other western North Carolina writers—offer very positive treatments of a past culture centered around the yeoman farmer. In each case, the North Carolina mountains appear as an extremely insular space, one that is depicted—with all of its hardships—as being purer and in many ways more healthy than the modern culture that has replaced it.

Because, in the wake of the civil rights movement, the plantation tradition is no longer viable as a pastoral mode, pastoral literature has taken root elsewhere, largely in the rocky soil of Appalachia. In later years even Reynolds Price has found it increasingly difficult to employ the pastoral as a means of exploring race relations in eastern North Carolina. Although rarely is it entirely absent, race plays significantly less of a role in the fiction by contemporary writers from Appalachia, making pastoral, with its idealization of an agrarian social order, more viable. The rapid development of tourism in western North Carolina, along with the crowding of indigenous populations by summer homes owned by absentee landlords, has created in the late twentieth century a further pastoral impetus toward cultural preservation.

In light of the history of his family and region, as well as the ever-present contrast during his boyhood of his family's farm with the polluting Champion paper mill, it comes as no great surprise that Chappell became a pastoralist. It is more surprising, perhaps, that he did not, like Reynolds Price, *begin* his career as one. Very unlike Price's debut novel, which celebrates the childhood farming town he knew as a rural utopia, Chappell began his career by rebelling against his past. (This difference between the early careers of Price and Chappell can be explained, in part, by the fact that Chappell was actually required to work on the farm where he lived, whereas Price observed with fond detachment the lives of farmers who frequently lived nearby.) After twenty years away from the mountains—first as a student at Duke University and then as a professor at the University of North Carolina at Greensboro—Chappell began to reassess his troubled relationship with his own Appalachian past, and the rebellion of his earlier novels became replaced by reconciliation.

It is difficult to imagine a career more bifurcated than Chappell's—the first decade of major publications dominated by a fascination with alienation and degenerating states of the self—including alcoholism, deviant sexuality, prostitution, accounts of paranoid schizophrenia, and nihilism—and the later three decades characterized by the qualities of pastoral—a reverence for nature and family, a preoccupation with social order out of which meaning and value are derived, and an imagining of the past as an innocent golden age. Chappell's first four novels were out of print until they recently reappeared in Louisiana State University Press's invaluable *Voices of the South* series. Most scholarship on Chappell has focused on the later work. Even in recent scholarship, critics seem in a quandary to reconcile these two very different modes of fiction from the same pen. This chapter will briefly investigate the earlier studies in alienation before studying at greater length the later pastorals, examining how both are very different reactions to the same Appalachian yeoman culture, especially with respect to the region's insularity and the resulting tension between the mountaineer's fierce *independence* and his *interdependence* with family and community.

The amazing diversity of Chappell's literary productivity was already apparent during his years at Duke University, where he earned a B.A. and in 1964 a M.A. in English literature. Chappell studied under the legendary William Blackburn, who also taught William Styron, Anne Tyler, and Reynolds Price. In writing workshops Chappell demonstrated a raw genius that much later prompted Blackburn, in conversation with George Garrett, to call him "the most gifted writer and the best of the bunch," even while admitting his doubts whether Chappell would "ever 'succeed' as a writer" the way the others had.[9] Chappell's "success" in the form of widespread recognition was slower in coming than it was for the other writers mentioned, which may be because of his penchant for experimentation. If Price's career began with considerably more fanfare, a critical reevaluation over the last two decades—sparked, in part, by the appearance of *The Fred Chappell Reader* (1987)—has begun to bring Chappell the attention he deserves. Among the many prestigious awards offered in recognition of Chappell's diverse achievements are the Best Foreign Novel Prize from the French Academy (for *Dagon*), the Bollingen Prize in Poetry, the Ingersoll Foundation's T. S. Eliot Award for Poetry, a Rockefeller Grant, the Award in Literature from the National Institute of Arts and Letters, and the World Fantasy Award. In 1997 Chappell became the fourth official poet laureate of North Carolina. George Garrett places Chappell "among the best American poets alive" and, recognizing his vast skills in long and short fiction as well as criticism, calls him "our preeminent man of letters."[10] Lee Smith has famously written that "anybody who knows anything about Southern writing knows that Fred Chappell is our resident genius, our shining light, the one truly great writer we have among us."[11]

His first decade of major publication was devoted to novels: *It Is Time, Lord* (1963), *The Inkling* (1965), *Dagon* (1968), and *The Gaudy Place* (1973). The first three novels are wonderful examples of gothic fiction and, like many of his short stories, demonstrate the important early influence of Poe. *The Gaudy Place* is an abrupt shift toward comic realism, an urban satire showing the influence of Twain and other southwestern humorists. *The Gaudy Place* marks a transition from his earlier studies in alienation, one that anticipates his later pastorals. Throughout the 1970s, Chappell's attention shifted to poetry with the appearance of *The World between the Eyes* (1971), followed by *River* (1975), *Bloodfire* (1978), *Wind Mountain* (1979), and *Earthsleep* (1980). These latter four volumes were conceived of as equal parts of one long poem and in 1981 were published together as *Midquest*, which won the prestigious Bollingen Prize. In *Midquest*, Chappell continued to employ the elements of southwestern humor that he had used in *The Gaudy Place*; however, the dark satire of the former novel gives way to an elegiac pastoral vision, which he continued to employ in the tetralogy of novels that follow: *I Am One of You Forever* (1985); *Brighten the Corner Where You Are* (1989); *Farewell, I'm Bound to Leave You* (1996); and *Look Back All the Green Valley* (1999). These autobiographical novels, which chronicle the maturation of a poet named Jess Kirkman, serve as a counterpart to the four volumes of *Midquest*, thus comprising an octave. The pastoral quality of the Kirkman tetralogy may be observed not only in its celebration of an agrarian culture but by the fact that, with the exception of the last novel, each part is set in the past of the poet's boyhood on the farm, whereas Chappell's first four novels all have contemporary settings. Since 1980 Chappell has also produced numerous other works, including two volumes of short fiction, seven additional volumes of poetry, and two collections of criticism.

The majority of his writing exhibits the basic tension between a longing for unity with his Appalachian past and his recognition of his alienation from that past. He has named Faulkner, Eliot, Pound, and Joyce among the numerous important models especially of his earlier writing, and, like these and other great writers of the high modernist period, Chappell has responded to his loss of a traditional culture by reconstructing the raw materials in forms borrowed from both within and without the culture. Many readers have noted what Michael McFee calls Chappell's "split literary personality." "On the one side," McFee explains, "we have 'Ole Fred,' the kind of persona readers tend to remember, a character of extreme Romantic temperament and habits. Ole Fred is feisty; he cusses, he jokes, he drinks, he misbehaves; he is cheerfully politically incorrect; he overstates and exaggerates. . . . On the other side . . . is Professor Chappell, a neo-classical polymath of the first order, deeply and widely read, profoundly learned: a genuine scholar."[12] This split literary persona arguably indicates an actual "split" within the writer, who understands himself and his world by means of two divided cultures, one belonging to his present life in the Piedmont city of Greensboro, where for four decades he served as a professor of English at that campus of the University of North Carolina, and the other to his childhood on the Appalachian farm of his ancestors.

Just as McFee observes the tension in Chappell between a Romantic and a neoclassical temperament, Chappell's literary influences, while impressively diverse, are dominated by the antithetical traditions of Romanticism and neo-classicism. These two antagonistic aesthetic tendencies manifest themselves in Chappell's work as competing attitudes toward the yeoman culture of Appalachia he knew from boyhood. His later pastorals have been largely indebted to writers who were themselves of or largely indebted to the literature of classical antiquity, figures such as Virgil, Dante, and Pope, poets who were concerned with depicting a vision of an ordered, ideal society and were acutely aware of how their depictions were informed and limited by a long cultural tradition. To the contrary, Chappell's earlier novels were more inspired by the "dark" Romantics, writers such as Poe, Baudelaire, and Rimbaud, who—even when they were impressively cultivated—conceived of themselves as inventing something wholly new, writers who saw themselves as alienated artists working in opposition to the conformist tendencies of their publics.

What cannot be emphasized too strongly is the extent to which this bifurcated literary personality derives from Chappell's Appalachian heritage and its competing values of independence and interdependence, values reflected both in the pattern of farm settlement in the mountains and the resulting social structure. Ronald Eller notes of the settlement of the mountains that "houses were seldom constructed within sight of each other but, instead, were spread out, each in its own separate hollow or cove. Solitude and privacy were such dominant cultural values that they fostered dispersed settlement patterns and the continual penetration of the deeper mountain wilderness long after the passing of the frontier."[13] Several pages later, Eller discusses the "familism" that characterized Appalachian farming culture, observing that in "preindustrial Appalachia, as in most traditional rural societies, the family was the central organizing force of social life. . . . Obligations to the family came first, and this economic condition created intense family loyalties that not only insured the survival of the group, but also provided a strong feeling of security and belonging for individuals."[14] Eller, astonishingly, does not seem to recognize the inherent conflict between the mountaineer's independence and his interdependence with family, but perhaps such a consideration concerns the historian less than the creative writer, who responds to the culture not as an objective observer, viewing the culture through the lens of multiple texts, but as an individual participant, in whom these contradictory impulses are intensely and personally felt. Certainly this tension between independence and interdependence is one of the most pronounced features of Chappell's oeuvre. He seems to have begun writing in oedipal rebellion as a declaration of independence from his family and community, portraying Appalachian families that are extremely dysfunctional and depicting independence taken to the extreme of alienation. Later, having found that position spiritually depleting, he began to chronicle interdependent farming families and communities in a much more positive light, finding the isolated family farm not a prison to be escaped but, rather, an Arcadia to be preserved.

"Darker Vices and Nearly Incomprehensible Sins": Chappell's Early Novels

Although Chappell claims that Jess Kirkman is by far a more autobiographical figure than the protagonists of his earlier novels, he admits that Jess has been "highly romanticized and cleaned up a great deal."[15] Unlike the earlier protagonists, Jess's attitude toward his family and community is characterized by innocent acceptance and an often reverent attentiveness to detail that demonstrates the adult narrator's longing for a vanished past. Two autobiographical essays chronicling Chappell's adolescence—"First Attempts" and "A Pact with Faustus"—provide a very different picture of his relationship to family and community. As a boy with an intense interest in books and writing, it comes as no surprise that he was less than content with life on the farm. Just as Thomas Wolfe had felt about his native Asheville twenty miles to the east, Chappell grew up seeing the hills around Canton as a prison, holding him back from the cosmopolitan experience—and the career of a writer—of which he dreamed. Remembering his adolescent penchant for melodrama, he writes that it was clear to him that as an artist he was "never going to catch up with the twentieth century," that he was already "starting from too far behind."[16]

By the age of fifteen, he had determined to become a writer and was already publishing stories in various science fiction and fantasy magazines, whose editors gave him what little encouragement and instruction he received. "My experience with [these] editors," he writes, "was that they were sinister spectral entities who occasionally scribbled crabbed notes on little blue rejections slips: 'Your exposition is silly'; 'This is not how Martians talk to each other.'"[17] Despite the thanks he gives to certain high school teachers who at least did not discourage him from writing, Chappell's account of his own adolescence is one that might be expected from an aspiring writer growing up on an isolated mountain farm: the dreamy autodidact, who began teaching himself to write through "an eon of trial . . . followed by an infinitude of error."[18] His parents were, at times, both school teachers, and so they instilled in him a sense of the value of education and made books readily available, including the classics of Western literature. Of his high school years he remembers that he "was reading Shelley and Shakespeare by wholesale acreage and had bought a copy of Yeats's early plays for twenty-five cents from a junk dealer."[19] Although he believes that his parents had themselves once entertained literary aspirations, they strongly discouraged his because they found them impractical.

In "A Pact with Faustus," Chappell recalls his adolescent friendship with Harry ("Fuzz") Fincher, another Canton boy, who aspired to become a composer. Chappell recalls their mutual "conspiracy against the placid town and against [their] perfectly nice parents": "We felt—God forgive us!—superior in some way that we could not articulate, and much put upon, despised for our interests and aspirations."[20] The boys felt cut off from any meaningful discussion of the arts beyond their own company of two, and in typical adolescent fashion they luxuriated in their alienation and eventually joined in a spree of vandalism through the nighttime streets of Canton, "breaking random store windows and wreaking other damage," a night that for Fred resulted in "severe" and "unforgettable" punishments involving "physical ordeals" and an "interminable" ban on reading, an activity his parents associated with his waywardness.[21]

If he was taught that reading was a guilty pleasure, writing seemed to have been doubly so. In a community of farmers and mill workers, a pursuit of the arts was seen as self-indulgent. Parents, teachers, and "everyone else" constantly lectured Fred about the valuelessness of his pursuits.[22] He remembers his family's attitude toward the long evenings he spent secluded upstairs writing. "My bedroom was too small to accommodate a desk and typewriter, but I had found a niche in the upstairs hall. When I set the Royal clattering the sound could be heard all over the house. Visitors who asked about the racket were informed that Oh, that's only Fred working on his typing. Their embarrassment was just that acute; I was not trying to write, I was learning to type. Typing was a useful skill that might come in handy someday. Writing was impractical and impracticality was worse than heresy, thievery, or some kinds of homicide. These were the tag-end years of the Depression; it was imperative to be practical."[23] He had discovered that to be a writer was to be at odds with his culture, and he clung to this newfound identity of the outsider. What a contrast Chappell's situation offers to that of Reynolds Price, who in *Clear Pictures* describes family and teachers only as being thoroughly supportive of his artistic ambitions. Even though there were no literary members of Price's family, the family's genteel history made possible the identity of the artist for young Reynolds in a way that such an identity was completely alien to Chappell's frontier, yeoman culture. At the same time, Chappell's embracing the role of the alienated artist is a manifestation of the fierce independence so prevalent in Appalachian culture.

Chappell makes comically clear in "First Attempts" that, in fact, what attracted him as a young person to the literary profession was the extreme eccentricity—and, thus, the glamour—that his people associated with "being a writer." At the same time, the problem he faced was a lack of models:

The only other writer [besides Hemingway] of whose personal life one
ever heard anything was Poe—and he was regarded as both scandalous
and tragic. Whenever my parents, teachers, and ministers tried to dissuade
me from a life of writing—as they did regularly and assiduously—it was the
fate of Poe they threatened me with. They pictured him as a wild-eyed
genius who was an alcoholic and drug addict, and they hinted too at
darker vices and nearly incomprehensible sins.

Well, I could see that being Edgar Allan Poe had it all over being
Ernest Hemingway. . . . To all of us [writing] seemed such an exotic occupation, such a dangerous ambition, that when we tried to imagine the way
of life a writer might trace we could come up with only the most lurid and
improbable scenarios, visions that horrified and repulsed my elders while
they attracted me with all the force a two-ton electromagnet exerts on a
single crumb of iron filing.[24]

Poe would serve as an appropriate icon to represent the alienation he felt, and,
along with the French Symbolists, would fix very firmly in his mind the image
of the young genius at odds with his world, composing obscure lyrical gems that
would some day after his early death bring him the fame he had deserved.

How striking it is that the young Chappell did not find in Thomas Wolfe a
model of the alienated artist—considering that Wolfe grew up in and wrote
about Asheville, just twenty miles to the east. Like Reynolds Price, however,
Chappell missed reading Wolfe, recalling that, as a teenager, he had only read
later works, The Hills Beyond and "Only the Dead Know Brooklyn."[25] Perhaps
like Lin Harper, the teenage founder of a literary club called the Skylark Society in The Gaudy Place, the young Chappell felt that Wolfe, a "local" writer
"too much lauded by parents and teachers," would have nothing to say to him
of the outside world.[26] While Chappell names Poe as his "first and most lasting
influence,"[27] the influence of Camus and Faulkner is also evident in his first
four novels.[28]

In fact, the protagonists in the first four novels might be seen as Appalachian Quentin Compsons, trapped and determined by their environments
and by their personal and familial pasts. James Christopher, the protagonist of
his first novel, It Is Time, Lord, describes the past as "an eternally current danger, in effect, a suicide. We desire the past, we call to it just as men who have
fallen overboard an ocean liner call. . . . it sours and rots like old meat in the
mind."[29] In addition to confronting the repressed trauma of sexual molestation
he seems to have suffered during childhood, James Christopher is still wrestling
at age thirty-one with the guilt of having as a nine-year-old burned down his
family's ancestral homeplace. His fixation on the past has produced a midlife

crisis, the symptoms of which include alcoholism and the loss of purpose in his professional and family life. James tells his wife of his plan to straighten himself out by visiting his parents in the mountains, whom he has not seen or corresponded with in five years. "Isn't it true," he says, "that if I could get my past settled in the right groove my present life would trundle along the way it's supposed to? It's like getting a nut cross-threaded on a bolt: you have to twist it back and try until it fits correctly" (160).

His attempts to "settle" his past depend largely on making peace with his father, a plan that fails abruptly. When James first enters the front yard, his father begins a withering speech, rehearsing—in a lazy and "preoccupied" voice, a "good voice for reading Tennyson"—all of his son's failures, past and present. In effect, he verbally divests James of his manhood, just as he had done throughout James's boyhood, constantly criticizing his bookishness and his disinclination for farm labor, making James re-experience the guilt of having burned his family's homeplace. After showing anything but enthusiasm for his son's visit, the father mentions plans for having James's wife and children make an extended visit—without James:

> "In the first place, I don't like to think about your kids inheriting your hatred—or do they call it an allergy now?—whatever—of clean air and sunlight. But if they do come, I want *them*. And every time I see you around I'll just try to drive you off with a shotgun."
>
> "Why?"
>
> "Well, that's hyperbole, of course. I don't like the thought of turning a gun on a mewling baby, especially one over thirty years old. What I can't understand is how you ever thought of coming up here. You could have everything that's on my mind, and I believe I can speak pretty fairly for your mother too, over the telephone in a few minutes."
>
> "I don't know."
>
> "The only thing I could figure was that you've been reading too many novels. Telemachus. Stephen Dedalus. The boy with the golden screw for a navel. The search for a father. All that literary stuff. I've read it myself, one time or another. It's hogwash. Bull shit. I've just about stopped reading, and only just now I've started hoping that I've stopped in time. Even our damn barn cat has got enough sense to chase its younguns off when they get old enough." (157–58)

Like James, his father is a man threatened by any degree of intimacy, and his rejection of his son appears to be a spontaneous response to that threat. Shortly thereafter, James's mother comes to his bedroom and explains that she is supposed to let him know that his father is still his "good buddy." "Your father's got in his head," she says, "that the only way a real masculine man ought to talk is in grunts and profanity. But the trouble is, he likes to talk too much for that to satisfy him. So he runs on. I've lived with him long enough to know he doesn't mean anything he says for an hour at a time." She further remarks that he "almost jumps out of his skin" when he hears the word "love" (161).

In *Look Back All the Green Valley*, Jess Kirkman observes that "to be well spoken is not in the tradition of the Appalachian mountaineer, whose sometimes inscrutable taciturnity is locally regarded as a virtue having something to do with valor and manliness."[30] If to show oneself a "well spoken man" in Appalachia is to invite suspicions of one's masculinity, to show oneself as "bookish" confirms those suspicions. In both cases, not only emotional warmth, but communication through language, is degraded in contrast to "action." James's father has obviously internalized these cultural values and, because, as his wife observes, he is a compulsive talker, he compromises by divorcing any emotional warmth from his speeches to his son. Chappell acknowledges "the taciturn farmer father" as a staple of American realism, finding examples in Hamlin Garland, Sarah Orne Jewett, Mary Wilkins Freeman, and "all the regionalists."[31] Such taciturnity and emotional paralysis appear throughout Chappell's fiction as the downside of yeoman independence. *It Is Time, Lord,* especially, launches a steady critique against Appalachian ideals of manhood, viewing the figure of the yeoman farmer as insensitive, alienated, and completely incapable of nurturing.

Interestingly enough, even in this darkly pessimistic first novel, Chappell shows signs of the pastoralist he would later become. The novel depicts James Christopher's intense preoccupation with his rural past and his desire to reconcile himself to that past—and to his father—even if that desire is thoroughly balked. Moreover, the description of James's boyhood on the farm is in many ways idyllic, though the idyll is corrupted by self-loathing: James recalls himself as "the toad in the garden of what [his] family . . . might call Eden" (95).

The psychological/supernatural thriller *Dagon* also depicts a return to a family homeplace in the mountains that goes awry. Peter Leland returns with his wife to his family's Appalachian farm, which he has just inherited and finds to be literally haunted by a familial past that he, like Poe's Roderick Usher, cannot escape. Upon first exploring the downstairs parlors, Leland remarks that "the pastness which these two rooms . . . enclosed was not simply the impersonal weight of dead personality but a willful belligerence, active hostility. Standing still in the center of the first room, he felt the floor stirring faintly beneath his feet, and he was convinced that the house was gathering its muscles to do him harm."[32] Over the following weeks, the house does in fact do him serious harm, exerting an influence over his moods and his frame of mind, leading him to morbid thoughts and ultimately to the brutal and motiveless murder of his wife. Up until the murder it seems that if Leland could only escape the homeplace of his ancestors he could avoid the malaise that has overtaken him.

Like Poe's stories of dementia that Chappell so admired growing up, the energy driving Chappell's first three novels[33] derives from within the self rather than from the social milieu in which the self finds itself. For all their intensity and frequent lyricism, the first three novels lack the breadth and social scope typically associated with long fiction. Admittedly, the length of each stays under 200 pages, and, considering the economy and intensity of the narratives, these novels have the advantage—which Poe attributes to the short story—of possibly being read in a single sitting.[34] Nevertheless, W. H. Auden's criticism of Poe's stories would equally apply to Chappell's. According to Auden, there is "no place" in any of Poe's fiction "for the human individual as he actually exists in space and time, that is, as simultaneously a natural creature subject in his feelings to the influences and limitations of the natural order, and an historical person, creating novelty and relations by his free choice and modified in unforeseen ways by the choices of others."[35] As with Poe's stories, each of Chappell's first three novels demonstrates an unease with society, and in particular, an unease with the yeoman society of Appalachia. The characters' self-destructive behaviors result not from interactions with others so much as from their withdrawal from society and the internal compulsions they cannot escape.

Even though Chappell has acknowledged this problem, noting a "claustrophobic feeling" that he "could not get out" of his early fiction,[36] in my estimation the "claustrophobia" of Chappell's earlier work is not necessarily a problem; as with Poe's stories, Chappell's early novels are so engaging precisely because of the characters' withdrawal into dementia. Alienation is not only a very real part of the modern experience but also the traditional yeoman experience in Appalachia as well. James Christopher or Peter Leland might be described in the very words Joe Robert Kirkman uses to describe one of his shy rural students who is more comfortable alone in the woods than in a high school classroom: "It was the mountaineer strain in his blood as pure . . . as it might have been a century ago" (*Brighten*, 57). Nevertheless, having acknowledged the insight of Poe and of Chappell's early work into the alienated psyche, Auden's critique of Poe is equally applicable to Chappell, prompting us to declare that not all the world looks so dark and determined. Even in the loneliest valleys of Appalachia, people form communities, however small, which they creatively engage and in which they define themselves. Chappell obviously recognized this same dilemma, having remarked of his fourth novel, *The*

Gaudy Place (1973), "I set myself very deliberately the challenge . . . of writing a novel about the same length as the others, but having scope in it, and trying to draw a larger social picture . . . [and] more variety of character."[37] *The Gaudy Place* marks Chappell's first attempt in long fiction to escape the prison of the self and to describe a social world.

The Gaudy Place is Chappell's first and only fully urban novel, taking in all of the bustle of the Gimlett Street red-light district of Braceboro, the fictional version of Lexington Avenue and Flint Street in Asheville, where Chappell spent numerous hours doing research.[38] A strikingly different sensibility is at work in this fourth novel; although the earlier fiction is replete with delicious irony, this is Chappell's first fully comic novel, a social satire reminiscent of Twain that pokes brutal fun at the American myth of the self-made man. With its Kafkaesque interest in the dissemination of power, *The Gaudy Place* is easily Chappell's most explicitly sociopolitical novel, one in which not family so much as economics and politics determine social and personal realities. But, then again, as the novel's Andrew Harper discovers upon moving to Appalachia with his mountain-born wife, mountain politics is a *family* business.

As satire, *The Gaudy Place* takes the first step toward the pastoral vision of yeoman society found in *Midquest* and the Kirkman novels. Frank Kermode observes that, like pastoral, satire is an urban genre, designed to contrast the "degeneracy" of the "metropolis" with some "better way of life—that is, some earlier way of life; the farther back you go the better."[39] Such a dichotomy appears, for example, in *Adventures of Huckleberry Finn*, in which the pastoral life of the river is juxtaposed with the social quagmires the boy finds along the river's shores. *The Gaudy Place* offers no such easy geographic demarcations; however, strata of corruption are associated with the extent to which individuals have insinuated themselves into the city's social structures by which power, wealth, and status are acquired.

The lowest stratum represented in the novel is occupied by Arkie, a resourceful fourteen-year-old orphan, an urban Huck Finn who survives day to day by running cons on the slow-witted truck farmers, who have come to the city to sell their produce, and on the unsuspecting "johns" waiting for their "girl friends." Arkie speaks a tough, comic street slang, full of both hyperbolic boasting and self-deprecation and is known all along Gimlett Street for a subservient song-and-dance routine that has all the characteristics of minstrelsy; whenever a tense moment appears, he sings out his namesake couplet: "Fried cornbread and cold coleslaw, I'm traveling down to Arkansas" (26) or some variant thereof. At a slightly more elevated level of society there is Oxie, a Gimlett Street pimp, who also works as a bondsman and reads Dale Carnegie in an effort to ingratiate himself with the "respectable" racket of local politics.

The city's highest level of power and corruption is represented by Zebulon Johns Mackie, or Uncle Zeb, a local politician and self-made man described as a "dead ringer" for Benjamin Franklin. A member of both the city council and the board of directors for the local Green Ridge Construction Company, respectable Uncle Zeb has his own con in the works, one that involves someone with Oxie's contacts on Gimlett Street.

This novel's considerable power derives from the vertigo of watching what at first seems to be a random sampling of society drawn into a web of power that robs each of them of agency—demonstrating that in The Gaudy Place Chappell feels the same mistrust of society that appears in his earlier novels of alienation. Admittedly, the novel ends somewhat hopefully for Arkie, with him running from the law after singing out that he is "going down to ARKANSAS!" (177) and thereby eluding the city's corrupting influences that have entrapped the other characters. Nevertheless, like Huck Finn, Arkie's final statement that he plans to light out for the territory of the old Southwest suggests that, equally for Twain and Chappell, freedom only exists for the individual removed from society.

"The green poison of money has leached into the ground and turned it blue"

The Gaudy Place is easily Chappell's most class-conscious novel. It not only provides a complete overview of the social classes of this mountain city but also shows how power flows from the upper classes downward to determine the lives of those below, how market capital in general perverts society's better instincts, including the truck farmers who often spend in a single day along the city's red light district a good portion of the cash they earned from selling their produce.

Although industrialization and urbanization, which developed throughout Appalachia during the late nineteenth and early twentieth centuries, certainly accelerated the threat to the yeoman's economic independence and exacerbated class conflict, Wilma Dunaway dates the introduction of capitalism into the region to the arrival of the first European settlers in the early eighteenth century and finds that class conflict was already present during the antebellum period.[40] Paul Salstrom demonstrates the rapid expansion of a market economy in the region following the Civil War—even before the growth of industrialization. Because of the war's devastation, the rising imbalance between population growth and depleted resources, and the restructuring of the national bank system (which favored capital investment available only from and controlled by sources outside the region), Appalachian farmers increasingly fell prey to market forces. The rise of a market economy devalued labor, kept the landless poor in a state of dependency and struggling for subsistence, and made a "competency" more difficult for yeomen to secure. Ironically, Salstrom explains, even as this struggle for subsistence became more acute, Appalachian farmers "increasingly abandoned their subsistence-barter-and-borrow systems and increasingly adopted the capitalist system," which depended on "increasing quantities of money" for survival.[41]

Chappell investigates the deleterious effects of this dependence on capital in the darkly comic poem "My Father Burns Washington" from *Midquest*. The poet recalls his boyhood during the latter years of the Great Depression when, lying in bed, he and his sister would overhear his parents as they frequently talked through their financial troubles and stalked the "phantom dollar and ghostly dime," after which they "went to bed in the grip / Of money and dreamed of money" (81). One night, the boy's father came home in tears and railed, "In outrage: 'Money. Money. Money. It's the death of the world. If it wasn't for goddam money a man might think a thought, might draw a breath of freedom. But all I can think is, Money. Money by God is death.'" (82)

As if to defy the control of capital over the farm and their lives there, and its delimitation of the farmers' "freedom," the father strikes a match and sets fire to a dollar bill. The poem's title, "My Father Burns Washington," suggests the symbolism of the Appalachian farmer's defiance of the national bank and what a world-systems analysis would describe as the exploitation of poor farmers in a capitalist system's periphery for the benefit of the capitalist core in the industrialized Northeast.[42] The poem ends with the repentant father stomping out the fire, before the bill completely burns, and asking his wife, like "a beaten child," "*Mother, will it still spend?*" (84). In "My Father Washes His Hands," also from *Midquest*, the older Fred, now away at college, returns to find his father broken and ready to give up the farm and "sell / Cheap furniture to poor folks" (153). Declaring that a "man's a fool in this age / Of money to turn the soil," the father intends not "to die in the traces like poor Honey" (153), the mule that died two weeks before. He tells Fred of the ordeal of burial, which involved digging through "pipe clay as blue and sticky as Buick paint" (153). "The green poison / Of money," the father explains, "has leached into the ground / And turned it blue" (154).

One of the most unfortunate effects of capitalism in Appalachia, as elsewhere, has been the production of barriers between social classes and resulting class conflict. Ronald Eller locates the appearance of class consciousness in Appalachia during the period of industrialization that began in the late nineteenth century, largely in mining company towns, where the mine owners and supervisors were segregated in nicer homes but always in view of their impoverished work force.[43] Both Salstrom and Dunaway observe a rigid stratification of social classes to have developed much earlier. Throughout most of the region,

Salstrom finds that by 1880 the capitalization of agriculture had already stymied a spirit of entrepreneurship, making farm ownership available to fewer moun-taineers and producing a nearly insurmountable division between upper and lower classes.[44] Dunaway demonstrates how the prevalence of absentee land-lords even in the antebellum period exacerbated the exploitation of labor in the form of tenancy, sharecropping, wage labor, and slavery.

Contrary to the prevailing myth of a nearly slaveless mountain South, Dunaway demonstrates how pervasive slavery was throughout southern Appa-lachia. Her research shows, however, that, compared to Appalachian Virginia, Alabama, Georgia, and South Carolina, where one-fifth to one-quarter of households owned slaves, coming near the southern average, 1860 census data show that in western North Carolina, as in eastern Kentucky, only about 10 percent of households owned slaves.[45] And even in western North Carolina this figure varies considerably, with the foothills showing a higher incidence of slavery than the more remote mountainous regions.[46] Dunaway observes one of the most significant effects of slavery in western North Carolina to be the production of an inequitable distribution of resources and developing social classes, including the rise of a large population of landless poor. According to Dunaway, despite their relatively low representation in the population, North Carolina's Appalachian slaveholders "engrossed more than two-fifths of the farm acreage, leaving only one-seventh of the resources available to the poorer bottom half of the farm households."[47] Furthermore, whereas "subsistence pro-ducers made up nearly one-fifth of the owner households," they owned "only 4 to 8 percent of the farm land."[48] Even more troubling, while distribution of wealth elsewhere in the United States remained fairly unchanged throughout the antebellum period, in Appalachia, Dunaway demonstrates, the polariza-tion of wealth between slaveholders and nonslaveholders increased dramati-cally.[49] This disparity in landholdings during the antebellum period produced widespread landlessness, forcing a significant portion of the agricultural popu-lation into wage labor, tenancy, and sharecropping, and thereby threatening the yeoman ideal of a classless, egalitarian society.

Chappell's fiction depicts the persistence of these class divisions well into the twentieth century. The legacy of slavery in the form of conflict between Appalachian whites and descendants of slaves is not entirely absent in his work, as exemplified by "My Father Allergic to Fire" from *Midquest* or in the acknowl-edgement of racism by Jubal Henry, Tipton High School's African American janitor in *Brighten the Corner Where You Are*. Nevertheless Chappell's concern with class conflict focuses much more often on the tensions between white ten-ant farmers and their yeoman landlords, with both groups struggling for subsis-tence in response to market pressures. Class conflict is most troubling in his

early fiction. If *The Gaudy Place* represents Chappell's most conscious engagement of the strata of Appalachian social classes, *Dagon* yields the most unnerv-
ing depiction of conflict between yeoman and tenant. Peter Leland, a Methodist
minister, and scion of an Appalachian yeoman family, returns to the abandoned Leland homeplace to complete a book that treats, among other subjects,
the spiritually deadening influence of capitalism throughout American history.
Leland concludes, "And wasn't the power of money finally dependent upon the
continued proliferation of product after product, dead objects produced without any thought given to their uses? Weren't these mostly objects without any
truly justifiable need? Didn't the whole of American commercial culture exhibit
this endless irrational productivity, clear analogue to sexual orgy? And yet productivity without regard to eventual need was, Peter maintained, actual unpro-
ductivity, it was really a kind of impotence" (70–71). This preoccupation with
capitalism, coupled with his return to his family's farm, produces in Leland psychological instability, which results in his motiveless murder of his wife, followed by his flight from the family homestead to the home of a sharecropping
family named Morgan, who for generations has sustained itself on the sale of
moonshine. Leland gives himself over to the Morgans' moonshine and spends
the rest of the summer drunk in the bed of the daughter Mina, who serves as
his dominatrix, subjugating him to her every whim, delighting in his increasing degradation. At the end of the summer, Mina uses Leland's automobile to
drive eastward with Leland and another young man to a Piedmont town where
they settle into an abandoned house. Mina employs two other women as pros-
titutes and begins a campaign of ritually desecrating Leland's body through
torture and tattooing. The story ends with Leland emaciated and covered in
tattoos, reduced to a state of bestiality and total withdrawal, grunting and moo-
ing being his only forms of communication, and a metal bar that he identifies
as his "man-thing" being the only object he values. When Mina finally takes
his life in ritual sacrifice, Leland welcomes the knife.

A reduction of this novel to a mere diatribe against the unhealthy influence
of market capital on Appalachian social classes would represent a serious
misreading—or at least an incomplete one. Nevertheless, as the descendant of
an established yeoman family, Leland's aberrant behavior toward the Morgans,
who have for generations occupied the position of tenant farmers, certainly
deserves investigation. His sexual behavior toward Mina obviously bears all the
marks of masochism, which, when considered in light of the economic relationship of their respective families, along with Leland's developing thesis on
capitalism, suggests a manifestation of his repressed class-based guilt. The same
dynamic appears in *It Is Time, Lord:* James Christopher, a successful middle-
class editor at a university press, leaves his job, undertakes an extended drunk,

goes on the lam with a cast of lower-class characters, and becomes masochistically involved with a "redneck" woman named Judy. This relationship may, in part, be a failed effort at reconciliation with his own past and, in particular, with his family's tenant farmer, "Uncle" George, who served the young James as a surrogate father while nevertheless neglecting and abusing his own son. Other than Uncle George's nurturing of James, no healthy relationship appears between poor whites and yeomen (and their middle-class descendants) in Chappell's early work. The yeoman fathers are cold and distant. Their sons are self-loathing drunks—not unlike the besotted aristocrats in decline who appear in Faulkner or Percy or Styron. And the poor whites are brutish, narrowminded, and cruel.

Chappell's later work marks a departure from such negative portraits of Appalachian society, a difference particularly evident in the Jess Kirkman tetralogy. In these four novels interactions between social classes appear less frequently or are downplayed, given that three of the novels focus on relations within the Kirkman family or within what appears to be a seemingly classless, agrarian society. When, for example, the Kirkman family hires Johnson Gibbs to work on their farm, paying him primarily with room and board, providing a better life than that to which he had been accustomed growing up in an orphanage, little mention is made of the economic incentives for his presence, so thoroughly is he embraced as a part of the family. The various elderly figures who proliferate the stories that make up *I Am One of You Forever* and *Farewell, I'm Bound to Leave You* are either kinfolk or apparently of the yeoman class.

The Kirkman novel that most directly addresses issues of class is *Brighten the Corner Where You Are*. Here, Jess's father, Joe Robert Kirkman, is a yeoman farmer/educator of modest means, who, with quiet grace and humility, assumes a position of noblesse oblige toward the less fortunate of his community. Contrary to the paternalism typically displayed by planters toward their dependents, however, Joe Robert takes pains to diminish any sense of social hierarchy or difference of status that might appear between himself and other members of his community. When as a high school science teacher he stumbles upon Jubal Henry's hideaway in the school's basement, Joe Robert absorbs without retaliation the African American janitor's repressed aggression toward "white folks." Even though Joe Robert advises Jubal to stand up to the perpetrators of racism rather than taking out his anger on a man who "never did [Jubal] a bad turn," he seems to understand when Jubal explains, "The man that will give me trouble is the one that will just as soon kill me. I rather take it out on you. A little backsass don't do you no hurt and does me a profit of good" (123).

Joe Robert takes a similarly pacifist stance toward the wrathful tenant, Hob Farnum, whom he employs on his dairy farm, as described in the central chapter of *Brighten,* entitled "Shares." When counseling his son not to fight back against tenant children, even when attacked, he tells Jess, *"Poor people have got plenty enough problems without you hitting them"* (109). Jess, who is being emotionally abused by Hob Farnum and physically bullied by the tenant's son, Burrell, counters, *"But what if I had to? What if he was to start picking on me, or we had a quarrel?"* Joe Robert responds, *"Oh, you've got a quarrel, all right. You had a quarrel before either of you were born"* (111). Joe Robert's efforts to enlighten his son about the complex of emotions involved between the *"haves and have-nots"* (111), however, are lost on his young son (but not on the adult Jess, who serves as the novel's retrospective narrator). Young Jess is thoroughly invested in the values of manly honor that come to him from Hollywood westerns (values that Bertram Wyatt-Brown finds pervasive throughout the Old South); filled with self-loathing as a result of his own cowardice, Jess thinks to himself, *"Roy Rogers wouldn't [even] spit on me"* (112). After months of cowering before the abuse of the tenants, feelings of dishonor drive Jess nearly to the brink of madness. *"It was all upside down,"* he reflects. *"They were the tenants and lived in the little weathered house with its bare yard pecked over by listless chickens; I lived in the brick house under the trees. Yet I was the one who was getting bossed around, the one who felt petty and subservient"* (110). Finally, after standing up to and defeating Burrell, Jess remarks, *"I wish I was grown up now already and owned me a farm with some poor folks on it. I wish I had me some tenants on a farm. I'd whip their ass three times a day"* (114). The abyss of self-loathing and alienation into which young Jess sinks here in this twelve-page chapter resembles the demented psychological states suffered by the protagonists of Chappell's first three novels. Unlike the earlier novels, however, Jess's suffering in the role reversal recounted in "Shares" is necessary for his maturation and his willingness as an adult to embrace his father's yeoman ideal of an egalitarian society, one in which no one should have to feel "petty" or "subservient."

Despite the conflicts that will arise in any society—and that are necessary for any fiction—the octave composed of the Kirkman novels and the four volumes of *Midquest* emphasize the possibility for social harmony grounded in the basic unit of the yeoman family farm. In "Shares," Jess observes, *"My father and Hob Farnum found one point upon which they enjoyed perfect agreement. They both hated and passionately despised the system of tenant farming"* (103). Both men realize that this system is necessitated by their participation in the market economy, which is equally for the tenant and the yeoman landlord an unavoidable trap. Implicit in this critique of capitalized agriculture, which deprives both men of independence and autonomy, is the ideal of a farm free of market pressures, providing economic competency for all willing to work, and freedom from hierarchies based on wealth. This yeoman ideal fairly characterizes the society that Paul Salstrom finds more prevalent throughout Appalachia in its earlier frontier stages, before capitalism so thoroughly ensnared the vast majority of the region's population.[50] In *Midquest* and the Kirkman novels, just such a golden age informs the vision of the pastoralist Chappell would become by his second decade of publishing. Quite in contrast to his earlier studies of alienation, in which the Appalachian tendency toward independence is taken to its extreme, in his later work there emerges the possibility of a balance between independence and interdependence, as he explores the lives of individuals whose identities emerge not exclusively in rebellion *against* the social order but nurtured *within* it, as well.

Midquest: "When You Got True Dirt You Got Everything You Need"

In "The Poet and the Plowman," Chappell ponders what he considers to be one of the fundamental issues facing poets ever since the classical age: the fact that it is impractical, if not impossible, to pursue both a life of poetry and a life of farming. As the essay begins, Chappell recalls long Sunday afternoons in the mid-1960s when he and·his guest Allen Tate (who was then a guest lecturer at the University of North Carolina at Greensboro) would watch football on television and bemoan the disappearance of their Latin skills, along with the diminishing allure of the "traditional attractions of farm life."[51] Chappell recalls Tate's conclusion that poets should be only "spectator farmers": "Then he would smile and say in his breathy ironic genteel Kentucky accent: 'But we would make dreadful farmers, Fred, you and I.'"[52] In Chappell's portrait of the aging Agrarian, "genteel" Tate comes off unmistakably more comfortable in his resignation than does Chappell himself, who goes on restlessly to ponder the age-old kinship between the poet—or, more generally, the writer—and the plowman. This connection between the writer and the farmer is one that Chappell explores throughout the long poem *Midquest* and the subsequent Kirkman tetralogy of novels.

In the preface to *Midquest,* which Chappell therein calls a "verse novel" (ix), he describes the poem's "protagonist," Ole Fred, as a "demographic sample" of the twentieth century: "He was reared on a farm but has moved to the city; he has deserted manual for intellectual labor, is 'upwardly mobile'; he is cut off from his disappearing cultural traditions but finds them, in remembering, his real values" (x). This contrast between an ideal agrarian childhood and a corrupted urban age is one of the principal hallmarks of pastoral, which, as Frank Kermode notes, is always "an urban product."[53] Kermode observes that the "first condition of pastoral . . . is that there should be a sharp difference between two ways of life, the rustic and the urban. The city is an artificial product, and the pastoral poet invariably lives in it, or is the product of its schools and universities."[54] Kermode's description fits both Chappell and "Ole Fred," the autobiographical protagonist of *Midquest*. Chappell grew up observing the remnants of a traditional culture, as well as the emergence of industry in western North Carolina. The "loud, smoky, noisome" Champion Paper and Fiber Company[55] is a ubiquitous presence in Chappell's pastorals (appearing under the name of *Challenger*), as is the figure of the farmer father tenaciously scratching out a living from the soil, and the dreamy adolescent boy destined to leave the farm for the Piedmont cities of Durham and Greensboro. The world Chappell describes is one very much in flux, which makes his recollections of childhood appear all the more valued. Kermode has noted that pastoral "flourishes at a particular moment in the urban development, the phase in which the relationship of metropolis and country is still evident, and there are no children (as there are now) who have never seen a cow."[56] This precondition for pastoral sounds very like the necessity of the "backward glance" to the Southern Literary Renascence, or, more generally, to the experience of modernism. In each case, the artist has witnessed the disappearance of the old verities, an experience that leaves him dislocated, alienated, full of epistemological uncertainty, and longing for some source of truth by which to reorient himself. *Midquest* is full of folk tales, jokes, and convincing accounts of farm life, and at the same time it abounds in literary allusions. Chappell's style conflates examples of high and low cultures and derives a high lyricism from a rural Appalachian vernacular. In its largest design, *Midquest* attempts to heal the schism between Ole Fred and Professor Chappell, to restore a sense of wholeness by employing the breadth of the poet's learning to recreate the world of his childhood.

Following the model of Dante's *Divine Comedy*, each of *Midquest*'s four volumes begins with Ole Fred awakening on his thirty-fifth birthday in a state of spiritual longing. Of the eleven poems that compose each volume, most take the form of dialogues with family members remembered from the poet's childhood. These recollections serve as a source of inspiration and direction for Ole Fred, who at mid-life finds himself disenchanted with his suburban existence. In "Birthday 35: Diary Entry," the second poem in the first volume, Ole Fred pessimistically considers—from the comfort of his living room—the results of his life's work: "On paper I scribble mottoes and epigrams, / Blessings and epithets, O-Holy's and Damn's— / Not matter sufficient to guard a week by. / The wisdom I hoard you could stuff in your eye" (4). The heroic couplets enhance the comic deflation of his vocational crisis. Throughout the poem Ole Fred employs humor to shield himself from raw feelings of despair and loss, as well as from the fear that the spiritual restoration for which he yearns is no longer available. Ultimately, though, he achieves that restoration through memory.

The past is no longer a "suicide," as it is described by James Christopher in *It Is Time, Lord,* but, rather, an antidote for the aridity of modern existence, a touchstone by which the poet finds meaning to live in the present. Nearing its conclusion, the tone of "Birthday 35" shifts from witty erudition to genuine desperation, as wasteland imagery proliferates:

> A wilderness of wind and ash.
> When I went to the river . . .
> . . . .
> I saw, darkened, my own face.
> On the bank of Time I saw nothing human,
> . . . .
> . . . only moon
> Upon moon, sterile stone
> Climbing the steep hill of void.
> And I was afraid. (7)

This sterile landscape is characterized by dryness and dreary uniformity. In addition to conjuring images of mountains denuded by timber companies, these lines express Ole Fred's anxiety concerning his own tendency toward solipsism and the possibility that, as in the case of James Christopher, the world he observes or remembers is merely a projection of his own subconscious. These lines clearly echo the language from the final section of *The Waste Land*:[57] "Here is no water but only rock / Rock and no water and the sandy road."[58] Chappell's reaction to the dilemma is a parody of Eliot's climactic prayer, with Ole Fred praying for transcendence in the form of "Elysium . . . plentifully planted // With trout streams and waterfalls and suburban / Swimming pools, and sufficient chaser for bourbon" (8). In characteristic fashion, he switches back and forth between adolescent cheekiness and heartfelt sincerity; these lines are immediately followed by a shift in tone from cynicism to reverential pleading. Note also that the suburban references are absent from the concluding lines:

> Lead me then, Lord, to the thundering valleys where
> Cool silver droplets feather the air;
> Where rain like thimbles smacks roofs of tin,
> Washing away sin;
> Where daily a vast and wholesome cloud
> Announces itself aloud.
> Amen. (8)

The wasteland imagery in "Birthday 35" evokes Ole Fred's spiritual estrangement and draws a distinction, in typical pastoral fashion, between the emptiness of his present urban/suburban condition and the spiritual sustenance to be
found in a long-past rural golden age.

The prayer for cleansing and quenching that ends "Birthday 35" is provisionally answered in the following dramatic dialogue set in Ole Fred's boyhood,
"My Grandmother Washes Her Feet." While washing her feet, the grandmother lectures the boy Fred about the dangers of pretension and the unrecognized history of his family's less respectable plain folk, which she accepts as
family, despite what might be seen by mainstream society as undesirable idiosyncrasies. Again, intellectual pursuits occupy an antagonistic position to the
farming life, as indicated in the grandmother's warning to the boy:

> You're bookish. I can see you easy a lawyer
> Or a county clerk in a big white suit and tie,
> Feeding the preacher and bribing the sheriff and the judge.
> Second-generation respectable
> Don't come to any better destiny.
> But it's dirt you rose from, dirt you'll bury in.
> Just about the time you'll think your blood
> Is clean, here will come dirt in a natural shape
> You never dreamed. . . .
> . . . .
> . . . When you got true dirt, you got
> Everything you need . . . (12)

The shift in consciousness that occurs from "Birthday 35" to the following
"My Grandmother Washes Her Feet"—from a jaded scholar, listening to himself pontificate in the prison of his suburban living room, to the mostly passive
and humble boy auditor, receptive to the wisdom of another—reveals the strategy Chappell will employ in the following poems, many of which take the form
of dramatic dialogues, letters, prayers, and metaphysical love poems, all forms
that emphasize the desire to make contact with another rather than only
pursuing introspection. He will consistently seek to escape self-absorption and
alienation, which he identifies as the problem of his age, and make contact
with the concrete and authentic world of his plain-folk relatives, evoked in
"My Grandmother Washes Her Feet" and elsewhere as "dirt."

Dirt has multiple connotations: the basis of agriculture and the source of all
life; a symbol for the cycle of life and death; and a representation of the eternal and substantial versus the ephemeral and superficial. *Dirt* also contains the
biblical allusions to the creation of Adam, as well as original sin. As in Betts's

fiction, original sin becomes changed by Ole Fred's pious grandmother into a positive attribute of the human condition, reminding us of our common proclivities to error, and thereby requiring the assumption of humility that comes with the acknowledgment of our common humanity. Classical pastoral relies upon a concept of human nature not altogether inconsistent with such a vision of original sin; as Kermode notes, classical pastorals frequently portray the people of a golden age in their natural states as "hedonistic and sinless, though wanton."[59] The grandmother's list of cousins in their "natural" states includes drunks, womanizers, a "Jackleg" preacher, and a great aunt named Paregoric Annie who would beg for drug-money by removing her glass eye and asking for assistance in replacing it. Fred idealizes these cousins as still vitally connected to the earth through farming, and thereby exempt from the fallen state and subsequent need for salvation attributed to civilized humanity. Furthermore, their connection with the earth diminishes differences of social status, which contrasts sharply with the urban future the grandmother foresees for Fred.

Fred longs to forge a lost connection to this extended family that the grandmother and her generation took for granted. In an effort to visualize better these shadow cousins he has never met, the boy Fred—like God creating Adam—shapes their earthen effigies from the mud produced by his grandmother's footbath water. The adult Fred concludes the poem dejectedly, contemplating the economic necessity that forced his father to give up farming, then comparing himself unfavorably to his imagined cousins: "I never had the grit to stir those guts. / I never had the guts to stir that earth" (13). The reciprocal substitution of the terms "grit," or its synonym "earth," with "guts" in these lines equates the terms syntactically, thereby conflating their meanings, an effect enhanced by the consonance in "grit" and "guts."

This same tendency to ennoble mountain folk by equating them physically with the land itself is found in *Brighten the Corner Where You Are* when Joe Robert Kirkman is visited by Pruitt and Ginny Dorson, an extremely rural couple whom he characterizes as "silent farm folk from the genuine old-time mountain stock. . . . Salt of the earth: That was the common phrase for families like the Dorsons, but my father considered that it was all too common. Soul of the earth, he thought, earth's own earth" (56). The purest expression of Chappell's longing for a complete reunification with his Appalachian heritage is found in his desire to be one with the earth itself, which Jess Kirkman symbolically achieves at the end of *Look Back All the Green Valley* (also the culmination of the entire octave), when he finds himself on a rainy night covered in the mud of his father's grave.

The Dorsons, Fred's "shadow cousins," the "dirt poor" as Fred's grandmother calls them (12), and all the other "genuine old-time mountain" folk in

Chappell's narratives figure the same way that shepherds do in traditional pastoral poetry, as a liaison between the pure and simple world of nature and the complicated and impure urban world of the pastoral poet. As J. E. Congleton explains, "The shepherd, actually, is half man and half Nature; he has enough in common with man to be his universal representative and has enough in common with Nature to be at one with it. Because the shepherd is so close to Nature, man, through him, can become united with Nature and consequently feel that he is a harmonious part of the whole and that his ideas are reconciled with the fundamental truths."[60]

Kenneth Lynn similarly observes how frontier storytellers often presented their characters as part man, part beast. Lynn quotes Christian Schultz's 1808 report from Natchez, Mississippi, where Schultz heard two drunken rivermen competing for a Choctaw woman: "One said, 'I am a man; I am a horse; I am a team. I can whip any man *in all Kentucky*, by G-d.' The other replied, I am an alligator, half man, half horse; can whip any man on the *Mississippi*, by G-d. . . . I am a Mississippi snapping turtle: have bear's claws, alligator's teeth, and the devil's tail.'"[61] Although the frontier humorist's "shepherds" are considerably more violent and bawdy than the shepherds of pastoral poetry, they perform one of the same essential functions—vicariously reconnecting the civilized reader with the wildness and simplicity of the natural world. In *Midquest* and the Jess Kirkman tetralogy, high and low cultures meet as Chappell employs elements of both classical pastoral and frontier humor to get in touch with the simple, the concrete, what he feels to be his own essential nature.

The error of leaving the farm and forgetting one's birthright of "dirt" involves the dominant theme of *Midquest*: the loss of the concrete world through a process of abstraction. Pastoral promises a reunification with nature by means of considering human culture at its most basic level, and yet, as Kermode observes, the challenge to the pastoral poet is to avoid merely an inauthentic imitation of established conventions. This challenge is one familiar to any reader of southern literature. Just as the earlier pastorals often tended toward derivative accounts of shepherds and nymphs, southern writers have felt the temptation toward predictable representations of pastoral types: the pure and virtuous belle, the noble colonel-father, the faithful Negro retainer, the hillbilly farmer.

In *Midquest* Chappell frequently calls attention to this problem, as in the poem "Firewater," in which the boy Fred listens to his father, J.T., and his father's drinking buddy Virgil Campbell as they lament the passing of the old ways and of the genuine Appalachian farmers. What their dialogue makes obvious to the reader is the difficulty of knowing or representing a "genuine" Appalachian farmer—and how the label itself implies a level of self-consciousness in which the organic and traditional have been extracted from their living medium to be displayed for their picturesque value. Virgil begins the poem by describing his recent visit to rural Clay County—where some of his backwater cousins live—for the purpose of watching their centennial celebration. The festival's main attraction was the "Grand Parade, / Celebrating their most famous products" (78), with moonshine topping the list. In an effort to celebrate their culture, the local officials have traveled up Standing Indian Mountain to invite Big Mama and her family (whom they have been trying to prosecute for ten years) to "build a model still" and "waltz it down Main Street in broad daylight" (79). The plan backfires during the middle of the parade when a mule following behind Big Mama's float staggers and then collapses, "Drunk as an owl, / Just from breathing the smoke that was pouring out / From Big Mama's *model* still" (79). A deputy attempts to make an arrest, but "smiling so the crowd would think / It was part of the act" (80), at which point

> Big Mama's boys stood up—
> Wearing phony beards, barefoot with beat-up hats,
> Just like the hillbillies in the funny papers—
> And threw down on the deputy three shotguns.
> Whether they were loaded I don't know.
> He didn't know. Except Big Mama's bunch
> *Nobody* knew. (80)

The use of disguises here calls attention to the stereotype and thus forces the reader to guess at the authentic identity hidden from view. These are the pastoral's real shepherds wearing shepherd masks. As Houston Baker notes of the minstrel mask and its adoption by black speakers during the Jim Crow era,[62] Big Mama's boys assume their hillbilly disguises as a means of protecting their genuine identities. That they alone know whether their guns are loaded further suggests their control over their own identity and culture, thereby invalidating Virgil Campbell and J.T.'s nostalgic lament of cultural erosion.

By choosing in *Midquest* to differentiate experience into four rubrics associated with the four pre-Socratic elements, Chappell examines experience at its most fundamental level. The effect of the repeated images of water, fire, air, and earth relentlessly locates human experience in a natural, primitive context. The speakers in these poems are constantly in contact with the natural elements and interpret their lives by means of metaphors derived from the natural world. In "Second Wind," for example, the grandmother tells the boy Fred the story of his grandfather's funeral and embodies the despair she felt in the hot, still August weather. Similarly the freshening of a breeze breaks her emotional stasis and leads to hope. Time in *Midquest* is cyclical, which is reinforced by the book's four-part structure; in each volume, the poet's birthday begins with first light and progresses toward evening. The farming community depicted in *Midquest* measures time in a premodern way, planting crops by the phases of the moon, paying attention to the progress of the seasons, locating memory by references not to calendar dates so much as significant events, often natural disasters, such as the storm described in "My Father's Hurricane" the flood in "Dead Soldiers," or the fire in "My Grandfather's Church Goes Up."

Midquest's structure reinforces this vision of a society in harmony with the cosmos. Unlike the montage of fragments in *It Is Time, Lord,* which resists not only closure but also the production of any sort of stable meaning, *Midquest* presents an ordered repetition of image and event, which reflects a psychic balance and harmony, rather than discord. And, in contrast to the five isolated perspectives that comprise *The Gaudy Place,* the multiple subjectivities represented in *Midquest*'s dramatic monologues and dialogues create the sense of a community of interdependent speakers. In addition to the numerous parallels between *Midquest* and the Kirkman tetralogy, Chappell alerts the reader in *Midquest*'s preface that the poems in each of the four volumes balance each other and make orderly connections with similarly placed poems in each of the other four volumes. Just as Lucinda MacKethan argues that southern pastorals have always been motivated by the "need of people in a rapidly changing world to have a vision of an understandable order,"[63] Chappell's attention to a carefully ordered structure throughout his octave underscores his desire to preserve in poetry a disappearing social structure: the network of relationships that define the farming family, the basic unit of yeoman society.

Like Thomas Jefferson, Chappell promotes yeomanry as the ideal society, one that makes possible the difficult balance between individual freedom and social integrity. Further still, Chappell's reliance on classical aesthetics suggests metaphysical implications, as he makes clear in his essay on Virgil's *Georgics,* "The Poet and the Plowman." Chappell examines Virgil's dictum, *"Nudas ara, sere nudus,* Plow naked, naked sow," and declares, "The words are there to remind us of the ceremonial, and ultimately religious nature of farming; they remind us of the selfless rituals we must undergo in order to keep faith."[64] Further on, he continues this theme: "The largest purpose of the *Georgics* is not to dignify, but to sanctify, honest farm labor. A reader who has not looked at it in a long time finds he has forgotten that the poem is full of stars. Even the smallest task must be undertaken in due season under the proper constellations. These prescriptions are not mere meteorology; they connect the order of the earth to the order of the stars. The farmer moves by the motion of the stars, and his labors determine the concerns of the government. The Roman State is not founded upon the soil, it is founded in the universe. And so were all the other civilizations which managed to endure for any length of time. If poets do not wish to study these matters and treat of them, they shirk their responsibilities and fail their society."[65]

In this passage Chappell makes explicit his belief in the spiritual harmony that exists between yeomen and the cosmos. Chappell's conviction that the artist bears a responsibility to his public—that he should show that public a vision of its better self—is a distinctly premodern notion, and indeed *Midquest* comes as close to the epic as anything likely to be found in contemporary poetry. As with Virgil, for Chappell poetry's greatest value lies in its ability to capture not only a life but a world. One of Chappell's most notable frustrations with contemporary poetry derives from his observation that the vast majority of it, good and bad, takes the shape of the "autobiographical lyric" with little in the way of "social scope" (*Midquest,* x). How ironic it is, of course, that Chappell would himself first come to find the full expression of "social scope" in his poetry, rather than in fiction, the more natural genre—at least in contemporary writing—for such explorations. However, when he returned to writing long fiction, after devoting his greatest energies during the 1970s to *Midquest,* the vision of an ordered life—rooted in the yeoman farming community—remained a guiding principle.

Frontier Humor in *I Am One of You Forever* and *Farewell, I'm Bound to Leave You*

As in the companion quartet of long poems that make up *Midquest,* the Jess Kirkman tetralogy features an autobiographical figure who struggles to access the Appalachian culture of his childhood. The entire octave serves as an extended kunstlerroman, which depicts Jess's maturation as a poet. Like Ole Fred of *Midquest,* Jess Kirkman discovers the unavoidable tension—common to all pastoral—between the necessity of employing the individual imagination and the danger of falsifying or abstracting the concrete experience he seeks to recover. In his effort to recreate Appalachian culture authentically, Chappell reconstructs personal experience and family legend according to models indigenous to his folk culture—principally, the tall tale, the windy, and the fairy tale.[66] As in *Midquest,* the characters spend considerable time telling each other tall tales, which lends the tetralogy its prevalent element of fantasy. Like the episodic collections of frontier humor from the nineteenth century, the term "novel-of-stories" might be applied to the first and third novels, *I Am One of You Forever* (1985) and *Farewell, I'm Bound to Leave You* (1996). The tetralogy's second and fourth novels—*Brighten the Corner Where You Are* (1989) and

Look Back All the Green Valley (1999)—also form a pair in that they both dramatize Jess's attempt to connect with his father and, through him, the culture of
the yeoman farmer Jess recalls from childhood.

A comparison of *I Am One of You Forever* and *Farewell, I'm Bound to Leave
You* is especially fruitful when considering how the model of the frontier storyteller facilitates and limits Chappell's ability to immerse himself in his Appalachian culture. These two novels balance each other in that *One of You*
focuses on the many solitary men in the extended family and *Farewell* focuses
on a community of women, a difference that helps to illustrate the development
of Jess's poetic vision and the tension he feels as a young artist caught between
his Romantic impulse to follow the lead of his own individual imagination and
his constant longing for unity with an interdependent family and farming community. This tension is dramatized by the playful contestation between Jess's
father, who aligns himself with the masculine ideal of frontier independence,
and Jess's mother and grandmother, who seek to domesticate the frontier and
promote order through the maintenance of family ties.

Four of the chapters in *One of You* dramatize a series of visits by Jess's maternal uncles, solitary men who pay brief visits to the farm. Jess's memories of
these visits focus on the uncles' eccentricities and the extent to which they
remain separate from the family. Jess begins the tale of Uncle Zeno's visit by
observing, "Uncle Zeno came to visit us. Or did he? Not even the bare fact
of his visit is incontestable" (97). Zeno is a legendary storyteller, one who fits
Twain's description of the frontier tale teller in that he consistently appears
oblivious to the reaction of his audience. Furthermore, even though he periodically entrances them with his stories, Zeno never once engages Jess or his family in even the simplest of dialogues. Like Uncle Zeno, each of Jess's other
visiting uncles is physically but not mentally or emotionally present. Each
uncle is absorbed by his own subjective reality to the extent that communication with the family is severely limited. Each has his own individual obsession.
Like Uncle Zeno, bearded Uncle Gurton will not be tempted into dialogue.
Gurton will speak only one sentence, and only after mealtime: "I've had an elegant sufficiency; any more would be a superfluity."[67] Uncle Luden is so driven
by his dependence on whiskey and women that he finds it difficult to fit in time
for his family whom he has traveled all the way from the far west, California,
to visit. Luden, too, has his favorite expression: he sums up his renegade individuality in the melancholy war cry "Wahoo!" Uncle Runkin prefers the world
beyond the grave to the world of the living; he is obsessed with graveyards
and sleeps in the casket he has brought with him for his visit with the Kirk-
mans. Each of these uncles is larger than life, eccentric to the point of inspiring legend—or tall tale, which is essentially the genre that each of the chapters

devoted to the visiting uncles best fits. In assuming the role of frontier story-teller, Jess understands his responsibility to let the tale grow larger than life, as for example in the chapter entitled "The Beard," which ends with Uncle Gur-ton's fabled long beard pouring down the steps of the farmhouse, flowing out the windows and blending with the stars in the night sky. Additional chapters of *One of You* feature a talking horse, storm angels, a shape-shifting telegram, a storyteller who creates the future by speaking his tales, and numerous other fantastic instances.

Because Jess *receives* the stories in *Farewell, I'm Bound to Leave You* from his mother and grandmother, the stories (and the values encoded therein) have been more faithfully rendered this time, less transformed, less tampered with than they were in the earlier novel. In contrast to the string of visiting uncles in *One of You*, who are treated more as grotesques than as fully human charac-ters, the stories in *Farewell* typically present legendary women who, never-theless, appear to be flesh and blood and capable of interacting with their community. The association of these differences of representation with the gender of the respective narrators is supported by Carol Mitchell's research of gender differences among joke tellers. She observes how men "often seem to enjoy competitive joke-telling sessions," whereas women "very rarely partici-pate" in them,[68] Women prefer to tell jokes in more intimate settings involv-ing one or two close friends or family members, whereas men are "much more likely than women to tell jokes in the presence of casual acquaintances and even strangers."[69] Furthermore, a woman is more likely to "speak amusingly or wittily about herself or others in an informal way rather than using the formal con-ventions of the joke."[70] In contrast to the intimacy that develops as a result of women's humorous anecdotes, Mitchell finds that the aggressive competitiveness among male joke tellers prevents "friendships from becoming too intimate."[71]

A similar difference distinguishes *Farewell* from *One of You*: much more actual dialogue takes place between the boy and his mother and grandmother than between him and his father. As in the dramatic dialogues of *Midquest*, in Chappell's novels the women are more capable of responding to Jess's ques-tions, and their dialogue is marked by an emotional directness that is lacking between the father and son. Chappell himself observes, "It's noticeable in my work that the father actually *says* very little, except when he is showing off and teasing."[72] The women's stories contain an explicit moral purpose, while the father's are filled with humor and hyperbole; he delights in the tales for their own sake as artistic performance. Furthermore, the competitive aspect of Joe Robert's tale telling becomes quite clear when the renowned storyteller Uncle Zeno visits the family, and Joe Robert feels that his very existence is called into question.

Considering the degree to which in Appalachia an "inscrutable taciturnity is locally regarded as a virtue having something to do with valor and manliness,"[73] such a premium on silence creates serious obstacles for an Appalachian storyteller, and, in its broadest sense, *I Am One of You Forever* involves Jess's struggle to find an appropriate voice to articulate his experience. Reviewers have often acknowledged *One of You* as an initiation story; as such, it describes the paradoxical initiations into the norms of his community and, by doing so, into the independence and emotional isolation of frontier manhood. Although Jess seeks to preserve his family's Appalachian culture by becoming its spokesperson, his very assumption of this role—in which he speaks in the detached voice of the frontier teller of tall tales—perpetuates his isolation from his community.

Like *One of You*, the third Kirkman novel, *Farewell, I'm Bound to Leave You* is very much an initiation story, though initiation not into the isolation of manhood but rather into the adult community defined by his mother, grandmother, and all the other mountain women they visit both literally and in their stories. These stories are told within a domestic space—around the kitchen table, out on the front porch, down in the cellar—and they usually coincide with some shared chore such as peeling apples, stringing beans, or washing dishes. One of the most obvious purposes of these stories is to feminize the young Jess, to expose him to both women's labor and women's stories. Often the subjects of the stories are women who exemplify some quality that the men of their frontier community have exclusively associated with masculinity, such as marksmanship, physical toughness, or shrewdness. In stories with fairy tale titles that clue the listener/reader into the story's moral purpose—such as "The Figuring Woman," "The Fisherwoman," and "The Feistiest Woman"—Jess's grandmother and mother seek to deconstruct chauvinistic gender stereotypes and simultaneously promote "feminine" values of nurturing and collectivism versus what they identify as destructive masculine values of the frontier, based upon competition, domination, and exploitation.

"The Child Is Father of the Man": *Brighten the Corner Where You Are* and *Look Back All the Green Valley*

Though Chappell pays tribute to Appalachian women in *Farewell, I'm Bound to Leave You* and in many of the poems in *Midquest*, the figure of the farmer father remains for him the most significant door to his native culture. Whereas that door remains firmly closed in the early novels, in the second and fourth novels of the Kirkman tetralogy Chappell explores the relationship between father and son as a means for Jess Kirkman to reconnect with his homeland. Except for demeanor, Jess's affable father, Joe Robert Kirkman, very closely resembles James Christopher's emotionally abusive father from *It Is Time, Lord.* Each father is a farmer-teacher who abandons a job teaching science at the nearby high school because of his unwillingness to refrain from teaching evolution. Both men are rugged individualists who cultivate a friendship with a local grocery store owner named Virgil Campbell, the hard-drinking epitome of Appalachian independence. In these respects, both fathers closely resemble Chappell's own father. What changes, obviously, is Chappell's attitude toward his father. An oedipal struggle appears in the early work that is absent or at least muted in the Kirkman tetralogy. In these later four novels, the father is a benign, harmless, fun-loving trickster figure, whom the boy idolizes and emulates. For all his adolescent pranks, Joe Robert Kirkman demonstrates an emotional distance from his son, which the adult Jess seeks to close. Whereas James Christopher's father ridicules the son's search for the father found throughout Western literature, from Homer to Joyce, in the Kirkman tetralogy, Jess successfully enacts just such an epic quest.

The first three novels chronicle Jess's maturation from elementary-school age to late adolescence, and in each the adult narrator almost entirely effaces himself. The final novel, *Look Back All the Green Valley,* skips ahead to Jess's middle age, collapsing the distance between Jess the narrator and his dramatic self-characterization. He finds himself returning to the mountains (after living away from them for twenty-one years) to help arrange for his terminally ill mother and his father, who died ten years earlier, to share a final resting place. As he assumes the task of traveling the countryside looking for an appropriate site, Jess ends up tracking down kin and family friends whom he has not seen since childhood. In the process, he retraces his father's old stomping grounds in the still extremely rural Hardison County, searching for the world his father knew. In this attempt to become reconciled to a father from whom he always felt estranged, Jess simultaneously seeks to become reconciled to the mountain culture.

Upon his return home, he meets his sister, Mitzi, who has become successful in the business and politics of Asheville. In contrast to her active life—which he likens to their father's faith in the practical benefits of education—Jess finds that his scholarly work at the university does not lead him into a vital connection with his community. He recalls beginning the composition of a steamy novel based upon departmental gossip, "a tale of intrigue, betrayal, sabotage" that "involved a married chairman of a Romance languages department who was carrying on a weird affair with a junior colleague" (13). After observing that he was not busy "describing telling incidents at all, but paying off ancient grudges and unforgiven slights," he abandons the novel and decides "ruefully but not reluctantly, that Jess Kirkman was not born to write novels. [He] was condemned to poetry. . . . a dreamer: nose in a book, head in the clouds" (13). Jess is presently busy translating Dante's *Divine Comedy* into Appalachian vernacular and finishing, under the pen name Fred Chappell, a book of Appalachian poems called *Earthsleep*, the last in a series of four volumes (that is, *Midquest*). In retreating to poetry and poetry translation, Jess withdraws from his actual community in Greensboro and returns to the purer, more ideal worlds of Dante's medieval Europe and the Appalachian farm of his own boyhood.

Similarly, by imaginatively inhabiting his father in *Brighten the Corner*, Jess finds an avenue to escape his own tendency to introversion. He manages to live the active life vicariously, to immerse himself—through his father, a teacher in a public high school—in the life of the farming community of Tipton. This strategy of escaping the self is suggested in the text; in his civics class, Joe Robert struggles with the challenge of drawing out some of his shy rural students and happens upon a strategy of role playing that enables his very shyest student, Scotty Vann, miraculously to overcome his stuttering and speak with the authority of Socrates. Joe Robert identifies "the principle of the mask" at work in his student (158), and the reader should recognize the same principle at work in the novel's narrative voice, which involves Jess—as first-person narrator—assuming the consciousness of his father. Except for several instances, Jess effaces himself from the narrative, usually referring to his father neutrally as "Joe Robert" and assuming the detached voice of an omniscient narrator; the reader easily forgets that the novel is actually told in first person. If Jess's role as narrator is kept in mind, however, Jess's personality becomes readily apparent in the character of his father, or at least in his father's voice. Joe Robert's chameleon ability to speak both down-home language around the campfire with a group of old farmers and not only correct but highly cultivated English in the classroom (while operating a dairy farm in the mornings and evenings) is more than heroic; it is not quite believable. Despite Chappell's assertion that his father, J. T. Chappell, actually was multivoiced like his fictional counterpart,[74] the very act of assuming his father's point of view throughout the novel makes it nearly inconceivable that Jess would not, to a large extent, project his own voice, especially when we consider his powerful desire to connect with his father. This connection is best illustrated by a scene late in the novel when Joe Robert steps into his son's bedroom to find him asleep with a volume of the *Aeneid* by his side, dreaming of his father's heroic deeds, so that the entire narrative can be read as the son's Virgilian dream of his father. The point of view is, in fact, even a little more complicated: the adult Jess imagines his father thinking of his son lying in bed thinking of him (201–2), a point of view that approximates a hall of mirrors, so that ultimately the father's and son's consciousnesses merge into one, which is exactly Jess's purpose in telling the story about his dead father. The entire action of the novel occurs during this one day in which the dreaming boy imaginatively follows his father to work at Tipton High School. Indeed, it is *the* pivotal day of Joe Robert's career as an educator; he has been called upon by the school board to address the concerns of certain parents who have questioned his teaching of evolution in his science class. By imaginatively reconstructing that single day from the past, Jess (the adult classical scholar and poet) not only observes the classical unities but combines elements from Virgil's *Aeneid* and *Eclogues* in order to idealize his father as a hero of classical proportions.

Joe Robert serves Jess as an apt conduit to the Appalachian culture because, like Jess, he, too, is something of an outsider and so acts out the drama of struggling to integrate himself into the culture, a struggle Jess would himself find impossible. Having grown up not in the mountains but in the middle eastern part of the state (like Andrew Harper of *The Gaudy Place*), Joe Robert is capable of observing the mountain folk with some degree of detachment, which allows him more fully to idealize and seek to emulate them, while nevertheless finding it necessary to bring to them an alien perspective and thereby disrupt their homogenous world. As a science teacher and a believer in the Enlightenment philosophy of progress through "the advancement of knowledge" and through "education and biological and cultural evolution," Joe Robert is often opposed by the more conventionally religious members of his community, whom he refers to as "our local medievals" (*Look Back*, 26). Jess is one step further removed from them, finding his father's Victorian optimism "quaint and outdated" (26), though Jess frequently yearns for his father's innocent faith in progress.

Of all of Chappell's novels, *Brighten the Corner* confronts the issue of cultural change most relentlessly and with the most explicitly universal ramifications. Joe Robert may be an optimist, but he is not a blind one. Early in the novel he confronts the question of whether the Promethean gift of knowledge will lead to mankind's enlightenment or its demise. More specifically, he questions the uncertain results of his own mission to bring scientific enlightenment to his corner of the world, which has for generations lived according to traditional folkways and beliefs. When the parents of one of his former students visit the school to tell him that their son has recently committed suicide, Joe Robert is forced to consider the influence of his classroom discussions on the boy's decision. Lewis Dorson had recently returned from World War II decorated but physically and psychologically damaged, alienated from his rural family; after a brief visit, Lewis left for Detroit, where he took his own life. Lewis's father, Pruitt, who claims that for generations his family had read only the Bible, blames Lewis's death on his education. Although the mother explains that Pruitt's reaction is only temporary, Joe Robert is left to ponder the connection between science and the world-shattering technologies derived therefrom. If he'd been "a praying man," reflects Joe Robert, he "would have prayed that Pruitt Dorson was wrong, that it wasn't the lessons and the books and the teachers that had brought this century to nothing but disaster. But how could you be sure? Every time you looked anywhere, there was the schoolhouse smack in the middle of it with its fool ideas and its silly hopes. Maybe it was not the cure but the disease, maybe it would have been better always to let well enough alone" (*Brighten,* 66). The rest of the novel involves a series of dialectics, which, in one form or another, engage this question of enlightenment—thus, informing the novel's title. As in Virgil's eclogues, which feature shepherds who engage each other in a variety of philosophical topics, *Brighten the Corner Where You Are* takes the shape of a series of debates through which Joe Robert, as philosopher in shepherd's disguise, seeks to define his relation to his world—in his case as an apostle of Enlightenment idealism in this rural backwater.

Joe Robert's function as philosopher-shepherd is underscored by the fact that he spends the entire novel literally in the guise of a yeoman farmer. Early in the novel, after saving a drowning girl from Trivett Creek on his way to teach school, Joe Robert stops by his friend Virgil Campbell's Bound for Hell Gro. & Dry Goods and, after getting the girl dry and warm, exchanges his own wet suit for the only clothes Virgil's store carries, a pair of overalls and "a pair of new brogans of the cornball old-fashioned sort" (45). He wears this farmer outfit while teaching school, which helps to provide a comic contrast between his erudition and his good-ol'-boy posturing.

Joe Robert's characterization as an incorrigible paramour further aligns him with the shepherds of classical pastoral, who wile away their days fashioning not only philosophical speculations on the nature of life but also, more frequently, plaintive ballads for the nymphs they are wooing. *I Am One of You Forever* begins with his construction of an elaborate bridge that will lead his wife, Cora, into a pastoral garden, in which he no doubt imagines a variety of amorous possibilities. In *Midquest, Farewell,* and *Look Back,* we hear three different versions of the family legend regarding his unorthodox courtship of Cora: how, while they were both teachers at Tipton High School, he attempted to duplicate for his general science class Ben Franklin's famous electricity experiment by fashioning a kite out of Cora's red silk slip and then flying it outside her classroom window. Throughout *Brighten the Corner,* Joe Robert comically pretends a serious flirtation with one of his female students, Janie Forbes. In *Look Back,* Jess finds a map of Hardison County that he at first suspects to be a record of his father's amorous adventures across the rural countryside, only later realizing the absurdity of such a notion. While Jess frequently depicts his father as playfully amorous, Joe Robert's flirtations take the form of an adolescent boy's mischief rather than genuine erotic passion. Nevertheless, this constant posturing, like that of the shepherds from classical pastoral, aligns Joe Robert with the generative processes of nature and thereby connects Jess with these same processes and draws him out of the spiritual stasis to which he has succumbed while living in the city.

As in Virgil, Joe Robert's amorous adventures concretely locate him within the pastoral milieu, balancing the more serious philosophical and social issues he engages. Whether discussing race relations with Tipton High School's elderly black custodian, arguing for scientific skepticism with his general science class, or defending his right to teach evolution before the inquisition of "Socrates," Joe Robert addresses the possibility of effecting positive changes in society. In *Look Back*, Jess calls his father "your classic folklore trickster" (26), and, like most trickster figures, Joe Robert is an agent of unpredictable change. From the opening chapter of *Brighten the Corner* in which Joe Robert steals the moon from the sky and holds it captive in a milk can, this "wizard" appears as a threat to the natural order. His entrance into the community disrupts the present order but thereby makes the creation of a new order possible. Whether that new order is preferable to the old is in this case, as in most, a matter of debate. The inevitability of change from a simpler to a more complex state has always been central to pastoral. Kermode notes that, during the Renaissance, pastoral flourished in part as a response to the discovery of the New World and its inhabitants, who were "living in a state of nature, unaffected by Art, and outside the scope of Grace" (40). Western society divided into two positions regarding those New World natives: those who recognized the duty of civilizing them and bringing them into "the scope of Grace" extended by the Christian church and those such as Montaigne, who saw them as "virtuous because unspoilt."[75] In bringing modern science into the Appalachian hinterlands, Joe Robert confronts just such a dilemma, one that by the end of *Brighten the Corner* he is unable to resolve completely.

The novel ends with Joe Robert's dream—inspired by the school board's debate about allowing him to teach Darwin in the schools. In his dream Darwin is brought up to a scaffold in a back lot of the high school and Joe Robert is called upon to defend him. He begins eloquently defending the theories of evolution and cultural progress but ends by expressing repressed doubts: "We began as innocent germs and added to our original nature cunning, deceit, self-loathing, treachery, betrayal, murder, and blasphemy. We began lowly and have fallen from even that humble estate" (211). Despite his belief in the doctrine of modern science, Joe Robert is a reluctant missionary. His respect for—and idealization of—the yeoman independence of his community gives him pause, even though his pursuit of science derives from the same instinct for independence that he observes in the most rugged mountaineers. Before teaching school, he worked for Carolina Power and Light stringing electrical lines across the remotest mountains, bringing light into the darkness. Joe Robert views his role as an educator in the same terms: he is a Promethean liberator from the darkness of superstition. While religion subjugates the individual to the authority of the church—an authority outside the self—Joe Robert embraces the Enlightenment values of human perfectibility and promotes the scientific attitude because he believes that it locates authority for truth within the individual. Thus, he believes that by following science rather than religion the essential yeoman spirit of Appalachian independence will best flourish.

If in *The Gaudy Place* the image of Ben Franklin is borrowed for the sake of undercutting the myth of the self-made man, in *Brighten the Corner* Joe Robert is associated with a positive image of Franklin as scientist and Renaissance man. Whereas in his characterization of Uncle Zeb, the corrupt Asheville politician, Chappell shows how the yeoman spirit is degraded by society, politics, and money, in Joe Robert, Chappell offers the pure ideal of the public man, one whose private nature has not been compromised by his public role. Whereas Uncle Zeb seeks to impose a social hierarchy that will subjugate the masses to a position of relative powerlessness, Joe Robert consistently champions the individual liberty and egalitarianism at the heart of the yeoman ideal. By defending his right to teach Darwin's theory of evolution in his general science class, he promotes independent thought and expression. In his brief role as high school principal, he similarly seeks to dismantle social hierarchy among the faculty; he combats their tendency to be "too concerned with personal status among equal colleagues" by inventing "the Ungodly Terror, a mysterious and utterly rotten kid, a student who was a danger to them all" (51). To convince his faculty that the threat is real, he spends a significant part of his time as principal exploding firecrackers in lockers, painting doorknobs with kerosene, filling teachers' desk drawers with wet oatmeal, and virtually every other "naughty schoolboy fantasy he could remember. / It must have been for him the Earthly Paradise" (52). Joe Robert plays the trickster to bring about a siege mentality and thereby foster an egalitarian community spirit among his faculty.

At home on the farm he embraces the same defiance of authority—in the form of his mother-in-law—by pulling an ongoing string of pranks, or "rusties." Whenever he dons his working clothes to milk the cows, he imagines that he is wearing his "Peasant Costume" and says, "Every time I get into these duds . . . it makes me want to overthrow the Czar" (*Brighten*, 31). This Romantic antagonism to authority finds a very real outlet in Joe Robert's opposition to tenancy, a system that presses landless farmers into a feudal dependency. Joe

Robert is fully aware that tenancy is a system that perpetuates itself, for a lack of economic independence often leads to a lack of spiritual independence that keeps the tenant "poor forever" and that "breaks his pride. Turns him mean sometimes" (103–4). Unfortunately, Joe Robert is pressed by financial necessity into hiring the tenant, Hob Farnum, whose Dickensian characterization suggests deprivation and perversion of nature. Hob is "a short man, slightly hunchbacked . . . filled with an angry narrow energy" (104). By creating the loss of economic and social independence, tenancy degrades the sharecropper's connection to nature and even potentially reduces the spiritual act of farming to the materialistic function of production, not unlike the mill jobs so many sharecroppers found preferable to tenancy.

As opposed to the "angry, narrow energy" of his tenant, Joe Robert finds his own life so rewarding because he is capable of channeling his energies into such a broad scope of freely chosen activities. He has worked as a farmer, schoolteacher, school principal, lineman for Carolina Power & Light, and, in his off time, a tinkerer. As a self-proclaimed jack-of-all-trades, Joe Robert approximates the whole man whose disappearance from any specialized society Emerson laments in "The American Scholar." Emerson examines an ancient creation story in which the gods "divided Man into men" so that Man "might be more helpful to himself"—an act that nevertheless left the disassociated men longing for the original wholeness. In an ideal state, Emerson finds that "Man is not a farmer, or a professor, or an engineer, but he is all. Man is priest, and scholar, and statesman, and producer, and soldier."[76] The yeoman farmer, out of necessity a generalist, comes as close to fulfilling Emerson's ideal of the whole man as any profession—except that of the poet, whom Emerson identifies as "representative. He stands among partial men for the complete man."[77] Echoing Emerson, in the preface to *Midquest* Chappell explicitly identifies his task to be one of writing the "widely representative" experience. Throughout *Midquest* and the Jess Kirkman novels, Chappell strives to capture the wholeness of life, for which the farming community serves as an apt model. By making Joe Robert a generalist, someone with a wide range of vocational interests and diverse friendships, Jess (and Chappell) solves the dilemma that faces him as a poet who earns his living in the "ivory tower" of the university. Separated even from his immediate colleagues by his academic specialty, Jess recovers a sense of wholeness through his idealization of the self-reliant yeoman farmer.

In *Look Back All the Green Valley*, Jess similarly makes use of Joe Robert's avocation of tinkerer to gain for himself proper orientation as a poet. As he seeks a final resting place for his parents, Jess stumbles across a secret workshop his father had kept in the basement of an antique clock store. In his readings of the notes and journals he discovers there, Jess reconstructs his father's

identity as a self-educated scientist: a botanist, engineer, and natural philosopher. Among the records of his father's intellectual life, Jess finds a hand-
drawn, cryptic map of Hardison County, which Jess finally discovers to be a key
to his father's horticulture experiments; Joe Robert has planted diverse culti-
vars of roses all across the rural county, partly in an effort to determine the
effect of environment on growth. Jess finds his father's diagram for a mechanism that would enact revenge on an engineer at the Challenger Paper and
Fiber Company, whom Joe Robert holds personally responsible for the factory's
egregious pollution. Jess also finds a collection of epigrammatic meditations on
time entitled "The Thoughts of Fugio"; adolescent fantasies of space travel;
and Joe Robert's theories for a "Floriloge," an ideal timepiece that would be
"organic" rather than mechanical, a clock that would be a "living thing, connected with the cosmos" (78).

These various artifacts point Jess toward the discovery of his father's private
life of the imagination, and this inner journey coincides with Jess's search for
traces of his father upon the landscape of Hardison County. The two ultimately
converge, in a Dante-esque vision of paradise, in the pristine region of True-
love, where Jess witnesses a flourishing yellow rose that his father had planted
years before. His father's interest in horticulture and his pseudo-scientific design
of the Floriloge coalesce with Jess's immersion in the task of translating The
Divine Comedy into Appalachian vernacular, signifying their common idealization of unspoiled Appalachia as a fitting image of the golden age, a place and
time where life is unified and "connected with the cosmos." Jess's ability to
recognize the spiritual affinity between his own profession as a poet and his
father's interest in science and agriculture becomes a final means of reconciliation, a reconciliation he has sorely needed, considering his father's silence on
the subject of Jess's profession and Jess's mother's clear denunciation. According to Cora, "Poetry explained [his] wayward and drifting existence. . . . It was
the vice that had brought [him] low and made [him] crazy" (175). It is not surprising that she had a similar reaction to her husband's excessive absorption in
his "projects." In his short fiction, Chappell has explored the lives of a variety
of historical scientists, including William Herschel, Carl Linnaeus, and Benjamin Franklin. As in these stories, Joe Robert the tinkerer/scientist is interested in seeing the world accurately. Seeing accurately requires a right relation
to the universe, which Chappell, like Virgil, finds equally necessary for the
farmer and the poet.

As Fred Hobson observes in his treatment of I Am One of You Forever,
Chappell's attempt to become utterly one with his native Appalachian culture
forces him ultimately to recognize the impossibility of doing so, to recognize—
and celebrate—the importance of the individual imagination in the process of

cultural recovery. In fact, the individual imagination is still as distinct and separate from the concrete world it observes in Chappell's pastorals as in his earlier dramas of alienation. Indeed, extravagant products of the imagination proliferate throughout the octave of *Midquest* and the Jess Kirkman novels. Even after adopting a classical aesthetic, Chappell is no less of an "experimental" writer than when he worked from a darkly Romantic sensibility. What has profoundly changed is the orientation of the imagination—from an inward to an outward gaze—as well as an affirmation that the efforts of the imagination can be a collaborative effort, one that balances the *independent* perspective with involvement in an *interdependent* community for the production of meaning. By using the father—who is farmer, teacher, scientist—as a means to access the world of Appalachia, Chappell manages to reimagine that insular world and to transform it from a hill-ringed prison into Arcadia. As the entire octave comes to a conclusion, Jess tells his wife, "You know, I am the son who went searching for his father, just like the characters do in all those important well-received literary novels. But I didn't find a man. I found a boy" (*Look Back*, 271). Jess's words suggest both his father's perpetual adolescence and that, in finding his father, Jess has reclaimed the wholeness of his own Appalachian boyhood.

LEE SMITH
The Yeoman's Wife

Like Chappell's Kirkman quartet, much of the recent literature from Appalachia reveals a fascination with a lost yeoman past. Charles Frazier's *Cold Mountain* (1997), Robert Morgan's *Gap Creek* (1999), and Tony Earley's *Jim, the Boy* (2000) are three examples of contemporary novels by North Carolina writers that have adopted the pastoral approach of exploring the life of the yeoman farmer as a past golden age either explicitly or implicitly contrasted with a modern technological, consumerist age. A very different vision pervades the fiction of Lee Smith; even when she employs pastoral, she carefully qualifies it. Despite the obvious contrasts she acknowledges between an earlier yeoman culture and a present-day Appalachia overwhelmed by K-Marts, fast-food franchises, and theme parks, Smith emphasizes the continuities between the two and demonstrates how more recent cultural erosion is a product of the same cultural insecurity and economic impoverishment that caused yeomen to allow their mountains and themselves to be exploited by timber and mining industries earlier in the century. Her novels frequently focus on how such broad cultural upheavals have affected the lives of mountain women; in particular, she explores the themes of entrapment and self-fulfillment she sees common to the yeoman wife. In *Oral History* (1983), *Fair and Tender Ladies* (1988), and *The Devil's Dream* (1992)—novels that relate family sagas that span generations—Smith depicts the struggles of mountain women to achieve wholeness in the world they inherit, rather than imagining a past innocence based on the ideal of the yeoman farmer.

Although Lee Smith grew up in the Virginia mountains, she has lived in North Carolina since 1974 and taught creative writing at North Carolina State in Raleigh for two decades. Furthermore, although the coal mining industry never caused the kind of widespread economic and cultural upheaval in North Carolina that it did in Smith's southwestern corner of Virginia, the experience chronicled in her novels and stories (including the rise of the timber industry in southern Appalachia) resembles the experience of North Carolina mountain folk in many respects, notably the effects of cultural isolation followed by the confrontation of remote mountaineers with mainstream modern American culture. Her hometown of Grundy lies in the center of the coal-mining area of southwest Virginia—in the poorest county in the state—and remains today a town with fewer than 2,000 residents, among whom are counted numerous relatives from her father's side of the family.

Smith is the author of twelve novels and three collections of short stories. Her many awards include the Lila Wallace–*Reader's Digest* Writer's Award, the Robert Penn Warren Prize, a Lyndhurst Fellowship, the John Dos Passos Award, the Weatherford Award for Appalachian Literature, the North Carolina Award for Fiction, two Sir Walter Raleigh Awards, listing of three books among the *New York Times* Notable Books, the 1999 Academy Award for Fiction from the American Academy of Arts and Letters, two O. Henry Awards, and the Southern Book Critics Circle Award.[1]

Place as Class in Appalachia

The marriage of her mountaineer father and her genteel mother from Tidewater Virginia appears in many of her novels as the antagonism between plain folk Appalachians and genteel flatlanders. Her father, Ernest Lee Smith, was an entrepreneur who began a successful dime store in Grundy and managed to fund his daughter's private education, first at St. Catherine's Girls School in Richmond and then at Hollins College, closer to home. The Smiths were even able to afford a Porsche for their daughter to drive to Hollins, as well as a year's study in Europe. Although Smith grew up a town girl, she went to school with children from nearby rural farms, and during her years of private education, when she experienced the class-based elitism of many of her fellow students, she began to identify with the rural folk of her home county.[2]

Uncomfortable in Appalachia, Smith's mother, Virginia Marshall Smith, had grown up on the island of Chincoteague, just south of Delaware on the Atlantic coast, and always "aspired to be a lady"; for Smith her mother was very much a "product" and a "victim" of a distressed aristocracy clinging to the antebellum ideal of the southern lady. Recalling her own childhood, Smith says, "I grew up to some degree feeling that if you didn't fit right in, if you didn't conform, you would go crazy. My mother, see, came from eastern Virginia and she was always trying to be a lady, and there was this notion that if you fit right in, if you were a lady and went to a nice school and married a doctor and so on, that that was somehow comforting and would somehow keep you from going crazy. But the idea of being artistic was being outside of norms in a certain way, and it was sort of dangerous."[3] As a teenager, Smith longed—like her mother—to "escape from the circumscribed life of Appalachia,"[4] but by the time she began publishing fiction she had embraced rural Appalachia as her primary subject matter, and the self-sufficient yeoman farmer, or his plain-folk descendants, is typically contrasted to the social-climbing spouse or descendent, who seeks to overcome a lack of self esteem by acquiring artificial indicators of success, such as wealth and social status.

This dichotomy between plain folk and social climber appears frequently in Smith's fiction. In *The Last Girls* (2002), the school teacher Harriet Holding feels like "country cousin come to town"[5] when she is reunited with her prosperous former college classmates, especially Courtney Gray, who was "on the Honor Court and yearbook staff" in college and now is president of her gentrified community's Friends of the Library group and its Historic Preservation Society. When she married into wealth and position, Courtney was informed by her mother-in-law that the family home, Magnolia Court (which had been featured in *Southern Living*) had not been "restored," it had been "*maintained*" (39).

In *Family Linen* (1985) the contrast between plain folk and social climber is even more starkly drawn—within the same family—by Candy and Myrtle Hess, cousins raised as sisters. Candy is a beautician, who, despite her profession, shows little concern for her own appearance, is happy in her simple home, and is the most centered member of her family. Myrtle, on the other hand, restlessly seeks to fill an enduring emotional void by attempting to measure up to society's expectations, a habit she has inherited from her socially conscious mother. Myrtle and her dermatologist husband Don have joined the local racquet club, which fills her with anxiety about fulfilling the expectations of the other women members, who all seem to be pursuing careers. In her marriage she is also insecure. As if quoting advice from a woman's magazine, she observes, "You can't afford to get fat . . . or let yourself go. You have to throw out your old lingerie and have sex in the afternoon."[6] When describing her marriage, she can only resort to hollow clichés, saying, that she loves her husband "*with all her heart*" and that they "share everything—their hopes, fears, plans, a laugh or two" (48). Although Myrtle asserts that hers is "one of the few truly successful marriages of the eighties" (48), both she and her husband are, in fact, involved in secret extramarital affairs. Don is involved in a twenty-year relationship with Candy, who, unconcerned with surfaces, is able to provide genuine nurturing. At this point in her life, the primary purpose of Myrtle's marriage seems the maintenance of an upper-middle-class lifestyle. Myrtle has "typed her fingers to the bone putting Don through medical school" (46), so that they can live in "their own white colonial" in Booker Creek's exclusive neighborhood of Argonne Hills. At 3,800 square feet, the house is twice the size of Myrtle's mother's (62), though, like her other siblings, Myrtle can never measure up to what she believes to be her mother's expectations. If Myrtle has been damaged by her emotionally distant mother, her half-sister Sybill suffers even more acutely. Not only has Sybill inherited her mother's obsession with order and cleanliness, but these traits have also become intensified in Sybill's lifelong attempt to repress the memory of her mother murdering her philandering father with an ax.

The appearance of emotionally distant and psychically unbalanced parents common in Smith's fiction can be traced to her own childhood. Smith admits that mental illness was common in her family and that at one point both of her parents were in "separate psychiatric hospitals at the same time."[7] Her fiction is full of female Huck Finns who have essentially been orphaned by detached parents, such as the nine-year-old Susan Tobey of her first novel, *The Last Day the Dogbushes Bloomed* (1968), written while Smith was a student of Louis Rubin's at Hollins College. Susan fancifully refers to her social climbing mother as "The Queen" and constructs for herself an imaginary world to sustain her in the absence of adequate care by her distracted parents, whose marriage is in the process of disintegrating. By the end of the summer, Susan will be raped by a neighborhood boy, and neither of her parents will know. In "Tongues of Fire," from her collection *Me and My Baby View the Eclipse* (1990), a similar situation occurs, with an Appalachian father (from northern Alabama) overworking himself into a nervous breakdown in a vain attempt to please his gentrified wife from Birmingham, while their daughter Karen attempts to make sense of her world by beginning to attend a Holiness church with a lower-class school friend named Tammy. Karen rejects her mother's "social ranking" of churches with "Methodist at the top, attended by doctors and lawyers and other 'nice' families; Presbyterian slightly down the scale, attended by store owners; then the vigorous Baptists; then the Church of Christ."[8] Karen finds the Methodists boring and prefers the lower-class Maranatha Apostolic Church, where they "speak in tongues" as a sign of divine revelation. Although Smith portrays the lower-class evangelicals as earthy and more vital than the solidly middle-class churches, she resists the temptation to idealize them; for example, Karen's lower-class friend Tammy longs for what she believes to be the greater stability of Karen's middle-class world. Furthermore, after her adventures among the working poor, Karen goes on with her solidly middle-class life, becoming a cheerleader and attending college.

As in the work of Fred Chappell, Lee Smith's fiction shows a strong pastoral impulse, identifiable by the frequent tension between an isolated, rural, yeoman past and a present-day Appalachia overcome by consumerism and technologies imported from the mainstream society outside Appalachia. This tension especially appears in the later novels beginning with *Oral History*, which often take the form of family sagas, spanning as much as a century and chronicling the historic transition of Appalachia from a region of isolated yeoman farms to a region devastated by the mining of its natural and cultural resources. Smith's pastorals are problematized, however, in that the binary opposition of an idyllic past and a corrupted present typically does not remain a stable one; rather, she is more interested in discovering the ways in which the present merely repeats the past. As Fred Hobson has observed of *Oral History*, "Folk society is hardly idealized in the novel: it contains neither the strong sense of community nor the religious sense one idealizes, and the proof of its relative weakness is that it falls so easily before popular culture in the end."[9] The very fact that so many of her characters desperately long to escape the mountains and their families demonstrates what she characterizes as the region's widespread cultural and emotional deprivation. Nancy Parish remarks that "Smith uses the image of the mountains as a metaphor for the cultural entrapment of women that is reflected in her fiction."[10] Elsewhere Parish broadens Smith's critique of Appalachia as representative of America, noting that one "constant feature in the development of Smith's writing has been her increasingly open consideration of the victimization of women in American society and the way women have learned to overcome that condition."[11] Anne Goodwyn Jones identifies one of Smith's primary themes to be the acquisition of assertiveness by her female characters, in the form of either "sexual, violent, linguistic" or "religious" expression. According to Jones, Smith's women "find it all too easy to center themselves outside themselves,"[12] a problem that must be overcome in their journey toward complete selfhood. Often, this journey leads women away from the farm, though eventually they return, if only for extended visits. This quest motif is true for Sally in *Oral History*, Katie Cocker in *The Devil's Dream*, and even for the virtually farm-bound Ivy Rowe of *Fair and Tender Ladies*. In each case, the heroine must escape the limitations of her culture to gain the critical distance necessary to become autonomous when she reclaims that culture. Ironically, to develop fully the yeoman values of independence and self-sufficiency, these women are forced to leave the farm.

Oral History: "None of the womenfolks do much traveling"

Oral History, *The Devil's Dream*, and *Fair and Tender Ladies* all take the form of family sagas, and each begins with an Ur-story depicting the family's pioneer ancestors and their settlement of a specific place, a story that shapes the course of each respective family throughout the successive generations that follow. The yeoman family farm becomes iconic for the descendants of the pioneer generation; they come to identify deeply with the landscape and the myths associated with it. They associate the homeplace with their own personal identities to an extent that *place* often obstructs personal development. Unlike plantation literature, in which the name of a house or cultivated plantation serves as the dominant indicator of place, in Smith's fiction, place names nearly always derive from a landscape that predates settlement, such as Hoot Owl Holler in *Oral History,* or Grassy Branch in *The Devil's Dream,* or Sugar Fork in *Fair and Tender Ladies.* Geography figures so largely in the imaginations of Smith's characters that even buildings and social groups—such as the musical Grassy Branch Girls—take their names from the landscape. The Chicken Rise Church was founded as Hebron Old Primitive Baptist but, over the years, yielded to the pressure of the surrounding landscape (46). Like the Hesses of *Family Linen,* both the Cantrells in *Oral History* and the Baileys in *The Devil's Dream* are families haunted by their pasts. And just as Sybill Hess is obsessed with the bones of her father in the capped well beneath her half-sister's swimming pool, the Cantrells and the Baileys each have a family homeplace that is believed by descendants to be haunted and that descendants ultimately turn into a museum and theme park attraction, respectively. Both *Oral History* and *The Devil's Dream* begin with the story of the family's pioneer settlers and the tragic deaths that the family remembers. These stories, full of biblical imagery, serve as creation myths for the respective families, providing them and their communities with an articulation of the values that are perpetuated generation after generation. It is unsurprising that many of these values are not only yeoman but patriarchal, and therefore many of the female descendants spend their lives struggling to escape the limitations imposed upon them by the patriarchal worldview they have inherited.

Oral History and *The Devil's Dream* resemble each other in many respects. Structurally they are virtually identical; an italicized frame story in present time begins and ends each novel, and the intervening narrative provides the explanatory history of the family that allows the frame to signify. After the introductory frame, each novel begins with the family's originary tale narrated in first-person by an elderly native of the region, obviously speaking his or her tale long before the time of the introductory frame. This narrative is then followed by a fragmented plot told in numerous voices, with most of these speakers related by blood or marriage. Chronologically, each novel progresses from the time of the originary narrative to the contemporary period presented in the frame story. In either novel—though especially in *The Devil's Dream*—keeping up with the many characters can be a dizzying process, and it seems we are hardly expected to do so; rather, as with the Bible or Faulkner or Gabriel García Márquez, the reader keeps track of character *types.* For instance, in *Oral History,* the women fairly well divide into two categories: the object of desire, and the oracular granny, who is masculinized and unsexed by her community. Other dichotomies obtain with respect to men and women in the novel: nearly all the men conceive of women as either virgins or whores, and similarly the men are divided into silent, potentially violent masculine types and feminized talkers. These binary opposites prevent real communication between the sexes and between members of the same sex. Part of the overarching intent of the novel is to deconstruct these dichotomies that are expressed in the originary myth of the pioneer Almarine Cantrell and in the subsequent stories that repeat his story. The novel's considerable energy derives from the momentum of the family's and region's history, in which, according to the elderly jaded minister Aldous Rife, "Nothing ever changes that much."[13] With each successive Cantrell who succumbs to the pressures of this history, change becomes progressively more necessary though less available.

Almarine Cantrell's story begins in the late nineteenth century and is told by Granny Younger, the novel's archetypal granny-oracle, the voice of her community. Ironically, while deliberately setting out to codify and support the yeoman values that she believes Almarine's history to represent, she subtly subverts them, in ways of which she is unaware, by portraying the pioneer yeoman society as thoroughly patriarchal and repressive of its women. In Granny Younger's story, Almarine is the epitome of the yeoman—fiercely independent and seemingly at one with the land. He has inherited a large tract of land that covers Hoot Owl Holler, Hoot Owl Mountain, and parts of nearby Snowman and Hurricane Mountains. After surviving a difficult childhood, one in which he suffered the neglect of his mother and the abuse of his father and brothers, Almarine leaves home for five years and then returns home in 1902, content to find Hoot Owl Holler deserted. Even while she finds it odd, Granny admires the fact that Almarine lives alone on Hoot Owl Mountain, identifying in him the epitome of the impulse toward privacy and independence she and the other mountaineers feel. "Almarine sits now in the cabin door in his daddy's chair," says Granny, "and he owns all the land he sees. Truly this holler is so much a part of Almarine that he doesn't even think of owning it, not any moren a man would think of owning his arm nor yet one of his legs. The whole time Almarine was gone, most of him stayed right here. He wasn't nothing but a half-boy, a half-man I guess you'd say, but now he's back here with all of them dead as stumps and he won't have to leave again, he won't have to go noplace ever again. Almarine's soul swells out over this whole holler" (32). Two antithetical relationships appear in this short passage: Almarine's strong ties to the land where he was reared and the absence of any ties to family. He shows no signs of remorse upon finding the rest of his family "dead as stumps"; on the contrary, their absence means that he will not have to leave the farm again. Granny quickly excuses his lack of grief by cataloguing the abuses of his family and declaring that "any sweetness in the family . . . went straight to Almarine" (31). The reader, however, should find something strange, almost sociopathic, about

Almarine's contentment upon returning to Hoot Owl Holler. Julius Rowan
Raper argues that the southern dependence upon place may often signify a
weakly formed self and demonstrate the result of improper parenting. Raper
notes that "what we in the South lack from parents and community we find
mirrored back to us from the landscape. . . . By default, we may employ the
landscape . . . to mirror our desire, or our rage. Or we may use a strong sense of
place . . . as a ballast against the chaos of rage. Either way, we tend to fuse what
the Greeks called *edos*, our dwelling-place or foundation, with *ethos*, our custom or habit, and then confuse both place and custom with *ethnos*, the Southern people. In short, we find our character in our place."[14] Raper's argument is
doubly convincing when applied to southern Appalachia, or at least to Smith's
vision of it. Almarine Cantrell's childhood is hardly an anomaly in Hoot Owl
Holler. The mothers in his family either die young or become emotionally
distant, and the fathers either leave home or become abusive and emotionally
distant. As a result, the children grow up, like the Hess children in *Family
Linen*, without attachment to others, without security or confidence. They feel
an inchoate longing for something outside themselves. Almarine serves as an
example; Granny Younger says that he "allus wanted something—who knows
what?—and that's why he kept staring out beyond them hills" (31). Despite
the fact that Almarine lives on a remote yeoman farm, his attitude of longing
for fulfillment outside himself denies the purported spiritual independence
associated with yeomanry.

One of the frequent images in Smith's fiction is that of the farm-bound
woman obsessively looking at the pictures of fashionably dressed models in the
catalogues and magazines her husband brings back to the farm from the near-
est town. After meditating over such magazines and "page after page of women
dressed to the nines," Nonnie Hulett Bailey of *The Devil's Dream* orders a bolt
of expensive silk that she uses to sew a dress like the ones she sees in the magazines, and then every evening she wears that dress while sitting on the porch
of her mountain cabin, rocking her baby, "with noplace to go."[15] In *Oral History*, Almarine's first wife, Pricey Jane, lives at Hoot Owl Holler three years
until her early death without ever leaving the farm. "None of the womenfolks
do much traveling," she realizes and is content that her husband, who is frequently "gone off trading," "brings it all back" to her (*Oral*, 70). Of the various purchased items, the ones she seems most to prize are the newspapers and
magazines with the pictures she likes to cut out and glue to the wall with flour
paste. Like the sharecroppers chronicled in James Agee and Walker Evans's
Let Us Now Praise Famous Men, Pricey Jane decorates her spartan home with
pictures of a world she will never see. It is tempting to view the entrance of
commercialism in the form of magazines to the yeoman farm as the source of

corruption that leads to the downfall of Arcadia. The omniscient narrator who serves as the voice of the community and tells the story of Nonnie's seduction away from the farm in *The Devil's Dream* makes just such an assumption, remarking, "It might be that the magazines were the most damaging of all" (*Devil's*, 67). A close reading of both novels, however, shows that the susceptibility of the housebound wife to moon over pictures in magazines merely demonstrates an emotional lack she already feels. And Nonnie's great-granddaughter, Katie Cocker, will follow in her ancestor's footsteps, pursuing a career in country music that will keep her perpetually on the road and away from home, a journey that takes Katie through decades of despair and personal fragmentation but that inevitably leads her to greater fulfillment than she might have known had she remained on the farm.

Throughout Smith's fiction, both outsiders and the mountaineers themselves often idealize the Appalachian experience as an innocent pastoral. In *Oral History*, the Tidewater schoolteacher Richard Burlage makes his "pilgrimage" to the mountains in part to escape the decadence of the Tidewater's more cosmopolitan society and journey back to a "simpler era" and the uncorrupted values and belief in God he hopes to experience among the mountain folk (97). His oversimplifications and prejudices severely limit his ability to understand the Appalachian people at any meaningful level. Similarly, the college student Jennifer, a descendent of Almarine Cantrell (and, illegitimately, of her grandfather, Richard Burlage) who returns to the mountains for a folklore project, fills her journal with notes that reflect little more than her own preconceptions. After one evening in Hoot Owl Holler, she gushes about her "new knowledge of [her] heritage and a new appreciation of these colorful, interesting folk. My *roots*. . . . I feel nothing so much as an outpouring of consciousness with every pore newly alive. I shall descend now, to be with them as they go about their evening chores" (19–20). The falseness of the pastorals witnessed by the outsiders Jennifer and her grandfather are instantly apparent, especially with respect to their need to view the Appalachians as innocents. However, the Appalachians often falsely view themselves as innocents, as well. This is particularly true of the young Almarine Cantrell and those who tell his story.

Early in her story, Granny Younger devotes considerable time to an enumeration of the folkways common to mountain farm families: all of the many tasks done on the Cantrell farm, such as the building of a log cabin, making quilts for the beds, picking down off of the goose for the house's single down-filled tick, drying fruits and vegetables grown in the nearby garden and apple and pear orchards, boiling clothes in the kettle over the outdoors fire, then using the ashes from that fire to make lye soap (32–33). Out of necessity, the yeoman learns to be a conservationist, to depend upon nature, and also to recycle his waste. Almarine's is the only farm on all of Hoot Owl Mountain and is described as a self-contained, self-sufficient paradise. Sitting alone on the porch of his cabin, surveying this paradise, Almarine appears as an Adam figure. The reader, upon considering the list of farm chores enumerated above, quickly observes how many in this list fall under the category considered by Almarine's traditional community to be women's labor. As Stephanie McCurry observes, the self-sufficiency of the yeoman farm was largely dependent upon the labor of women, even though the men alone retained many of the privileges of independence produced by this labor. Women's *dependence,* she asserts, "was the stuff of which independence—and manhood—was made."[16] Understanding the need of a woman to complete the young man's paradise, Granny Younger advises Almarine to find a wife, and, as if considering the proposition for the first time, he begins a series of courtships. Smith can be considered a romance writer in that the acquisition of a proper mate, the maintenance and potential rupture of an erotic, romantic, or marital relationship, occupies much of the characters' energies. As a feminist writer, she is concerned with the power dynamics that obtain within these relationships and with the social norms that maintain inequitable power dynamics.

The aged Granny Younger's tale focuses on Almarine as a young, "sweet," virile man, during the time of his courtship—rather than the later bitter and violent older man after the death of his first wife. Granny, of course, dies without knowing this older Almarine. After summarily describing his childhood, she skips ahead to Almarine's return to Hoot Owl Holler as a very eligible bachelor, whose legendary good looks and ownership of a vast expanse of property easily leads him, after Granny's prompting, into the company of a succession of sweethearts. Each courtship defines a pattern of conquest and retreat. Unverified rumors have spread around the mountains that Almarine spent the five years away from Hoot Owl Holler in prison, and he seems likewise to identify romantic commitment as a prison that would limit his freedom and uncompromised control of his world. Granny approvingly describes his flight from two successive relationships, saying, "So Almarine got home free, that time" (40) and "Almarine mounted that horse again while the getting was good" (41). The next time Almarine goes "a-courting," he comes upon a beautiful redheaded woman named Emmy bathing in a stream on the deserted side of Snowman Mountain. He becomes aroused at the sight of her naked body, and, though she escapes his advances, he searches the mountains for her during the following weeks until he comes upon the cave where she lives with her father, Old Isom. Isom shoots at and scares off the prospective suitor but later dies—at the hands of his daughter, according to Granny.

Granny warns Almarine to forget Red Emmy, whom she claims to be a witch. Granny explains that Isom has "pledged" his daughter "to the devil" (44), by which it might be understood that he has been committing incest with her alone in the caves on top of Snowman Mountain. Granny advises Almarine to "go back over to Black Rock . . . Find you a sweet God-fearing town girl" (45). Her reasons for participating in—or helping begin—the area's prejudices against Emmy and Old Isom are not completely clear, though one explanation involves Granny's earlier relationship with Emmy's father. Granny grew up with Isom on Hurricane Mountain and says, "I knowed him bettern I ever knowed ary a soul" (46), indicating the likelihood of sexual knowledge and at least the possibility that Emmy might, in fact, be the daughter whom Granny has allowed Isom to raise alone on Snowman Mountain and to "pledge to the devil." Granny describes Isom as a "mountain man" and tells the story of how his mother died and how he was abused by his father. According to rumors, he "kilt his brother and beat his paw before ever he took to the mountains" (46). Isom and Emmy are the novel's two most extreme cases of isolated mountaineers and are called "crazy as coots" (57) by Joe Johnson, who owns the one store in the vicinity.

Johnson is a friend of Granny Younger's and provides her masculine counterpart as the voice of community norms and judgments. His store serves as the locus of a community consciousness, a consciousness that is thoroughly masculine, considering that farm women remain at home. Because Granny Younger is unmarried and old and constantly traveling the area to birth children and tend to the sick and the dying, she is granted at least a peripheral position among the men at Joe Johnson's store. She smokes a pipe and drinks liquor like them and, to some extent, is masculinized. One of the most interesting and disturbing aspects of Granny's tale is the ways that it supports a patriarchal yeomanry that regularly denies rights to the women in the community. One of the fundamental rights denied a woman is to be a whole person, not only to have the same freedom to travel as a man, but also the freedom to express her sexuality.

Red Emmy's sexuality, more even than her isolation, elicits from her community the label of "witch." Aside from the rumors that her father has "pledged her to the devil," the openness of her sexuality provokes even Granny to condemn her, indicating the degree of Victorianism in rural Appalachia. After Emmy has moved in with Almarine at his farm, Granny pays a visit and spies on the two of them working in the field together. She notices Emmy's long red hair and remarks, "You know a woman orter bind up her hair. But Emmy did not. It was the only way you could tell by looking that she differed from other womenfolks" (49). According to Granny, Emmy also made the first explicit sexual advances in the couple, coming to Almarine in the middle of the night and undressing. Granny is disturbed not so much by Emmy's sexuality as by the fact that she is openly sexual at the same time that she desires to be domestic. Granny is surprised when she notices Emmy "a-dusting, and a-sweeping, and a-cooking and milking the cow" (49). Attempting to reconcile Emmy's sexual nature with her domesticity, Granny says, "She wanted to be a witch and a regular gal both" (48), then concludes that "twerent natural, no moren a snow in July" (49).

Granny and the rest of the community ostracize Emmy because she does not neatly fit into a category of either housewife or sexual object. According to Granny's reckoning, Emmy is at least forty, despite her youthful looks (47), and therefore nearly twice Almarine's age, an age when women in this culture are relegated to the role of granny rather than sexual object; as Richard Burlage later notes, "They age quickly here—the men appearing, by and large, much less the worse for wear" (108). Because she is older than Almarine (and there-fore likely more experienced, especially more sexually experienced), she prom-ises to be an equal, or more than an equal, in their relationship. That Emmy "was a woman as big as he was, a woman near about six feet tall" (44), and that she has grown up learning to live in even greater isolation than Almarine rein-forces the prospect of an equal relationship. Neither Almarine nor his commu-nity can accept such gender equality. Granny summarizes the attitude of the farmers down at Joe Johnson's store: "Everybody that had liked him so good, turned their back now. You don't want no truck with a witch" (50). Granny similarly counsels him to extricate himself from the relationship: "You better go back over to Black Rock. . . . Find you a sweet God-fearing town girl" (45). To Granny, the rugged experience of the frontier may be appropriate for a man, or even for an old woman like herself, but not for a woman who would make an appropriate spouse for Almarine. Because Emmy grew up in a cave, she may make a suitable lover for Almarine, but not a suitable wife, as would some domesticated girl from town, suggesting that the identity of the rugged, in-dependent Appalachian yeoman depends as heavily upon Victorian gender dichotomies as does that of a Richmond businessman, whose "angel in the house" allows him to engage in the cutthroat world of business (and even enjoy the occasional prostitute) without irrevocably sullying his soul. Rather than collaboratively evolving identity, the passive wife merely mirrors back to the husband the identity of assertiveness and independence that he has created for himself. Unlike the town girls from Black Rock, Emmy is not sufficiently sub-servient; she does not respect Almarine's authority in the home and in the bed.

The male fear of feminine sexual assertiveness underlies a folk tale that appears in Granny's narrative and later in an extended comic version by Parrot

Blankenship (201–5). Both accounts center on the witch "riding" her lover in his sleep at night, resulting in his progressive physical deterioration. Of Emmy and Almarine, Granny observes, "He was servicing her, that's all, while she liked to rode him to death" (53). Both her tale and Parrot's involve bodily transformation. Parrot tells of his younger wild days when he was cohabiting with a "widder lady reputed to be a witch" (201), and each night she transformed him into a horse and rode him until dawn, leaving him a bit weaker and more emaciated each morning. According to Granny, "Witches'll leave their bodies in the night, you know, and slip into somebody else's. . . . They can take on any form" (53). By associating the witch's sexuality with her transformative powers, these tales contain subtle clues to this culture's sexual norms: appropriate sexual intercourse does not threaten the male's ego boundaries. The woman should be appropriately passive and should remain the object of the male's desire, rather than expressing her own sexual desire. When Emmy becomes pregnant, Almarine turns desperately to Granny for advice. He "cries down into his hands" and says, "I come back here a free man . . . . I served my time. I growed up here, Granny. . . . I love this holler. . . . I ain't a-going to lose it. . . . I won't have no witch-children in my holler. . . . I don't know what come over me" (55). Almarine fears a loss of control, as well as the limitations that commitment will impose on his freedom and independence.

In light of Granny's association of Almarine's body with Hoot Owl Holler— "Truly this holler is so much a part of Almarine that he doesn't even think of owning it, not any moren a man would think of owning his arm nor yet one of his legs"—Almarine's fear of losing control of the holler to Emmy and her children can be taken both literally and metaphorically as his fear of how her sexuality is changing his identification of his own body and psyche—from a sense of self as inviolable and complete, to a more fluid sense of self in an interdependent relationship with another. This anxiety may derive largely from his lack of nurturing as a child, which was then exacerbated by his family's isolation. Remembering Almarine's childhood, Granny explains, "Nobody ever knowed what he was up to" and that he would spend hours sitting alone up in a tree "just waiting to see if anybody ever come up the trace, which nobody ever did" (27). In what seems a rewriting of the biblical story of Adam and Eve's expulsion from Eden, Almarine makes Emmy the scapegoat for his own rash behavior and sends her out of his holler alone and pregnant to wander across the mountains.

The men at Joe Johnson's store support his decision. Johnson tells Granny, "Almarine took up with a crazy girl, and now he has run her off. There ain't a man among us mought not of done it nor worse. That gal and her daddy was crazy as coots" (57). Out of their own self-interest, these men join together to restore Almarine's independence and his innocence. To exonerate his selfish behavior, they label Emmy "crazy," and a "witch," and a "whore" (91). This male solidarity largely accounts for the yeoman farmers' means of maintaining their own hegemony in the home and the rural community. Two decades later, Richard Burlage writes in his journal that a poker game has been going on at Johnson's store for forty years (125), vividly demonstrating one way men in this community maintain a level of freedom and power unavailable to women, who are typically home-bound and separated even from close kin.

The Ur-story of *The Devil's Dream* depicts similar effects of such familial and cultural dislocation. When the religious Moses Bailey marries Kate Malone, he takes her away from Cana, her family's community, to live alone with him and their children on Grassy Branch. This physical dislocation from Cana—her family's version of the biblical promised land of Canaan—is exacerbated by Moses's prohibition against fiddle music in their house, an especially harsh deprivation for Kate to bear, because she had grown up hearing the fiddle. The narrator, Old Man Ira Keen (Granny Younger's counterpart in *The Devil's Dream*), reports that "you couldn't of found two families more different-like than the Baileys and the Malones" (23). In this culture the patriarchal family values clearly prevail.

By traveling frequently to aid in childbirth, illness, and death, Granny Younger transgresses the men's monopoly on freedom of movement. She smokes a pipe and drinks liquor like the men and even enjoys a limited membership in the camaraderie down at Johnson's store. But, because of the threat she poses as a woman to the gendered exclusivity of their fraternity, her position among them is never secure. Immediately after hearing Johnson justify Almarine's expulsion of pregnant Emmy because she was "crazy," Granny turns to leave the store and hears the same word used in judgment of her: "'Crazy old woman,' that Stacy boy says, and I hear him alright, but I never look back nor give any sign. Thinks he is a power with the U.S. Mail" (57). This Stacy boy, obviously a young man, enjoys a certain clout with the other men because of the air of authority he derives from his connection to the U.S. government and from the extensive traveling and connections to many remote farms required in his job as a mail carrier. Because of their similar occupations (Granny is also constantly on the move from farm to farm tending to illnesses) she is the Stacy boy's obvious rival for power and influence in the community.

Families throughout the region of three mountains are completely dependent upon Granny for her lore in the areas of health, nutrition, and the supernatural. This dependence is illustrated in an episode involving Almarine Cantrell; several years after Almarine sends Emmy away, he comes home from town to find his wife Pricey Jane and their first child sick with "dew pizen" from drinking a sick cow's milk. Helpless, he rides across the mountain to Granny's house where he finds her on her death bed. The omniscient narrator of this chapter relates that Almarine "will not remember how Granny lay in the bed with her face turned toward the wall, or how . . . Granny . . . got up out of her sickbed and took off the white socks she had put on for dying, her burial socks, and put on her boots instead" (77). That Almarine is oblivious to Granny's situation indicates his worry about his dying wife and child, but it also indicates his complete self-absorption and lack of awareness or appreciation of Granny's sacrifice and her heroic effort to help him. The behavior of men at Joe Johnson's store reveals this attitude to be common among men in the area.

The most unsettling question raised by Granny Younger's narrative concerns her complicity in maintaining the power of the patriarchy in her region, suggested, for example, by her involvement in Almarine's series of courtships. When Granny advises Almarine to forget Emmy and go back to Black Rock and find himself a "nice God-fearing town girl," she encourages him to choose a wife in the same way that he might leave the farm to purchase salt or coffee. In fact, when Almarine eventually takes a wife, he does so by purchasing her or, rather—relying on the primary mode of exchange among yeomen—by bartering. One Saturday while visiting Black Rock, Almarine and a group of local men encounter a wagon on its way to Kentucky, pulled by a team of emaciated mules. In the wagon is one man with children and single women, all of them "foreigners." While the man is busy trading with the local men, Almarine meets and courts one of the young women. When they return, Almarine arranges to trade one of his healthy mules for the girl, to which the traveling man readily assents, so readily, in fact, that he seems to have filled his wagon with marriageable women precisely for the purpose of collecting such dowries. The description Granny Younger gives of Almarine's bride emphasizes her value as a commodity: "Everybody said it and I'll say it too—this was about the prettiest gal you ever laid eyes on. She was slight and just as dauncy as a little fancy-doll, the smallest, whitest hands and the littlest ankles" (59). She wears golden earrings that she refuses to take off even during childbirth (66), and even her name, "Pricey Jane," calls attention to Almarine's purchase. Granny has only the highest praise for Pricey Jane as an appropriate bride, remarking that "this time he done hisself proud" (58) and "Almarine got him a bargain" (63).

In contrast to the tall, experienced, and powerful Emmy, Pricey Jane is "frail" (64), small of frame, young and inexperienced, "not even sixteen" (62), with a "low voice what reminds Almarine somehow of a dove" (59). Furthermore, she in no way imposes on his liberty. Orphaned by her family, and nominally marginalized in her community as a "gypsy-gal," she is without a support network in the region and completely dependent upon Almarine for her material and emotional sustenance. The daughter of immigrants, Pricey Jane is accustomed to such powerlessness; when her parents died in eastern Virginia and "the men were there with the paper to claim the land," she was forced to move farther west with relatives (69). In Granny's imagined version of their domestic life, Pricey Jane is completely subservient to Almarine's wishes and, though she longs for his return, is content to remain at home while he frequently travels to the nearby towns to trade and enjoy the company of men at Joe Johnson's store—as long as he remembers to bring her some gift to purchase her complacency. Pricey Jane is not only passive, but also naive about Almarine's "trading" trips to Black Rock, the sight of much of his earlier courting. "Pricey Jane knows he's not like the other men" (70), even though he "won't ever say anything" about "what all he did in the lumber camp" (71). Compared to Emmy's open sexuality, Pricey Jane's notions are strikingly conservative, reflecting Rhoda Hibbits's advice that "Hit's a woman's duty and her burden" (71).

It comes as no surprise then that Almarine is deeply conflicted between his adoration of a chaste wife and his longing for sexual fulfillment such as he had known with Emmy. Pricey Jane glimpses evidence of his struggle when "sometimes he'll cry in the night and when she wakes him she'll feel his wild heart in his chest when he pulls her close. What's he afraid of . . . ? Of losing her, he says" (70). Almarine also experiences conflict between his feelings toward his wife and his place in the company of other men. Returning home partly drunk from several days in Black Rock, he visits Joe Johnson's store, where he intends only to stop for a moment but ends up staying all night long to best Harve Justice in poker. Harve has teased Almarine about his wife at home, asking "if his gypsy-girl had put him on a leash or under a spell, or maybe he was still under a spell from the first one" (74). The poker game signifies more than a contest of skill with cards; it becomes a safer version of the duel. After spending all night in the back room of Johnson's store, Almarine gloats in his triumph over Harve and, along with the other men, watches the defeated Harve "stumble off down the trail toward Hurricane and that sharp-tongued woman of his" (74–75).

When Almarine finally makes it home to his own farm, he finds his son dead, his wife dying, and their infant daughter crying of hunger. After Pricey Jane dies, Almarine reacts first by blaming himself for playing poker all night at Joe Johnson's but then shifts the blame away from himself on to Red Emmy, who supposedly has placed a "curse" on his holler. This scene ends with Almarine running through the night toward Snowman Mountain, where Emmy was reared, "screaming out like a crazy man, or like a man bewitched" (81). Afterward, rumors spread that he has murdered Emmy in retribution for the death of his wife, and all of the men who spread this rumor find him completely justified in this action. Emmy becomes a scapegoat for the male neglect of the farm and family and for his possible infidelity. For generations afterward, the rumor spreads that Emmy's curse lingers upon the Cantrell family, causing deaths, broken families, and a perpetual void of meaning in the lives of many of Almarine's descendants. Emmy's curse serves as an apt metaphor for the continuing social fragmentation that results from a commitment to patriarchal inequities.

When Almarine purchases Pricey Jane with a mule, the only person to object is the Judge's sister, Miss Lucille Aston, who tells Almarine, "You can't trade a mule for a girl, boy" (62). Even Granny Younger opposes Lucille Aston, portraying her as a shrew and a meddler, who ought to leave a man to his business. "Young folks just gets them a roof and moves under it," Granny explains, "and when the circuit rider comes around he makes it legal by saying the words, or they don't fool with it one way or the other. It's nothing but words, what I say" (62). Granny appears not to be bothered by the lack of legal protection for women's rights on the frontier, even finding it humorous that the sheriff "has daddied more children than ary other man in these hills" (62), implying, of course, that most of them are illegitimate. Lucille Aston forces Almarine and his new acquisition to accompany her to the house of her brother, the Judge, so that he can marry the couple. Granny doubts the legality of the perfunctory ceremony and denigrates Miss Aston's behavior by observing of the Judge, "What it is, he's scared of his sister" (63). In much the same way that the mountain folk later are suspicious of the Tidewater educator Richard Burlage, Granny likely resents how the city-bred Miss Aston assumes power on the frontier, relying upon distinctions of class and education that relegate Granny to a position of powerlessness and obsolescence. Two decades later Richard Burlage will remark of the mountain people that their "insularity astounds" and that they use the term "foreigner" to refer not to someone from another country, or even another state, "but simply to *anybody* who was not born in this area of the country" (125). On this point Burlage may be trusted; such insularity prevents Granny Younger from sympathizing with Lucille Aston and leads her to find her base of support within the power structure of her own community— among the men down at Joe Johnson's store.

There is another, less political, reason for Granny's lack of sympathy for Lucille Aston and Red Emmy: her feelings for the young Almarine Cantrell. In her protective attitude toward Almarine, Granny demonstrates maternal, as well as romantic and erotic interest, all of which blind her to his mistreatment of women. Granny's account of Almarine's courtships is complicated by her own involvement in the tale. Early on she denies involvement, saying, "Iffen twas my story, I never would tell it at all. . . . And iffen twas my story, why I'd be all hemmed in by the facts of it like Hoot Owl Holler is hemmed in by them three mountains. I couldn't move no way but forward. And often in my traveling over these hills I have seed that what you want the most, you find offen the beaten path" (37). Properly translated, Granny's statement offers instructions on how to interpret her tale: the reader should not be misled by the stated intentions of her story but should look off of "the beaten path" at the repressed truths of her experience, which are all the more clear since she believes she is not telling her own story. Granny takes pains to show how her feelings for Almarine are purely maternal: "Now I loved him as a baby, you recall. I said he was always so sweet" (50). The word "sweet" recurs frequently in her descriptions of Almarine; this insistence on his childlike innocence seems in part designed to protect her own repressed sexuality from responding to him as a sexual object.

One motive for her antipathy for Emmy might involve simple jealousy, though such an explanation oversimplifies the complexity of Granny's involvement with both Emmy and Almarine. Considering the possibility that Emmy is Granny's daughter by Old Isom—as discussed above—her reasons for dissuading Almarine from courting Emmy run much deeper than jealousy or maternal protectiveness. If Emmy is, in fact, Granny's daughter, she is an illegitimate one—and thus proof of Granny's own past sexuality—and her involvement with the "mountain man" Isom, whose history appears very similar to Almarine's. As long as both Isom and Emmy are ostracized to the far side of Snowman Mountain, Granny is not forced to confront the reality of her own past. In an effort to prevent her own psychic fragmentation, Granny denies her daughter; this abandonment by the yeoman mother becomes a trope that is repeated throughout the novel, and one that Smith suggests to have ancient origins. When Emmy sees Granny spying on her and Almarine, Emmy shows Granny a face that is "older and meanern time." Granny says, "Red Emmy stares me right in the eye and she spits one time on the rainy ground. . . . Well as soon as she spits, I get a pain in my side that liked to bend me double, it is all I can do to get outen that holler that day and get over on Snowman Mountain where I belongs to be curing the thrash, stead of going spying on a witch and her business" (52). These pains that bend Granny double resemble birthing contractions and might be identified as the psychosomatic reaction of a mother to the presence of her abandoned child. In light of her comments about straying "offen the beaten path," Granny seems to have learned the danger in this instance of wandering too close to repressed truths of her own history.

Even if Emmy is not Granny's child, her identity as a "witch" and a mountain woman closely associates her with Granny, and so she potentially becomes a surrogate for Granny in her sexual relationship with Almarine. That Granny

is hardly willing to acknowledge her vicarious interest in their sexual relationship is clearly illustrated when she travels all the way to Hoot Owl Holler to
spy on the couple: "All I want to do, I says to myself, is see how Almarine is
a-doing. That's all I want, I says. I says I'll look my fill, and then I'll be traveling directly" (51). The scene that Granny witnesses has a transformative effect
on her. As she comes upon the holler and hides herself behind a pair of cedar
trees, Emmy is out in the field, planting corn with Almarine, when a thunder-
storm comes on. Instead of running for the house, as Granny observes "most
womenfolks" would have done (51), Emmy stays in the field and embraces
Almarine in a passionate kiss. The image of natural and open sexuality outdoors in the elements awakens Granny's own libido, allowing her for the only
time in her narrative to speak directly about her erotic involvement in the couple's affair. "You never saw such kissing in all your life!" she exclaims. "Made
me feel like I had not felt for years and if that surprises you, you ain't got no
sense. Now a person mought get old, and their body mought go on them, but
that thing does not wear out. No it don't" (52). These feelings are dangerous
to Granny for obvious social reasons—if she is already considered a "crazy old
woman" by some down at Joe Johnson's store, this revelation would certainly
not ingratiate her with the men there. Granny may safely involve herself vicariously with Almarine through the surrogate of a Victorian town girl; to do
so through Red Emmy would dissolve the categories of chaste, domesticated
housewife and natural whore, categories held by her society that Granny has
thoroughly internalized.

Granny Younger's long narrative is one of the strongest in the novel; she is
the finest sort of unreliable narrator, charming the reader through her richly
idiomatic telling of a fascinating tale, so that, in suspending disbelief, the
unwary reader is likely to put too much trust in this granny-oracle's wisdom.
Specifically, the reader is likely to accept Granny's overly sympathetic account
of Almarine Cantrell, at the same time that her account produces an ill-
defined unease with his behaviors. Smith places the reader in the position of
insider, inviting us—through the charismatic Granny Younger—to suspend
our political judgments and cultural biases, as if we too had been reared in the
isolation of those mountains. As the first main narrative beyond the opening
frame, Granny Younger's story establishes the main themes and tensions that
recur in the subsequent episodes, told by a third-person narrator and by seven
additional first-person narrators. The reader's quandary of finding a reliable
perspective on the dilemma of the Cantrells is not much improved throughout
most of these points of view. The effaced third-person narrator who continues
Granny Younger's story of Almarine and Pricey Jane provides an essentially
neutral access to the thoughts of the characters and allows the reader to bring

to the continuing story the same attachments to the characters developed in Granny Younger's story. Anne Goodwyn Jones has observed Smith's unease with omniscience, finding that, when Smith uses the third-person narrator, it is "either very close to one character" or serves as the voice of the community on which it reports.[17] Jones also remarks Smith's "commitment to oral over literary traditions, individuals over omniscience,"[18] which is especially notable when comparing the "oral" first-person narratives with the long "written" narratives of the visiting schoolteacher and photographic anthropologist, Richard Burlage.

After the death and burial of Pricey Jane, the story skips ahead roughly fifteen years to 1923 and we are immersed in Burlage's journal. Burlage is young and idealistic, and his notes consistently require the reader to appreciate the irony of his misperceptions. His elder friend, the Methodist minister Aldous Rife, whose thoughts Burlage frequently records in his journal, offers a more reliable perspective. Rife has resided in these mountains for thirty years, busy compiling a history of the region and, in the process, being "ruined" by the loss of his own idealism (134). Although Rife's dispassionate account of the region provides us with many useful facts, he lacks the moral perspective to see in these details anything more than a long, painful, and essentially unchanging history. Fred Hobson has compared *Oral History* to Faulkner's *Absalom, Absalom!*, pointing out that in both novels "the reader finally knows more of the truth than any of the individual narrators" and that "the deeper truth of both novels is that truth itself is not only a relative but a highly elusive thing."[19] As in *Absalom, Absalom!* in *Oral History* truth emerges over time as a part of a pattern that begins to repeat itself in the procession of relationships that take place over the course of nearly a century.

Richard Burlage becomes sexually involved with Pricey Jane's daughter Dory. His abortive courtship, despite cultural differences, in many ways duplicates Almarine's series of conquests. Like Pricey Jane's, Dory's name—which Granny Younger gives her, telling Almarine that it means "gold" (68)—emphasizes her value as an object of desire. Like Almarine, Burlage divides women into categories. In contrast to the coquetry of Melissa, the Tidewater girlfriend who left him for another man, Burlage views Dory as an innocent, protected in this pastoral setting from what he considers the corrupting influences of modernity. As he dreams of her while transcribing into his journal Marlow's "The Passionate Shepherd to His Love," Burlage clearly places Dory into the role of the virginal rustic. This dichotomy of woman as "vamp" (102) and innocent remains intact until Burlage initiates sexual contact with Dory and is "distressed" by her "apparent knowledge of lovemaking," a dilemma he provisionally resolves by returning to a pastoral vision of her sexuality and viewing her "desire to be a kind of purity" (147). By viewing her sexuality within the realm of pastoral, he essentially objectifies her in the same way he does the rest of her culture, and this objectification allows him to enjoy her sexually without making a commitment. Like Red Emmy, Dory is abandoned by each of her sources of emotional nurturing: by her lover, who returns to the Tidewater; by her mother, Pricey Jane, who dies while Dory is an infant; and by her father, Almarine, who dies in a dispute over money with a partner bootlegger.

Similarly, Dory's young half-brother Jink feels abandoned by emotionally detached parents and by the fleeing Burlage, whom he has identified as a surrogate father. As his father did when a child, Jink spends his time away from his family, alone up in a tree, spying on the path down below. Of his secret hiding place in the tree, he says, "I call it the mother-seat. Don't ask me why" (187). His distance from his actual mother, Vashti, is emphasized by his calling her "Mamaw," a name typically used for the grandmother, and by her habit of locking him in the root cellar as a form of punishment (190). Just as Dory whiles away her time dreaming of a life distant from the mountains with Burlage as her cultivated lover, Jink dreams of a life with his sister Mary and with Burlage and Dory as surrogate parents (193). In the few months under the schoolteacher's tutelage, Jink is able to imagine a better life than the one of violence and deprivation he experiences at home on the farm with his bootlegging family. Unfortunately, when Burlage leaves, Jink withdraws into his own fantasy world, treasuring a copy of *The Adventures of Tom Sawyer* Burlage has left with him, along with one of the oranges, now shriveled and black, the schoolteacher passed out at Christmas. Jink takes an active part in his first hog killing—helping in the slaughter, singing along with the men's misogynist ditties, drinking whiskey for the first time, and eating greasy cracklings until he vomits. This hog killing is intended to serve as a rite of passage into manhood, which will signify the boy's entrance into the rights and responsibilities of his community, but afterward Jink resolves to run away, saying, "I hated them ever one" (207). In light of the ongoing feud that leaves the male Cantrells scattered across the mountains, Jink's decision to leave with *Tom Sawyer* under his arm may be one that spares his life. The fate of Twain's Buck Grangerford suggests how Jink's life might have ended otherwise.

The dilemma of an absent father and an emotionally distant mother repeats itself in the next generation. Throughout the fourteen years following her abandonment by Richard Burlage, Dory frequently walks down by the train tracks near the mining camp where her family lives, all the time dreaming of the Tidewater life of refinement she missed. Eventually her self-absorption leads to a gruesome suicide, when she lies down on the tracks and the oncoming train beheads her, turning her funeral and her family into a "tourist attraction"

(245). All of her children are devastated. Sally describes the effect of her mother's suicide on Lewis Ray, at nine years old the youngest of the children: "Lewis Ray went into a shell of a kind, serious and pigheaded as ever. He's still in it if you ask me! Anyway he packed his own lunch, for instance, even though I would have done it. I packed everybody else's. He went off to school every day like a little businessman going to work, and saved all his money in a sock under his bed-tick and got it out and counted it every night. He never mentioned Mama once and hasn't since in all the years, so far as I know. Would not let you touch him, either. Once when I put my arm around him . . . he jumped back like he'd been licked by fire. I didn't do it again" (251). By his withdrawal into a world of beginner's accounting, a world he can control, Lewis Ray seems nearly autistic and as emotionally distant as his grandfather Almarine. Although he cuts all ties with his family and its culture, he nevertheless perpetuates the negative qualities of yeoman isolation that the Cantrells have been unable to escape.

Similarly Lewis Ray's half-sister Pearl, the illegitimate daughter of Richard Burlage, repeats many of the negative qualities of her mother and grandmother. Like Pricey Jane and Dory, her name implies her worth as a commodity, as an object of desire, an identity that she tragically embraces, turning her back on the mining town of her youth and attempting to overcome the loss of her mother by marrying a wealthy businessman who goes into debt to build her an extravagant house complete with columns and servants. Sally describes Pearl as someone who was "never satisfied, not for one minute. . . . If I think of Pearl even right today, with her now dead and gone, what I see in my mind is those thin pretty white hands of hers grabbing and grabbing out at the air. Pearl was the worst one for wanting, of all of us. And the biggest fool" (241). Sally's description of Pearl's hands repeats Granny Younger's description of Pricey Jane who had the "smallest, whitest hands" (59), just as Pricey Jane's obsession with ear jewelry expresses itself in Pearl, who covets her grandmother's golden earrings and is caught stealing a pair of "cut-glass earrings" (241). Sally also recalls Pearl's habit—like her grandmother's before her—of spending hours with the magazines her relatives collect for her (241). Pearl's story ends tragically in a scandalous affair with one of her high school art students, which results in her being labeled "unfit" (273) and returning home to Hoot Owl Holler with a pregnancy that will kill her. This affair begs the obvious comparison to the affair between her mother and father, but it also calls to mind Tennessee Williams's Blanche DuBois, and, like Blanche's, Pearl's actions can be read as a rebellion against the constraints of her conventional society, a final desperate attempt to act upon impulse rather than in response to expectation. In her last visit with Sally, Pearl realizes that her insatiable desire for material success and "self-improvement" is merely in response to the early loss of her mother; "It's all about love" (266), Pearl tells her sister. Moreover, because, in this final visit, Sally compares Pearl to both Granny Hibbitts (271) and Ora Mae Cantrell (270), two of the novel's prominent granny figures, Pearl seems to have finally made an attempt to escape the role of passive sexual object and to achieve what Sally identifies as being her goal even as a child: "several lives. One was just plain not enough" (242).

Of all the Wades and Cantrells, Pearl's half-sister Sally most successfully integrates the novel's two types of women into a whole self. Contrasting herself to her beautiful mother and her sister Pearl, Sally describes herself as a "chicken hawk" more closely resembling her grandfather Luther Wade than any of the women in her family. Spiritually, though, she resembles her stepmother Ora Mae Cantrell, as well as the other granny-oracles in the novel, masculinized women who possess the social independence that allows them a freedom and mobility typically unavailable to women in their society. With each of the grannies before Sally, however, this independence comes at the price of repressing feminine sexuality and maternal instincts. In passing on to Ora Mae the lore of healing, Granny Hibbitts tells her that the power comes only to a woman who "never knowed her daddy" (209), which indicates the emotional cost—as well as the liberation from the father—that comes with matriarchy in this community. At Pearl's funeral on top of Hoot Owl Mountain, Ora Mae vividly demonstrates the sacrifice she has made when she throws from the cliff the heirloom earrings she believes to have doomed Pricey Jane, Dory, and Pearl, in succession. Despite her judgment, Ora Mae longs for the chance to have been, like her kinswomen, the object of romantic and sexual longing. Sally remembers watching as Ora Mae "got one of them in each hand and held them up . . . to her own ears. That old, old ugly woman! It was just about the worst and saddest thing I ever saw. . . . Then she slung both arms straight out and threw the earrings into the swirling clouds. . . . Gone. Ora Mae had the right idea. But she stood there with her arms flung out . . . for the longest time" (277).

Like Granny Younger, Ora Mae stifles sexual desire, sending away Parrot Blankenship, the one man she ever loved romantically, because she understands that, like the young Almarine Cantrell, Parrot's romantic interests in women are characterized by conquest and retreat. Ora Mae has the foreknowledge that if she were to express a desire for him he would leave her. She begins cohabiting with Luther Wade more out of practicality than desire. In practicing the renunciation of desire, Ora Mae eludes the endless search for romantic fulfillment that preoccupies so many of Smith's women characters. Ora Mae develops a creed based on necessity that sums up the determination and resignation

of the yeoman wife; "All it is," she says, "is what you have to do, and you have
to do what you have to do" (212). Her stoicism is born of experience and an
understanding of the realities of her culture. Nevertheless, like Granny Younger,
Ora Mae is a woman whose equanimity has come at the price of denying a substantial portion of her potential selfhood.

By discarding Pricey Jane's earrings, Ora Mae ritualistically opposes what
seems a never-ending cycle in the Cantrell family. Because Sally reports this
event near the end of her narrative, it does carry the force of a new beginning.
As already stated, Sally dissolves the categorization of women that has so
plagued the Cantrells throughout their history. Like the other grannies, Sally
possesses an intuition that approaches foreknowledge (266), and, like Ora
Mae, she is a caregiver to her siblings. Looking back, she says, "I just did what
I had to" (264), but Sally has managed to assume the role of caregiver without
emotionally detaching herself from those for whom she cares. Furthermore,
after the failure of a long and conventional first marriage to a man from Ohio
who "didn't believe in talking to women," and whose sexual interest in her was
little more than hygienic, Sally rejects convention and explores her own fantasies, first living in Florida with a disc jockey and then returning home to
marry Roy only when she is already a granny, "over the hill" (234). Sally enjoys
with Roy what seems a perfectly harmonious union, one that allows her to
express her sexual self without being objectified—and then discarded—in the
process. Unlike her first husband from Ohio, and most of the Cantrell farmers,
Roy is a talker—and a listener. Sally begins her narrative by saying, "There's
two things I like to do better than anything else in the world, even at my age—
and one of them is talk. You all can guess what the other one is" (233). Of
course, her ability to exercise her two favorite avocations depends upon her
finding the appropriate spouse, of whom she says, "Roy likes cars and boats.
And Roy can fuck your eyes out, Roy can, and talking all the time. 'Talk to
me,' he says. Well I like that" (233).

Unlike all the other first-person narratives in the novel, Sally's has an
implied auditor. At his prompting, she tells Roy the concluding episodes in the
history of the Cantrell family. Roy is the kind of man Smith seems to be calling for, someone who can accept a woman as both sexual and a source of wisdom, not one or the other. Furthermore their relationship is one based upon
mutuality, which Sally particularly notes of their sexual life. "Because him and
me we are two of a kind," she says, "and sometimes when we're there in the bed
it's like it all gets mixed up some way, like you kind of forget where your body
stops and his starts or who did what to who and who came when and all that.
I said we are two of a kind" (234). The mutuality and physical transformation of
their sexual relationship, in fact, recalls that of Emmy and Almarine—though,

unlike Almarine, Roy is capable of interdependence. As a couple, Roy and Sally demonstrate the self-sufficiency and independence central to the yeoman ideal. Unlike most of Sally's siblings, including Almarine Wade, who is determined to make a fortune selling AmWay products, Sally and Roy prove themselves capable of finding their centers in themselves and in each other. Although Sally and Roy live amid the same consumer culture as Pearl and Almarine, they are immune to its appeals and enjoy the simple pleasures of plain folk's domesticity. Sally claims that they are "*down to earth*" (234) and offers as proof the fact that she and Roy are the only people on their street who have not planted any grass in their yard so that they "won't have to mow it" (235). Sally also demonstrates a healthy attitude about her family's past. She acknowledges how her life has been a process of self-discovery that has largely depended upon accepting and understanding how her family's history has helped to shape her own. Like Katie Cocker of *The Devil's Dream*, Sally could say, "I know who we are. The hard part has been figuring out who I am, because I'm not like any of them, and yet they are bone of my bone" (*Devil's*, 14).

"Nothing lasts . . . not nary a thing": Overcoming Memory in
Fair and Tender Ladies

With Ivy Rowe, the protagonist of *Fair and Tender Ladies*, Smith again explores the themes of entrapment and self-fulfillment she sees common to the yeoman wife. Like Sally, who must learn to sort through the emotional baggage she has inherited from her family history, Ivy spends a lifetime gaining autonomy from the stories she has heard from her family, as well as the stories she has lived. *Fair and Tender Ladies* is a unidirectional epistolary novel—Ivy's story is told in a series of letters she sends over a period of more than sixty years to the world beyond her mountain home. Because the novel contains none of the replies that she receives, the narrative structure serves to emphasize Ivy's isolation in the mountains, but it also foregrounds Ivy's imagination, which is especially evident in the letters she writes to her dead sister Silvaney and to an imaginary pen pal named Hanneke—letters that Ivy obviously writes for herself.

Ivy's self-portrait in these letters differs from what one might expect from a farm-bound Appalachian woman from the early twentieth century. Rather than a conventional mind that relies purely on traditional modes of interpreting the world, Ivy's might even be considered an emerging postmodern consciousness: she takes a progressively eclectic approach in understanding her life, basing her interpretations in one moment on the model of a folk narrative and in the next on nineteenth-century British gothic novels—and later in her life she even bases a fundamental statement about her position in the world on the lyrics of a pop song she hears on the radio. As she ages, Ivy learns that the body of myth she inherited in girlhood will not wholly suffice as an interpretation of life's various experiences, especially experiences of loss. Julius Raper makes the distinction between *modern* and *postmodern* consciousness as a difference between the relative primacy of memory and imagination,[20] and to the extent that Ivy Rowe uses her imagination to achieve freedom from the dominance of both personal and cultural memory, we might call this yeoman farm woman a postmodern. Raper argues that "in the postmodern world the dependence of character on stability of place is inevitably doomed by the speed with which modern environments are changed."[21] This statement surely applies to Ivy Rowe, whose mountains are irrevocably changed by the growing lumber and mining industries and whose family is decimated by sickness and death. What ultimately distinguishes *Fair and Tender Ladies* as a postmodern work from the modernist pastoral elegies of Chappell, and even from *Oral History*—essentially a modernist montage of subjectivities in the tradition of Faulkner—is the manner in which the protagonist, Ivy Rowe, finally accepts and celebrates the change that comes to her life and region.

Ben Jennings notes that Smith's "fiction is impressive as a record of the psychological dislocations that have occurred in women, particularly during periods of rapid cultural change."[22] In *Ladies,* Ivy Rowe tells the story of pioneer Appalachia coming into the twentieth century. She suffers the hardships of pioneer life and its attendant mortality rate, and she likewise experiences the disappearance of traditional cultural values and ways of knowing the world—so that the continuity of her life is doubly threatened. Ivy's earliest childhood memories are of watching her sick father as he lay close to the fire trying to stay warm and waiting for death. As a young girl, she associates his imminent death with life's general mutability. "Daddy allus said Old Christmas was a time to stay home and think on what will last," she muses. "And what will last? I said to myself rigt[23] then, and I looked over at Daddy ther fixing to die, and the fire was dying too. It was real late but I wasnt one bit sleepy. Nothing lasts, I said to myself, nothing not nary a thing."[24] She loses her father when she is very young, and of her mother she remarks, "Nobody ever did know Momma I think except Daddy, and that so many years ago before she was burdened by all her cares" (125). Like so many of the children in *Oral History* and *Family Linen,* Ivy grows up without sufficient nurturing from parents and so spends the rest of her life attempting to heal the psychic wounds of her childhood.

The norm among Ivy's children and her siblings is to associate their childhood experiences in rural Appalachia with both material and emotional deprivation. After Ivy's sister Beulah dies of alcoholism, her husband returns to the mountains to tell Ivy, "I think she was desperately lonely. . . . Beulah wanted to get away from her past, from where she'd come from, what she'd been. From you. From all of you. She felt like the past was holding her back" (285). Smith studies the private drama underlying major societal upheavals occurring in Appalachia. She places the mechanism of cultural change in the efforts of individuals to resolve—or to avoid dealing with—adolescent trauma. Most of her characters, in fact, are able to manage the psychological pressure of past crises only by repressing them, by looking forward and embracing change, often accepting change with little critical self-awareness in order to break with the past. Just as Almarine Wade converts his family homeplace into the theme park Ghostland for the pure sake of profit, Ivy's son Danny Ray moves away from home to become a successful urban lawyer, and, despite his mother's exhortations to "stick with the Democrats" and represent the rural poor of his roots, he finds his political opportunity with the interests of big business and the Republican Party (294). When they were both young women, Ivy's friend Violet Gayheart fled the aftermath of a coal-mining disaster that killed her husband, leaving Ivy with the responsibility of raising Violet's daughter, Martha. Later in life Violet manages the guilt of separation not by dealing with the immediate cause but by becoming a leading union activist in Appalachian coal mining camps. Molly Bainbridge, another one of Ivy's girlhood friends, goes on to become a widely known and successful leader in the movement to bring public education to the mountains. Like Violet, Molly chose a career over family, and, similarly, Ivy raises at least the suspicion that Molly's success is overcompensation for the years of girlhood she spent without parental care in the Catholic girls' school.

The changing landscape of Appalachia suggests the visible manifestation of a wounded collective psyche. The behavior typically exhibited by the Appalachian people to repress the past is mirrored by their frantic efforts to cover up the old familiar landscape with a facade of billboards and "jerrybuilt buildings." Ivy, who consistently emphasizes the need to remember, is not impressed. She writes her daughter that "it is getting real built up around here, Joli, and real tacky. People are throwing these jerrybuilt buildings up anyplace, even out into the river which is not a good idea as they say that's what caused the flood—that and all the strip mining. But Bill says you can't stand in the way of progress. This makes me sad to hear. I wish he hadn't of quit farming, and let that tobacco field fall to weeds. I keep thinking about this land and how Daddy said, *Farming is pretty work*. It hurts me to see the scrub pines taking over what used to be the garden" (291–92). Ivy's description of flimsy buildings erected over the river prone to flooding functions as a metaphor for the repression of psychological trauma, which likewise perpetually threatens to resurface and flood the consciousness. In turning away from farming, Ivy finds that they become even less centered and more susceptible to the endless pursuit of instant gratification, attempting to distract themselves from the void of meaning gaping ever wider.

The citizens of Majestic stop shopping at the Branham store in favor of the Magic Mart, not only for the sake of novelty but also because they associate the Magic Mart's newness with the outer world, which has been denied them for so long. By exchanging their authentic agrarian identity for the semblance of modernity, the mountain people demonstrate en masse a cultural insecurity. The tacky, jerrybuilt buildings are "thrown up" to cover up and fill the emotional and cultural void of these people. In a letter to Silvaney, Ivy identifies herself as representative of her culture—she admits a deep personal insecurity and a subsequent search for fulfillment outside herself: "I have spent half of my life wanting and the other half grieving, and most often I have been wanting and grieving the same thing. There has been precious little inbetween" (275). In fact, Ivy begins her story with a search outside herself for validation of her experience. In a series of unanswered letters to a European girl named Hanneke, whom Ivy hopes to win as a pen pal, she tells all about her life at Sugar Fork. After waiting in vain for a letter in return from Hanneke, Ivy feels that her experience has been invalidated. "I hate you," she fumes. "You do not write back nor be my Pen Friend I think you are the Ice Queen insted. I do not have a Pen Friend or any friend in the world, I have only Silvaney who laghs and laghs and Beulah who is mad now all the time and Ethel who calls a spade a spade. I know you are so rich with all your lace and those fine big cows. I know you have plenty to eat. I know I am evil and I wish evil for you too. Mister Brown told us one time that God is good, but He is not good or bad ether one, I think it is that He does not care" (25). Ivy associates this particular case of indifference with a more general cosmic indifference. She suffers the plight of a child in a large family in which each member is preoccupied with his or her own life. In her school books she has read stories depicting the closure and fulfillment denied her. She has used such myths of completeness to construct the pen pal Hanneke through whom she hopes to access a world that is both materially and emotionally more satisfying than her own.

Her letters to Hanneke serve as Ivy's first experiment of self-understanding. They let her articulate her fantasies of wish-fulfillment and seek some vital relation between the world of her experience and that of her imagination. She slowly begins to accept the indifference of her pen pal and to internalize the presence of the imagined other outside herself. In a later letter to Hanneke, she calmly writes: "Dear Hanneke, I know you will not get this letter. I know I will not send it, you are the Ice Queen so cold. . . . But it is snowing now and so I think of you, and sometimes it seems to me like you are more real than all of my Family. . . . It seems like I can not talk to my Family they is so many of us here" (31). Her letters to Hanneke become a means of poetic expression, of emotionally engaging and articulating her experiences. After some practice, her voice in the letters becomes less artificially constructed and more personal— and gradually more grammatical, too. Ivy's increasing literacy might, in fact, be viewed as a visual metaphor to suggest her lifelong transition from fragmentation to wholeness. That Hanneke will, in fact, never see the letters allows Ivy to write for herself. "I cant tell it to nobody else," she realizes, "so I have writ it down for you cold Hanneke, Hanneke Queen, or for nobody, or may be it is for me" (39). In constructing an imagined audience for her letters, Ivy, in effect, carries on a dialogue with herself and, by doing so, eventually internalizes the presence of that other self for whom she writes. On Christmas day, while the rest of her family prepares for the community ritual of firing shotguns into the morning air, Ivy walks away from them to lie down alone in the snow and make the shapes of angels. "I must of made a thousand angels," she says. "Lord it was a pretty pretty day. . . . And I says, I am the Ice Queen, rigt out loud. I felt so good" (26). She has appropriated for herself the qualities of indifference and self-sufficiency that she imagines Hanneke to possess.

In a deeper sense, Ivy relies on the same technique she developed in her letters to Hanneke when she spends the rest of her life writing to her lost, older sister Silvaney. As a result of a "brain fever" she suffered as a child, Silvaney retains her childlike innocence and responsiveness to life, while all the other members of Ivy's family retreat into their shells of subjectivity and become preoccupied with private concerns. If Ivy projects onto Hanneke her desire for the completeness of an imagined exotic world that she might potentially realize in the future, Silvaney—whom Ivy imagines as being eternally young—expresses Ivy's pastoral longing for the imagined wholeness of her past. Years after Silvaney has been taken away to a mental institution, Ivy confronts her loss, saying, "I have felt like I was split off from a part of myself all these years" (182). In writing to Silvaney throughout the rest of her life, even after she realizes that Silvaney has died in a flu epidemic, Ivy seeks to heal that psychic wound by imaginatively projecting and then internalizing her absent sister. Just before Ivy dies, she writes to her daughter Joli, explaining that "Silvaney, you see, was a part of me, my other side, my other half, my heart" (313). This tendency of a woman to project a sister or alternative self imaginatively is a common trope in much of Smith's fiction, as, for example, with the character of Rose Annie in The Devil's Dream, who even as an adult believes in the presence of a "little-girl ghost," her double, who has befriended her since childhood. These characters compensate for an actual lack of nurturing by filling the absence imaginatively. This personal mythmaking may further serve as a metaphor for the function of fictions for readers and writers; Ivy's letters to Sylvaney are her "novels," in which she gains the freedom to regain control of her life.

In every letter she writes, Ivy constructs an audience and thereby internalizes a sense of the other, expanding her imagination. Even though she spends nearly all of her life in a remote hollow of the Blue Ridge Mountains and, in fact, never travels out of those mountains, Ivy gains a much wider experience through her reading and letter writing. In a letter to her daughter, she affirms, "Oh Joli, you get so various as you get old! I have been so many people. And yet I think the most important thing is Don't forget. Don't ever forget. . . . A person can not afford to forget who they are or where they came from, or so I think, even when the remembering brings pain" (265). Unlike her friend Violet, who has changed so dramatically that Ivy remarks how her old self "has been burned clean out of her," Ivy maintains a connection with each of her past avatars. Her emphasis on the need to remember and reconcile herself to every part of her experience—including the trauma—indicates the nature of Ivy's triumph: she has gained the ability to recreate the past, internalizing and reconfiguring it by means of alternative narratives of her life, rather than being overwhelmed by a static mythology located outside and beyond herself.

Although Ivy finds her past a source of emotional sustenance, the past provides, throughout her life, the fundamental obstacle in her attempt to see the world from a fresh perspective. Not only her own past, but the collective past of her family, its mythologies and clichés of folk wisdom, establishes itself as a nearly incontrovertible authority in Ivy's consciousness. The past imposes itself upon Ivy, because she allows it to. Unlike all of her siblings and children, Ivy remains geographically rooted at Sugar Fork, reinvesting the landscape with memories of her family and making it ever harder to leave.

A series of important passages in which Ivy meditates upon the landscape at Sugar Fork reveals her evolving conception of herself in relation to her past and the possibilities she imagines for her present and future life. The first and most important extended description of landscape appears on the third page of the novel and is periodically alluded to thereafter. Ivy retells her mother's story of elopement with John Arthur to his family farm at Sugar Fork. The couple rode double on horseback all night long and arrived at the farm just before dawn as the sun

come peeping up then over the top of Hell Mountain like a white hot firy ball. . . . Momma looked around.

She saw Sugar Fork sparkle in the sun like a ladys diamond necklace.

She saw Pilgrim Knob rise up direckly behind the house, and Blue Star Mountain beyond. They call it that because of how blue it looks from

down below, along Home Creek and Daves Branch, why you can see Blue
Star mountain clear from majestic on a pretty day. And you can see the
Conaways and the Rolettes and the Foxes cabins, coming up Home Creek
from the schoolhouse like her and daddy had done that morning, now you
can see all them neghbor peoples houses fine but you cant see ourn, nor
get to it nether, without wanting to. You are not going to happen upon
us, is what I mean. And Blue Star Mountain don't seem so blue nether,
when your up here. But it is the prettest place in the world.

And so my momma looked all around, and she seed all of that.

She seed the shining waters of Sugar Fork go leaping off down the
mountain into the laurel slick. And she seed that this is a good big double
cabin here with a breezeway in between where it is fine to set and look out
and do your piecework. And she seed the snowball bush in the yard and
the rosybush here by the porch all covered with pink-pink flowers. It was
June. And Momma looked up in the sky she said and she seed a hawk glid-
ing circles around and around without never flapping his wings, agin that
big blue sky. She said that hawk made three circles in the sky, and then
Daddy turned to her real formal-like and cleared his throat and said Maude,
it is what I have to give you. It is all I have. But she said she knowed this,
she had knowed it all along. It will do, John, is what she said. Then she
busted out laghing and my daddy picked her up and carried her in the
house which is where I live today, in Virginia, in the United States of
America. (13–14)

Like Granny Younger's account of Almarine Cantrell and Pricey Jane, and like
the story in *The Devil's Dream* of Moses Bailey and Kate Malone, this narrative
carries with it the importance of a family legend. As the originary story of Ivy's
immediate family, it provides them with a common point of reference and
becomes a part of their collective memory.

As in the case of any story preserved in the oral tradition, the various tellers
of this narrative selectively refine the details of the story and even invent missing details to satisfy their respective psychological needs. The mother high-
lights her acceptance of the new life on the remote farm away from the city.
She makes the proposal of rural life and her acceptance the dramatic climax of
the story. The choice of language—that she looked and saw that the home was
"good"—echoes the creation myth from Genesis, and for Ivy, who refuses
throughout the novel to be dominated by the authority of religion, this family
story serves as a creation myth. It is the story of *her* genesis.

The detail of the circling hawk at first appears anomalous, and even more
striking is the fact that the mother remembered—or invented—the detail of

its three circles in the sky. Such a detail that does not serve to further the narrative suggests at least the possibility of symbolism. For Maude, who has had perhaps more religious training than her daughter, the hawk might serve as a replacement for the manifestation of the Holy Spirit in the form of a dove from the Christian gospels, just as the hawk's three circles echo the trinity symbolism that pervades Western culture. Maude is arguably influenced by the same collective consciousness that prompted Columbus upon discovering the new world to name Trinidad in honor of the holy trinity, when he saw the three mountain peaks rising from the center of the Caribbean island.

The most important details from Ivy's version of the narrative are likely her own embellishments. Maude might have seen or later added to her story the images of the "snowball bush in the yard and the rosybush," but the exact phraseology from the narrative indicates the importance of these details to Ivy. The presence of the mountains in the background serve as the ultimate borders for her world, but the "snowball bush in the yard" and the "rosybush here by the porch" identify local details that connect the absent place of the myth with the present landscape that continues out of the past into Ivy's lifetime. After telling that the rosybush was in bloom, Ivy adds the explanation "It was June" perhaps not from a memory of the narrative but from her memory of her own personal experience of the landscape, indicating the continuity of myth and life that affords such stories their power and relevance. Ivy recreates her parents' experience of the landscape by describing the scene as it appears to her when she returns from the schoolhouse. By extrapolating this one opportunity for reflection to her daily walk up the mountain from the school on Home Creek, we see the repeated reinforcement of collective myth upon her personal consciousness.

According to Ivy's narrative, her family's farm is superlative not only because of its beauty but because of its remoteness. She says that of all the houses in the region hers is the only one not visible from or accessible to the outside world. She turns what might seem a detriment into the defining attribute of Sugar Fork, the singular feature that differentiates her family from all others. Like Hoot Owl Holler, Sugar Fork is a self-contained Eden, where, she says, "we grow nearabout all we eat. . . . we raise what we need, we don't go to the store for nothing but coffee and shoes and nails and to get the mail" (16). She clearly embraces the yeoman values of self-sufficiency and independence. Like the biblical pastoral of Eden (and even more like Milton's version), Ivy's first depiction of Sugar Fork is of a self-contained, bountiful Arcadia, devoid of death or loss or want. In Ivy's third letter to Hanneke, in which she describes the family cramped in their cabin in winter, where her father and younger brother are wasting away from unknown illnesses, she divulges that her family does, in fact, sometimes have less than plenty to eat and that the emotional life of her family is less than perfect. Because of these facts, not despite them, this initial narrative of plenitude maintains its importance to Ivy.

This first narrative of Sugar Fork exerts such a primary influence over Ivy's imagination that she can only measure her life in relation to it. This narrative expresses the wholeness of early childhood that Ivy experienced or imagined. Whenever her experience varies from this myth of plenitude, Ivy suffers inchoate feelings of desire and insufficiency. When her father dies, for example, her mother retells the story of the midnight ride to Sugar Fork, and Ivy reports that upon hearing it she is "full up with wanting, wanting something so bad, [she] culd not of said what it was" (46). Ivy witnesses what Raper describes as the incongruity between memory's insistence on stability—especially when associated with place—and the ongoing change experienced in the present, which might lead to fragmentation unless she is capable of imaginatively responding to change by re-envisioning her world.

Her father's death is the first in a series of losses that forces Ivy to confront the extent to which life's reality varies from the pastoral myth of her childhood. However, the circumstances of her father's burial allow Ivy to revise the myth without doubting its viability. Upon descending from the burial ground high on the mountain, the family discovers that Ivy's sister Beulah has given birth to a boy, whom they name John Arthur after his grandfather. The seemingly supernatural coincidence of the two events, reinforced by the family's ritual of naming, suggests to Ivy some order of compensations that fits into her worldview based on an incorruptible Eden. Instead of blotting out her Sugar Fork myth, her father's death simply adds a complementary chapter and convinces Ivy of the viability of returning to the perfection of her childhood Eden by finding an appropriate means of compensation. The folk wisdom of her great aunt Granny Rowe adds to Ivy's revised worldview the sanction of familial authority: "Granny Rowe says that sometimes it happens like that, one spirrit goes and a nother one comes direckly" (50).

Like Granny Younger of *Oral History*, Granny Rowe functions as the voice of the remote past. Representing the unnamed and unremembered generations, she appears to speak for the land itself. Exemplary of the yeoman values of self-sufficiency and dependence only on the earth, Granny Rowe is a druid who passes on to her children a knowledge of medicinal herbs and the rules for planting by the phases of the moon. Immediately before she dies, Granny takes Ivy into the woods in order to instruct her about edible plants. Ivy remembers, "Granny's hand was like a claw on my arm. *Look at me*, Granny said. *Here's how you boil your bitters*, and I looked straight into her bonnet, at her apple-doll face. *Remember*, she said, and I have. I saw the clouds already forming in her sharp blue eyes, and I have always remembered, and now in the spring of the year I go out and gather the greens the way she told me, and boil them like she said, and give everybody a good dose of bitters whether they want it or not, to thin out their blood for the summer. . . . The sharp bitey taste of the greens takes me straight back to that sunny blowing day by Sugar Fork when we sat on the rock ledge and Granny said, *Ivy. Remember*" (197). Ivy remembers Granny in connection with the landscape. Her sensual experience of the "bitters" recalls her visual memory of a scene located in a specific landscape at Sugar Fork, so that the ritual of preparing bitters in the spring becomes a way for Ivy to recapture the past—and, more specifically, a past landscape. Ivy's connection to her past is not unambivalent: she remembers Granny's hand as a "claw" clutching her arm. Despite her deep attachment to Sugar Fork, Ivy senses the truth of Welty's famous statement about the dangers to the imagination of too deep an involvement with place. Welty explains that for "the artist to be unwilling to move, mentally or spiritually or physically, out of the familiar is a sign that spiritual timidity or poverty or decay has come upon him; for what is familiar will then have turned into all that is tyrannical."[25] Ivy spends her life trying to negotiate between loyalty to her past and freedom to live in the present. This tension reveals itself most clearly in her sexual and romantic life.

In the same way that the birth of Beulah's son provides a partial compensation for the death of Ivy's father, Ivy seeks a more complete compensation and return to past perfection when she marries Oakley Fox. She and Oakley both grew up in the same part of the mountains, and Oakley was the first boy she kissed. Then she goes "astray" and has a baby by a "foreigner" named Lonnie Rash, who comes to the mountains to work in the lumber business. To avoid scandal she leaves town and lives with her sister Beulah in a coal mining town. After having her baby in the mining town, Ivy has a scandalous affair with Franklin Ransom, the son of the superintendent for the Diamond Mines Company. Significantly both of Ivy's first two lovers are from outside the mountains and are aligned with the logging and mining interests that forever change the landscape. Ivy's sister Beulah, who constantly strives to "get away from her past" (285), urges Ivy to pursue the relationship with the wealthy Franklin, which Ivy does until she views her adventure as a threat to the main narrative of her life—marrying Oakley and returning to Sugar Fork. When Oakley barely survives an explosion in one of the Diamond mines, he and Ivy decide to discontinue their separate residences at the mining village and to return together to Sugar Fork.

Ivy clearly views her return with Oakley in relation to her mother's story of coming to Sugar Fork for the first time with John Arthur Rowe. Ivy sees her journey back to the farm as a return to the perfection of her childhood and its myths of completion. Despite how close she comes to recreating her mother's experience, the factuality of her return will never obtain the grandeur and wholeness of memory. In a letter to Beulah she tells of her disappointment upon returning to Sugar Fork: "But everything is smaller than I thought, or remembered, or imagined. This may be because I was a child then, and now I am grown, but I find that all has shrunk some way, and I do not like it" (188). Similarly, Ivy learns that the actuality of marriage and rearing children pales in comparison to her imagined narrative of nuptial completion. Her gothic romances, no doubt, end with marriage and do not attempt to deal with the quotidian nature of life on a farm.

Throughout most of the novel, Ivy conceives of herself in terms of a present self and a past self, and she consistently privileges her girlhood. Until she finds herself in a house full of her own children, she maintains her sense of an integrated self by imagining a continuity of experience between her girlhood and her present self. She writes to her brother Victor, "I remember as a child, I thought all the older people around us were grown up. Now I think they were just old. Because although I am a married woman now, I still feel like the girl that grew up here, the one I used to be" (182). Ten years later, after sacrificing herself to the responsibilities of motherhood, she loses her imaginative connection to her own girlhood and she perceives an irreconcilable schism between her past and present. She explains to Silvaney, "It is like I was a girl for such a long time, years and years, and then all of a sudden I have got to be an old woman, with no inbetween" (195). Because all of her siblings have either died or moved away from Sugar Fork, Ivey lacks an audience that might creatively engage her memories; instead they become monolithic and inaccessible, and they become even more so with the loss of Silvaney to a flu epidemic that spreads through the mental hospital. Ivy waits ten years before she is able to overcome the "fact" of her sister's death and to begin to recognize how her letters to Silvaney are important not for their function as correspondence but for the way in which they allow Ivy to engage her own life imaginatively.

When Ivy rediscovers Silvaney as an audience for her "letters," she begins the process of reconnecting imaginatively to her past and escaping the self-absorption of static memory. "I am not old yet, Silvaney," she declares,

> 37—that don't sound so old! But I have fallen down and down and down into this darkness. I can see it all so clear now, and bits and pieces of me have rolled off and been lost along the way. They have rolled off down this mountain someplace until there is not much left but a dried-up husk, with me leeched out by hard work and babies. I feel like a locust— like a box turtle shell! . . .

I have been down in that darkness now for years.

Although in a way it seems short, like one long day that has lasted for years and years. I feel like I've been frozen, locked in time.

Oh Silvaney, all of a sudden I am thinking about that game Statues we used to play, and how you loved it. Don't you remember? Victor was the one that would fling us around, and however we landed we'd have to stay. . . .

Now I feel like I've been playing Statues and got flung down into darkness, frozen there. I see myself frozen this way, frozen that way.

I look down in my mind and see my statues. (195–96)

Ivy continues her letter for several pages, discussing various important scenes extending from her girlhood through her recent past. She represents her past not in fluid images that change and evolve—evolving eventually into her present. Rather, they are statues, remote in time from her, but standing in her memory like landmarks that overshadow and dominate her present. Ivy's conception of her past as a series of statues echoes the imagery of Wordsworth's *Prelude*, in which he conceives of his past as "spots in time," significant moments from his life that inform his present. Ivy and Wordsworth share the same dilemma: how to overcome a preoccupation with mortality by imaginatively reclaiming the past in order to achieve a unified awareness of life. While Wordsworth manages to integrate the past and present in an organic whole, Ivy—at this point—conceives of her life as a series of unconnected fragments, as "bits and pieces" that "have rolled off and been lost along the way."

Ivy overcomes her fixation on the past by becoming imaginatively involved in the present, by entertaining the idea—perhaps for the first time in her life—that change might be positive. Since girlhood, her evening ritual has involved sitting on her front porch and staring out at the landscape, which changes only predictably with the seasons. In girlhood she sat on the porch beside her father, and now in womanhood she sits in the very same place beside Oakley, while he whittles and she shells beans. Ivy makes it clear that her husband's struggle to maintain his emotional health under the rigors of farm life is no less intense than her own (201), though their methods of coping vary considerably. Whereas he finds solace in religion, she learns to find hope in the possibility of the unexpected. This difference is nowhere more movingly depicted than in the contrast of their responses to the view of the landscape from their front porch:

Oh Silvaney. Silvaney. I recall one Sunday about a year ago when I was sitting here, Oakley was gone to church all day, to a baptizing I think, and when he came home he sat in that chair and we looked at Bethel

Mountain together which we have done so many years and Oakley said, *Ivy, you can look out on that Creation and know there is a God.* I reached over and got his hand and held it. I couldn't see his face. And I couldn't see God's face neither.

But *now*, Silvaney, now we sit and watch the lights on Bethel Mountain twinkling like fairy lamps through this blue haze. I feel like there's a big change coming on somehow, when I look down this holler and see light. It makes me feel all electrified, myself! But it ain't got up here yet. (207)

Oakley seeks certification of a concept in the same way that Ivy has looked out at the landscape for years seeking an outward verification of her girlhood myth of completeness. She is ready to see the landscape through new eyes only when the myth has exhausted its ability to revitalize her imaginatively.

Although change comes to Ivy in the form of rural electrification and shortly thereafter in the form of the bee man, Honey Breeding, Ivy imaginatively extends herself outward to meet change halfway. When she describes her response to the golden-haired woodsman who has come to their area to find and transport bee hives, Ivy says, "I thought about Rapunzel spinning gold. I thought about the Brownies in the MGuffey Reader. For Honey Breeding did not seem quite real. He seemed more like a woods creature fetched up somehow from the forest, created out of fancy, on a whim. Honey Breeding seemed like a man that I had made up in the cool dark springhouse, like a man I had imagined until he came true" (214). Honey Breeding engages her interest because he taps into a wellspring of frustrated sexual fantasy and associated pubescent images. But what begins as mere projection of wish-fulfillment ends in a dialogue in which he imposes his own reality upon her, so that Ivy moves out of her interior monologue into a dialectic in which she is forced to engage the world. For the first time in years, she finds herself telling her stories to someone besides herself (in the guise of letters to Silvaney). She says, "My own voice sounded funny in my ears. It sounded rusty. I felt like I hadn't used it in such a long time except to say something like, *The wooden paddle is broke,* or *Close the door*" (224). The episode in which Ivy follows Honey Breeding up the mountain, telling stories of Sugar Fork all the way, parallels her first letter to Hanneke, in which she seeks a pen pal, a connection with the outer world. In the Honey Breeding episode, however, Ivy successfully engages in a two-way line of communication. Not only do they enjoy a sexual union, but he responds to her stories with stories and songs of his own. His presence becomes so real to her that he obscures the landscape, which for Ivy represents much more than mountains and trees. Recalling the relief of having the landscape and its attendant psychic pressure eclipsed, she says, "When I stood on the cliff with him that day in the last of the sunshine, I couldn't see nothing but him, nothing. I couldn't see the valley below, nor any part of the world. I was blinded and dazzled by his shape" (234).

That Ivy has allowed Honey Breeding to obscure her view of the landscape surrounding her mountain home is, as might be expected, not without its repercussions. The guilt she experiences upon coming down off the mountain and finding her infant daughter LuIda dead is compounded by her guilt for violating what she sees as the moral order of her world expressed in her narrative of family and its relation to the landscape at Sugar Fork. Ivy has replaced her mother's narrative of Edenic harmony with the figure of Honey Breeding and a new story in which Ivy leaves her family to pursue her own private fantasy. The censure of community narrative reasserts itself upon Ivy's return home by its physical manifestation in the landscape. After hearing the news of her daughter's death, Ivy sees the tall lilac bush blooming by the back door and says, "Granny's voice sounded strong in my ear. *Never let a lilac bush grow tall enough to shade a grave, or death will come to fill it*" (239). The lilac does not appear in Ivy's first performance of her mother's elopement narrative, but in a subsequent letter Ivy does associate the lilac with the rosybush Maude saw on her first morning at Sugar Fork. Upon returning to Sugar Fork from Diamond, Ivy writes to Beulah and tells her, "The rosybush by the front porch steps is still in bloom, and the lilac by the back door never had so many flowers" (184). The two flowering bushes balance each other as images of birth and death. Furthermore, the lilac is associated with Honey Breeding, who identifies himself as a "backdoor man" (231).

The Honey Breeding episode likewise balances Ivy's account of her father's funeral. When the family descends from the mountain burial, they come home to find that Beulah has given birth. When Ivy descends from her sexual and potentially procreative experience with Honey Breeding, she comes home to find her baby dead. The coincidence of such an occurrence reinforces her conception of a moral world order that she has transgressed, and, though change continues to come to the world around Sugar Fork in the form of the Second World War and coal mining strikes, Ivy retreats once again to the interiorized landscape of her memory; she writes to Silvaney: "I can not get past this little grave up here in the orchard on the hill. I can't get over it" (244).

After a period of grieving and of rededicating herself to her children, Ivy does begin to overcome her guilt, and, despite the death of LuIda, does not sink to the depths of self-absorption and abstraction that she had reached before her affair with Honey Breeding. Two years afterward, she writes to Silvaney, "It *is* true that time softens things. I feel now as I write that I am better than I was.

. . . At least I am alive now, since I ran off with Honey, there is *that*, come what may. And I do have all these children to take care of" (248). Ivy's transgression and its repercussions echo Milton's account of Eve's disobedience. Both transgressions are described in explicitly sexual terms, and both involve a new awareness of the world that comes at the expense of death. Ivy's story is a retelling of Milton's, in which Ivy's expulsion from Eden brings the promise of freedom, freedom from the domination of her mother's "creation myth." Like Milton's Satan, Honey Breeding serves as a catalyst for change that ends in the necessity of a greater mutual dependence between a man and woman. Ivy remarks, "Honey Breeding was full of tricks, full of stories, full of songs" (235). Indeed, he is a trickster figure, who disturbs the stasis of the old social order in Ivy's world and allows a new one to form. Ironically, after a period of grieving, Ivy and Oakley communicate much more successfully, both sexually and verbally, than they had in the past. Before her affair, Oakley had become so preoccupied with his own labors and personal struggles that he never looked at his wife. After Ivy's affair, she notices, "Well, now he is paying attention. He is looking at me dead-on" (246).

Because Ivy can not incorporate her affair with Honey Breeding into the previous monolithic narrative of her life, it serves her as an alternative text that challenges the dominance of her former worldview. It allows her to consider her present experiences in relation to some context other than that unflawed narrative of childhood perfection, whose germ is to be found in the story of her mother's elopement. The story of Honey Breeding serves Ivy in the same way—but to a much more fully realized extent—that a romance novel might. When Ivy writes her daughter Joli to congratulate her on the publication of her first novel, she cannot help but add the criticism, "I think you could of used more of a love interest. Or may be that is just me! Anyway it was real good even if they do *just think* an awful lot. You might put some more plot in it next time, for an awful lot does happen in this world, it seems to me" (290). Evidently, Ivy finds that the dilemmas of Joli's self-absorbed characters hit too close to home. Ivy does not want fiction that serves as a mirror for her own experience. Rather, she prefers stories about *other* people with lots of *other* experiences, which will serve her by taking her *out* of herself and thus allowing her to imagine other possibilities for her own life—even if these possibilities remain in the realm of fantasy.

As she ages, Ivy learns to live with flux, to be influenced, but not dominated, by her past. She begins to read again, replacing the canon of her childhood with the paperback romances she buys at the Rexall drug store. And she has developed a passion for pop music, especially Elvis Presley, to whom she pays subtle tribute in one of her last letters: "I think a person will go one way or the other, don't you? Either they will get more set in their ways, or they will get all shook up. I am shook up, myself" (296). After suffering so many losses in her life, Ivy learns to accept death and change. In a letter to Silvaney, after Oakley's death, she writes,

> I know that not one hour for the rest of my life will go by without me missing Oakley and that's a fact. But I will tell you another fact which is just as true, it hit me yesterday.
> I can read every book that John O'Hara ever wrote.
> I can make up my own life now whichever way I want to, it is like I am a girl again, for I am not beholden to a soul.
> I can act like a crazy old woman if I want to which I do.
> I can get up in the morning and eat a hot dog, which I did yesterday.
> I don't know what I might do tomorrow! (277)

Ivy learns that possibility opens up to her only when she is willing to relinquish control; the past becomes accessible only when she no longer worries about losing it. Shortly after bearing her first child, Ivy had written to her sister, "I think this is one reason I write so many letters to you, Silvaney, to hold onto what is passing. Because the days seem to go faster and faster, especially now that I have got Joli, the days whirl along like the leaves blowing down off the mountain right now" (147). Before she dies, in her final letter to Joli, Ivy describes her experience of burning the letters she has written throughout her life to Silvaney. She realizes, at last, the futility of her effort to hold onto time through writing. "The letters didn't mean anything," she says. "Not to the dead girl Silvaney, of course—nor to me. Nor had they ever. It was the *writing* of them, that signified" (313). When she burns the letters and relinquishes her fixation on the idea of a preserved past, she becomes aware of the possibility of the present moment. With a new vision of the world, she exclaims, "I gathered them up and took them out back to the firepit. . . . Now and then I would stop and look all around, but you know how quiet the land lies in the snow. And it all looks different. The shape of Pilgrim Knob looked different, and Bethel Mountain down below hung in wreathy mist, and even the slope of the orchard looked different, strange and new. I don't know—it was kindly *exciting*! It was a new world, with even the shape of it changed" (312–13). Her description of the snow-covered landscape here is remarkably similar to a winter scene she witnessed as a young girl. In a letter to Mrs. Brown, her teacher who first introduced her to "high" culture, to a world of possibilities through reading, Ivy describes an important early experience of seeing the landscape at Sugar Fork.

"It was like I looked out on the whole world," she says, "and I culd see for miles, off down the mountain here, but it was new. The whole world was new, and it was like I was the onliest person that had ever looked upon it, and it was mine. It belonged to me" (26). These two passages are essentially identical—with the important exception that her later statement lacks the expression of a need to possess. She has learned finally that the landscape, like moments in time, can be experienced, but it cannot be owned.

Her final letter to Silvaney, which reads more like an interior monologue than a written letter, catalogues a list of images from Ivy's life. By the end of the passage, in this moment of dying, she has clearly attained a state of detachment that allows for her transcendence. She remembers her various love affairs without imposing a hierarchy of importance among them. She mixes images from early and late periods of her life along with phrases from canonical poetry, nursery rhymes, oral folktales, and very recent dialogue between herself and her nurse. And as the "letter" progresses, the minimal degree of logical organization completely breaks down and gives way to a free association of words and images. In contrast to her earlier meditation upon the "statues" of her past, in this final monologue, the fragmentation of images does not fill Ivy with anxiety, nor does she attempt to impose control. Rather, she allows them to flow freely toward the final series of images that combines both transcendence and affirmation of memory: "The hawk flys round and round, the sky is so blue. I think I can hear the old bell ringing like I rang it to call them home oh I was young then, and I walked in my body like a Queen" (316). In her last several letters to Silvaney, and especially in these parting words, Ivy demonstrates that she has overcome her earlier dependence on the stability of memory as a recovery of a fixed order outside herself. Instead, she shows confidence in the autonomy of her own imagination.

Consistently in her fiction Lee Smith presents Appalachian women who are entrapped by their circumstances and often spiritually impoverished by their inability to find their centers within themselves. She convincingly demonstrates how life on a self-sufficient farm does not necessarily lead to spiritual self-sufficiency. In fact she implies that such a supposition is the result of false consciousness on the part of male pastoralists, who privilege a masculine conception of the whole self as one defined by rigid ego boundaries rather than a more feminine self based upon interdependence. Sally Wade (*Oral History*), Katie Cocker (*Devil's Dream*), and Ivy Rowe (*Fair and Tender Ladies*) each escapes the farm—at least temporarily—in order to pursue a personal vision of self-actualization that conflicts with the traditional roles for women they have inherited.

The very image of life as journey, as process, instead of location, contradicts the pastoral vision of completeness associated with place. By leaving home, both literally and imaginatively, Smith's Appalachian heroines engage in political action and restore to themselves—and potentially to their communities—a sense of wholeness.

CHAPTER 5

CLYDE EDGERTON
The Embattled Yeoman

If the women in Lee Smith's fiction suffer deprivations associated with the isolation of farm life and the lack of community, the men and women in the fiction of Clyde Edgerton experience the mixed blessing of *too much* community. In the fictionalized small towns of Edgerton's Piedmont dwells an embattled yeomanry, attenuated by the forces of encroaching civilization. Although few actual farmers figure prominently, the children and grandchildren of farmers most certainly do, and, although these descendants have left the farm for towns, they nonetheless retain varying degrees of allegiance to the values of self-sufficiency and independence held by their yeoman forebears. Very unlike the loosely organized frontier patriarchy of Smith's *Oral History*, in most of Edgerton's novels a rising matriarchy rules by promoting collectivism and undermining (often unwittingly) the yeoman values of independence and autonomy. Whereas men dominate kinship in Smith's Appalachia by removing their wives from the network of support found in extended families, Edgerton's women typically control kinship. Since they also control the influence of the church, these two forces coalesce to locate community power decidedly with the women. The frontier value of personal independence manages to survive only at the margins of the community, occasionally in an openly confrontational position, but more often in a state of carefully maintained unobtrusiveness. This situation is most fully developed in Edgerton's small-town novels of manners, such as *Raney* and *Where Trouble Sleeps*. On the other hand, *In Memory of Junior* features a more open war of the sexes, which takes the form of a yeoman farming family aligned with the matriarchy pitted against a fading masculine remnant of frontier individualism. The Copelands of *The Floatplane Notebooks* are a family still more fully invested in the masculine values of frontier individualism than in the feminine collectivism of the small town. Even though the main narratives of all of Edgerton's novels are set in the latter half of the twentieth century, the families who populate these novels represent a spectrum of values associated with the history of the yeoman farmer, from his emergence with the settlement of the frontier to his disappearance with the rise of the urban and suburban South. Edgerton's novels suggest that a fundamental aspect of this history was the transition from masculine values of independence to feminine values of collectivism and interdependence.

With the exception of *Redeye*, which takes place in the American West, all of Edgerton's novels are set in the eastern Piedmont of North Carolina, in or around the communities of Listre, Bethel, and Summerlin, in the fictional Hansen County. Listre is roughly based upon Bethesda in Durham County, where Edgerton grew up, and, like the neighbors Edgerton knew, his fictional communities are fairly homogeneous: white, middle class (or lower middle class), and predominantly Baptist. Like Bethesda,[1] these fictional communities are thoroughly segregated. With the exception of *Killer Diller*, a sequel to *Walking across Egypt*, each novel presents a completely new cast of major characters, although minor characters and allusions to major characters do appear in more than one work. For example, Preacher Gordon and Wilma Fuller from the Baptist Church in Bethel figure in both *Raney* and *In Memory of Junior*. In *Junior*, Faison Bales mentions that his relatives are the Copelands (from *The Floatplane Notebooks*), and Faison's brother Tate teaches at Ballard University, which provides the setting of *Killer Diller*. Lamar Benfield from *Egypt* makes a brief appearance as a gravedigger in *Junior*, as does the music of his nephew Wesley's band, the Noble Defenders of the Word. This minor overlap creates with each novel a deeper sense of community networks. Since Edgerton typically narrows his focus in each novel to members and acquaintances of one extended family, allusions to other characters, families, and nearby communities allow the reader familiar with Edgerton's oeuvre to observe each family in relief against the panorama of a larger community and to observe the extent to which each particular family shares or diverges from a common ideology.

Edgerton's novels often portray provincial communities in the throes of social and economic change that accompanies regional "progress." At *Killer Diller*'s Ballard University, the administration is attracting federal dollars for an aggressive outreach program of social reform and is even making plans to build an airport. In *Junior* the farmland is being gobbled up by TechComm Commons (the fictionalized Research Triangle Park), and the occupations of successive generations reflect this change: from farmer, to traveling salesman, to college professor, to computer specialist. In each case, as the level of social organization broadens from the frontier, to family farm, to small town, to an increasingly cosmopolitan and suburbanized region (not to mention the virtual society of the Internet), we witness successive losses of autonomy: from individual to clan to community to larger economic and political networks. Edgerton suggests, however, that in many ways such changes are superficial. Even though occupations and physical environments change, they often leave ideologies and family structures intact. In *Junior*, Summerlin enters the information age with computers at TechComm Commons that process data at rates measured in nanoseconds, and Tate Bales has moved off the farm to become a professor of psychology, yet he experiences the same problems communicating with his son that his father and his father's father experienced. The changing landscape around Summerlin foregrounds the stasis within the Bales family. For Edgerton, family provides by far the most significant determinant of identity, as well as the greatest challenge to personal autonomy.

Because of the profound influence of family and community on identity, Edgerton affirms the necessity of the individual to find the will and the imagination to act independently. Edgerton's oeuvre depicts how at every level of increased social organization the perpetuation of frontier individualism becomes more difficult. As matriarchal farming families and small towns adapt the masculine, frontier value of self-sufficiency to the collectives of family and community, the result is an insular society that militates against individualism. Edgerton's characters' habits of thought and behavior are largely part of their cultural inheritances, accepted and passed along often with little critical self-consciousness. Nevertheless, all of the protagonists in Edgerton's fiction struggle toward greater self-awareness and self-determination by gaining a critical distance from their respective cultures. In *The Floatplane Notebooks*, for example, Meredith questions the uncritical patriotism he learned at home and in public school, which led him to the horrors of Vietnam. His younger sister, Noralee, becomes a dissenter at home. In *Raney*, Raney Bell Shepherd gains sexual independence from the taboos against eroticism she learned from her mother and her church and, in doing so, salvages her marriage and gives birth to a generation to whom she will pass both her rich family tradition and some level of freedom from the constraints of that tradition.

Edgerton's personal history reveals a similar tension between himself and his community. Sterling Hennis describes the political transformation Edgerton underwent during his late teens and early twenties:

> Edgerton came to the small university community [University of North Carolina at Chapel Hill] a staunch conservative who supported Barry Goldwater in the 1964 presidential campaign. He even wrote a right-wing poem that was published in the *Daily Tar Heel*, the student newspaper. When he returned for graduate work in 1972, however, he worked for George McGovern for president. He attributes his move from a conservative political attitude to a more liberal one to his experiences during his active duty in Vietnam, as well as to the atmosphere he encountered while a student at Chapel Hill. Even in high school, however, he had been fascinated with issues of conformity and nonconformity . . . he

remembers being impressed by the essays of Ralph Waldo Emerson, Henry David Thoreau's "Civil Disobedience," and the works of Mark Twain.[2]

After serving in the Air Force in Vietnam, Edgerton returned to Chapel Hill to earn a Ph.D. in English education, followed by eight years of teaching education at Campbell University, the Southern Baptist institution in Buies Creek, North Carolina, which serves as the inspiration for Ballard University in *Killer Diller*. At Campbell, Edgerton again experienced the kind of thought control he had suffered growing up in a Baptist home, and in 1985, upon the publication of his first novel, *Raney*—which satirized some of the beliefs and folkways of Baptists—the tension between his more progressive worldview and the conservative university administration reached a head. The administration withheld Edgerton's teaching contract while awaiting his response to their question of how his novel "furthered the purposes of Campbell University."[3] Ultimately, Edgerton found it necessary to leave Campbell and has since pursued a writing and teaching career at more liberal schools, such as St. Andrews College, Duke University, and the University of North Carolina at Wilmington. His eight novels, five of which have been *New York Times* Notable Books, include *Raney* (1985), *Walking across Egypt* (1987), *The Floatplane Notebooks* (1988), *Killer Diller* (1991), *In Memory of Junior* (1992), *Redeye* (1995), *Where Trouble Sleeps* (1997), and *Lunch at the Piccadilly* (2003). In 2005, Edgerton published a memoir, *Solo*, which treats, among other subjects, his years as an Air Force combat reconnaissance pilot during the Vietnam War.

In a tribute to the influence of Emerson's essays (originally entitled "Birddogs, Intellectual Rebellion, and Ralph") collected in David Perkins's *Books of Passage*, Edgerton describes the pressures to conform he felt growing up. As a high school sophomore, his "life and death musings were tied mostly to the teachings of [the] Baptist church."[4] When he read Emerson's essays "Nature" and "Self-Reliance," however, he felt as though his "mind was set afire as if soaked in gasoline."[5] In Emerson, Edgerton found a model of a "believer" who could "question 'truths' handed down from his elders," a man who was "moral, but not dictatorial and narrow."[6] Emerson's writings led Edgerton to Thoreau's "Civil Disobedience" and Edgerton began to find a voice for the vague sense of resistance he felt toward his community's pressures to conform. In the writings of these Transcendentalists, he discovered the idea that "'America' and 'democracy' were not so much about accepting God as handed down to me by other humans; America and democracy were more than that. America and democracy had to do somehow with my being free to search for truth. I could think for myself."[7] Emerson's deification of nature also validated the spiritual aspect of Edgerton's experience hunting and fishing as an alternative to the Baptist services by which he had come to feel constrained. In his fiction, such activities are often performed as a ritual, by which the individual exercises his better nature and reclaims the yeoman values of self-sufficiency and independence that have been diluted by life in a small town.

Edgerton's novels borrow from a range of southern literary traditions: satire and humor from the tradition of Twain and the other frontier humorists; family saga and an experimentation with point of view from Faulkner; from O'Connor, a fascination with grotesques who represent states of spiritual degeneracy; and from Welty an awareness of the effects of insularity and a prose style that eschews rhetoric. In 1998, Edgerton discussed the effect, twenty years earlier, of hearing Welty read "Why I Live at the P.O." on public television. "Jolted, shaken, taken—stung, but without pain," he recalls, "I went straight to my journal and wrote, 'Tomorrow, May 15, 1978, I will get up and start writing fiction seriously.' I got up next morning and started writing fiction seriously. I'm still not over it. . . . It dawned on me that 'Why I Live at the P.O.' was about my people. It was like a relative."[8] As in the socially incestuous family of "Why I Live at the P.O.," the families in Edgerton's novels often threaten to smother their individual members. And the eponymous narrator of his first novel, *Raney*, resembles the narrator from Welty's story. Just as Raney's chatty and discursive voice echoes Sister's, so does her predicament; like Sister, Raney struggles to overcome her dependence on the approval of her parents and to gain some distance and independence.

Like Welty, Edgerton focuses on the observable surfaces of language and experience, writing an economical prose that some have called "minimalist," often requiring the reader to dig out the significance buried in every line of dialogue. Throughout Edgerton's oeuvre there appears hardly a single passage of explanatory rhetoric. This coproduction of the text with an active reader suggests a more democratic approach to writing, one in keeping with the yeoman ideals underlying the cultures he describes. His often nearly folkloristic attention to recording and preserving the traditions and idiom of the people of the North Carolina Piedmont has provoked Joseph Flora to remark that Edgerton writes "a fiction that seem[s] to revel in its southernness."[9] Less satisfied by this attention to a "mimetic" representation of the culture, Scott Romine objects, "Although I do not doubt that every detail has an actual referent somewhere in the contemporary South, the cumulative effect is one of overkill; in the end *Raney* crosses the limit at which the mimetic representation of 'the South' devolves into performative self-indulgence."[10] Romine's criticism of *Raney* errs in its assumption that Edgerton's novel is an attempt at "realist narration" any more than *Huckleberry Finn* is. As with Twain's work, or that of any of the southwestern humorists, overstatement and "overkill" are the basis of satire, in which the trick is to convince the reader that as outlandish and overstated as a depiction might seem, it is nevertheless accurate. M. Thomas Inge notes, for example, that "hyperbole and comic exaggeration . . . have characterized American humor from William Byrd to John Barth."[11] Furthermore, first-person narration, by definition, includes performative aspects, whether conscious or—as with Raney, Sister, and Huck—unconscious.

Like Mark Twain, Eudora Welty, Lee Smith, Jill McCorkle, Harry Crews, Lewis Nordan, Flannery O'Connor, William Faulkner, Reynolds Price, and just about any other southern writer who employs comedy, Edgerton well understands how to flirt with the boundaries between character and caricature, between comedy and tragedy. In each case, the technique is remarkably similar: tempt the reader to laugh at what seems ignorant, expected, low-class —subhuman—and then with a flourish reveal the buffoon's humanity in a way that suddenly elicits the reader's sympathy and guilt at having laughed at the character. Twain pulls this trick with Jim throughout *Huckleberry Finn*, letting Jim wear the minstrel mask and shuck and jive for Huck's—and the reader's— amusement, and then the next moment provoking in both an awareness of how laughter debases the audience more than the minstrel. In "Letter from Sister: What We Learned at the P.O." Tony Earley points to a similar technique at work in Welty's story, showing how the "bright surface" of grotesque comedy covers a deep pool of human suffering. "What is difficult," Earley says, "is to take the poor, the uneducated, the superstitious, the backward, the redneck, the 'trailer-trash,' and make them real human beings."[12] Whereas Edgerton writes about *plain* whites rather than "poor white trash," his characters typically represent an insular culture whose eccentricities, like Sister's family's, can alternately be exploited for their comic and tragic potential. Edgerton acknowledges that humor can be both a "distancing technique and an endearing technique." "If I have disarmed a reader with humor," he says, "then the chances of the reader thinking more deeply about his or her life or behavior may increase. . . . Another important reason [for the use of humor] is my own natural inclination—humor helps keep me from being depressed about my doubts when they're strongest."[13] Edgerton is a "comic" writer whose subjects are most often the very serious matters of death, loss, and cultural change. Louis D. Rubin, Jr., has remarked, "I think Clyde is in a definite tradition of religious writing—I mean the same kind of tradition that Flannery O'Connor . . . and Walker Percy are in. He deals with the questions of *How do you maintain religious values in today's society?* The novel [*Raney*] is essentially about people in change, trying to hold onto the past and at the same time adapt themselves to the future. It's a hard thing to do."[14] Rubin's observation calls attention to the ambivalence Edgerton typically demonstrates in his depictions of the characters in his novels, whose frequent racism, rigid conservatism, and xenophobia are inherited from their culture. Edgerton's novels might be described as "small-town novels of manners," and, as in the fiction of Austen or James or Wharton, the individual's struggle for freedom and self awareness brings into relief all of the community taboos that individual behavior transgresses. Edgerton's first novel, *Raney*, and his seventh, *Where Trouble Sleeps*, provide his clearest examples of the novel of manners, dramatizing the extent to which frontier individualism has been restrained in the small town. Both novels most clearly present the connections between an entrenched matriarchy and the church as the primary vehicle for disseminating feminine values of collectivism.

Raney: Life under the Blinker Light

Two of Edgerton's most autobiographical novels, *Raney* and *Where Trouble Sleeps*[15] depict families that closely resemble the author's own: the strong, religious mother; the quiet, retiring father; the obedient child; the disruptive, alcoholic uncle who lives with the family. Based on Edgerton's own Bethesda, North Carolina, during the 1950s, the Listre of *Trouble* is little more than a wide spot in the road, with the recent addition of a traffic signal at the crossroads, which is flanked by a filling station, several locally owned stores, a barber shop, and Listre Baptist Church. Throughout the novel characters watch each other across the open crossroads; the new blinker light even suggests the presence of an electric eye, omnipresent, always capable of observing their sins and secret desires. The daily gossip and the omniscient point of view (a first for Edgerton's novels) also suggest an awareness of surveillance on the part of all the characters. Six-year-old Stephen Toomey is frequently seen watching the men drinking beer across the street at Train's Place filling station, and, with guilty pleasure, he sips his Big Top Grape pretending to join them, even though his mother has preached to him about the evils of alcohol. Listre is a thoroughly dualistic community, one in which all of its members share a set of norms, whether they choose to abide by them or not. The opening chapter presents Alease Toomey taking her son Stephen and the neighbor boy Terry Daniels to the state penitentiary for a look at the electric chair in order to impress upon them the dangers of misbehavior. The rest of the novel follows Stephen's indoctrination into the rigid small-town morality at the direction of his mother.

Stephen is roughly based upon Edgerton himself as a young boy, and he comes as close as anyone to being the novel's protagonist; however, *Trouble* focuses more upon the town as a collective, rather than upon any of its individual citizens. Frequently the narrative is interrupted by indented passages of collective stream-of-consciousness, in which the omniscient point of view quickly slides from one perspective to the next. One of these passages occurs, for example, during a church service, creating a montage of thoughts among congregation members: the minister who is trying not to lust for one of his teenaged parishioners; the toddler trying to pry gum loose from the bottom of a church pew; the husband who retires from the sanctuary to the foyer where he can enjoy the relative secular comfort of conversation with the other ushers. Each of these behaviors derives its relevance from the shared context, from the minister's sermon that makes clear the choice of heaven or hell, from the ritual chicken dinners that will take place in homes across Listre after the service is over. More than anything else, *Trouble* is a close study of the nearly unconscious manner in which the citizens of Listre are socialized, how they learn the fears, values, and taboos of their town, and how they each come to relinquish some degree of autonomy in order to belong.

Like the depiction in *Trouble* of Listre in the year 1950, the nearby town of Bethel as it appears twenty-five years later in *Raney* has changed very little. Like Listre, Bethel is an extremely insular community, dominated by the local Baptist church. The community's insularity has allowed for the development of extended families with deep roots and entrenched worldviews, which tend to be conservative and dualistic, fearful of any degree of difference, clearly demonstrative of what W. J. Cash called the "savage ideal." Like Cash's "man at the center," Raney and her family view themselves as representative of the mainstream of their community: middle class, church-going, and white. However, in light of Edgerton's vision of a small-town matriarchy, Cash's expression might be rephrased as "the woman at the center."

Raney articulates her community's vision of a natural order, in which she and her family occupy a central position; their identity is defined by the marginalized blacks in their community. In her opposition to her liberal, outsider husband's protest for equality, she remarks,

> I thought of all the years the colored people around Bethel and Listre had lived in real low conditions and had never amounted to anything and I figured if Charles thought skin didn't make a difference then he must be blind. . . .
>
> If it was natural for white and colored folks to marry then they would do it. God made us all to do natural things. . . . That's why dogs are so happy—they do natural dog things. You never see a dog doing something God didn't intend him to do. You never see a dog doing a cat thing or a bird thing. Never.
>
> Now when you look out that window you don't see colored people and white people getting married. That's very simple because God didn't make

that as one of the natural things for people in the world to do. . . . It's as plain as the nose on your face and some of these ideas of Charles's must come from a part of his brain which has never known about the natural and unnatural things God has intended for us to do.[16]

Implicit in Raney's conception of a "natural" order, created by God, is the imposition of a hierarchy. She sees the world in medieval terms, as a great chain of being with white Christian Americans at the top of the chain and closest to God. The presence of "colored people . . . in real low conditions" living on the margins of her community only serves to validate her position in the center.

Raney's habit of perceiving the world hierarchically extends itself beyond race to matters of gender, sex, and ultimately to the basic dichotomy of good and evil. In each case a privileged entity gains its identity in opposition to one that is subordinate. For the same reasons that Raney fears miscegenation, Aunt Naomi fears the threat of communism. "'I'll tell you what I don't like,' says Aunt Naomi, 'is the idea of all this government day care stuff. That's pretty much like the communists, ain't it, Preacher Gordon? Seems like we're getting more like them and they're getting more like us. They're wearing dungarees all over the place. Pretty soon we'll be all the same. That's what I'm afraid of'" (186). In the above passages, Raney and Naomi oppose miscegenation and communism because they fear a loss of identity. Both women require a clearly identifiable *other* that serves as a threat to what they identify as the purity and order of their own family and Baptist community. This dependence upon a subordinate *other* for the maintenance of personal identity is even more visible in Raney's Uncle Nate, the most vocally racist member of the Bell family, whose virulent racism derives from his near unemployment and dependency on alcohol and the goodwill of his sister and her family.

Issues of race occupy a more central position in *Raney* than in most of his novels; however, frequently in Edgerton's fiction issues of race, usually unspoken or only hinted at by white characters, threaten to surface and disrupt the placid, homogeneous white communities, where African Americans are relegated to the margins of town and of consciousness. In *Trouble*, the reader is constantly reminded of Traveler's Rest, the black neighborhood on the edge of Listre, while the main streets of Listre appear thoroughly white. The con man and drifter Jack Umstead attempts to ingratiate himself with town folk by repeatedly mentioning that he is in town to visit relatives at Traveler's Rest; that he is oblivious to the fact that the settlement on the edge of town is occupied exclusively by blacks becomes increasingly comic every time the whites in town silently and confusedly nod at his statement, each time reminding the reader of the extent of Listre's segregation. As in *Trouble*, elsewhere in Edgerton's fiction, blacks are typically an unseen and unheard presence, lurking somewhere on the margins and threatening to sully the purity of white families and communities. In *Floatplane*, Noralee Copeland has a crush on her high school's star halfback, J. W. Potts, though she is afraid to agree to date him, because of her parents' racism. In *Raney*, Charles's long-distance friendship with his black army buddy Johnny Dobbs becomes a source of tension in his marriage. In *Killer Diller*, Wesley Benfield's black fellow band member, Ben, smokes pot in their room at the BOTA halfway house sponsored by Baptist Ballard University, mocking the university's pious pronouncements that these young men are "back on track again." Ted Sears, the president of the university is, in fact, quite anxious about sponsoring BOTA, despite the considerable federal funds available for the project, because "this halfway house business" involved "known criminals, black criminals in some cases."[17]

In a 1990 interview, Edgerton remarked about the role of the Baptist church in his community in promulgating racism: "It's a paradox. . . . In my church, the same older people who loved me like aunts and uncles also refused to consider letting black human beings, created in the image of God, have entry into our place of worship."[18] This statement is consistent with observations made by Price and Betts about the failure of white Protestant churches in their hometowns to be racially inclusive. For Edgerton, this "paradox" has been one of the most significant motivations behind his "need to write it out, to understand it."[19] Throughout the novel, Raney and her family rely upon biblical authority to justify not only racism but also their general intolerance of difference. As in *Killer Diller* and *Redeye*, organized religion appears in *Raney* as the primary means of consolidating and disseminating power, of maintaining a society's insularity and policing the thoughts and behaviors of its members.

The prominence of the church in Edgerton's fictional small towns provides the best indication of the degree to which the relative freedom and heterogeneity in the depictions of the Appalachian frontier such as we find in works by Chappell and Smith have suffered decline in the Piedmont. Reynolds Price argues that mountaineers settled the frontier in flight from the racial heterogeneity of the flatlands.[20] Geography accomplished in the West what the church was used to accomplish in the Piedmont. The lack of racial conflict in Appalachia might, therefore, be one of the reasons for the relatively diminished role of the church in social organization. Or, to be more generous to the mountaineers, the church was not needed to justify a system of racial exploitation, as it was in the lowlands. Certainly religion was never absent in Appalachia; however, the proliferation of Jack tales throughout the region—many of them featuring a parasitic minister at odds with a resourceful yeoman's son named Jack (as in Orville Hicks's rendition of "Jack and the Heifer's Hide"[21])—suggests a healthy resistance to excessive influence of organized religion. Rarely in the fiction of Chappell or Smith does the church significantly undermine the yeoman value of independence so prominent in the culture. Religious zealots in Chappell's works are relegated to the margins of society, as is the evangelical, self-righteous Canary of I Am One of You Forever, who attempts to pester Virgil Campbell into salvation. In Chappell's Midquest, even Ole Fred's religious grandmother remains tolerant of the idiosyncrasies of others, as her lecture to the boy in "My Grandmother Washes Her Feet" demonstrates.

In Smith's fiction, religion is typically of a Pentecostal variety and proves to be a vital force in the lives of individuals, one that brings them into closer contact with their deepest selves. Smith's characters speak in tongues ("Tongues of Fire"), handle snakes (Saving Grace), and express their prophetic visions in what folklorists typically call "outsider art" ("News of the Spirit"). Religion is often associated with sexuality in the lives of Smith's characters, as in the intertwining of the spiritual and sexual awakening Richard Burlage experiences in Oral History. Sex and spirituality are also interdependent forces in the work of Betts and Price, as in The Sharp Teeth of Love and A Long and Happy Life. In Edgerton's fiction, on the other hand, religion and sex are completely incompatible; of all forms of thought and behavior control furthered by the church and community, Edgerton suggests that the undermining of a person's sexuality serves as the most deleterious to individual autonomy and independence.

In Clear Pictures, Reynolds Price asserts that of all the contributions made by African Americans to the white South, one of the most significant and "paradoxical gifts . . . was sexual health" (107). Because of what he acknowledges as a history of "hidden and often monstrous sexual exchange between the two races," Price argues that the white South accessed the more natural and healthy sexuality of black Americans and avoided the "merciless body-hatred that blighted so much of the white republic" (109). Whether Price's argument is accurate or tainted by romanticism, his observations shed light on a very different situation in the fundamentalist families and more thoroughly segregated communities who populate Edgerton's fiction. Just as Price recognizes a sexual component (most often a homosocial one) as integral to the daily intercourse between the two races in Warren County, Raney's community exhibits a fear of sexuality that can be linked to their fear of social intercourse between blacks and whites.

In Killers of the Dream Lillian Smith writes convincingly about the widespread connections, throughout the South, between racism, religion, and sexual repression:

By the time we were five years old we had learned, without hearing the words, that masturbation is wrong and segregation is right, and each had become a dread taboo that must never be broken, for we believed God, whom we feared and tried desperately to love, had made the rules concerning not only Him and our parents, but our bodies and Negroes. Therefore when we as small children crept over the race line and ate and played with Negroes or broke other segregation customs that were known to us, we felt the same dread fear of consequences, the same overwhelming guilt that was ours when we crept over the sex line and played with our body or thought thoughts about God or our parents that we knew we must not think. Each was a "sin," each "deserved punishment," each would receive it in this world or the next.[22]

For Lillian Smith, the three principal "lessons" of childhood—fear and love of God (and parents); love of one's own white skin and fear of black skin; and fear of one's own sexuality—become inextricably linked in the subconscious, and so to transgress one taboo is to transgress them all. Within this paradigm, the behavior of Raney and her women kinfolk stems not so much from a calculated effort to establish a white matriarchal power base but, rather, from a fear of trespassing what they view as a divinely ordained order. Their insularity, racism, xenophobia, and sexual frigidity are all subconsciously associated, just as Raney's gradual sexual liberation is necessary for her increasing racial tolerance. In Edgerton's fiction women accept the role of housewife and nurturer equally out of desire and fear—believing that the reproduction in successive generations of a familiar order of social norms, religious beliefs, and taboos is necessary not only for the continuation of community values but for the avoidance of eternal damnation. The rise of matriarchal power in Bethel and Listre is motivated not by a desire for gender equality so much as by a need to maintain a social order the women view as necessary for spiritual and psychological wholeness.

The obvious paradox in the idea that a matriarchy would make use of fundamentalist Christian religion to promote its own power base is that many fundamentalist sects are themselves built on very clearly male chauvinistic tenets, traceable to biblical male chauvinism. For an example of how clearly male chauvinistic Raney's Baptist church is, consider the scene in which Preacher Gordon visits with Raney's family for Sunday lunch. The dinner table discussion moves to a debate about Raney's desire to take a part-time job working in her father's feed store; after filling himself on Doris Bell's fried chicken, the preacher presents his biblically authoritative position on gender roles. "I believe the scripture is quite clear on this," says Preacher Gordon. "The man is the head of the household, the breadwinner so to speak, and the woman is the natural mother of course, whose principal responsibility is to the home itself: especially the raising up of the children under God's word and laws. And then too we understand, or I understand, from the Old Testament that Adam was made by God, in the image of God, *for* God, and that Eve was made by God, from the man, *for* the man" (183). According to Preacher Gordon, a transgression of the biblically sanctioned gender roles, in which women are subordinate and obedient to men, involves the transgression of both a social and a cosmic order.

Both Aunt Naomi and Doris identify Preacher Gordon as an ally against the secular, "liberal" ideas of Raney's new husband, Charles, who proposes that he and Raney share in both career opportunities and childcare responsibilities. These matriarchs clearly identify their primary responsibility of childrearing as central to the maintenance of autonomous Bible-based community values, free from the meddling of a national government and Raney's husband, who threaten to disrupt their carefully maintained relationship to God. "You know," says Preacher Gordon, "the whims of society and government shift like the sands. What's in today is out tomorrow. We need to—" "Build our houses on a *rock*," says Aunt Naomi. "God's truth has been God's truth for so long," says Mama, pointing with her fork. . . . "and I thank God for people like you, Preacher Gordon, who have been called to interpret the Gospel" (185). Naomi and Doris have been conditioned by their culture to accept inequitable gender roles and to accept a passive position relative to the masculine authority of their minister as head of the community, but their behavior in this discussion is anything but passive. Consider, for example, Naomi's readiness to interrupt Preacher Gordon in mid-sentence. And Doris's "pointing with her fork" at the preacher while she thanks God for him is a comically aggressive gesture that at least temporarily silences him. These matriarchs clearly do not perceive masculine forces within their community as a threat to their power; rather, they desire to maintain the familiar order of their community and oppose disruptive forces that threaten to intrude from without.

Marxist feminists ever since Frederick Engels have argued that this division of labor between the sexes provides the foundation for the capitalist patriarchy and all the class inequities resulting from such an economic system. In *Origin of the Family, Private Property, and the State*, Engels describes the relation between husband and wife in terms of class and economics, with the man representing the bourgeoisie and the woman representing the proletariat.[23] In *The Reproduction of Mothering* Nancy Chodorow combines with Engels's emphasis upon socialist reform a neo-Freudian examination of the psychoanalytical dynamics within the family. "Parenting, as an unpaid occupation outside the world of public power," she writes, "entails lower status, less power, and less control of resources than paid work. Women's mothering reinforces and perpetuates women's relative powerlessness."[24] She calls for a correction of this problem by demanding greater involvement of men in the nurturing of children and by demanding socio-economic changes that would allow them to do so (exactly the sort of changes Charles is asking Raney to accept). The other major premises upon which Chodorow bases her argument against the exclusivity of "mothering" by women are related to the isolation of women from a social base of emotional support and political power. This separation of women from one another occurs because of kinship rules, which "organize claims of men on domestic units," and by which "men dominate kinship. Culturally and politically, the public sphere dominates the domestic, and hence men dominate women."[25]

Chodorow discusses geographic rootlessness in an industrial, capitalistic society as the main cause of male domination of kinship. Of course, such an economic basis for these kinship rules is relevant only to cultures in which the men uproot their families because of economic factors. Smith's Appalachian novels provide a geographical motive that yields similar results. However, if women were able to dominate kinship and thereby dominate the domestic units, they would at least theoretically be able to reverse the hierarchical relationship between the domestic and the public spheres—and thereby dominate men. This reversal is exactly what has happened in Raney's community, or at least in her family. That the women have dominated kinship is demonstrated by the lack of bonds among related men and the constant reminder of bonds among related women (where relation includes both "blood kin" and relatives through marriage). In the case of Raney, she dominates kinship by removing her husband from his kinship group and incorporating him into hers. Raney's mother, Doris, dominates kinship by building strong emotional bonds with both her own and her husband's (mostly women) relatives. She then has at her disposal this broad base of emotional and political support as leverage to influence her husband's behavior both in and away from the home.

Raney's aggressive control of kinship in her own family is illustrated not only by her discomfort during her Atlanta mother-in-law's visit but by her frequent insistence that Charles comply with her requests to accompany her on visits to her family more often than the Sunday dinners at her parents. She tells him, "Charles, the entire foundation of my entire family is built on visiting. The family that visits together stays together" (188). To further her case, she explains to him how all her uncles have always dutifully accompanied their wives on family visits. Similarly, Raney's mother expends a considerable amount of energy maintaining family bonds and has therefore become the center of her familial community. Every Sunday she provides dinner at her house for children, brothers, sisters, and in-laws. She enjoys a close relationship with Aunt

Naomi and Aunt Flossie, and she acts as a mother to her brother Nate. She takes care of Uncle Newton whenever Aunt Minnie needs to be away from her house. Doris has even extended her network of nurturing beyond her family to include visits, along with other women, to elderly people or "shut-ins" in her church. With all of these people Doris has established meaningful emotional connections.

By contrast, the three visible men in Raney's family—Charles, Thurman, and Nate—are solitary and incapable of emotional involvement with other men. The level of conversation between Charles and Thurman, for example, is virtually limited to baseball scores. Though Nate and Thurman work with each other daily at the feed store, during one of his drinking binges Nate curses his brother-in-law (91) and reveals that, despite their friendship, he identifies Thurman primarily as a rival for the attention of Doris. Because of a similar rivalry over Raney, Nate regularly shows his antipathy for Charles. Though Thurman and Nate spend considerable time at the store with other men, their most significant relationships are limited to the nuclear family. They do not actively seek relationships with extended family but maintain them only passively through the initiative of the women, principally through the opportunity for visiting created by Doris's Sunday meals. Doris enjoys a closer relationship with Aunt Naomi and Aunt Minnie (Thurman's sisters) than Thurman himself enjoys. When Minnie's husband, Uncle Newton, dies, Doris assumes control of the situation and takes her children and Charles over to Minnie's and then to the funeral home to view the body before the wake proper begins. While even Mrs. Fuller from the church is there with Minnie, Thurman is conspicuously absent from his sister's side. With respect to nurturing and emotional support, in this culture gender is clearly more of a determinant than familial relations. Women not only serve as nurturers for the men and children in their families, they serve as nurturers for each other. As a result, women have a large network of emotional support among other women. Men, by and large, have only their mothers and their wives.

The difference Chodorow notices between men and women in societies where women are the primary nurturers—that "the basic feminine sense of self is connected to the world" while "the basic masculine sense of self is separate"[26]—is evident throughout Raney's extended family, as it was in Edgerton's own extended family. Of family gatherings he recalls,

> When I grew up, I had twenty-three aunts and uncles and was an only child and my mother's two favorite sisters were often at our house and we were often at their houses. So in a way it was as if I had three mothers. I grew up with these three women who loved to talk and who loved to tell

stories. Of my uncles, only one really liked to tell stories, and the others, for example, on a Sunday afternoon when family was together would sit on the front porch and their conversations would go something like this. (Long pause. . . .) "Yeah. Looks like it might rain." (Long pause) "Yeah." . . . And then it'd be (Sound of snoring. . . .) But I could go into the kitchen and the women would be talking ninety miles an hour about people, usually about people in our family, stories about an incident that had happened the day before, or decades before, and little details about things going on in their lives. I heard many stories about family members I'd never met. So, I grew up listening to women talk.[27]

Like Raney and her siblings, in Edgerton's family the many articulate women—especially the two childless aunts who virtually became additional mothers of an only child—provided the family history, values, and emotional support system, while the men remained outside in their respective silent solitudes.

Although Chodorow argues that paid work in the public sphere entails higher status than parenting, which "reinforces and perpetuates women's relative powerlessness,"[28] little evidence of such appears in Raney's community. Quite the contrary, by virtue of their solidarity—and the virtual lack of solidarity among working men—the housewives in Raney's family and community not only dictate family values but ensure the propagation of those values in the public sphere. The Sunday dinner scene with Preacher Gordon serves as a case in point. Although Raney's mother and her Aunt Naomi fervently voice their support for Preacher Gordon—as when Doris Bell says, "I thank God for people like you, Preacher Gordon, who have been called to interpret the Gospel" (185)—both women exhibit relative indifference to what the preacher actually has to say. He attempts to give them a sermon about gender roles, and they are much more concerned about ensuring that the pickle dish makes its way around the table and that everyone has lemon in their iced tea. This scene comically dramatizes the resistance of the *domestic* to domination by the *public* sphere. In their easy acceptance of Preacher Gordon's authority, Naomi and Doris demonstrate that he poses no threat to their autonomy. He is, rather, their ally in the perpetuation of matriarchal values, represented by the primacy of "the family."

In her examination of the Sunday school movement from 1865 through 1915, Sally G. McMillen finds a widespread condition throughout white southern Protestant churches to be that despite the fact that "females formed the majority of Sunday-school teachers and pupils" and that the Sunday school movement accounted for "75 to 85 percent of all new church members,"[29] women were systematically excluded from leadership positions. During this

period, men exclusively "managed Sunday-school boards and publishing depart-
ments and served as colporteurs, superintendents, and missionaries."[30] (Decades
later in Raney's church, notably the minister, the head deacon, and all other
leaders mentioned are men.) In her examination of Sunday-school literature
from 1865–1915, McMillen finds a deeply entrenched male chauvinism. Although all denominations "insisted upon women knowing their rightful place,"
"white Baptists were most insistent upon reinforcing this message."[31]

Ironically, despite the church's role in promulgating female subordina-
tion to men, the church, and more specifically the Sunday-school movement,
provided the South's primary vehicle for empowering women. In the same
Sunday-school literature that insisted that women know their rightful place,
females—and, more significantly, *young* females—were portrayed as "society's
moral force; they corrected the errant and supposedly engaged in exemplary
behavior. In Sunday-school fiction, boys inevitably disobeyed; girls often reminded them to behave. . . . As long as the goal was Christian in nature, apparently women's assertiveness was acceptable."[32] Within a value system that
privileges obedience to God's laws as found in the Bible and disseminated by
one's teachers and elders, the behaviors identified as female—obedience, self-
sacrifice—logically are privileged over behaviors this society associates with
maleness—disobedience, rowdiness, self-assertion (notably, the very frontier
values that are threatened by the encroachment of civilization). Furthermore,
as McMillen points out, Sunday school provided an opportunity for girls to
compete with boys intellectually, usually besting them not only as examples of
appropriate comportment but at memorizing Bible verses and demonstrating
an understanding of scripture. Their typically female teachers also provided
vivid role models of female assertiveness. For these teachers, Sunday schools
"added a new dimension to women's duties; not only could mothers influence
their children in the home, but they could teach youngsters in the Sunday classroom as well. . . . For women accustomed to being confined to the home, the
Sunday school offered a sphere in which to spread their influence and develop
a sense of community."[33] So thorough was this feminization of Sunday school
that churches found it increasingly difficult to find young male teachers to
serve as appropriate role models for boys. According to a 1904 edition of the
North Carolina Baraca Newsletter, three quarters of the boys left Sunday school
as they entered young manhood.[34] This same gendered division between a
feminized church and a masculinized secular world appears throughout *Raney*.

That the church represents the interests of women in Raney's community is
suggested by the men who congregate around Thurman Bell's store and com-
plain about "the people down at the church" (191). Thurman's store represents
the geographical center of maleness and secularity in the novel—in opposition

to the church, which represents an extension of the family unit. Men frequent Thurman's store to find some level of personal independence from the domination of women in the family and the church, but Thurman's store is situated at the political and ideological margin of the community—on the darker side of town—and its identity is threatened by the political clout of the center, situated in the church and the family. Thurman's store, with its oil-can spittoons, the rough wooden floor, and a quarter inch of dust on the tops of the canned food, seems more a men's hangout than a center of commerce. In contrast to the order and neatness of their homes, this is a place where men can come and feel comfortable, without needing to keep up appearances. They can tell crude jokes and buy pornographic magazines and relax—as long as the women don't find out. Train's Place occupies a similar position in *Trouble*. With its coolers of beer and pinup calendar, Train's Place is under constant attack by the Baptist Church and the church mothers like Alease Toomey, who prohibits her son from entering the store and allows her husband to enter only when paying for gasoline.

The fact that Thurman's store is a public place, accepted—or at least tolerated—in the community, requires that all participants practice a certain degree of subterfuge: the pornographic magazines are sold from under the counter. When Raney discovers them during her part-time work in her father's store, she complains to Sneeds, the manager, saying, "I just don't think it's right. If it was, they wouldn't have to be under the counter." "Well, yes," Sneeds explains, "but if you put them out where everybody can see them, old Mr. Brooks [a deacon in Raney's church] is liable to have the sheriff on us" (192). The matriarchal imposition of "family values" poses an even greater threat to the independence of the public sphere when Sneeds is wrongfully accused of attempting to purchase the services of a prostitute in White Level. Over Sunday dinner, with the righteous indignation of a sermon still ringing in their ears, Doris, Raney, and Aunt Naomi pressure Thurman to fire his store manager. When Thurman refuses, saying simply that he refuses to fire a man who has not been convicted, his normally voluble wife laconically answers, "It's your store." The irony in her statement rings loud and clear during the following silence that envelops the dinner table; the reader cannot help but wonder if it is indeed his store. How secure is his autonomy over its affairs? If Sneeds were, in fact, proven guilty, Thurman quite likely might yield to the pressure from the women in his family to fire his store manager.

Although Thurman's store gives him control of the family's monetary resources, he shows no signs of exploiting this control to gain leverage either in his family or in the community. Nancy Chodorow's generalization about the correlation between the woman's lack of control over financial resources and a lack of social and political status does not apply in this instance. The one political body in which Thurman and Doris actively participate is the Bethel Free Will Baptist Church, and if their church is like most a correlation certainly exists between the size of their tithes and the influence they have in the political decisions of the church. However, because such tithes generally represent the contributions of the *family* to the church, both Doris and Thurman thereby gain political clout. And considering that Doris is more outspoken and more involved in church affairs, she is more likely than her husband to exercise this power.

More significant, Thurman makes no attempt to use his control of finances to gain control of family decisions. Thurman allows his wife complete autonomy over the propagation and enforcement of values in the home. Whenever a debate arises over religion or race or Uncle Nate's alcoholism, Thurman quietly slips out of the room. In exchange for his deference in family matters, he expects control of his own business affairs. His reluctance to allow his daughter to work part time in the store may result from his ideas about gender roles; he perhaps worries about exposing Raney to the male environment of the store. However, Thurman probably worries at least as much about *her* effect on that environment. When Raney tells him of her plans to clean up the store to attract more customers, he answers, "Honey, don't nothing much but farmers come in there. We sell more cigarettes, drinks, chicken wire, fence posts, and such than anything else. No need to try to make it into something that won't have no market" (176). He is noticeably reluctant to see his store transformed into a place in which a woman would feel comfortable.

Although the Marxist aspects of Chodorow's argument do not apply to Raney's family, her psychoanalytic insights into the need for shared parenting are very applicable. Both Raney and her Uncle Nate suffer as a result of absent father figures. When Nate shoots himself, for example, Thurman seems suddenly to recognize the dangers of yielding all authority in family matters to matriarchal control. Raney tells how at the wake, "Daddy just sat like somebody had slapped him, and mother told about what had happened over and over and all about how she had tried through the years to get Uncle Nate straight and that she guessed she had failed" (138). His silence at the wake most likely stems in part from a sense of guilt for consistently deferring to Doris rather than involving himself in his brother-in-law's problems, beyond supplying him with the job at the gas pumps. By remaining silent while Doris infantilizes Nate and preaches to him about his sins, Thurman is complicit in Nate's domination by an overbearing mother figure and the puritanical moral imperatives that she imposes upon him. For this very reason, however, it is highly unlikely that Nate would have responded to any of Thurman's further efforts.

If Charles is struggling with an Oedipus complex, Nate's case is much more severe. He identifies with his sister as if she were his mother; she is doubtlessly the most physically and emotionally recognizable image of their mother available to him. Each time he comes home drunk, he looks for Doris, even though he knows she will chastise him (84–86). In fact, that she does so makes her behavior even more recognizably maternal to him. On one of the occasions he comes home drunk, Raney scolds him and tells him, "You're in trouble," to which he responds, "I was in trouble when I was born" (89), thereby associating his present behavior with his "naughty" behavior as a child, which is reflected in the attitude of Raney's younger brother, Norris.

It is impossible to know all the causes of Nate's alcoholism and whether his war experience is indeed the main cause or whether it is simply a convenient rationalization for his family. But an equally likely source of trouble may be located in his childhood. The tyrannical puritanism of Edgerton's mother characters like Doris (and her mother?) creates a situation in which it is potentially impossible for a child to gain a reasonable degree of independence from his primary identification with his mother and thus successfully resolve his oedipal behavior.

Although his timing is poor, Charles offers one insightful suggestion: he tells Raney—after Nate has died—that her mother's care for Nate was the one thing Nate did not need, that "maybe what he needed was to take care of himself" (142). Thurman's employment of Nate at the feed store is a case of too little too late. If, indeed, Nate's troubles are related to his childhood, he needed the presence of a nurturing father figure in the home earlier in life to diffuse the primary identification with his mother. Nate exemplifies a certain type of southern male, estranged from the father and overly dependent upon the mother.

This observation was borne out by Edgerton, in a personal interview, where he commented on his own close bond with his mother as well as his own efforts to gain some independence from her. This close bond, he says, was

> a consequence partly of her having lost a child before me and being forty when I was born, and it was a curious mixture of being protective, in some cases overprotective, and pushing me out to do things on my own, making me be independent. . . . My father taught me baseball and took me hunting. He kind of introduced hunting and baseball to me, but he was less directly involved with what I did than my mother, who was sort of pushing me into music, pushing me into this, pushing me into that and the other. . . . You know, my having close ties to my mother was a norm for me as a person growing up. I didn't know people didn't have their mother also taking piano when you're taking piano, for example. On the other

hand, my father, who was less involved in my upbringing, was very fright-ful of water and airplanes and stuff. He wouldn't let me swim in the deep end of the pool. He didn't want me to play football. He couldn't go to the airport when I left to go into the Air Force. He just couldn't quite handle that. Whereas my mother, of all things, was saying, "Join the Air Force. Fly airplanes." She was the first person who flew with me, too . . . when I got my private pilot's license. She was sixty-two, and she had never been in an airplane. And I took her up, the first ride, the first of anybody. So you've got that kind of interesting contrast, her being there, number one, but look at what she's about: she's saying that her son can fly an airplane, maybe kill himself. She's being supportive of that, but, at the same time, she's going to be there.

So when I was older, I had the experience . . . of talking to her about all this and saying to her, "I want to have a friendship with you. I don't want to have a mother-son relationship with you." Hell, I don't know how old I was when I said that to her, but it was after the Air Force. And, she was standing at the kitchen bar, and she turned around and looked at me, and she said, "You're right. I grant you your leave." Just like that. So that was pretty amazing, that she would be able to say that and that I would be able to hear it. You know you don't know unconsciously what kind of ties are there and how they're there, but at least you have this sort of agree-ment that this is the way it is now, and it's not the way it was, right or wrong. But there was a powerful bond there. Again, it was the conse-quence of my being an only child, her having lost a child, her believing that she was not going to have children, and her believing that a child would be a gift from God.[35]

If men in this culture suffer under the domination of their mothers, women are even more vulnerable, as demonstrated by a comparison of how Raney's younger siblings, Mary Faye and Norris, are socialized. Already, at the age of eleven, Mary Faye practices the role of mother, repeating to her younger brother the prohibitions of their mother. When Norris recalls how he promised his mother that he would "try not to sin," Mary Faye corrects him, insisting, "She said not to *do* it . . . not just 'try' not to" (114). For Norris there is some leeway, allowing him a certain amount of freedom and independence to choose and experiment. Whereas both Mary Faye and Raney are likely to benefit from the expectation that they will participate in a circle of female nurturers, they also suffer from the greater loss of freedom that comes with such an expectation.

Raney can be identified with a tradition of female Huck Finns who populate much of the twentieth-century fiction by southern women writers—teenage female characters such as Carson McCullers's Frankie Addams, Bobbie Ann Mason's Samantha Hughes, and Doris Betts's Violet Karl and Mary Grace Thompson—characters who rebel against societal expectations to find a greater degree of personal independence. Granted, Raney's rebellion is not nearly as extravagant or free-spirited as in these other cases, and the muted rebellion she finds possible comes much later, during her early twenties, after she has married; nevertheless, just as Huck narrowly escapes the clutches of Widow Douglass and Miss Watson, who are trying to "sivilize" him, Raney gains a sufficient distance from her mother—and thereby from their insular culture—in order to think and act more independently. Although Raney acts as an apologist for her culture throughout the novel, she does gradually begin to reconsider critically its many judgments and values. This reevaluation of her culture results principally from her ongoing debate with her liberal husband about matters ranging from race relations to the role of sex in their marriage. One of the most disruptive, "liberal," changes Charles pursues is his insistence in sharing with his wife the responsibilities of childcare, wage-earning, and housework. Because Charles refuses passively to accept the gendered division of public and private spheres that characterizes Raney's community, he threatens to dismantle its matrilineal transmission of power and to rear a future generation that—as Chodorow proposes—will include both males and females capable of nurturing.

What does this change in parenting—and, thus, the disappearance of such rigid gender roles—predict for the legacy of the yeoman value of independence? In one sense, it certainly suggests its obsolescence. In such a society, there is hardly a place for the masculine frontier ideal of the independent, solitary male. Considering that Charles himself is largely influenced by his own mother and is one of many examples in Edgerton's fiction of the civilized (or feminized) male, he is likely to pass on to his own children the values of coalition building that likewise appear among the women of Raney's family. On the other hand, the presence of two parents as nurturers, who will bring competing values and interests to a family, will help break down the monolithic role of the mother as authority and thereby create greater personal autonomy and independent thinking on behalf of the children—male and female. Furthermore, as the gender divisions between public and domestic spheres break down, and women and men find their own identities constructed less exclusively in one or the other, the nuclear family—as opposed to the extended family—is likely to become the basic unit of society, which will become even more the case as families become more geographically mobile. In such a changed world, the primary threats to individual autonomy may appear not from the family so much as from outside sources.

In Memory of Junior: Welcome to the Farm

In Memory of Junior presents even more dramatically than *Raney* the transition from a rural farming culture to an urban one. In his fifth novel, Edgerton bypasses the small town in his depiction of a farming community rapidly suc-cumbing to the expansion of a corporate information technology park, Tech-Comm Commons. The issues raised by the novel are similar to those that appear in *Raney:* What changes will people from an insular, traditional culture have to make to survive in a radically altered world? What ideals hobble them from generation to generation? Which values will they painfully and gradually discard, and which will they preserve?

In *Junior,* the lives of the Bales clan are as circumscribed and determined—or more so—than that of the characters from *Raney* and *Trouble* living in Listre and Bethel. Just as family, church, and community in *Raney* all function to establish rigid social norms, in *Junior* this function is served equally well by family alone, suggesting how even at such an early stage of social organization —the farming clan—frontier individualism has suffered decline. In fact, the novel's depiction of the Bales family suggests that the yeoman family serves as the basic unit of social organization in Edgerton's fiction, upon which the small town merely expands.

The theme of ancestor worship, an impediment to personal freedom in both *Raney* and *Trouble,* becomes even more of a problem in *Junior.* Raney remarks, "Rules get set by somebody hundreds of years ago and they are hard to break, like rules about what you can and can't talk about" (162). In *Junior,* Evelyn McCord Bales similarly observes of her mother- and father-in-law, "The two of them, Mr. and Mrs. Bales, were as set in their ways as stumps. They had learned to survive like ants, foxes, rabbits making their appointed rounds. They didn't have time to develop new tactics, plans, or ideas that weren't in their blood when they were born or passed down to them to live by, to stay alive by."[36] Evelyn's comment echoes the perspective of Henry Adams, for whom south-erners "had no mind" but only "temperament."[37] Like Welty's Fairchilds, the Bales family is virtually oblivious to the world outside the confines of their family and its farming history. As in *Delta Wedding*—and as in Twain's tale of the Grangerfords and Shepherdsons in *Huckleberry Finn*—marriage presents a crisis in so many of Edgerton's novels because it threatens to undermine, through cultural exchange, the continuity of family values and traditions. In fact, Raney's husband's surname, *Shepherd,* suggests a direct comparison to Twain's Shepherdsons.

Unlike the successful marriage between Raney and Charles, however, the Bales family of *Junior* fails to resolve this crisis in a positive manner and suffers the subsequent collapse. Because Glenn Bales cannot break his emotional dependence upon family, his wife Evelyn, who is desperate to leave the farm and move to town, abandons her family and escapes with a lesbian lover named Honor Walters. Evelyn later observes of her husband, "Glenn was bound to the farm, to his mother and father, brothers and sisters. Bound in a way he was never bound to me, bound with thick cords, while his binding to me was with tiny, weak strings" (104–5). Glenn suffers from the same problem that plagues Raney: a socially incestuous veneration of one's own family and the inability to break away from parental authority. In twice remarking that Glenn was "such a baby" (17, 108), Evelyn notes his inability to assert his independence from the domination of his parents. Similarly, Glenn's aging sisters venerate their dead elders to the extent that they reject both of Glenn's wives and remain single and childless themselves. In the same way that Raney fears miscegenation, Bette and Anse fear the dilution of Bales blood through any form of intermarriage. Bette remembers that, when Evelyn abandoned her sons, Mama Bales said, "getting the Devil's blood out of them boys would not be easy, if at all possible" (75). "Blood," which manifests itself primarily by loyalty to kin and reverence for parental authority and family order, is the primary determinant of character for the Bales women.

One very significant difference between the social order of the Bells and the Baleses—associated with the difference between life in town and life on the farm—is that the former is obviously matriarchal and the latter is seemingly as obviously patriarchal, with the long deceased Papa Bales serving as paterfamilias whom his children acknowledge as the ultimate source of authority. Papa Bales is a "rock" (95) in the same way that the scriptures are a "rock" (185) for Raney and her family. Glenn "worships" Papa Bales, whom he remembers being "as serious and stern as God Himself" (102), calling to mind Lillian Smith's observation regarding how southern parents so often "represent God, in the family" (79). Papa Bales's imposing presence in his family likely results, in part, from his daily regimen of farm work, the kind of hard labor that cultivates sternness and, in some cases, aggression; notably, Raney's gentle, retiring father is exempted from such labor by his ownership of a community store that services farmers. Furthermore, out on the farm the women do not have at their disposal such an extensive support network as that enjoyed by Raney's mother in town. Finally, the patriarchal structure of the farm family is furthered by the primacy of land as a commodity, inherited by male children, thereby allowing them to control kinship. In the Bales family, the male child, Glenn, has inherited the family farm, and his wife Evelyn, who also grew up on a farm, moved to the Bales farm. Despite the protestations of Glenn's sisters, Bette and Anse, that they have spent their lives "working" the farms, as long as their brother lives they have no legal claim to the property and fritter away their long spinsterhoods in "those little houses over on Tully Drive" (214).

Unlike Raney Bell, whose primary filial identification is with her mother, Bette and Anse have invested most of their emotional energy in their father, and they even more closely fit Freud's description of "persons who never overcome the parental authority and never or very imperfectly, withdraw their affection from their parents."[38] For either of these sisters to *overcome* their allegiance to family would involve serious costs, both emotional and economic. If Bette or Anse left the farm, they must realize that they would put themselves in the same helpless position in which Evelyn finds herself when she marries Glenn and moves to his family's farm, where she finds herself and her children dominated by women in-laws. The advantage Raney enjoys from living in a small town is that she can maintain the network of emotional support with women of her own blood kin while gradually extending her emotional connection beyond her family. When she marries Charles, she remains in a position of relative power because of her family network. Furthermore, by living in town she has access to Listre Community College and the possibility of working part time away from home, opportunities less available to the farm-bound women of *Junior*. Even if the small-town matriarchies in Edgerton's fiction limit the autonomy of both men and women, such communities at least offer significantly greater autonomy to women than do the patriarchal yeoman farms that preceded them.

As with Lee Smith's novels, Edgerton's invite a feminist critique of the yeoman farm in their depiction of the numerous women who abandon their children to escape the domination of their husbands' extended families. Like Evelyn in *Junior*, in *The Floatplane Notebooks* Rhonda leaves her husband Meredith and their newborn son to the care of in-laws who deny her any identity other than mother of the newest Copeland boy child. "It's just one big happy family that cooks, and talks about dead people," Rhonda complains, "and don't never ask anybody about their family, and if you don't *have* a family, or if you have a shitty one, you feel like shit. . . . Goddamn, *you* birth a baby and then put up with five or six in-law mamas and I don't know what all else. I just want to sing a little music with a band. That's where my life is."[39]

If women suffer from such rigid gender norms, so do men, who usually lack any ability whatsoever to function in the role of nurturer. One of Edgerton's most common characters is the taciturn father, incapable of communicating with his family, lacking in male role models who serve as nurturers. These men have been socialized to function in roles such as farmer, soldier, and factory worker, which require them to endure long periods of emotional and communicative deprivation. In the home, their role is limited to the role of lawgiver.

Unlike Raney's father, Thurman, a gentle, retiring man whose wife has allowed him to abdicate this traditional male role, the men in *Junior* dutifully assume the role of lawgiver. For example, when Glenn Bales returns home on the weekends from his job as a traveling salesman, he listens as his sisters Bette and Anse report on the bad behavior of his boys and then metes out the appropriate punishment, just as his father before him had done:

> And there's no choice in the world in the years to come [after Evelyn leaves] when I get home on weekends—from Wadesboro or Salisbury—but to, of course, whip Faison for all he's done wrong, and to whip Tate for all he's done wrong. . . . If I didn't whip the boys for doing wrong then there would be a great worry around in the air, a great uncertainty. If I didn't whip them, I might be whipped, still, by Papa, who was as serious and stern as God Himself. Papa feeling like whipping me would be as bad as him actually doing it because Papa's bad feeling would bring me to shame at what I would be doing to him, hurting him, shaming him, putting him in such a fix that he might crumble apart, fly apart, in front of my eyes.
>
> You know, about Papa. He could always stand hard field work. He was a real man. He could bring his raging up to the surface, but it seems to me now when I think on it that he couldn't somehow stand any other feelings rising up to the surface. That's the way he had to be. All that other was never there because it would have made him weak somehow, you see. It would have. He was steady, a rock. That way he could keep his bearing. We all needed him to keep his bearing, his power. Even now we all need that. Even now that he's dead.
>
> I think I kind of worship—or something—them all, standing there, all dressed in white, working in the fields, tending crops, plowing. . . . And this must have been the same with Mama and Papa. They must have remembered the ones before them that way. (94–95)

As in Chappell's Appalachia, where "taciturnity is locally regarded as a virtue having something to do with valor and manliness" (*Look Back*, 183), Edgerton's male characters learn communicative dysfunction from their fathers. Just as the primary narrative development in *Raney* involves the hope of Raney avoiding a repetition of her mother's frigidity and conservatism, *Junior* involves the possibility of Tate Bales overcoming—in his relationship with his son Morgan—his father's (and his father's father's) communicative dysfunctions.

In *Junior*, however, the catalyst for change comes not from the future but from the past. Whereas Raney's new husband from Atlanta—to whom she must accommodate herself and her culture—represents a future urban and suburban South, in *Junior* change is initiated by the return to town of aged Grove

McCord, Tate Bales's maternal uncle, a renegade and representative of frontier independence who challenges the ordered life of the Bales family farm. Ever since boyhood, Tate and his brother, Faison, found in their Uncle Grove a surrogate father—while their actual father, Glenn, was emotionally absent and literally absent as a result of his job as a traveling salesman—leaving the boys to the mercy of their domineering Bales aunts, Bette and Anse. Grove McCord interrupted the ordered farm life of endless chores by taking the boys fishing and hunting, flying in his airplane, and generally initiating them into the freedoms of frontier manhood. Furthermore he was willing to listen to them and to tell them irreverent stories and jokes that their Bales kinfolk deemed inappropriate. Grove's return, in old age, to North Carolina from his home in Arkansas coincides with Glenn's death, and his presence facilitates Tate's grieving, as well as Tate's attempts to break through the communicative barriers that separate him from his son and brother.

Having convinced himself that he is dying of cancer, Grove returns from Arkansas to be buried near family in North Carolina. A drifter, lawbreaker, and general hell-raiser, Grove has long been for his nephews Tate and Faison a refuge from the rigid order of the Bales family and an alternative to the role model of lawgiver provided by their father. Grove's return provokes the smoldering animosity of Bette and Anse Bales, who have never forgiven his sister Evelyn for bringing that "queer" McCord blood into their family. The antagonism between these sisters and Grove represents the same conflict between the order of civilization and the freedom of the frontier present in most southwestern humor and in Chappell's Kirkman novels. In each case, women represent the order of farm life, as opposed to the rootlessness of male drifters and agents of change. Indeed Grove McCord bears numerous similarities to Chappell's Uncle Luden, who likewise returns from the West to his kinfolks' farm in North Carolina, where he drinks and womanizes and generally stirs up trouble. As a rambler and adventurer and a lover of the West, Grove represents the earliest phase in the history of the yeoman, the settlement of the frontier, a phase that has long been superseded in the Bales and Bell families by civilization, roots, church, family order, and upward social mobility.

In his 1949 study, *Plain Folk of the Old South*, Frank Owsley describes how consistently the frontier of unsurveyed lands was first occupied by two waves of immigrants. First came the hunter-trappers, who led a seminomadic life, occupying the Indian territory, where game and rich pastureland were most abundant. Next came the "main body of frontiersmen," the "genuine herdsmen" who occupied the "zone of unsurveyed lands at a reasonably safe distance from the Indian border."[40] Until nearly the end of the eighteenth century, Owsley finds that the Piedmont was "devoted primarily to grazing livestock"—often wild swine, cattle, and horses of Spanish origin, and not infrequently appropriated from Indians.[41] These herdsmen, often cowboys living in tents, led a markedly more independent life than the farmers who pressured them to move farther west. Contrary to the widespread belief that slaveowners forced plain white farmers onto the poor soil and rugged terrain of the pine barrens and mountains, Owsley shows how the more prevailing conflict in the evolving South arose between herdsmen and the yeoman farmers. This latter group was constantly moving westward to occupy newly surveyed territories, forcing the herdsmen to move themselves beyond the reach of farm settlements with their fenced-in fields and pastureland. Owsley calls this conflict an "old phenomenon," one dating back to ancient times. Indeed, the myth of Cain and Abel alludes to the ancient conflict between herdsmen and agriculturalists. According to Owsley, nearly always has an "agricultural economy . . . driven the livestock grazier into the deserts and the mountains."[42] During the nineteenth century, William H. Sparks observed Mississippi herdsmen, whom he calls "refugees from a growing civilization consequent upon a denser population and its necessities."[43] As civilization marched steadily westward, the pioneer herdsmen were faced with the choice of advancing westward along with the frontier or becoming farmers themselves and adjusting to a life rooted in a place, which frequently included demands of family, church, and community, demands that challenged the complete autonomy and independence the former herdsmen had known on the frontier.

The antagonism in *Junior* between Grove McCord (the rounder who has returned from the West) and his farm-bound sisters-in-law implies just such a conflict between herdsman and yeoman farmer. Whereas Grove restlessly pursues adventure and independence, Bette and Anse obsess over the inheritance of the family farm. Much more than the Bales men, they are deeply invested in preserving familial order, represented by maintenance of family bloodline and appropriate behavior. The conflict between Grove and the Bales sisters points to the gendered quality of the conflict between herdsman and yeoman. Although the Bales family appears to be patriarchal, the ordered life of the farm actually furthers the collectivist interests of women, just as Grove's frontier individualism threatens those interests. The contrast between Grove and the domesticated (feminized) Bales men suggests a similar reading. Significantly neither Tate nor Glenn (nor even Papa Bales?) assumes the role of lawgiver out of a desire to promote their own personal interests. Rather, they do so because it is expected of them, because to abdicate the role would be to violate the social contract into which they were born.

Although Grove opposes the order and tradition associated with farm life, he restores to the male descendants of that farm the masculine frontier values of autonomy and independence that have been attenuated by the feminine values of order and stability. Edgerton suggests that such a restoration is necessary both for a healthy sense of self and for healthy relationships among men. In his forties, Faison remembers spending more *quality time* hunting and fishing and "stuff like that" during the six months as a teenager that he spent with his uncle out west than he spent in his whole life with his father (53–54). In modeling himself after Grove ever since, Faison has rejected the family of his father and the tyranny of their value system. Like Grove, he has refused to compromise his liberty by finding a career, preferring instead to do odd jobs that give him time to hunt and fish with his stepson, Junior. Faison's brother, Tate, also fondly remembers their uncle. He remembers flying in Uncle Grove's 1946 Super Cruiser as a child.and buys a replica of the plane to share the experience with his son, Morgan. He identifies with Grove, but Tate has not allowed Grove to replace his father in the way that Faison has. Unlike his older brother, Tate has not replaced the Bales value system with Grove's. Rather, Tate has become a workaholic like his father. He becomes emotionally invested in the Bales farm (Faison wants to sell it) and reverentially submits to the authority of his father and his aunts in a way that Faison refuses to do. When their father dies, however, Tate becomes more capable of challenging the values of order and parental authority so firmly entrenched in the Bales family.

Junior culminates with a fishing trip to North Carolina's Outer Banks, where Tate and Faison hope to relax after enduring their father's funeral. Grove, Faison's good-ol'-boy friend Jimmy, and Tate's son, Morgan, are along for a weekend of fishing, poker playing, drinking, cursing, trading tall tales, and other exhibitions of male bonding. Tate and Faison work through their differences, admitting the secretive jealousies they each have harbored over the years. Morgan, who has always resisted the advances of his domineering Bales relatives, is won over (like Tate and Faison) by his Great Uncle Grove's joking and storytelling and general rebellion against authority. Still struggling to acclimate himself to the loss of his father, Tate's sense of an ordered world suffers further diminishment when he and Faison discover from Grove the story of their mother's escape from the farm with her lesbian lover—a story the Bales family has suppressed for four decades.

As in most of Edgerton's fiction, the changing family order in *Junior* represents the changing social and economic order of the entire region. As the farmland around Summerlin is paved over by the expanding TechComm Commons, the Bales and McCord families undergo the painful generational transition from farmer to, eventually, computer specialist. As the novel ends, Tate's son matriculates at Duke to study computer science. Like the son of Raney and Charles Shepherd, Morgan is the bearer of values and traditions from diverse families, from the rural Bales and McCords, as well as his mother's more cosmopolitan family. As a result of this cross-cultural exchange, Morgan will likely accept a wider diversity of people—including the gays and lesbians whom his uncle Faison cannot accept and the "rednecks" to whom his cousin Adam condescends. This evolving inclusiveness is a dynamic present throughout Edgerton's fiction: the breaking down of a social order defined by hierarchical difference and exclusion—to allow for a new, more inclusive and tolerant social order. Despite how desperately the Bales spinsters Anse and Bette cling to the idea of pure blood, the family must change to survive. Nevertheless, the novel presents a contrary impulse to idealize and elegize the purity of the past—the cultural traditions and values that will disappear as each generation becomes increasingly removed from a rural way of life.

More specifically, *Junior* promotes an antiquated frontier ideal of masculinity, while very consciously problematizing that ideal. Edgerton recognizes the threats to male liberty imposed by the feminizing influence of civilization—just as Twain and other frontier humorists had throughout much of the nineteenth century. Contrary to the frontier romances of William Gilmore Simms and James Fenimore Cooper—in which, as Elizabeth Jane Harrison argues, women appear as property of the white patriarchy, analogous to the property they have wrested from the wilderness—in the tradition of the frontier humorists, women serve primarily as a threat to male autonomy in that new wilderness. Of Simms's historical romances, Harrison rightly observes that "white southern womanhood represents this virgin land . . . and by protecting her, the cavalier upholds his patriarchal ideals and defends his homeland from defilement by intruders."[44] In both Simms and Cooper, Harrison observes that white women play a supplementary role to their male counterparts, bringing a "civilizing, moral influence" to the wilderness.[45] In focusing on the pastoral romance, Harrison ignores that other prominent pastoral impulse of nineteenth-century southern literature—southwestern humor. Contrary to the aristocratic vision of Simms, these writers interested in the low-brow experience of the frontier tended to see women not as a passive supplement but rather as a very active threat to the masculine Arcadia they fled the civilized East to find. Just as Simms's cavalier defends his women and homeland from the "defilement by intruders," chroniclers of the old Southwest often identified women as the "intruders" who would defile the wilderness. As Augustus Baldwin Longstreet aphoristically notes in "The Fight": "It is said that a hundred gamecocks will live in perfect harmony together if you do not put a hen with them."[46]

If in some yeoman past the Bales family was truly patriarchal, the family's present and future clearly lie in the hands of women and feminized men: Tate's step-sister, Faye, a corporate lawyer from Charlotte who threatens to possess

the Bales farm to which she has no legitimate claim; Bette and Anse, the spinsters who do ultimately inherit the farm; Tate and his son Morgan (both the
products of overprotective or domineering mother figures), whose college
educations align them with the social and economic orders that have come to
supplant the world of the farmer. In contrast to these characters, the overtly
masculine Grove McCord appears a besieged anachronism. Like the yarn spin-
ners from the Old Southwest, Grove returns to the East from Arkansas, and, to
the delight of his civilized nephews, he never stops telling stories of the grand
old days—when he ran moonshine or revived a poodle by mouth-to-mouth
resuscitation—extravagantly humorous tall tales in which he appears larger-
than-life.

Grove continues to exemplify the frontier individualism of his youth when,
convinced that he is dying of cancer, he plans his own suicide and burial—
instead of submitting to the medical machinery that will rob him of bodily
autonomy. "I ain't gone get hooked up on no tubes," he insists, "and all that
with them foreign juices flowing in my body from no telling where, full of
germs, little blip blip machines going off all over the place, people I don't know
from Adam coming in sticking their finger up my ass" (128). Grove views the
loss of physical autonomy in terms of both a literal and a figurative rape. His
rapists, an anonymous medical establishment, are associated with the other
"foreign" corporate presences in his homeland, and, since in Edgerton's fiction
these forces of order are associated with the feminine impulse to civilize, Grove's
fear might be identified as the fear of a retributive femininity, a reading that
becomes more reasonable in light of the revelation, late in the novel, that he
had years earlier threatened to rape his sister's lesbian lover. The disclosure to
the reader of such a brutal act forces a reconsideration of the charming Grove
McCord and the long-lost, lawless culture he represents. The brutality of
Grove's assault appears even starker, since it is described retrospectively by the
victim herself; however, it might be argued that Honor Walters stands outside
the main narrative, and, because she is ignorant of the intensely close—and
sexual—relationship between Grove and his sister, she fails to understand the
full nature of Grove's act, or of Evelyn's ready forgiveness of it. Although his
attack is clearly a male chauvinistic and proprietary gesture, intended to rescue
Evelyn from the clutches of her "queer" lover, within the novel's larger theme
of blood ties, his act might be seen as an expression of his own helpless attachment to his sister, a love that might help explain Grove's own series of unsuc-
cessful marriages.

Although Grove's male chauvinism will likely prevent a reader from too
thoroughly identifying with him or trusting his judgment, he is clearly the most
colorful character in the novel; compared to the rigid and narrow Bales family,

his irreverent humor is a breath of fresh air—as his real-life model most certainly was for Edgerton. Edgerton collected most of Grove's stories from the five hours of audio tape recordings he made of his own eccentric Uncle Bob, who lived in Florida and enjoyed a variety of careers as carnival worker, "truck driver / moonshine hauler," and the owner of a general store and trailer park.[47] Like Grove, Uncle Bob was a flamboyant outsider from the mainstream of Edgerton's Southern Baptist family, and, as Grove does with his nephews, Uncle Bob made a lasting impression on the young Edgerton through his stories, his candidness, and his treatment of Edgerton as an equal. Edgerton remembers,

> He was very good to me. He was a great uncle. He was always very straight with me and very honest with me and talked to me as if I were an adult and would say anything around me, which could have been dangerous if he had been abusive in any way, but he wasn't. He would tell me stories, straight to me, nobody else, just for me. Here I'm ten years old, eleven years old, and you have this grown man sitting down talking to you, telling you these stories—it was a wonderful experience. I was crazy about him. . . . He would say anything, and he would tell me a lot of stuff that the other family wouldn't tell me, you know, the dirt, family stuff, and he would drink and no one in my family would dare touch a drop of alcohol, much less around me. And we would be going fishing or hunting and he would always have to stop and get a tall Busch. That's what he would always drink, a tall Busch. He'd go into a 7-11 or wherever and come out and pop that thing, and we'd go riding on. So you can imagine someone "sheltered" like me being turned loose around someone like him, with tattoos on his arms, and he would roll his own cigarettes . . . he ran a bar in a trailer park and a service station and grocery store, and his hand was broken where he had hit somebody in the side of the head, and he had shot at him with a gun and there was a hole in the wall—and this was Uncle Bob. . . . He was a little crazy in a way.[48]

Uncle Bob served as the model for not only Uncle Grove McCord but also the slightly tamer Uncle Hawk Copeland of the earlier novel *The Floatplane Notebooks*. Edgerton has remarked that, although he exaggerated Uncle Bob's wildness somewhat for the character of Grove, he slightly understated it for Hawk.[49] Edgerton's black-sheep uncle can be recognized in other outlaw characters in his fiction, including the con man Jack Umstead of *Trouble* and the freelance evangelist L. Ray Flowers of *Lunch at the Piccadilly*. Just as Umstead represents the return of the repressed to the sleepy little Baptist town of Listre in 1950, Edgerton identifies with his Uncle Bob as the repressed masculine element in an otherwise matriarchal family. Not to be confused with the alcoholic

Uncle Nate in *Raney* or his counterpart in *Trouble*, Uncle Raleigh, whose repeated failures at self-control merely serve to further justify the matriarchy's crusade for greater order, as well as its vision of a dualistic universe, both Uncle Grove and Uncle Hawk unrepentantly refuse to be tamed, and the reader seems expected to applaud their rebellion.

The Floatplane Notebooks: Innocents Abroad

If for the purposes of illuminating the world of Edgerton's fiction the dichotomy of masculine and feminine is limited to its respective associations with the principles of liberty and order, or independence and interdependence, then the Bales family of *Junior*, which at first seems thoroughly patriarchal, actually more closely resembles the matriarchies of Edgerton's other novels. The Copelands of *Floatplane* (and their McCord cousins from *Junior*) then stand out as the one truly patriarchal family in all of Edgerton's oeuvre. Unlike the men of the other novels, who have been subjugated to the demands of family order, the Copeland men appear blissfully unfettered, and, by and large, even the Copeland women demonstrate the "masculine," frontier values of liberty and personal autonomy. With the exception of Aunt Esther, the family's lone religious zealot, the Copelands are nominally "Christian" but far from regular churchgoers.

Occasionally the Copeland men find it necessary to hide their doings from the women, as when they routinely hunt on posted land in Florida, but, for the most part, the men and women live in relative harmony. Unlike Esther, who anxiously overprotects her only child, Mark, and hopes that he might one day become a Baptist missionary, Albert's wife, Mildred, is much more lax in her approach to discipline. In contrast to the matriarchal network in *Raney*, Esther is alone in her opposition to the freewheeling behavior of the men. Other women in the family obviously find her prudish, such as elderly Aunt Scrap, who is not above unearthing a little family dirt—against Esther's protests ("Why don't you tell some nice stories?")—or the teenaged Noralee, who eggs Scrap on, saying "I like the ugly ones. . . . Nobody ever tells any of those" (258). The men generally ignore Esther or purposefully bully her into silence, as when Albert responds to her request for "some nice stories" by telling how as children they were told that "a baby started growing in a woman's stomach after a man peed in her mouth, and nine months later the baby came out her asshole" (258).

Of all Edgerton's families, the Copelands are closest in spirit to life on the frontier. Earthy and self-sufficient, they are relatively free from the ideological pressures of the church and small town. In contrast to the landscapes of Bethel and Listre, where the steeple and the blinker light are ubiquitous presences, Summerlin appears to be a more rural area. Since *Floatplane* is set during the period from 1956 to 1971, the farmland around Summerlin has not yet been overwhelmed by urban sprawl and TechComm Commons, as it has been by the time of *Junior*, the early 1990s. Furthermore, whereas the Bales family of *Junior* perpetuates by force a veneration of elders and ancestors, the Copelands do so by charm.

Floatplane is the most pastoral of Edgerton's novels. For more than a hundred years the Copelands have lived an Arcadian existence, resiliently surviving periodic intrusions from the outside world—the Civil War, the typhoid epidemic of 1911—to live a life that is close to nature and that maintains its continuity with the past through shared family stories and family rituals. In fact, the novel's structure derives from the two annual events for which the extended family ritually gathers: the Christmas hunting trip to Uncle Hawk's in Florida and the May grave cleaning at the old family homeplace in North Carolina. The recurrence of these events throughout the novel invokes the pastoral theme of sustainability, of nature's ability to restore life after the death-like state of winter[50]—a restoration essential to the amelioration of the story's tragic ending, when Meredith returns home critically wounded from Vietnam.

The repetition of family rituals also serves to highlight the opposition between the sustainable natural order of the family's insular, Edenic existence, and the intrusion of an artificial and disruptive order from the outside world. This opposition is a hallmark of Edgerton's fiction. In *Raney* and *Junior*, change is a mixed blessing; although Edgerton elegizes the loss of cultural stability that occurs in each novel when an insular culture is breached, he recognizes how the ensuing change is necessary for the continued vitality of the family and culture. In both *Raney* and *Junior*, the disturbance of a long-standing order has the healing effect of lancing a festering sore. Change restores life and health. In *Floatplane*, however, change and the disruption of an insular culture are presented in more purely negative terms. As in Milton's version of Eden, death intrudes from the outside (in the form of the Vietnam War) to destroy the sustainable and essentially healthy order of the Copeland clan.

Even though the Copelands are no longer farmers, they still thoroughly demonstrate the self-sufficiency of the yeoman. Uncle Hawk, who brags that he is "too tan" for "paper work," owns a "combination gas station, café, hardware-grocery store, and fruit stand." He explains his profession to strangers as "transportation and digestion" (53–54), a phrase that suggests his association with the most basic level of social organization, the nomadic hunter-gatherer, an association supported by his hosting of the family's annual Christmas bird hunts. These hunts, which always take place on posted land, demonstrate how the Copelands exhibit the hunter-gatherer's *and* the frontier herdsman's non-proprietary attitudes toward the earth. Bliss, who has married into the family, is shocked when she accompanies the men for a hunt and watches as Uncle Hawk pulls a barbed wire fence out of the ground so that they can drive over it. Afterward he fixes the fence and cuts a pine branch to erase their tire tracks. On their annual southern migrations to Florida, the Copelands take their hunting dogs along in the car, as well as any food they will eat along the way. Bliss describes the trip: "We stopped about once every hour to let the dogs out. We stop at the same side roads every year. It's a good way to notice how things change because every now and then a side road will be gone, with something built there, and we'll have to find a new side road" (106). The changing landscape—cluttered with new buildings and other signs of private property—becomes increasingly inaccessible to the lifestyle of the Copelands. Just as earlier generations of seminomadic and land-squatting herdsmen were displaced by full-fledged farmers, the Copelands are forced constantly to seek new side roads that they can use as public property on their wanderings.

Of all the Copelands, Albert best illustrates their inveterate self-sufficiency. Much of the novel's comedy derives from Albert's do-it-yourself schemes, such as his elaborate frogman rescue of the pickup truck from the pond, which he accomplishes by tying a cinder block to his ankle and breathing through a water hose. The truck sank into the pond as a result of Albert's son Meredith's improvisation: Meredith drove back and forth along the pond's dam while towing his cousin Mark on a pair of water-skis. The novel's title points to the story's central do-it-yourself scheme involving the floatplane that Albert spends fifteen years building and rebuilding, while performing test runs out on Lake Blanca, waiting patiently for the plane to become airborne. Like prior generations of yeoman farmers who flourished in what Paul Escott identifies as a "practically cashless economy"[51] by bartering with neighbors, Albert collects hickory chips from the sawmill he runs and uses them to barter for flying lessons from Joe Ray Hoover, who uses the chips to smoke meat in his restaurant. Relying on incomplete building plans and a lot of imagination, Albert constructs the plane from aluminum tubing, powers it with two chainsaw engines, and uses lawn chairs for seats and football helmets for headgear. In addition to the plane's comic appearance, the test runs are farcical failures, and with repetition they reinforce the image of Albert the do-it-yourselfer as an ineffectual clown.

The records Albert keeps in his notebooks to satisfy FAA requirements further emphasize how unofficial—and therefore presumably doomed to failure —his project is. His oldest son, Thatcher, frequently points out how Albert regularly fudges test results, as in the case of his "first successful in-air operation"; Albert records that the "aircraft lifted into air on eight separate occasions," which Thatcher corrects by pointing out that he merely "run it across this speed boat wake twice and it bounced eight times" (66). Albert is much more concerned with accurate records of his children's birthdays or their heights and weights, which he includes in the floatplane notebooks along with his doctored test results. Over time he becomes more obsessed with the notebooks as a means of preserving his family's history; he records family trees, includes clippings from the local newspaper about the family's grave-cleaning ritual and the frogman episode with the garden hose, as well as his own private records of significant family events, such as the elopement of his son Meredith with Rhonda, and the initial report of Meredith's mine accident in Vietnam. Early in the novel, when Thatcher points out that the FAA might not approve of such irregular records, Albert defensively responds, "It's my record. You want a record of something, *you* write it up. But don't you go complaining about my record or how I keep it, or I'll hide it. You ain't no government official" (19). The notebooks become a testament of Albert's belief in independence and personal autonomy. As such, they highlight the opposition between the private and the public, and, given the novel's title, the notebooks serve as a metafictional device, suggesting that, like Albert's records, Edgerton's novel represents an insider's report on a passing culture and protests the forces of cultural erosion.

One of the basic components of most pastorals stemming from the tradition of classical Greece and Rome is the recognition that Arcadia is doomed, that change and death are inevitable. Within the youngest generation of Copelands, there appear signs of an encroaching outer world. Mark goes to college to study industrial relations. Thatcher works for Strong Pull Construction Company, and, though he prefers to work outdoors, he decides to take a promotion to an administrative position. The name "Strong Pull" itself suggests the irresistible seduction of the economic incentives to leave a life rooted in a history of subsistence farming. Similarly, the saw mill Albert operates represents one of the earliest forms of industrialization in the area. The family is made even more vulnerable to change by their ignorance of its inevitability—and by their ignorance of their status as innocents. Their very insularity prevents them from recognizing the difference between their egalitarian existence and the hierarchical order of the outside world that militates against the principles of autonomy and self-sufficiency they take for granted. The Copelands retell stories of their ancestors who fought in the Civil War, and notably of the farm-bound Caroline, who poured scalding water on the Yankee soldiers who plundered her smokehouse. By the time of the Vietnam War, however, any "rebel" impulses have subsided and they view themselves as a thoroughly American family, whose children will, of course, fight in their nation's cause against communism. Like the rest of America, they fear the abstract threat of communism and fail to see how America's own capitalist military machine presents a more real threat to their liberty. Only after Meredith returns broken by the war are they capable of viewing their innocence critically.

As in the story of Eden, knowledge of good and evil becomes a compensation for the loss of innocence, which is most demonstrably presented when the novel's principal innocent, Meredith, returns home from Vietnam after stepping on a tank mine and losing an arm and a leg, nearly all motor functions, the capacity for speech, and control of his emotions and his bladder. His cognitive capacity, however, remains virtually intact, which forces him into an awareness of life he had previously chosen to avoid when he was capable of acting physically. He reflects, "It's amazing how much time you get to think when you can't talk or go nowhere. And you start to figure out what life is, which is doing things. Things you've already done, or are getting ready to do. Like I am, you can't do nothing but think" (219). Meredith's dramatic change from the active to the contemplative life is further emphasized by the fact that the reader only gains access to his point of view in the final third of the novel, after the accident. Throughout the first two-thirds of the novel his antics are reported by the other first-person narrators, who include his cousin Mark, his siblings Thatcher and Noralee, and Thatcher's wife Bliss. (Notably, all of these narrators belong to the same generation.) Throughout childhood Meredith remains self-absorbed, though in a relatively innocent and harmless way; his endless pranks make him the center of his family's attention, inspiring the jealousy of Thatcher and Mark and the adoration of Noralee and Bliss.

Like most other members of his family, the reader is likely to forgive Meredith his boyish excesses and his lack of self-awareness; in fact, because of his lack of self-consciousness, he is more at one with his family and culture. By contrast, his cousin Mark, who grows up under the protection of his religious mother and is coddled by the adults at the Baptist church, is trained to be hyperconscious of his behavior, to dissect each action for the possibility of guilt that could lead him to perdition. Mark's frequent religious angst results not in a greater sense of empathy for others or accountability for his actions but, rather, in a calculating duplicity, by which he seeks to ingratiate himself with others and to avoid punishment. Compared with Meredith's simple, knee-jerk tendency to avoid trouble by blaming Mark, which becomes all the more comic with repetition, Mark's duplicity takes on a darker tone. When, for example, Meredith and Mark get into trouble for starting the well digger, Meredith quickly resorts to his culture's typical scapegoat and reports that they saw a "big nigger" around the well digger, who was probably responsible; Mark corroborates the lie, and afterward he dwells upon his complicity to the point of losing touch with reality. "I thought about the nigger," reflects Mark, "until I could see him in the darkness by the welldigger, moving slowly, white eyes in the dark, moving in the darkness around to the far side of the welldigger. The nigger had been there. Jesus would still love me if the nigger had been there and he probably had been. He could have been there, but in case he hadn't been there at all, I prayed: "Jesus, I'm sorry—if the nigger won't there. I think he might have been there, though. Dear Jesus, I'm sorry—if the nigger won't there" (33). This compulsion to preserve his innocence, to rationalize any behavior by denying responsibility or consequence is one that follows Mark throughout the novel—from his adolescent guilt for masturbation to the bombing raids in Vietnam to committing adultery with Meredith's wife, Rhonda. Thoroughly trained in the dualism of the Baptist church, Mark fears external retribution for his actions, rather than recognizing—as Emerson points out in his "Divinity School Address"—that "in the soul of man there is a justice whose retributions are instant and entire. He who does a good deed, is instantly ennobled himself. He who does a mean deed, is by the action itself contracted."[52] By all worldly standards, Mark is a success: he earns a college degree, becomes an officer in the military, has lots of dates, and drives a fast car. But he lacks the common sense not to brag of these successes to his crippled cousin, Meredith. With the character of Mark, Edgerton critiques America's superficiality, commercialism, and, most significantly, its willful innocence.

Such innocence, the blind determination not to mature or acknowledge one's mistakes, is necessary for the preservation of the national "manifest destiny" that sent troops to Vietnam and then would not admit either the reckless devastation or the possibility of losing the war. C. Vann Woodward writes that after the Civil War the South was spared such innocence, but Edgerton convincingly tells a different story. The "tragic view" of life that followed in the wake of Sherman's march has obviously disappeared with those who suffered it firsthand, leaving subsequent generations once again innocent and naive about war and death. The Copelands' willingness to send their young men off to Vietnam is very clearly related to the fact that they have not lost blood kin to a war since 1865. Edgerton suggests that loss and death are experiences each generation must have for itself. After his accident, Meredith describes the naiveté of an entire American generation. "There are plenty of fools," he angrily asserts, "ready to get blown apart for what they believe in about this mess over here. The hell they are. Nobody's ready to get blown apart. The only reason they do it is they know they're not going to get blown apart. I knew better than anything I won't going to get blown apart. I would have bet my life on a butcher block" (213).

Meredith's education about warfare and loss is accompanied by subtle but palpable changes in the novel's structure. The hard lessons Meredith confronts begin to bear a resemblance to those of the preceding generations. Interspersed among the various first-person narratives in *Floatplane* are sections recounted in an omniscient voice, which represents the collective consciousness of the dead generations buried in the family graveyard, now overgrown with the wisteria vine planted more than a hundred years earlier by the family matriarch, Caroline Copeland. In addition to the omniscient voice of "the Vine," these chapters often include the individuated voices of the dead, who appear in rocking chairs by their graves on each "blue moon" to tell jokes and stories from their lives. In a humorous retreatment of Thornton Wilder's *Our Town*, these graveside chats provide a comically sublime counterpoint to the increasingly tragic events of both the main narrative and the narratives told by "the Vine."

Occasionally, the stories of the living and the dead overlap, and often the Vine presents a complete narrative that is only retained by both the living and the dead in the odd detail or a sketchy anecdote, dramatizing the inevitable decimation of family history. The frequent friendly debates about story details that arise among the living—and among the dead—suggest how these stories change and splinter into competing versions in response to the individual needs of the various tellers. Although the omniscient voice of the Vine does suggest that these competing visions of the past might coalesce into a shared whole, or that the past continues to exist and exert its influence in the present—even if it is not wholly remembered—the living individually bear the responsibility of using that past to define themselves. As Robert Penn Warren observes in "The Use of the Past," "There is no absolute, positive past available to us, no matter how rigorously we strive to determine it—as strive we must. Inevitably, the past, so far as we can know it, is an inference, a creation, and this, without being paradoxical, can be said to be its chief value for us. In creating the image of the past, we create ourselves, and without the task of creating the past we might barely be said to exist. Without it, we sink to the level of a protoplasmic swarm."[53] Despite the inevitable loss of much of their history, the Copelands nevertheless are a family that values its heritage and believes that individual identity is largely constituted by family history. At each grave cleaning, the family tells its stories, and Aunt Scrap, in particular, serves as the voice of the lost past to the younger generations. The family's continuity is emphasized by both the reproduction of incident and the reproduction of character types through several generations, as in the case of the first Ross Copeland, born before the Civil War, whose mischievous nature is repeated in the characters of Meredith and his son, Meredith Ross Copeland.

In choosing to cut himself off from his family and its history, refusing to understand the significance of his actions in the light of his own or his family's past, Mark (and, to a lesser degree, Thatcher) remains an innocent, capable of the most destructive behavior, and he chooses to become increasingly alienated from the shared future of the Copelands. Despite his upbringing in the bosom of the Baptist church—or, rather, because of it—Mark's behavior calls to mind the antiheroes whom Walter Sullivan, in "The New Faustus," regards as typical of the modern southern novel, characters who "live by the premise that there is no such thing as right and wrong."[54] Like Joyce's Stephen Dedalus and his many clones that Sullivan finds in the modern novels of the mid-twentieth century, Mark flees the pressures of his church and community and their shared values. But, unlike these antiheroes, Mark is the clear Judas of *Floatplane,* and his rejection of community serves only to emphasize further the novel's true heroes, the other family members who stay at home and collectively suffer, who, committed to a shared fate, grow into an ever clearer understanding of the values that bind them together. Sullivan argues that if the southern novel is to thrive then southern writers "will have to discover [their] own sources of moral organization" and that "we must see the world as larger than ourselves or our generation or our ability to send a space ship to the moon."[55] In *Floatplane,* Edgerton provides the clearest articulation of the "sources of moral organization" that he discovers in his culture as defined by yeoman and frontier-herdsman forebears. Furthermore, their values of independence and self-sufficiency are pitted against other sources of moral organization equally prevalent in the culture of Edgerton's Piedmont: namely, the Baptist religiosity represented by Mark, an ideology that emphasizes human depravity and militates against both self-sufficiency and a healthy sense of community.

Unlike Mark and Thatcher, each of the novel's other narrators grows into a deeper commitment to and understanding of their own individual moral visions, which are informed, but not controlled, by a commitment to family. When we first meet Bliss, she is an innocent young woman who describes her hopes for marriage in the comically romantic language of a girl who has read too many sentimental novels; she becomes a very realistic woman—like her mother-in-law Mildred—remaining in a less than satisfying marriage, shouldering the burden of holding her adopted family together, whom she has grown to love in the most unromantic of ways. Along with Noralee, Bliss opposes the Copelands' uncritical acceptance of their duty to send their boys to Vietnam. Noralee also secretly challenges her family's racist ideas, while remaining at home and helping Bliss to care for the children of the next generation. These women will likely pass along their more liberal ideas, while maintaining a continuity with their family's nobler traditions.

Meredith's voice, previously silent, dominates the final third of the novel. Unlike Mark, who observes Southeast Asia through the Plexiglas canopy of his jet fighter, or from the interior of a Bangkok bar or the officer's club, Meredith witnesses the horrors of war first-hand and includes his open criticism in his letters home to Noralee. When he returns home, Meredith spends his time adjusting to the new conditions of everyday life; he learns to maneuver without an arm and leg and communicate with his reduced speech capacity, he connects with his newborn son, he learns to accept the care of his family and resolves the inevitable separation from a wife who abandons him. But, mainly, Meredith spends time recalling his many childhood adventures. Because we the readers have shared these adventures from the perspectives of the other narrators and only now for the first time witness them with Meredith as memory, we share in the elegiac force of his recollections.

The first third of the novel is almost purely episodic and follows a series of seemingly unrelated boyhood incidents in which Meredith and Mark get into trouble, Albert unsuccessfully attempts to fly his floatplane, and the family travels to Florida in December to hunt and gathers for the grave cleaning in May.' The novel's structure reinforces Meredith's experience. As he passes through childhood and adolescence, the episodic story and seeming lack of narrative purpose underscores the extent to which Meredith contentedly lives in the present. The episodes stand alone upon the merits of their comic exuberance, and, as in the tall tales of southwestern humor, the self-contained miniplots that dominate the first half of *Floatplane* suggest an endlessly novel world, free from enduring consequence and, thus, free from change. Only in retrospect, when these various isolated incidents begin to reveal a pattern, do we perceive the wholeness of Meredith's life, which makes his physical alienation all the more painful. Furthermore, only in the latter half of the novel does there begin to appear a connection between the main narrative and the chapters narrated by "the Vine," which suggests how the individual lives of the Copelands are intertwined with the larger patterns of family and regional history.

This connection becomes most evident as the tone of both the main narrative and the "Vine" chapters darkens. Mark and Meredith's rivalry over Rhonda resonates in the Vine's story of the feud between the Copeland brothers Walker and Julius (161–62) and in the dead Ross Copeland's retelling of Harper McGuire's rivalry with his father for the affection of a black servant girl named Zenobia (173–76). Immediately following a chapter in which Mark passively witnesses drunken pilots in an officer's bar as they challenge each other to eat a live duck (202–5), the Vine reports on Walker and Caroline Copeland's youngest son William and his sadistic treatment of animals—how he would catch rabbits just to torture them and how he once skinned a fox alive (206–9). Having become desensitized to violence and addicted to the power trip of mastery over another creature, the pilots indulge themselves with increasing fervor, killing animals and Vietnamese with equal indifference; similarly William Copeland's mistreatment of animals inevitably leads him to kill a young white girl, whom he hides under the house of the Copelands' black field hand, Zuba. Reminiscent of the well-digger episode in which the young Mark and Meredith avoid punishment by inventing the scapegoat of the "big nigger," William tragically makes Zuba his scapegoat; when the lynch mob comes out to the Copelands' house and fashions a noose from the wisteria vine, Walker Copeland and his family attempt to stop the hanging but fail to do so because they are unwilling to reveal William as the true culprit. The use of the vine as a noose underscores how family heritage serves equally to connect and to ensnare the individual.

Because these two stories of Zenobia and her father Zuba are not told by the living Copelands, and because the Vine gives their full account only late in the novel, they have the effect of stories that have been long repressed. Their telling generates a catharsis, triggered by the family's grieving over Meredith's accident and their subsequent loss of innocence. Racism is not a major theme in *Floatplane*, as it is in *Raney*. Race never becomes a principal issue in the main narrative; it remains in the subplots of Noralee's flirtation with the black football star at her high school; Meredith and Mark's lie about how the "big nigger" started the well-digger; and the episode in which the young Meredith and Mark challenge some black children to a basketball game in the old school gym, during which they become covered in soot from a broken coal stove and are later scolded by Albert for "changing races" (115). What each of these side narratives has in common is its emphasis on purity—either through the use of a black as scapegoat to preserve innocence, or the fear of a loss of whiteness, or innocence, through contact with blacks. That these subplots fail to intrude into the main narrative only further demonstrates the family's success in segregating itself and thereby denying its shared history with the family of the ex-slave Zuba and his slave ancestors.

On initial consideration, it seems odd—if not an outright flaw—that the stories of Zuba and Zenobia are finally divulged in the Vine chapters without a concomitant confrontation by the family, in the main narrative, with its tradition of racism toward blacks. On further investigation, however, this unwillingness on the part of Edgerton to provide a simple and tidy—and unrealistically optimistic—resolution to the problem of racism represents perhaps the novel's greatest imaginative triumph. By connecting the Copelands' tragic southern history with its participation in a national tragedy, *Floatplane* transcends the purely regional and becomes an American story. The American experience in Vietnam and the southern experience of slavery and its aftermath are explicitly related in the text by the aforementioned adjacent chapters set in Vietnam and in the Reconstruction-era South. In the bar scene in which drunken pilots challenge one another to eat a live duck as preparation for indiscriminately bombing Vietnamese, and in the following story of young William Copeland's sadistic treatment of animals and Zuba's hanging, the theme involves one ethnic and national group's brutal subjugation of an *other*. Both involve the perpetration of injustice in the name of justice and thus imply a willful blindness and indifference necessary for imperialism and domination.

In a letter home to Noralee, Meredith comments on the disparity he observes in Vietnam between public mission statements and the widespread realities that are never acknowledged by the U.S. press and are therefore invisible to the American public. With his letter he includes an official military "notice," with his own monosyllabic commentary noted in the margins:

> a. Remember we are guests here: We make no demands and seek no special treatment. *Ha.*
>
> b. Join with the people: Understand their life, use phrases from their language and honor their customs and laws. *Ha Ha.*
>
> c. Treat women with politeness and respect. *Ha Ha Ha.*
>
> d. Make friends among the soldiers and common people. *Ha Ha Ha.*
>
> e. Always give the Vietnamese the right of way. *Ha Ha.*
>
> . . . .
>
> i. Above all else, we are members of the U.S. military forces on a difficult mission, responsible for all our official and personal actions. Reflect honor upon ourselves and the United States of America. *Ha Ha Ha.*
> (191–92)

Although Meredith quickly recognizes in Vietnam the same duplicity and false paternalism that made slavery possible, he fails to make the connection or to be startled into a newfound criticism of his family's racism, and he still unconsciously uses the word "nigger" himself (213). Edgerton leaves it up to the reader to make this connection, as he often does with the simple observations made by characters that are designed to provoke much larger implications. A good example of this technique appears in the scene in which, sitting in the float-plane in his father's shop, Meredith recalls the many times from his childhood when he and Mark would "go on bombing missions over Germany and Japan and Korea" (228). The memory provokes Meredith to break down into a fit of sobbing and regret, though he shows no signs of appreciating the irony—which the reader is most certainly meant to recognize—in contemplating how the fiasco of Vietnam was the inevitable culmination of an unbroken history of military victory. On the contrary, Meredith, who is constitutionally suited for the active rather than the contemplative life, tends to personalize his situations, and here he simply mourns his own personal loss. The closest Meredith comes to generalizing his suffering appears in his observation of how so many people awkwardly recoil from him after his accident. "It's damn terrible," he considers, "the way the human race don't know how to act around somebody that ain't the average talking Joe. Let somebody be a little off and people get turned on to this different frequency and they act like total assholes and don't even know it. I figured it out pretty much: Thousands of years ago they had to kill people that was screwed up, so now some of that instinct is still in the blood, and people feel guilty that they want to kill you, so they act funny" (239). Meredith is no willing martyr, and only at the very end of the novel is he able to begin passing out of the "angry" phase of grieving his loss. Nevertheless, his suffering provides for the family the opportunity to suffer vicariously, which is necessary to exercise their full humanity. Through vicarious suffering with Meredith, they overcome the isolation of the self and achieve a tragic view of life capable of encompassing the suffering of others, even the repressed history of Zuba and Zenobia.

That Meredith's loss serves to restore wholeness to his family is suggested in the novel's final grave-cleaning episode, in which Aunt Scrap tells of the family's terrible losses during the typhoid epidemic of 1911. "You ought to know about some of this," she tells the family's youngest members and goes on to report how four Copelands died along with many of their neighbors (255–56). Significantly, this chapter, which begins with the aged Aunt Scrap reverently remembering the deaths of family members, ends with Albert's telling the scatologically humorous tale of how as children they believed that life was conceived when a man "peed" in a woman's mouth. To further suggest how an acceptance of death and suffering is necessary to a healthy and whole life, Bliss reports that the "splendor of the wisteria has not abated one iota" (253). The group that has gathered for this final grave cleaning is predominantly composed of women and their dependent children and Meredith—acknowledging that, despite the celebration of the masculine, frontier values of freedom and independence that pervades the first part of the novel, ultimately the women and their commitment to community are most responsible for the continued possibility of those frontier values.

Albert is the only able-bodied adult male to join the family at the novel's final grave cleaning, which suggests that, through sympathy with his son's suffering and a commitment to his care, he has overcome the isolation that plagues so many of Edgerton's father characters. Meredith remarks the change in his father, who had previously been a peripheral figure in his family, spending most of his free time alone on his projects. After Meredith's accident, Albert becomes devoted and regular in performing the most personal chores, such as helping Meredith go to the bathroom, cleaning up his messes, and helping him bathe. "Papa don't mind," Meredith notes. "Papa is like a woman in some ways.

He don't mind a lot of stuff" (229). Albert has become something of an androgyn, combining the best of feminine and masculine values. Although he still avoids directly addressing his own or Meredith's feelings, Albert helps Meredith overcome his fixation on his victimization and dependency by designing the most ingenious ways to help him achieve some of the bodily and spiritual independence he so exemplified as a boy. Albert's do-it-yourself schemes, which provided so much of the farce in the first two-thirds of the novel, now become the means by which Meredith reclaims some of the self-sufficiency of his childhood. In addition to taking his son along on hunting trips, Albert transforms an old typewriter into a device that lets Meredith communicate, and he engineers a pulley system that lifts Meredith into the floatplane so that he can imaginatively reconnect with his childhood. Throughout the first half of the novel, the family ridicules Albert's reliance on "natural suspension" in his various engineering projects, but after Meredith's accident he speaks of his father's work with awe: "What 'natural suspension' is is nothing but this giant mystery. And what Papa does is figure out how to use it when something needs fixing or when things go wrong" (233).

Albert's ability to tap into the basic order of the physical universe recalls Chappell's yeomen, who, in planting according to the seasons and the phases of the moon, "connect the order of the earth to the order of the stars."[56] "Natural suspension" might be offered as a description of the spiritual ideology of the self-reliant Copelands and recalls Emerson's monistic philosophy of the "Over-Soul," or divine spirit, whose ubiquitous presence the individual must access, or affirm within the self, in order to become conscious of one's innate divinity. Edgerton acknowledges the essential influence of Emerson on his own early rebellion against the stifling dogma of the Baptist Church,[57] which he views as subjugating the individual to a parasitic dependency. In contrast to the spiritual degeneration and increasing isolation Mark experiences, largely as a result of his indoctrination into Baptist dualism, Albert instills in Meredith a faith in self-reliance, by which one is capable of accessing a unity with the strength of nature, democratically available to all. Meredith's allegiance to his father's creed is suggested in his christening the floatplane *Natural Suspension* (261), and the unexpected flight of the plane in the novel's climactic ending serves as a sort of apotheosis for Meredith as an adherent to this creed.

Floatplane ends with Meredith's spirit sitting in the graveyard, telling the other spirits of his family the story of the day he and his father took the floatplane for its maiden flight. The tone shifts here abruptly to euphoria; after Meredith's claustrophobic interior monologues that dominate the last third of the novel, the full restoration of his voice and his release from a broken body signal a similar spiritual restoration. Despite the optimistic tone of the ending and its implicit transcendentalism, *Floatplane*, like all of Edgerton's fiction, is shot through with elegy, a tone that was even more apparent in an earlier version of the novel, which included, as an epilogue, a newspaper article from 2088 describing a Boy Scout troop's discovery of the family graveyard, completely overgrown by wisteria.[58]

As with the writers of the Southern Renascence, the power of Edgerton's fiction derives from a backward glance toward a culture that is either long gone or quickly disappearing. As with Faulkner, however, Edgerton's efforts to preserve a passing culture are typically not without ambivalence and are characterized by a contemplation of the ways in which the better aspects of his culture are compromised and doomed by its inherent contradictions, making change inevitable and necessary. Both *Floatplane* and *In Memory of Junior* idealize masculine frontier individualism, while simultaneously inviting a critique of the naiveté and potential destructiveness of such a position. *Raney* and *Where Trouble Sleeps* celebrate the relative classlessness and community autonomy of the fictional Piedmont towns of Listre and Bethel while demonstrating how these communities are built upon religious and ethnic dualisms that exclude outsiders and impose severe limitations on the freedom of its members. The restoration and continuation of yeoman values depend, therefore, upon the dissolution of community boundaries and hierarchies within the community, as well as the dissolution of rigid gender roles. The individual is left with the challenge of internalizing the community's noblest values and of preserving them in a new social order.

RANDALL KENAN
The Black Yeoman

6

Although North Carolina politics historically have privileged the interests of the upper class of planters and industrialists—in the form of unfair taxation and legislation made possible by powerful lobbies and unequal political representation—no group of North Carolina plain folk has suffered discrimination like the state's African Americans. Furthermore, North Carolina blacks have suffered at the hands of both elite *and* plain whites. If Frederick Law Olmsted was correct in observing that the state's generally smaller plantations resulted in more humane treatment of slaves and "less lamentable" conditions than those found on larger plantations elsewhere in the South,[1] the antebellum slave narratives provided by North Carolinians such as Harriet Jacobs, Moses Roper, Lunsford Lane, Moses Grandy, and Thomas H. Jones reveal many of the traumas found in narratives of slaves from other states.[2] Among the cruelest treatments recorded in the state's history are the punishment of runaways by court-ordered burning at the stake; one such case occurred in Kenan's Duplin County in 1787. The despotism of abusive masters was facilitated by the fact that, as elsewhere in the South, North Carolina slaves were not permitted to testify against whites in a court of law.[3]

Nonslaveowners constituted more than two-thirds of the white population in 1860 and were often ambivalent about slavery, for economic as well as religious reasons. After 1830, however, proslavery sentiments experienced a marked increase. This solid public support of slavery and growing fear of freed blacks after 1830 was owing to the rise of northern abolitionism, fear of slave rebellions, the national debate over the westward expansion of slavery, and the increase in the free Negro population. Among these and other causes, the publication in Boston of "Appeal to the Colored Citizens of the World" (1829) by David Walker, a free black of Wilmington, North Carolina, increased among white North Carolinians the fear of slave uprising, promoting legislation that further restricted the rights of both slaves and free blacks. In 1830 the teaching of reading and writing to slaves was outlawed, and the distribution by slaves of abolitionist materials was made punishable by death. Although there were more than twice as many free blacks in North Carolina than in any state further south, an 1830 law required newly freed slaves to leave the state within ninety days or face re-enslavement. Furthermore, marriage between slaves and free blacks was made illegal, demonstrating the growing anxiety among whites concerning the state's large free black population and its perceived negative influence on the stability of the "peculiar institution."[4] Lunsford Lane's narrative provides a moving account of the state's many restrictions on the liberty of free blacks.

Although free blacks were not "legally disenfranchised" between 1776 and 1835, a North Carolina constitutional convention in 1835 narrowly repealed their suffrage rights, which would be reinstated thirty-two years later by the Reconstruction Act of 1867. Despite Reconstruction, between 1867 and the end of the century, blacks in North Carolina struggled to gain representation. Not only were they forced to contend with the race-baiting Democrats, but they also struggled with the racism pervasive in their own Republican party. Barred from participation in the North Carolina Farmers' Alliance, some black farmers participated in the southern Colored Alliance of farmers, which, nevertheless, refrained from overt political action—perhaps in response to pressure from whites. With the beginning of the twentieth century, black voters in North Carolina were again disenfranchised, this time by the notorious "Grand-father clause," an amendment to the state constitution requiring any registered voter to have paid his poll tax and to be able to "read and write any section of the Constitution"—unless he or his ancestors were entitled to vote on January 1, 1867. Disenfranchisement of blacks culminated in the ascendancy of the Democratic Party's white-supremacist push to control North Carolina politics. At the time, black North Carolinians hardly prevailed politically, as the state was represented by only one black congressman, four black state legislators, and a few black county officials. Nevertheless, Charles Aycock's gubernatorial bid, like that of Democratic predecessors, played to white North Carolinians' fears of "Negro domination." Aycock's campaign managers organized white-supremacist rallies in which hundreds of men in red shirts and toting rifles "broke up political meetings, fired on citizens in their homes," and "kidnapped and whipped political opponents as they carried out God's work in the coastal plains of North Carolina."[5]

The Red Shirt counterrevolution produced its bloodiest results in the port town of Wilmington, where the progressive Fusion Party had succeeded in placing blacks in several important leadership positions, including three black alderman on a board of ten. Speaking on behalf of the city's Democratic Party, Chairman Alfred M. Waddell declared, "We in Wilmington . . . will not live under these intolerable conditions. No society can stand it. We intend to change it, if we have to choke the current of Cape Fear River with Negro carcasses." On November 10, 1898, Waddell and his Red Shirts made good on this threat. They raided the city's light infantry armory, armed themselves, burned the Black Fusionist newspaper to the ground, and then marched to the city's black neighborhood, where they conducted nothing short of a massacre, breaking into homes, disarming blacks, and, according to one contemporary account, pouring "volleys into fleeing Negroes like sportsmen firing at rabbits in an open field." Representing the reaction of white North Carolinians to the events, Raleigh's News and Observer "hailed the massacre as imperative to save the city from degradation," and Wilmington's Messenger "praised the coup d'etat as an heroic act in liberating whites from Black tyranny."[6]

Just as Wilmington provided the setting for the culmination of North Carolina's reaction to congressionally imposed Reconstruction, in 1971 the city witnessed the high point of violence in the state's seventeen-year-long struggle against nationally mandated school desegregation. Race relations in the city had continued to deteriorate since the riots following the assassination of Martin Luther King, Jr., in 1968, and the desegregation of the city's high school the following year. After local efforts had failed to produce better treatment of blacks in city schools, the state's Commission for Racial Justice sent in field organizer Ben Chavis, who organized a school boycott by the city's black students. Chavis and other leaders of the boycott were stationed in the black community's Gregory Congregational Church, which became the target of white supremacist reprisals, organized variously by the Ku Klux Klan, local police, and a group of paramilitaries that called itself ROWP, or the organization for the Rights of White People. Chavis's petition to the city government for a curfew was denied, and during the nights of early February 1971 white supremacists terrorized the black community. At the height of the conflict, 5,000 rounds of ammunition were fired in a single night, and seventy people in and near Gregory Church were wounded. Ultimately, Chavis and nine other activists were falsely accused of arson and sniping at firemen and police. They were summarily tried and convicted and then sentenced to a combined term of 282 years in prison. Outrage over the miscarriage of justice surrounding the "Wilmington Ten" spread throughout the nation and the world. In 1976, Amnesty International took up their case, and in 1980 they were finally acquitted by a federal appeals court[7]

Randall Kenan grew up less than forty miles to the north of Wilmington and would have been nearly eight years old during the riots of February 1971. Nevertheless, he recalls hearing little discussion of the Wilmington Ten during his childhood. "I remember talk of the Wilmington 10 in the news," he says, "but not much talk of it in the community."[8] The rural black communities in Wallace and Chinquapin (Duplin County) were obviously sufficiently distant—at least culturally so—from urban Wilmington that the riots did not directly impact the lives of his family. Furthermore, he states that he "knew nothing about the Wilmington Riots [of 1898] until the 1990s. Have never heard anyone in Duplin Co. discuss it or mention it."[9] Although black resistance to white oppression is a persistent theme in Kenan's writing, at least in his fiction it remains local in scope, connected to the history of the black farmers around the fictional village of Tims Creek, who have for generations worked to define their own autonomous community. Without diminishing the injustice of racism, Kenan, like Zora Neale Hurston, tends to focus on the dynamics within the black agrarian community and resists the possibility of defining that community too thoroughly in terms of its reaction to white oppression. Even in his transcontinental travelogue, *Walking on Water: Black American Lives at the Turn of the Twenty-First Century* (1999), Kenan appears to share Voltaire's—and Booker T. Washington's—response to tyranny, finding that the healthiest course for black Americans to centuries of oppression is to return (at least culturally) to their agrarian roots and "tend their own gardens," rather than define themselves in relation to the white middle class within the urban spaces increasingly controlled by the power structure of white America.

Despite the lower wages paid to black farm laborers in North Carolina from the emancipation onward, as well as legislation that facilitated the profiteering of unscrupulous landlords, a number of black tenant farmers and wage laborers managed to acquire their own farms and thereby to better define the conditions of their lives. Furthermore, although the rate of tenancy was certainly higher among black farmers than whites, in the final decades of the nineteenth century tenancy was actually decreasing among blacks while it was increasing among whites.[10] In Kenan's fiction, black yeomen receive ample attention, and, notably, he focuses significantly more on the lives of black yeomen and their descendants than upon the more numerous black tenant farmers and theirs. Kenan fictionalizes the unincorporated black farming community of Chinquapin, North Carolina, as Tims Creek, which provides the setting for his debut novel, *A Visitation of Spirits* (1989), and the story collection *Let the Dead Bury Their Dead* (1992), a finalist for the National Book Critics Circle Award.[11] In addition to celebrating the patriarchs and matriarchs of Tims Creek who fought oppression to build an autonomous farming community, Kenan pays equal attention to the ways their descendants learn from that yeoman tradition in order to survive in "a world peopled with new and hateful monsters that [exact] a different price."[12] In *Walking on Water*, Kenan takes with him his concern for an autonomous black culture as he travels across North America exploring the present realities of African American communities, as well as their histories of resistance to white oppression.

"Enormous potential, lying dormant, waiting": The Yeoman Vision
of *Walking on Water*

Walking on Water offers an advantageous introduction to the breadth of
Kenan's interests—as well as a wealth of autobiographical information. Since
Kenan introduces *Walking on Water* by meditating on the subjectivity of his
American study, self-deprecatingly calling it "more a book about me than anyone else,"[13] it should come as no surprise that he frames his travelogue with
opening and concluding chapters devoted largely to the rural North Carolina
community where he grew up. Born in Brooklyn in 1963 to young parents, at
the age of six weeks Randall Garrett Kenan was taken to live with his paternal
grandparents in the coastal plains town of Wallace, North Carolina. Throughout the next several years, the boy gradually came to spend more and more
time in the nearby farming village of Chinquapin, with his great-uncle Redden
and his great-aunt Mary, whom he grew up calling "Mama" (607). Mary and
Redden lived in the family's ancestral homeplace, on land that had been in the
family for five generations (15).

Reflecting upon his childhood, Kenan revises the West African aphorism
that "it takes a village to raise a child," remarking that "in my case, it was largely
done by four people, with a village to back them up" (606). In addition to his
grandparents and his great-aunt and great-uncle, he describes a vast extended
family living in Duplin County and ever present during his childhood. He also
notes the importance of the community's two Baptist churches, which "made
an indelible mark" on his growing up, remarking that "no matter how far or
how fast I run, the lessons of Baptist protestantism and Southern Calvinism
will be etched on my brain—probably my soul—the way circuits are hardwired
to a motherboard" (608). He grew up in an integrated school, though until
high school the schools he attended were an extension of the black community; he notes that he had "more black teachers than white teachers" and
that these women knew his mother (that is, his great-aunt) and watched him
"and all the other black boys and girls like sentient hawks" and "would report
any crime or misdemeanor with the rapidity of lightning" (609). His grandfather was a virtual jack-of-all-trades, a successful entrepreneur who built a dry-
cleaning business and pursued a range of other independent ventures, including renovating and renting old homes, and dealing in scrap metal (616). The
county was still largely agrarian, and he describes Chinquapin as "unincorporated and rural, largely tobacco fields and cornfields and hog farms" (607).

Culturally, Kenan's community was quite autonomous and still very much in
touch with its ancestral past, a past that served to constitute individual identity.
The community he knew during his childhood from 1963 to 1981, he claims,

was virtually identical to the community as it must have existed in 1920, "with the exception of a few welcome gadgets," notably television (608). Nevertheless, even television failed to alter the basic values and outlook he inherited, because he was "surrounded by folk who had been on the planet for an entire century, and their view of the world began before any of these new-fangled machines were even invented." He notes, for example, that both of his maternal great-grandmothers were still living when he went to high school (608). Although he grew up during a period of tumultuous change nationally—"Vietnam, Woodstock, Watergate, rashes of assassinations, civil rights marches and boycotts and sit-ins, the Black Panther Party, free love, flower children, Kent State, Jackson State, men walking on the moon, the Great Society," the Wilmington Ten—Kenan claims that his community was virtually indifferent to these upheavals, because they were "focused on the more pressing matters: getting crops in, getting their children fed, grown and married, caring for the elderly, going to church and trying to be good, with occasional missteps" (607).

In retrospect he appreciates this rather sheltered upbringing and feels that it was responsible for making him "a fairly decent person . . . and probably a writer" (609). However, he also attributes the slow pace of village life as the probable source of his "wanderlust" (609), and therefore ironically responsible for the writing of the travelogue *Walking on Water*. From 1981 to 1985 he studied at the University of North Carolina at Chapel Hill, where he abandoned his boyhood dream of becoming a scientist and instead majored in English and studied fiction writing with Doris Betts and Max Steele (615). Afterward, he left North Carolina for New York, where he worked in the publishing industry until his own fiction was published and he made a career teaching creative writing. In 1994 he returned to North Carolina for a year as a guest lecturer at his alma mater and at Duke University, during which time he became "reacquainted" with his family and home community from which he had been geographically estranged for nearly thirteen years.

Upon his return he was shocked to find Chinquapin radically altered, the landscape covered, like most of the Sun Belt, with new supermarkets and convenience stores. The town now had city water, a state-of-the art ambulance service, cable television, and access to newly released videos. Nearby were the recent additions of Ellis Airport and the final extension of Interstate 40, which "created a line all the way from Barstow, California, to Wilmington, North Carolina" (611). Kenan muses that "thanks to satellite dishes and faxes and email, [his hometown] was not so far away from the rest of America, and not so quaint and Tobacco Road." Chinquapin "had finally been thrust—more like yanked—into the heady whorl of the postmodern era" (611). Kenan fears that this access to American popular culture has eroded the cultural autonomy of his region and that a way of life that was once organic to a specific place has now lost its specificity and its authenticity, that the experiences of children in Duplin County schools today are virtually identical to those of school children anywhere else in the country (613). Despite Kenan's frequently elegiac tone, he takes pains to undercut his own nostalgia for Chinquapin, declaring that "as early I can remember, I always wanted to get the hell out of there" (609). Kenan describes his childhood, in part, to show us candidly the biases he takes with him in his travels across the continent.

Kenan travels in an SUV he half self-mockingly calls Bucephalus, after the favorite steed of Alexander the Great, a word derived from the Greek *boukephalos,* meaning "bull-headed," which might be roughly translated as "stubborn" or, more generously, "persevering." Over the course of seven years, Kenan intermittently travels northeast as far as Maine, then heads west across the country via the Rust Belt and the upper Midwest all the way to western Canada and Alaska. Afterward he chronicles the west coast and the western "promised lands" of Las Vegas, Salt Lake City, Denver, and Cheyenne, Wyoming. Finally he makes what some might call an abbreviated tour of the South, stopping in Louisiana, Georgia, and North Carolina, before ending his journey with a brief look at New York, the place of his birth, to which he returned as a young adult to begin a career in publishing and writing.

In this book devoted to the question of what it means to be black in America, Kenan is unwilling to settle for an easy answer. At its base an aggressively intertextual work, *Walking on Water* makes use of a vast diversity of oral and written sources, including those that promote the healthiness of the very postmodern identity that troubles and entices him. For example, he quotes from *Life on the Screen: Identity in the Age of the Internet,* in which Sherry Turkle argues that the Internet helps one "to develop models of psychological well-being that are in a meaningful sense postmodern: They admit multiplicity and flexibility. They acknowledge the constructed nature of reality, self, and other. . . . We are encouraged to think of ourselves as fluid, emergent, decentralized, multiplicitous, flexible, and ever in process" (613). While Kenan affirms the freedom and fluidity that Turkle promotes, he is less than sanguine himself about the possibilities of the Internet or other information technologies for genuinely promoting self-determination among blacks. To the contrary, he finds that such technologies have historically subjugated blacks to a position of relative powerlessness. A theme to which he periodically returns throughout the book is the failure of the media—specifically Hollywood and television—to empower blacks. From *Amos 'n' Andy* to the blaxploitation films of the 1970s, he calls attention to white media's marketing of black stereotypes. Kenan is even troubled by the impact of black popular artists and media representatives on black cultural autonomy, noting how "those things that I had taken so for granted about being black, which had come from my mama and my grand-father and Uncle Roma and Aunt Lillian and Aunt Mildred in third grade, and Reverend Raynor and Miss Ruth, were now being dictated by the *Martin Lawrence Show* and Snoop Doggy Dogg and Dr. Dre and Russell Simmons and *Vibe* magazine and, yes, Paramount. Chinquapin was becoming more like the rest of America. It was being absorbed by the vast cultural soup of consumeris-tic we-think. The problem, as I saw it, had to do with the idea that blackness was not so easily beamed through a satellite or through an optic fiber" (613). This final statement suggests that for Kenan blackness is something tangible, concrete, and located in a specific place and tradition, and that to seek to extract and abstract it is to violate its very nature.

In *The Southern Writer in the Postmodern World*, Fred Hobson calls the black southerner "the quintessential southern *agrarian*," noting his "closer acquain-tance with the soil," his "emphasis on family and community, his essentially concrete vision, his feeling for place."[14] Although in *Walking on Water* Kenan seeks to reinscribe these very assumptions, as the above passage demonstrates, occasionally he balks at such a characterization of black Americans as limiting and possibly even stereotypical. For example, when he seeks out a black com-munity in Bangor, Maine, he anticipates the incredulity of his audience, for whom the "very possibility [of blacks in New England] goes against the grain of what the nation would believe of black folk; as if to be black came with an agreement; as if having origins—or a livelihood—geographically located outside an agreed upon, fixed, predictable location, somehow makes one less than black" (97). Kenan identifies a double bind for black Americans: to leave or forget one's heritage—usually in an attempt to emulate the dominant culture—intensifies the cultural erosion of Diaspora; however, an engagement with black heritage requires a confrontation of what Hobson identifies as the "legacy of failure, poverty, defeat, and those other well-known qualities of the southern experience."[15] In *Walking on Water*, even more so than in his fiction, Kenan finds it necessary to reject a tragic view of the black experience. He pro-poses instead the difficult challenge of affirming history but not being limited by it, of engaging a heritage of struggle in order to reinvent oneself in the present.

Contrary to Turkle's optimism about self-determination in the information age, Kenan finds the positive aspects of "multiplicity," "flexibility," and "fluid-ity" to be more prominent among blacks in a premodern age. "Black American culture was always a Creole culture," he says. "Long before the term was coined, black culture was a postmodern culture; folk made it up as they went along" (625). Kenan also calls attention to blackness as a cultural construct.

Unequivocally opposed to an essentialist position that posits race as a biological "fact," he nonetheless acknowledges that "Dr. Du Bois's essentialist, mystical connection to some mythical Mother Africa still holds profound emotional energy, even for me" (639). Even though, he argues, the concept of race was created by white society "for sinister purposes," black cultural identity grew into "its own state of being: being black. It is a desire toward some spiritual connection with some larger whole" (638). Kenan suggests that, more than anything else, this loss of wholeness—or the loss of a desire for it—marks the damages of the modern age to black identity and black community.

Kenan notes this loss of an organic wholeness in his own life. After studying predominantly European culture at the predominantly white University of North Carolina in the predominantly white town of Chapel Hill, and after working in a predominantly white publishing industry in New York, Kenan began to fear that his "Negro 'soul'" was put "in danger" (11). "Did I," he asks, "in my attempts to learn and to experience another world, somehow lose, divest, mitigate or disavow who or what I was? Did I, in mingling and comingling [sic] with white folks, dilute or pollute or weaken my legacy as a son of a son of a son of a son of slaves stolen from Africa?" (627). Though he confronts the postmodern experience of fragmentation and multiplicity, the confrontation typically fills him with anxiety and longing for a stable order—like the one he knew in his childhood in the farming village of Chinquapin, or like the one he imagines to have existed even more potently among newly freed slaves a century earlier: "I think of those black folk in the 1860s who had none of the modern baggage my contemporaries and I lug around. As deprived as they were, they were also lucky. They knew exactly who they were. There was no jangling television set, no blasting boom boxes, no candy-colored magazines, no Wal-Marts, Tower Records, Web pages, billboards. Marketing had yet to be invented, and consumerism was a mere glint in Rockefeller's eye. We—black, white, indifferent, but American—must now disentangle ourselves from the garbage of the information age; we must pioneer a new way of seeing ourselves; we must reinvent humanity" (625). Obviously, Kenan does not call for a return to the conditions of the 1860s—nor would he even if the promise of forty acres and a mule had been fulfilled; despite his recurring interest throughout *Walking on Water* in the histories of black farmers, he does not propose a literal return to an agrarian-based society so much as a return to its values: autonomy, community, self-determination, egalitarianism, and a call for a unified vision of African American identity rooted in a common agrarian history.

This longing for unity, for transcendence of a fragmented present, is most clearly illustrated throughout *Walking on Water* by his frequently self-conscious use of the pronoun "we" in reference to black Americans. He sets out across

America with the tentative hope that his travels will reveal to him within the multiplicity of black experiences an underlying cultural unity. He acknowledges the difficulty of pursuing a vision of society that is both multiplicitous and unified. As if at least provisionally to settle this quandary, he quotes from Whitman in the book's concluding lines: "Do I contradict myself? I contain multitudes" (639). Just as Whitman addressed the fragmentation of a nation sectionally and ethnically divided by holding forth a vision of unity that he located within the experience of the poet himself, Kenan addresses the fragmentation of contemporary black America by representing, through his own consciously subjective journey, possibilities for wholeness. Like Whitman, who positioned himself as the spokesperson for his nation (and like the more immediate examples of black ministers whom Kenan watched since infancy), Kenan presents himself as a black Everyman, sometimes a Christ-figure who sympathetically suffers for his people, saying, "I am black; nothing black can be alien to me" (156).

Kenan's ambition to "contain multitudes" (639) expresses itself most apparently in the hundreds of interviews he conducts with black Americans; however, it likewise appears in the rich diversity of historical, literary, and sociological texts—primarily black ones—from which he generously quotes. This assertive intertextuality, what Robert Stepto refers to as a canon-shaping "call" and "response,"[16] might be seen as the logical culmination of a trend established by those ex-slave authors who struggled to obtain literacy and, thereby, freedom and self-determination. By presenting the best of what has been thought and said (both spoken and written) by African Americans, Kenan seeks to "disentangle" African America from the chains and shackles of misinformation, from what he refers to as the "garbage of the information age" (625). Like Jean Toomer's *Cane* (1923), Zora Neale Hurston's folkloristic writings, or even the efforts during the late 1930s of the WPA to record the experiences of ex-slaves, *Walking on Water* is inspired by the impulse to preserve a passing culture.

Kenan's geographically aimless journey may at first appear to be essentially postmodern—open to possibility—and, to a degree, it is; however, the pattern of Kenan's travels and reportage finds him, in typical pastoral fashion, privileging the past to the present, the village to the metropolis. In very loosely planning an itinerary, Kenan writes that his plan "was to trust in fate and serendipity . . . to avoid the obvious places, the places written about ad nauseam" (17). In fact, he does visit, at least briefly, many of the "obvious" places, the major cities that represent the largest black populations in America—Chicago, Oakland, Los Angeles, Atlanta, New York. In each case, however, often after exhaustive research, he retreats from his earlier hopes of capturing the black experience in each of these cities. Finding that experience too vast and diverse to be contained within a single chapter of his travelogue, he often remarks, as he does of both San Francisco and New York, that such a treatment would require its own book (336, 636). Of Chicago, he notes, "Oh, I had big—enormous—plans for Chicago. . . . Why [though] add to the trillions of words [already written about Chicago] when so much of the country had yet to be written about?" (164). While such practical considerations certainly contribute to his disinclination to document urban spaces, other, more spiritual and emotional considerations also weigh heavily upon his tendency to flee the contemporary black urban experience in America.

As is his tendency throughout the book, in Madison, Wisconsin, Kenan allows the black folk he interviews to put forth in their own words what appears to be Kenan's vision of a better future for black Americans. Darryl, a graduate student who has left New York to study history at Wisconsin, argues, "Cities really do break spirits. . . . We have to get out of the cities" (147–48). Darryl and his friends argue that "land linkages" (149) in the South help maintain cultural continuity for blacks and that the commercialism more prevalent in urban America serves to deplete and inauthenticate black culture (147–49). Kenan echoes these sentiments in the next chapter, "My Own Private Chicago," when he flees what he finds to be a dreary and depressing landscape of South Side Chicago. "Feeling blue myself and out of time and space," he recalls, "I longed to be away from it [Chicago], away from cities altogether" (164).

Though acknowledging that his perception of Chicago is likely skewed by the inclement weather—it rains throughout his visit—and by his weariness of having been on the road for three straight months, Kenan finds in the city's South Side slums the quintessence of what he has already identified as "the utter sense of entrapment and doom hanging over black folk in America" (157). He also admits to being negatively prejudiced against the Windy City much earlier by Richard Wright's Native Son and his "unredeeming and unredeemable vision of how a hellish environment can produce a Bigger Thomas; how circumstances model and shape individuals, like Pavlov's canine" (153). Kenan admits that he "never cottoned to that book [Native Son]; I found it terribly chilly, lacking soul. . . . I reckoned that, like me, being a country boy himself, Richard Wright never cottoned much to Chicago, and Native Son was his assessment of the city" (153). Reminiscent of Wright's gritty realism, Kenan's chapter on Chicago represents the spiritual nadir of his journey across America. He confronts the fact that 70,000 black men and women are in America's prisons, more, he observes, than are enrolled in its universities (163). Unlike the "once-splendorous past" apparent in Harlem's urban landscape, he finds the architecture of Chicago's South Side to be "uniform and mercantile. . . . drab and grim. Of the many buildings on the many streets that were not con-demned, many looked as if they should have been" (154). Again reminiscent of Wright's often harsh criticism of black culture, Kenan's harshest, most direct indictment of black urban culture results from his visit to Chicago. "Too often, in writing about black folk," he concludes, "I have read what is romanticizing. It is much too easy: to make poverty holy; to make ugliness beautiful; to make violence valiant; to make weakness charming; to make stupidity wise; to make arrogance comic; to make disease health; to make squalor exotic; to make mean-ness noble; to make cruelty ingenious; to make stink perfume; to make laziness expression; to make anger pride; to make debauchery art; to make nothing something; to make blindness sight; to make evil good" (155). Nowhere else in the book does there appear quite so strong a statement of Kenan's antipost-modern tendencies, or of his dualistic training in Chinquapin's Baptist church.

His despair in Chicago is made even more intense by his awareness, like Wright's, that throughout the first half of the century Chicago remained for so many African Americans the hope of salvation from southern oppression and poverty—an illusory hope, provoking a migration that Kenan calls "the arche-typical African American move from the South of despair to the North of despair" (154). Alone and despairing in Chicago, Kenan's own alienation echoes Bigger Thomas's; ultimately, he asks, "Is this the American reality? . . . The end result of our manifest destiny? Our individualism? To be utterly and finally alone?" (151). Like his early mentor Doris Betts, Kenan rejects modern America's materialist seduction of individuals away from traditional values rooted in an agrarian community. In his description of Chicago and urban America in general, Kenan invites our comparison of such modern alienation and social fragmentation to the utopian vision of community he provides in his reminiscences of Chinquapin and of his heroic grandfather, who speaks of an agrarian past when independent black yeomen interdependently built an agrarian community seemingly ex nihilo.

Although he declares that "the move is turning around," that more blacks are presently returning to the South than leaving it, many more blacks, he notes, are remaining in the North. As in Chicago, in Buffalo he observes how economic depression has deleterious effects on black communities, which are being overlooked by city planners seeking to restructure industry and re-envision a brighter future for the Rust Belt. Even more discouraging, Kenan finds that black urban communities are less vital and interconnected than pre-viously. For example, Ken Holley, director of the Lutheran Unemployment Center and manager of the Harambe bookstore in Buffalo, informs Kenan, "If you're talking about a social infrastructure [in Buffalo], there's probably none. Even the black church here has gone inward, for their own survival, rather than trying to be a community resource for people" (118). Holley explains how so many southerners still arrive in Buffalo "full of expectation," only to be disappointed (118). Kenan finds this pattern of expectation and disillusionment characteristic of African Americans' urban migrations all across America; here he cites Jonathan Raban: "The country is littered coast to coast, with dream cities that either came to nothing or came to something so monstrous that their names are now pronounced like those of Sodom and Gomorrah" (315).

Kenan acknowledges this pattern of expectation and disillusionment in his own wanderings across America, a pattern that finally fully clarifies itself in Seattle. Proclaimed throughout the 1990s to be the new urban utopia, as so many other American cities had been proclaimed before, Seattle disappoints Kenan. After acknowledging a prominent black middle class and strong black leadership in the city, including Mayor Norm Rice, Kenan looks "through a broader lens" to recognize how Seattle's statistics fairly match those of other American cities: black unemployment in "the double digits," a nominal black presence in the major corporations of Boeing and Microsoft, and poor performance among the city's black high school students. "In short," he concludes, "same mess, different city. Looking at the ostensible failures [in Seattle] led me first into depression—in truth I had been sinking, sinking, sinking, for months now—for I had great hopes for Seattle: I wanted the hype to be true. Was there one city in America that defied trends, lived up to its promise? The chances were looking slim" (314). After briefly considering the histories of some of the city's most prominent black settlers, Kenan visits what he calls a "shadow Seattle," conveniently overlooked by tourists and residents alike: he visits a downtown needle exchange program, as well as a group home for men with AIDS. In both places, Jeffrey Henderson, an outspoken young man suffering from AIDS, serves as Kenan's guide. Kenan compares Henderson's courage to that of Horace Roscoe Cayton, a black leader and newspaper founder, who a century earlier spoke out against injustice in the city.

Throughout much of *Walking on Water*, Kenan adopts this same technique of placing current struggles within a historical context. In his efforts to make sense of the contemporary scene in California, he affirms, "My travels were beginning to teach me how central history was to any such understanding [of a given place]" (349). Struck by the "vast amount of African American history that either lay gathering dust in hundreds of libraries or had gone unrecorded" (347), Kenan assumes the task of historian. More than a simple travelogue, *Walking on Water* provides a history of the diverse struggles of African Americans across the continent. While calling attention to its difficulty, Henry Louis Gates, Jr., confirms the need for just the sort of historical work that Kenan undertakes. According to Gates, "the curse that the scholar of African and

African-American Studies bears is the *absence* of a printed, catalogued cultural memory."17 Kenan sets for himself the goal of remedying such an absence; for a goodly portion of the communities he documents, he seeks to locate origins of settlement, traces demographic changes over time, examines the history of local Jim Crow laws within a larger national movement (as well as strategies of resistance), and collects the stories of numerous African Americans, many of them seniors who reflect back on earlier times. In compiling such a history, Kenan seeks to reshape the image African Americans have of themselves and thereby to provide hope for a better future.

After visiting the Afro-American History Museum in Los Angeles, he interviews the museum's curator, Dr. Rick Moss, who argues that African Americans are routinely indoctrinated in a view of American history that neglects the contributions made by blacks and other ethnic groups, producing the erroneous view that Europeans and their descendants are "responsible for everything we have today" (347), thereby relegating nonwhites to a state of cultural parasitism. Later, Kenan interviews Los Angeles novelist Trey Ellis, who similarly observes that blacks have "internalized a belief in their own failure" (351). To counteract this belief in "failure," Kenan documents numerous success stories, both historical figures and living African Americans who tell their own tales. For example, he interviews Ida Leggett, the first black woman trial judge in Idaho; filmmaker Charles Burnette, winner of a MacArthur Foundation's "genius" fellowship; and internationally renowned sculptor, James W. Washington, Jr. More often, however, Kenan interviews middle-class blacks. Quoting Zora Neale Hurston, he calls such average, successful blacks the "best-kept secret in America" (16). Although Kenan engages in a "call" and "response" with a vast portion of the African American canon, including black militants, it is the tradition defined by Hurston and Booker T. Washington that most influences his vision. In the 1990s neither Kenan nor most of the blacks he interviews finds it necessary to mute feelings of bitterness resulting from white oppression; however, their emphasis remains not on that oppression but on the achievements of enterprising blacks despite such oppression. For example, of Oscar Micheaux, the pioneering filmmaker of the 1920s, Kenan asserts that his "vision was the vision of Booker T. Washington" (353). Kenan is attracted to Micheaux because he dared to think outside the box, moving west and portraying successful blacks in his films, which were marketed to black audiences.

As with the exceptional figures whom he interviews, in the cases of "average" African Americans, Kenan is likewise drawn to people who are anything but "average." Rather, he interviews individuals whom sociological or demographic studies might not adequately represent: a black real estate agent pursuing a successful career in nearly all-white Coeur d'Alene, Idaho; an army major living in North Dakota; a retired history professor in Bangor, Maine. These African Americans expand the possibilities for black lives in America in the new millennium. And, even though not typically associated with farming, they have found in moving westward across America the same possibilities for autonomy and self-definition that Thomas Jefferson imagined for a vast republic, built upon what he believed to be the limitless opportunities available to yeoman farmers. Also reminiscent of Jefferson's aversion to urbanization, Kenan seems to believe that black Americans would thrive if not for superfluous cities. In contrast to what Kenan depicts as the bleak existence of blacks whose descendants migrated northward and westward to America's major cities, he is considerably more optimistic about the possibilities for self-definition among blacks who have migrated westward to rural areas, small towns, and small cities. Even when such migration does not yield the benefits that the travelers themselves originally imagined, Kenan consistently celebrates the impulse to move to a place in which settlers can define their own existence. Among a current generation of black immigrants to the West and Midwest, Kenan finds the same spirit that inspired black yeoman farmers a century earlier to leave the oppression of the South and travel westward to places where they sought to reinvent themselves and their communities.

These historical black pioneers include the obvious figures, such as York, the chief translator for the Lewis and Clark expedition, but Kenan devotes much more space to an exploration of the lives of less well known pioneers—lives whose histories, in many cases, are accessible only in local libraries or in oral history. In Maidstone, Saskatchewan, Kenan seeks out evidence of the black community called Shiloh, settled in the first two decades of the twentieth century. The settlers had immigrated primarily from Oklahoma, after the Oklahoma state legislature repealed black voting rights in 1910 and legalized segregation in 1913. By 1911, over two hundred black homesteaders had settled in Maidstone and in 1916 built the Shiloh Baptist Church; they created a community where they could "live closely together in order to help each other and be socially independent" (255). Kenan notes that more than three thousand African American homesteaders settled in northwestern Canada, before the Canadian government began to discourage black settlement.

One of the most fascinating communities of black farmers documented in *Walking on Water* is Allensworth, California. Situated in the fertile San Joaquin Valley, Allensworth—like Maidstone, Saskatchewan—was settled in the first two decades of the century by a group of visionary men and women who sought to found a village where they could farm and build a life independent of white intrusion. These settlers were led by Colonel Allen Allensworth, a retired

Army chaplain. In his 1914 account of the young town, Charles Alexander describes the settlers as primarily middle-class blacks who were "moved by the independent spirit to break away from the servant class and try their hand at agriculture and trade on their own responsibility" (375). According to the town's resident historian, Ed Cornelius Pope, representatives of these settlers discussed their plans with Booker T. Washington and they decided to build a "Tuskegee-style institute" in California; this utopia would involve the efforts of "50,000 of the biggest, baddest, blackest, smartest, wisest, most courageous, pioneering, adventuresome, successful black folk in the nation." They would "isolate" themselves "from the whole world in a little colony" in order to "show California and the nation and the world just what we are capable of doing" (379). Although Allensworth never attained the grandeur of its settlers' original vision, it did make quite an auspicious beginning. The initial settlement included three hundred families, who built their own homes, a courthouse, a school house, and a library. In addition to farming, the community included master craftsmen, especially masons, and cement and well-digging companies. The rich cultural life of the community included a town orchestra, a string and brass band, and various church choirs and secular singing groups (379–81).

According to Ed Pope, large white farms in the area resented Allensworth and coveted its population as a source of cheap labor; arsenic was found in the water supply, leading to a declaration by the county government that the town was "nonviable" and therefore an inappropriate place for county funding (385). By the end of the 1930s the town had lost the majority of its population, its skilled workers, and its rich cultural ferment; it had become essentially what the area's major white farmers had long desired: a town of "migrant farm workers" (382). By the time Kenan visits Allensworth, it is essentially a ghost town, a museum of its former glory, preserved by the quixotic energies of Ed Pope. Pope clings to Colonel Allensworth's dream, in which he sees the hope for the eventual fruition of "an enormous potential" in black America, now "lying dormant, waiting" (391). The importance of Allensworth for Mr. Pope is history —as it becomes for Kenan, who says that he "found it curious how much of [his] own thinking came together in Ed Cornelius Pope and his mission" (391–92).

In Allensworth—the community founded in accordance with the separatist vision of Booker T. Washington—Kenan's agrarianism most clearly resembles Washington's. This resemblance might, in fact, provoke some critics to consider Kenan's national narrative as conservative, separatist, even reactionary, one that questions the fruits of integration and nostalgically praises the long-gone dream of a black agrarian past to the reality of a black urban present. The book's recurrent structure reflects this preference for a rural past: so many of the chapters begin with an overview of an urban present, cataloguing the many social ills of a particular city, followed by either a retreat to a nearby rural area or a retreat into the city's own past. This structure is most palpably present in the chapter on California. The section on Los Angeles begins, "I have seen the future, and it is not Los Angeles. Don't let anybody tell you different" (341). Kenan visits a "residential school" for severely emotionally disturbed youth from L.A. who are on probation for crimes and who, despite all the efforts of their teachers, will spend much of their young lives in and out of institutions and probably be killed by the age of thirty-five (371–73). Realizing their poor odds for survival, and still lower odds for success, Kenan laments, "How could they be rescued?" (374), a question he answers in the next sentence, which serves as his introduction to the history of Allensworth: "Escape from Los Angeles?" (374). Kenan effectively seeks a solution to the apparently insoluble problems of Los Angeles by removing himself from the city and spending the rest of the chapter considering at length a history that many sociologists and intellectuals might consider obsolete or irrelevant, one that Kenan holds out as the last hope for his people.

This same structural rhetoric appears in Kenan's chapter on Las Vegas. Kenan leaves the city dejected after interviewing Ed Brown, editor of the state's only black newspaper, which has a circulation of 5,000 in a state with a black population of 90,000. Brown paints a gloomy picture of black life in Las Vegas, arguing that all of the valuable property is white-owned, that the black community is fragmented, that the city itself is "adult-oriented" (416) with little in the way of cultural enrichment for its youth, that the city's churches could "play more of a role" in community affairs, and that blacks in Las Vegas are, in general, caught in a "catch-22 . . . a no-win situation" (419). The chapter ends hopefully, however, when Kenan accompanies a dice-pit manager named Joseph Spears home to his desert lot outside of town. "One of the fascinating things about Las Vegas to me," Kenan notes, "is that it just stops. Some streets end, and there before you is desert; it feels as if you've just stepped out of a mirage" (420). The "mirage" of Las Vegas contrasts starkly with Spears's home, which is located next to a very *substantial* feature of the natural landscape, a "great hill, a tall, squat, craggy red rock of incredible beauty" (420). Spears, who is half Narragansett and part black, describes for Kenan how when his son was born he took the infant atop the rock hill, both of them naked, as they "surveyed the world" (420). Kenan recalls that at this point, he "had traveled across the length of this country. . . . but I can testify I have never been so moved as by this simple harmony of earth and man, red in the red sunset, but more, a place beloved" (421). This passage demonstrates, perhaps as well as any, the limits of Kenan's postmodernity: he is encouraged by Spears's ability to reinvent himself in order to flourish in a world that has drastically changed since the time of his Narragansett and black ancestors, and yet Spears has managed successfully to transplant their values to a new landscape and a new economy: he works hard in the city in order to escape it, to build a life autonomous from it, one in which he can foster a very real connection between his family and the natural world in which they live, while the "mirage" of Las Vegas glitters on the horizon. Is this the postmodern yeoman?

As in his account of his visit to Las Vegas, Kenan concludes the chapter on Grand Forks, North Dakota, by leaving the city and offering a rapturous account of the nearby natural landscape. At the Minnesota border where he finds a marker locating the "'exact' geographic middle" of the continent, Kenan waxes transcendental. In Whitmanesque fashion, he catalogues the immensity of the natural world around him—from "the Arctic Ocean to the Gulf of Mexico, from Maine's coast to Oregon's shore"—and writes that he "was only beginning to come to a realization of how much space America takes up" (226). The next day, entering Montana, "Big Sky Country," he muses that to "live in such space must do something to the soul, must stretch it and expand it. I know how romantic a notion it is, but to see it is to think it possible" (226–27). This emphasis on human possibility and potential fostered by the landscape contrasts tellingly with the "utter sense of entrapment and doom" he witnesses among the towering condemned tenements in South Side Chicago.

Even when Kenan does not end a chapter by physically leaving the city, he often leaves via the narratives he records in interviews. For example, his chapter on St. Paul/Minneapolis ends in the reminiscences of Soyini Guyton, who contrasts her present life in a city that "just feels real white" (199) with her childhood on a farm in rural South Dakota, where, despite their isolation from a large black community, her family had no problem cultivating an authentically African American identity. Guyton asserts that, contrary to the prejudices she has often encountered among urban black people, "when a people are faced with isolation, they hold on to their culture more tenaciously" (197–98). Guyton suggests that in contrast to the daily challenges to cultural autonomy found in urban environments, agrarian life fosters autonomy. She explains that "just living on that land was such an equalizer. . . . Another [white] farmer would never look down the road and say, 'Well, he only got this because he's black or because of equal opportunity.' He got it because he had to work for it" (199).

Arthur Anderson, a retired attorney and educator whom Kenan interviews in Buffalo, makes the same case for the necessity of black economic autonomy. Mr. Anderson argues that "once your income comes from the whites, you are not independent" (103). Anderson argues that most of the social programs undertaken by whites to help blacks, including education initiatives, actually had the reverse effect, that they were designed to control blacks, to allow them to make "permissible progress" (110), rather than fully to empower them. Mr. Anderson views the results of integration that occurred in the 1960s as ultimately negative for black urban communities, making them less self-sufficient. He pursues the same argument when considering the effects of integration on the education of black youth—a lament that is echoed repeatedly throughout *Walking on Water*. For example, Judge Orion Douglas observes that many southern black colleges have lost accreditation resulting from the loss of their best students to white universities (573). Patricia Cormier says, "I really appreciated being in segregation, because they taught us that we had to be better than. That's something that doesn't happen now" (126). Even Kenan, who recalls the many committed black teachers he had before high school, attributes his own long-term academic success to what had been largely segregated schools.

The problem that Kenan repeatedly discovers in Buffalo, St. Paul/Minneapolis, Seattle, Los Angeles, and Idlewild, Michigan, is that—rather than empowering the entire black community—integration has simply facilitated the flight of the *talented tenth* from black communities to white ones. In Minneapolis and St. Paul, for example, where he finds "one of the most affluent black middle classes in the country" (183), fully integrated into the Twin Cities' professional and political life, there also exists a large black population plagued by poverty and crime. According to Minneapolis labor organizer Nellie Stone Johnson (who grew up on a Minnesota farm), the black middle class in the Twin Cities did not "pay anything back to the community. Oh, sure, they'd get out there and march and jump up and down, and honor Martin Luther King, Jr., and like that, but not the hard things that you have to do politically or by way of your own organization, to put people to work" (186). Class division in the Twin Cities is most vividly depicted by the affluent Pilgrim Baptist Church, which once featured two choirs that were segregated by class: the Gospel Chorus sat in the balcony, while the "lighter-complected, educated ones who could read music sat in the Chancellor's Choir" (173).

Filmmaker Charles Burnett finds a similar fragmentation of the black community along class lines in Los Angeles, a city that during the 1940s and 1950s, he claims, was "pretty much the South" (364). In addition to keeping livestock in their back yards, these southern transplants belonged to clubs named after southern towns. The city then was extremely segregated, and Burnette reports that police brutality was even more oppressive than in the South. Nevertheless, because of segregation, middle- and lower-class blacks lived in the same area, "all in the same boat," and there was a "strong sense of community" (364). Following "the civil rights thing," Burnett explains, "people started moving out, moving to Baldwin Hills, Echo Park. The black community of L.A.

disappeared with the riots" (364). Dr. Rick Moss, curator of the California Afro-American History Museum, offers a similar history of black communities throughout California's major cities: Central Avenue in Los Angeles, the Fillmore District in San Francisco, and the Western Addition in Oakland—these places were home to thriving African American communities up until the late 1950s or early 1960s, after which time, he explains, blacks started moving out and spreading themselves out across the respective cities (346–47).

As a further testimony to the difficulty of maintaining an autonomous culture in cities—or at least in California cities—Kenan quotes from Gerald Davis's introduction for a special exhibit at the Afro-American Museum, in which Los Angeles is depicted as a "nether world where Africans in America lose their ancestral minds," a place where "forms of traditional African-American culture cannot survive" (343). According to Kenan, being in Los Angeles is "like being in a movie" (341) or being trapped in a dream created by white capitalists, which has outgrown "even the dreams of its dreamers; it reached beyond its own destiny, and wrought a warped matrix of American ideals: loopy, lonesome and lone" (375). Unlike the "dream town" of Allensworth, California, which is rooted in the shared yeoman ideals of its African American founders, Kenan's nightmare images of Los Angeles—and of urban America, in general—focus on a deracinated black populace who have abandoned their collective struggle in favor of the individualistic and narcissistic desires of mainstream America. When these desires remain unfulfilled, Kenan depicts urban blacks given to collective despair and rage, as their dreams turn to visions of apocalypse.

In Atlanta, Kenan interviews one such apocalyptic prophet by the name of Lawrence Jeffries, the young (and naive?) leader of Students for Afrikan Amerikan Empowerment (SAAE), who, according to Kenan, is calling for "apocalypse now, the razing of the American empire, total overthrow, true revolution" (549). Borrowing a phrase from Malcolm X—one Kenan claims SAAE's members have "used nearly to death"—this militant group promises to "employ *any means necessary* to free and protect our people from the evils of imperialism, capitalism, classism, racism, and sexism!" Further on in their "organizational principles," SAAE proclaims, "We do not wish to be 'equal' to, or necessarily integrated with any other group. . . . We demand cultural autonomy! We demand freedom to practice our unique Afrikan traditions . . ." (545). Kenan sums up his response by remarking, "Perhaps too many exclamation points, but certainly their points could not be mistaken" (545). SAAE's goal of "cultural autonomy" corresponds with Kenan's; they simply differ with respect to the means they propose to achieve autonomy, recalling earlier debates between Malcolm X and Martin Luther King, Jr., or W. E. B. Du Bois and Booker T.

Washington. Despite his ambivalent portrayal of SAAE, Kenan engages them in an honest debate that calls into question his own more peaceful vision of a better future, a dialectic that makes him confront the extent to which he has abandoned what we might call his yeoman revolution of consciousness. "My dilemma," he confesses, "and I only came to reckon it more rightly years after I had left Atlanta and those undeniably courageous black students, had to do with what I had become—a BUPPIE down to my socks—when I had once dreamed I would become a revolutionary. Had I become, to use Ellison's term in *Invisible Man*, a 'spy in the enemy camp'? Or just another bourgeois Negro, running after his share of the American dream? Paying lip service to the 'need for change' while I was looking to 'get paid.' Such critical thinking must cut both ways" (550). And cut both ways he does. While recognizing their courage, Kenan implicitly criticizes their struggle as self-defeating, arguing that the "strength of African Americans has always been that their position was (is) a moral one. When morality is taken away from black folk's struggle for parity, we are left with only economics and the politics of might" (557).

In general, Kenan puts forth the belief that the commercialization of the civil rights movement has led to an unfortunate dependency of black America on white America; no longer is black identity the authentic product of concrete traditions and lifestyles of autonomous black communities, but, rather, it is mediated through artificial, and often negative stereotyped images promulgated through popular culture. In the 1960s and 1970s, Kenan argues,

> To be black became defined by "the struggle" and if you weren't down with the struggle, who were you? And though Gil Scott-Heron declared, "The revolution will not be televised," in the end it was. Televised, broadcast, filmed, photographed, written about. The most curious manifestation of this "revolution"—far from the type of Marxist revolution dreamt of by the Black Panther Power Party—was the blaxploitation films of the '70s. These films—*Shaft, Superfly, The Max*—exemplify, if not typify or even account for—a strange collusion between African American culture and the mass culture. Being black no longer arose from the reality of day-to-day existence, and upon dreams of equality, and health, and education, and a reasonably good life. (14)

By glamorizing the most negative elements in black society, and by taking identity formation out of the hands of autonomous black communities, whites further victimized African Americans. According to Kenan, by entering the media frenzy themselves blacks have simply perpetuated their own victimization. Formed in 1992 in the wake of the Atlanta riots that followed the Rodney King verdict, SAAE became very successful at broadcasting its militant pronouncements in the media, appearing on the Oprah Winfrey show, and captivating a regional media that "sought them out for sound bites" (544). Beyond their dependence on the media for identity, the very fact that SAAE's formation was in response to Atlanta riots, which might be criticized as a copy-cat reaction to the L.A. riots, suggests another source of Kenan's ambivalence toward the group, since he has only negative things to say about contemporary Los Angeles.

Kenan is reluctant to endorse such militancy in part because it effectively precludes other forms of revolution. He argues that by fixating on the "radical-ism of the sixties" African Americans have largely been guilty of "selective amnesia," unaware that African American militancy has a long, rich history and that there "is practically no decade in American history unmarked by 'race riots'" (542). Kenan attributes the prominence of the sixties to the "pervasive crystal ball of television" (542). Another likely reason for Kenan's desire to diminish the relative importance of the radical sixties in African American history is that it was predominantly an urban phenomenon and centered upon confrontation with whites and an acknowledgment of blacks as victims of oppression, rather than emphasizing the strengths of autonomous black com-munities.

Following his recurrent pattern of retreat from cities, Kenan leaves SAAE in Atlanta to journey east to St. Simons Island, where he takes a more rever-ential tone in his interviews with the elder descendants of one of the oldest African American communities in the nation. Formed by freed slaves who fol-lowed General Sherman in his march to the sea (581), generations have lived on St. Simons, a place that marks the culmination of the Middle Passage for thousands of slaves brought to America. Slave ships would stop at St. Simons and neighboring Jekyll Island to prepare their "saltwater Africans" for market (581). According to local legend, one such group of Africans chose suicide over slavery; while shackled together in a coffle, they stepped together into the sea. Other versions of the legend represent these Africans as miraculously over-coming their predicament by *walking on water* back to Mother Africa. In *Praise-song for the Widow*, Paule Marshall writes, "They just kept walking right on out over the river. Now you wouldna thought they'd got very far seeing as it was water they was walking on. Beside they had all that iron on 'em. . . . 'Nuff iron to sink an army. And chains hooked up to the iron. But chains didn't stop those Ibos none. Neither iron. . . . They feets was gonna take 'em wherever they was going that day . . ." (564). This legend serves as such an apt source for Kenan's title because of its double nature. While calling forth the horror and the pain of the Middle Passage, it also transforms that pain into deliverance—by focusing on the dignity and poise of those in bondage who refused to

acknowledge defeat, by identifying their strategies of collective effort and ostensibly supernatural resourcefulness. Kenan challenges current generations to
seek strength in their ongoing struggle against oppression by looking back to
the legendary strength of their forebears and by emulating their inventiveness,
their ability to overcome seemingly impossible odds, and their uncompromis-
ing commitment to an autonomous existence.

As in *Walking on Water*, in his fiction Kenan never loses sight of his fictional
community's past and the struggle of rural farmers to attain and maintain their
autonomy. Beyond the more recent history of Tims Creek, he incorporates leg-
ends concerning the original acquisition of farm land and stories that portray
the town's origins as a settlement of marooners, or escaped slaves, who defied
the odds of survival in inhospitable swampland, in order to control their own
fates. Kenan's fictional histories of Tims Creek resemble John Hope Franklin's
scholarly history of North Carolina's antebellum free blacks at least insofar as
they both portray ex-slaves who thoroughly separate themselves from white
communities in order to thrive. Franklin discovered two distinctive aspects of
the experience of these free blacks in North Carolina between 1790 and 1860
that are quite significant to our study: first, "In no State south of North Carolina were there half as many free Negroes as in that State" (6), and, second,
unlike most of the South's antebellum free blacks, who tended to live in cities
working as artisans or in various service industries, in North Carolina (where
there were few cities of any appreciable size), free blacks, "like most of the
other North Carolinians, were rural and, therefore, agricultural" (7). Considering the pressures of such a history—in which black yeomen fought to preserve a free and separate existence in North Carolina for at least seventy years
prior to the Civil War—it should come as no surprise that, throughout *Walking on Water*, Kenan feels uneasy in urban spaces and that when envisioning a
better future for African America he consistently looks to the past of rural
farming communities.

A Visitation of Spirits: "The terrible past they all had to remember"

Quoting from Gertrude Stein's "A Long Gay Book," Kenan ends *Walking on
Water* by exhaustedly babbling, "Not enough can be enough and being enough
quite enough is enough . . ." (639). Perhaps, even after culling his 5,000 pages
of notes down to 629 pages of published text, Kenan jokingly considers Stein's
title, "A Long Gay Book," a fitting one for his own project; however, most gay
readers of Kenan would likely be surprised by his lack of attention in *Walking
on Water* to gay concerns and themes, to which he gives so much attention in
his fiction. Notwithstanding several interviews with gay black men, in *Walking
on Water* Kenan has decided not to confuse and complicate the issues related

to gay and black identities. This confusion, however, constitutes the primary theme of much of his first major publication, the novel A *Visitation of Spirits*, and also of several of the stories in his collection, *Let the Dead Bury Their Dead*. Because both books are set in Tims Creek, a conservative community of black farmers and their descendants, gay sexuality, not surprisingly, challenges the masculine ideal upon which the community's patriarchal authority rests.

In many respects, the repression of gay sexuality in Kenan's fiction resembles the repression of female sexuality in Edgerton's *Raney*, in which rigid and parochial norms are codified in and disseminated from the local Baptist church. In contrast to the conflation of church and matriarchal power in Edgerton's fictional towns, in Tims Creek's two black Baptist churches the men occupy more than merely a puppet leadership. As in Edgerton's fiction, the town matriarchs exert their influence in the home, shaping and working through a younger generation of male leadership. However, the men—at least the older generation—hotly contest the efforts of the matriarchy seeking to assume too much influence in the community. In A *Visitation of Spirits*, the young black minister Jimmy Green is caught in the middle of a battle of the sexes that has been waged in his family for generations; this battle problematizes his identification with his male forebears, an identification already complicated by his own latent homosexuality. Before investigating how sexual orientation challenges the stability of patriarchy in Kenan's fiction, the historical development of patriarchy in Tims Creek must be further delineated.

Even more so than in Edgerton's fiction, in Kenan's, individuals identify themselves with the community, which historically they have done out of necessity—for the sake of survival. This sacrifice of individual autonomy to the collective results in the formation of hierarchical power relationships along lines of age, sex, and position within the church, in which the highest positions are reserved for male elders. While a feminist critique might identify this black patriarchy as merely an imitation of the oppressive structures in white society, the men (and often the women) in Tims Creek see it as the natural result of men assuming the first line of resistance against white oppression, which takes the forms of physical, economic, and cultural threats to the black community's autonomy. Because Kenan comes from one of the prominent black families in his community, he is in an opportune position to appreciate and to critique this history of resistance and its repercussions within the black community.

As they do in other respects, the fictional Crosses resemble Kenan's own family with respect to its bifurcated, biracial identity. Like the fictional white Crosses, the white Kenans are among the wealthiest and most influential families in North Carolina, far from the yeoman families we have thus far

examined. Doris Betts offers a valuable sketch of the Kenans from Duplin
County:

> When [Randall] Kenan was born in 1963, that county, 822 square miles
> of small towns imbedded among woods, swamp, and farms, settled by
> Scotch-Irish in the early 1700s, already had in its population . . . Kenans
> aplenty—white, established, often wealthy. The family had stamped its
> surname on Kenansville, the county seat [fictionalized as Crosstown by
> Kenan], and was known for two hundred years of leadership and philan-
> thropy to the state. The first white Kenan immigrant ancestor, a member
> of the British House of Commons, was listed in the 1790 census as owner
> of thirty-seven slaves; some of these became the novelist's forebears. The
> Duplin chapter of the United Daughters of the Confederacy is named for
> Kenan. Duplin was one of only seven counties in North Carolina that
> voted never to repeal secession. That old Southern family added new
> money when one of the Kenan girls married Henry Flagler, founder of
> Standard Oil and father of Miami, Florida. In 1971, when a volume of
> Duplin County history and government was compiled, white Kenans,
> Sprunts, Hills, and Herrings continued to be well-known surnames in
> Kenansville, Faison, and Rose Hill. . . . In the county history there was
> little indication that African American descendants of slaves had been
> steadily living out their own complex histories alongside the descendants
> of slaveholders, their names and stories intertwined.[18]

In *Visitation*, Horace Cross, a black teenager, witnesses a similar blindness
on the part of the white Cross family for its black descendants. He participates
as "best boy" (211) in the Crosstown outdoor theater production of *Riding the
Freedom Star*, the musical saga of the Cross family through the American Revolution, the Civil War, and the years of economic reconstruction following the
collapse of the plantation system. The play, written by Philip Quincy Cross and
underwritten by the Cross Endowment and the State Commission on Outdoor
Drama, is described by Horace as a "mish-mash of ill-conceived, ill-wrought,
cliché-ridden drivel," replete with "doggerel verse and the melodramatic romanticizing of Southern American history" (213). Not surprisingly the black
characters "were mainly there for buffoonery and hijinks that brought laughs
and chuckles from the audience" (213–14). Perhaps it is because of this history
of domination, exploitation, and then neglect, that Randall Kenan's family—
and its fictional Cross counterpart—took pains to preserve their own history.

Furthermore, the history of white oppression is central to the formation of
Tims Creek as a patriarchal, and not a matriarchal, community. While *Visitation* provides examples of black women resisting white oppression, such as in

the memorable scene in which Horace Cross's three strong aunts correct the white principal's punishment of their nephew (91–92), the community's narratives focus more on black male resistance to white oppression. The reigning patriarch and head deacon of First Baptist Church, Zeke Cross, makes plain the importance of physical strength and aggressive resistance to domination in the tale of his own confrontation with a white employer: Zeke pulled a pistol on the man after being denied two weeks of back pay (157–60). In *Let the Dead Bury Their Dead*, the story "Things of This World" tells of eighty-six-year-old John Edgar Stokes, who stands up to the abusive Percy Terrell, a textile baron and one of the wealthiest white landowners in the area. After one of Terrell's sons maliciously shoots Stokes's dog under the pretext that it had been trespassing on their property, Stokes gets his shotgun, visits the Terrells at their general store and blasts to death one of their prize hounds. Afterward, a group of elderly black men gather at Mr. Stokes' front porch awaiting the law and the Terrells—in a scene that, as Trudier Harris points out, closely resembles the developing action of Ernest Gaines's novel *A Gathering of Old Men*.[19] In "Run, Mourner, Run," Percy Terrell again appears, hatching a scheme to extort a family homestead from the prosperous black undertaker, Raymond Brown, by exposing Brown's homosexuality. Although Terrell's scheme succeeds, the story's climactic scene, in which the Terrells break into Brown's home to find him in bed with a young white man, portrays a dignified Brown, whose equanimity in the face of attack fully exposes the brutality and indignity of the Terrells.

The collection's novella-length title story, "Let the Dead Bury Their Dead," involves a similar confrontation generations earlier, in which Percy Terrell's ancestor, Malcolm Terrell, was killed by Elihu McElwaine after Terrell swindled him out of a tract of land.[20] This same story focuses extensively on the conflict (and possible sexual attraction) between the antebellum planter Owen Cross and one of his slaves named Pharaoh—or Menes—who had "bewitched" him. In a Nat Turner–like uprising, Pharaoh led a group of slaves away into the swamps where they formed a maroon society that sometime later led to the founding of Tims Creek. According to one source, this "Pharaoh," brought from Africa, may have been both a Yoruba king and shaman, "an unusual confluence of power as the two offices were normally kept separate." This same source further argues that Pharaoh may well have been the "Oni of Ife," or "'first among equals' among the Yoruba chieftains" (295), a title that might still be appropriate in the community of Tims Creek for the head deacon of the Baptist Church, a position held for generations by Cross men.

Like Reverend Jimmy Green, his teenage cousin Horace Cross feels the immense burden of responsibility such a legacy entails. With trepidation, Horace considers the prominence of his grandfather, Zeke Cross, currently the head deacon of the Baptist church: "As it was explained to him, his grandfather was the center, the source of the church's memory, the link to the terrible past they all had to remember. [Zeke's] father and his father's father before him were church leaders, and it had fallen upon him to lead, to guide, to counsel his people, their people. A chief, a great elder. His place was higher than the pastor's, and to Horace this seemed so very close to God that he realized, one day, that his grandfather was something of a David. He was grandson of a shaman" (71–72). Significantly, in none of the fiction we have so far examined, not even in Price's, does there appear this sort of family dynasty within a yeoman community. In the isolated Bales family of Edgerton's *In Memory of Junior*, the sons struggle to develop their own autonomous identities, as does the daughter in *Raney*. Even though Edgerton's characters are encumbered with an over-developed sense of blood loyalty and reverence for ancestors, they are virtually unencumbered by the social responsibilities to a larger community that descend upon heirs of a dynastic family, the sort of noblesse oblige we associate with aristocracy, with, for example, so many of the sons in Faulkner's novels. As heirs to the powerful Cross family, Horace Cross and Jimmy Green ironically find themselves in a position closer to that of Faulkner's Quentin Compson or Bayard Sartoris than that of the characters in novels by other North Carolina writers. Like Faulkner's young protagonists, Kenan's measure their own self worth by how well they are capable of fulfilling the roles of patriarchal leadership and the masculine ideal they associate with their male forebears.

Faulkner's major themes are likewise Kenan's: the decay of an agrarian society, the loss of traditional values with the disappearance of previous generations and leading families in the community, the alienation and fragmentation that results from modernity, the internalization of that failure as guilt in the succeeding generations, and the limitations imposed by a familial past upon individual freedom and individual identity. Kenan adds the element of explicit homosexual desire to the mix, and, in so doing, draws our attention to how the same element, though already thoroughly latent in Faulkner, must be fully recognized as integral to the texts, not only for an inclusive reading, but often for a logical one. Both Kenan and Faulkner examine the ways in which idealization of masculinity variously manifests itself in the antagonistic forces of patriarchal rule and gay desire. As in Faulkner, in Kenan's fiction the separation of these two masculine forces, and the exclusion of femininity, results in the deterioration of community. Faulkner thus provides a valuable touchstone for reading Kenan, and, conversely, Kenan calls our attention to the abundant homoerotic potential in Faulkner's work—especially with the figure of Quentin (with whom Randall Kenan says he fell hopelessly in love while first reading *The Sound and the Fury*).[21] A reading of Faulkner through the prism of

Kenan—specifically *The Sound and the Fury* and *Absalom, Absalom!*—identifies Quentin's involvement with the Charles Bon story as sexual and intensely personal rather than simply cultural. Such a reading might come nearer to offering a convincing connection between Quentin's violent exclamation that he does not "hate [the South]" (*Absalom!*, 303) and his eventual suicide half a year later. Arguably, what Quentin is reacting to about the South with respect to the Sutpen story is not the South's taboo against miscegenation, but rather its deeper (and, for Quentin, more immediate) taboo against homosexual desire.

In Kenan's first novel, *A Visitation of Spirits* (1989) and in the novella "Let the Dead Bury Their Dead" (1992), he presents the stories of two gay black men—Horace Cross and his cousin Jimmy Green—who tragically fail in their attempts to re-envision their lives within the boundaries of their traditional African American community. Like Faulkner's sons of aristocrats, the younger generation in Tims Creek, exemplified by Horace and Jimmy, feel the immense burden both to preserve their disappearing culture and to succeed in a new one. Of Jimmy Green, we are told, "To say that he loved the town would be not only a gross understatement but in many ways an indication of the shortcomings of the English language—James Malachai Green seemed to exist for Tims Creek" (*Let the Dead*, 277–78). Like Quentin, both Horace and Jimmy succumb to the pressures of their community because they are incapable of imagining an identity not completely constituted within its value system.

The parallels between *The Sound and the Fury* and Kenan's *A Visitation of Spirits* are numerous. Structurally, both novels are fragmented into multiple subjectivities. As in *The Sound and the Fury*, where the four sections devoted to Benjy, Quentin, Jason, and Dilsey are each identified with a specific date, in *Visitation* each section is labeled only by the date and time of the events it describes—alternating between April 29 and 30, 1984, and December 8 of the following year. The points of view described are that of sixteen-year-old Horace Cross, during the twenty-four hours leading up to his suicide, and, a year later, that of Horace's cousin Jimmy, and their elder relatives, Zeke and Ruth. Like the Quentin section of *The Sound and the Fury*—in which we follow a demented and suicidal Quentin as he wanders around Cambridge, while mentally and emotionally visiting various periods of his past in Jefferson, Mississippi—in the chapters of *Visitation* that depict Horace Cross's wanderings around Tims Creek during the early morning hours of April 30, we revisit significant events from his childhood and youth that precipitate his suicide later that morning.

Having grown up in the bosom of the Tims Creek Baptist Church, Horace is tortured by guilt for his homosexual desires and acts. Seeking to relieve the pressure, he contrives the idea of casting a magic spell that will transform him from a human being into a red-tailed hawk, a beast free from desire and guilt, though, significantly, a bird indigenous to his community. Horace's desire to escape the bondage of his flesh echoes a similar passage in *Narrative of the Life of Frederick Douglass:* the famous scene in which Douglass observes the freedom of sailing craft on the Chesapeake Bay. Like Horace, who contrasts his own hopeless situation to the freedom of the hawk, Douglass's vision of white sails leads to a contemplation of how all of creation excepting enslaved mankind is born free: "Could I but swim! If I could fly! O, why was I born a man, of whom to make a brute."[22] This allusion to Douglass's *Narrative* underscores *Visitation's* exploration of how contemporary African Americans relive struggles of their slave forebears, although the forms of bondage have changed.

Typically the struggles of African Americans depicted in Kenan's fiction are against the constraints of their own communities. Horace's magic spell, designed to transform himself into a hawk, goes awry, and instead he summons a host of demons (or imagines he has done so), which spend the next seven hours tormenting him and prodding him to the open rebellion against his family and town that he has so long repressed. In a final act of rebellion, he takes his own life with his grandfather's rifle, while standing in front of his cousin Jimmy, the minister who failed to help him a year earlier when Horace solicited advice about dealing with his maturing sexual identity.

Jimmy's failure to help his younger cousin is complicated by his own uncertain sexual orientation, by his role as spiritual leader in the community, and by his inheritance of his family's five-generation-old legacy of spiritual and civic leadership in Tims Creek. Here it is Jimmy who resembles Faulkner's Quentin Compson, whose grandfather and great-grandfather were a Confederate General and the Governor of Mississippi. Or perhaps he more closely resembles another version of Quentin, Faulkner's Henry Sutpen, whose father, Thomas Sutpen, with the odds stacked against him, mysteriously wrested a plantation out of the Mississippi jungle by thievery, brute force, and a legendary effort of will. Like Thomas Sutpen, Horace and Jimmy's great-great-grandfather, the ex-slave Ezra Cross, "had somehow amassed over one hundred acres of land, exactly how no one is truly certain. If you ask one person he'll tell you old Grandpap was given the land by his former master; if you ask another he'll tell you he went away and worked and saved and returned and purchased it; yet another will say he stole, killed, and cheated for it. But however he came about it, in around 1875 he had title to more land than most former slaves dreamed of having and he needed all the sons he could get to manage it" (115). Ezra Cross establishes the masculine ideal of the frontier by which his heirs each in turn measure themselves and find themselves inferior. Each in turn feels deep insecurity for not perfectly replicating his father or grandfather and for not fulfilling the dynastic imperatives established by previous generations. Jimmy Green, for example, considers his position as pastor of the Baptist church in which he grew up, reflecting upon how it is "commonly known among Southern Baptists that it's hard to preach to people you know and who've known you all your life and most of your family's life. It is formidable. And it happens rarely. But in this case it was the result of my grandmother's unearthly will. That and the will of a few dead folks. It actually began with her grandfather, Ezra Cross, who had given the land on which the present First Baptist Church of Tims Creek stands. It was his dream that one of his own progeny would stand before the altar as His, and his, minister" (115). Since the pulpit represents the center of power and respectability in this community, Ezra Cross's "dream" very much resembles the "design" of Faulkner's Thomas Sutpen. Like the former slave, Sutpen, a hillbilly, was intensely class conscious and by pure will to power sought to establish an aristocratic lineage that would extend beyond himself into perpetuity. Both Ezra Cross's dream and Sutpen's design can be then critiqued as imitative reactions to a mainstream culture that denied them dignity and legitimacy.

In his article "Toward a Black Gay Aesthetic," Charles I. Nero offers just such a critique of the contemporary black church. Despite its historical importance to the liberation of black people, Nero points out that the church is often used as a vehicle for upward mobility within the black community and thereby acquires the intolerances of the mainstream society. "The church is eager to oppress gay people," he notes, "to prove its worth to the middle class."[23] Numerous other scholars have acknowledged the role of the rise of a black middle class during the twentieth century as a cause for increasing homophobia in black communities. Cheryl Clarke argues that black communities prior to the 1950s and 60s tended to be more tolerant of sexual variance. "It is my belief," she writes, "that poor black communities have often accepted those who would be outcast by the ruling culture—many times to spite the white man, but mainly because the conditions of our lives have made us empathic."[24] Similarly, Marlon B. Ross explains that because "racial freedom could be gained only through racial solidarity," there existed "an understanding that the need for racial solidarity was much more important than the impulse to ostracize individuals whose sexuality seemed to vary from the norm."[25] Such arguments recall the broader critiques of the black middle class that we find in *Walking on Water:* the voices of numerous black people across the country who explain how, following the passage of civil rights laws which made integration into white communities possible, the black middle class abandoned black communities and black culture.

Having benefited from being born into the black middle class and having embraced the Baptist culture in which he was reared, Kenan is deeply ambivalent about both. In *Visitation*, Kenan's depictions of class differences within Tims Creek acknowledge criticisms such as those launched by Nero, Clarke, and Ross. Although Horace Cross's process of "coming out" ends in suicide, his first lover, Gideon Stone—who hails from a family of poor black bootleggers in Tims Creek—seems to be a well-adjusted teenager who has completely accepted his own sexuality, as his family likewise seems to have done. Unlike the boys at school, who have teased and ostracized Gideon since childhood for his effeminate mannerisms, the men in his family respect and even look up to him because of his high grades and promising future. Obviously, they recognize him as an asset to the family, and since, like Gideon, they are accustomed to being judged and ostracized by the community's leading families, they have little concern for keeping up appearances.

Like one of Faulkner's Snopeses, Gideon Stone usurps Horace's place as the smartest student in school and the "token" black (161) among the group whom Horace calls the "beautiful people" (161). Horace had been a straight-A student until his sexual anxieties began to overwhelm him. His family exacerbates his problems by disallowing him to socialize with his group of white friends, an eclectic group of boys, whose families have moved to Tims Creek, bringing new and more liberal perspectives with them. Horace joins them in the rebel act of piercing his ear, which his family views as a betrayal both of his black heritage and of its masculine ideal. In this pivotal scene, the Cross women notably take the initiative in criticizing Horace's behavior, which they do by calling into question his manhood with the hope of remolding it according to the model of Horace's male forebears. The scene ensues when the extended family has gathered for Thanksgiving dinner at the home of Johnnie Mae, the reigning Cross matriarch. Reverend Barden is in the middle of saying grace, when Horace walks in late. After the blessing, Horace mumbles an apology for his lateness; Johnnie Mae notices the earring and declares that he looks like "some little girl. Like one of them perverts" (184). She enlists Zeke's aid in rebuking the boy, and when Uncle Lester and Horace's cousin Jimmy try to argue in Horace's defense, they are silenced either by Johnnie Mae or one of her daughters, proving that in Tims Creek (as in Edgerton's *Raney*) women rule in the home, or at least at the dinner table. Johnnie Mae, who, significantly was her father's favorite, criticizes Horace's allegiance to his white friends in the light of historical racism, recalling the many times white men in their community had called her "girl and aunt" out of "disrespect" and "hatred," and how many times they had called her late husband "boy and uncle" (187). Her act of conflating his disloyalty to his race and family with his abnegation of a culturally inscribed ideal of black manhood both challenges and reinscribes patriarchal power in the community.

Aunt Ruth performs a similar act of critiquing and reinforcing this cultural ideal of masculinity when she calls what she observes as homosexual tendencies in the Cross men a curse or disease. Ruth has entered the Cross family by marrying Zeke's late brother Jethro, who became an alcoholic, it seems, as an act of self-torture, resulting from guilt over his sexual difference; defensively, Zeke and his other siblings have blamed Jethro's alcoholism on Ruth. At the peak of an argument with Zeke about Jethro's decline, Ruth exclaims, "Well, you'll see yourself one day, Ezekiel Cross. See what you and your family, your evil family have wrought. And it wont just on Jethro. It's on Lester. It's on this boy here [Jimmy]. It was on your grandboy [Horace, now deceased]. You all is something else" (197). Ruth's prophecy of doom is fulfilled as the Cross family navigates its way into the more progressive era of the 1980s, following decades of civil rights advances and sexual liberation. The heavy toll of subjugating *eros* to *ethnos*, of subjugating self to community for the sake of survival becomes apparent only after the threat of white oppression begins to recede and the reified ideal of black masculinity becomes self-defeating.

Following Horace's death, Jimmy Green meditates on his family's decline and how their yeoman values seem obsolete and counterproductive in a changing world. "I guess they didn't reckon the world they were sending him [Horace] into," he reflects, "was different from the world they had conquered, a world peopled with new and hateful monsters that exacted a different price. What has happened to us? Can I cry out like the prophet Jonah and ask God to guide my hand and direct me toward the proper remedy? Once, oh once, this beautiful, strong, defiant glorious group could wrestle the world down, unshackle themselves, part seas, walk on water, rise on winds. What happened? Why are we now sick and dying? All the sons and daughters groomed to lead seem to have fled . . . How, Lord? How? The war is not over. The enemy is encamped over the hill" (188). The cause of the fragmentation of America's urban black communities (as Kenan diagnoses it in *Walking on Water*) equally appears a problem in Tims Creek: rather than remaining at home to provide leadership to a new generation, the talented tenth of young blacks is fleeing their own community to access the opportunities in white, mainstream society made possible by integration. Conditioned by generations of resistance to oppression, in the vacuum left by the mitigation of white oppression, the older generation still seeks to condition their youth for the ongoing struggle, only to find that the youth have identified their own, quite different, battles and opportunities. Following the passage quoted above, Jimmy Green goes on to muse upon his ambivalent relationship to his heritage, suggesting that the "enemy . . . encamped over the hill" might be rising from the cemetery in the shadow of his church's steeple. "I have never lost my fear of the dead," he says.

"No matter how many eulogies I preach, no matter how many funerals I attend, perhaps no matter how old I get, I will fear the dead. In my dreams the dead rise, and they wear armor and are armed with bows and arrows and swords and guns and knives. Perhaps the fight goes on. Perhaps the war will be won" (189). Jimmy imagines a different future for his community and his church. "I want to introduce a new way of approaching Christian faith," he declares, "a way of caring for people. I don't want to be a watchdog of sin, an inquisitor who binds his people with rules and regulations and thou shalts and thou shalt nots" (110). This desire to break with the past, however, obviously fills him with dread and guilt. The military metaphor in the above passage suggests how similar Jimmy's feelings are to a war veteran's survivor's guilt and how similarly difficult it is for him to adjust to life after the war.

Despite his best intentions, Reverend Jimmy Green fails to revise the rules of his community sufficiently to make room for Horace's differing sexuality; when his younger cousin approaches Jimmy after church one Sunday and worriedly declares, "I think I'm a homosexual," Jimmy nervously counsels him to be patient, reassuring him that he will change in time, that even he, Jimmy, "went through a period," earlier in life, when he "experimented" (112–13). When Horace questions Jimmy about this "experimentation," Jimmy defensively resorts to his community's position on homosexuality, acknowledging "what the Bible says" on the subject, and encouraging Horace to pray and to ask "God to give you strength" to abstain (113–14), as Jimmy obviously has spent many hours doing since his college years of experimentation. Long after his wife, Anne, dies from cancer, Jimmy tentatively faces the years of self-deceit, admitting that memories "have a way of censoring themselves," and declaring boldly, "I have lied. To myself. When Anne died, things were not 'idyllic' and pastoral and perfect," as he had pretended to himself and his family. He attempts to become nostalgic about intimate moments with Anne, producing long, lyrical passages describing graphic conjugal bliss, which are periodically interrupted by the intrusion of Anne's remembered voice, taunting, "Look at me," "Do you really see me?" "Me?" "Do you even want to [have sex], really?" "Are you even capable?" Jimmy concludes this session of failed nostalgia by reflecting on how the metaphysical poets called sex "a little death" (172), which evidently is as close as he ever comes to admitting the degree of self-mutilation associated with his pretense of heterosexuality.

Because their family heritage is so central to their own personal identities, Jimmy and Horace both find it impossible to construct an identity separate from their community and family. Marlon Ross finds this tendency to be the rule rather than the exception among black homosexuals. Of the gay migration to the cities that began in the 1960s, and which he describes as a fundamentally white phenomenon, he writes,

> For the white homosexual integrating same-sex desire into one's sense of self meant necessarily leaving one's community behind . . . . For the black homosexual, nothing could be further from the case. Integrating same-sex desire within the self meant finding a way to remain integrated within the home community while remaining true to one's desire. . . . For the black homosexual, same-sex desire was a matter of finding a way to reaffirm continuity, rather than a matter of breaking with a dominant culture in order to gain a new identity through an awakened consciousness shared with others of a similarly oppressed status. After all, how could black gays break with dominant culture, since they had never been a part of it? (504–5)

Ross's statement goes a long way toward explaining the motive behind Kenan's fiction: by creating the world of Tims Creek, he comes as close as possible to reaffirming his continuity with his family and the yeoman community of Chinquapin, while being truthful about the individual suffering that community unavoidably imposes upon its members, especially its gay members.

A brief look at the two pastoral essays that frame the main narrative of *Visitation* calls attention to this problem of integrating individual desire within community tradition. These two essays describe in detail the community practices of hog killing and of growing and processing tobacco, two of the principal activities that once materially sustained the community and that provided the primary rituals that bound them together spiritually. These brief vignettes, one very near the opening of the novel, and the other at the very end, are told by the omniscient narrator who directly addresses the reader, as if she were a part of the community and remembered the folk traditions that are now quickly disappearing. "Remember," the narrator says, "how excited all the children would be on hogkilling day? Running about, gnawing at cracklings" (6). The narrator goes on to describe in detail the specific jobs divided between the men and women and the older children, then, in conclusion, laments, "Of course it's a way of life that has evaporated. You'd be hardpressed to find a hogpen these days, let alone a hog" (9); "requiem for tobacco," which concludes the book, proceeds in much the same language: "You remember, though perhaps you don't, that once upon a time men harvested tobacco by hand" (254). The narrator then carefully describes the season-long process of planting the beds, transplanting to the fields, cropping, harvesting, curing. He then explains how most of the individual farms have been sold to corporate interests and how "brown hands and sweaty brows and aching backs" have been replaced by the "clacking metal and durable rubber of a harvester" (256). He ends by arguing for the importance of preserving a long-gone agrarian past in a collective memory: "And it is good to remember that people were bound by this strange activity, this activity that put food on their tables and clothes on their backs and sent their young ones to school, bound by the necessity, the responsibility, the humanity. It is good to remember, for too many forget" (257). Significantly, these lines echo from several pages earlier the conclusion to Horace Cross's own personal requiem: a private meditation that ostensibly takes place shortly before his suicide (or possibly afterward in some eternal spirit realm).

Meditatively and patiently, Horace recalls his life; he catalogues his favorite foods, his favorite books, musical groups, and TV shows, recalls activities with family members, church rituals and teachings, and the gradual awakening of gay sexual desire. Horace concludes by focusing on the irreconcilable tension between sexual desire and community ritual. "I remember worrying that I was not worthy of taking Communion," he says, "because I was unclean, no matter how much I prayed and asked for forgiveness. . . . I remember the day I realized I was probably not going to go home to heaven, cause the rules were too hard for me to keep. That I was too weak. I remember me" (251). In its simple, direct language, unsentimental tone, and focus on concrete details of a lost past, this extremely personal, private elegy so powerfully echoes the following "requiem for tobacco" as to suggest their inevitable correspondence: perhaps the community has failed precisely because it denied individual desire. As Robert McRuer correctly notes, the two sections are "already and inescapably in dialogue"[26] and the pastoral account that concludes the novel is thereby problematized. McRuer continues, arguing that "the 'time when folk were bound together in a community, as one,' is exposed even as it is being constructed. The mythical, pastoral wholeness of this 'community' is ripped apart as surely as '[t]he bullet did break the skin of [Horace's] forehead, pierce his cranium, slice through the cortex and cerebellum. . . .' Bakhtin reminds us that 'sexuality is almost always incorporated into the idyll only in sublimated form.' Kenan's juxtaposition here of idyll and suicide foregrounds the murderous consequences of such a sublimation."[27] As if recognizing the perils of pastoral, Kenan moves away from that mode when returning to the story of Jimmy Green in the novella "Let the Dead Bury Their Dead." A comic tour de force that explodes and parodies Jimmy's own pastoral impulse to record with exactitude the history of his community, the novella's full title, given by the scholarly "Right Reverend James Malachai Green," is "Let the Dead Bury Their Dead; Being the Annotated Oral History of the Former Maroon Society called Snatchit and then Tearshirt and later the Town of Tims Creek, North Carolina [circa 1854–1985]" (271).

Let the Dead Bury Their Dead: "The best lie I ever heard . . ."

As *Absalom, Absalom!* does with *The Sound and the Fury*, Kenan's "Let the Dead Bury Their Dead" extends and complicates the previous novel, *A Visitation of Spirits*. And, like *Absalom, Absalom!*, "Let the Dead Bury Their Dead" is a text very much interested in the ways that its characters define themselves through narrative; the text is constructed of competing voices, though in perhaps a more Nabokovian form than Faulknerian. The novella's central narrative is the transcription of a recording made by the Reverend Jimmy Green of his Uncle Zeke's retelling of the community's central legend, a tale full of supernatural elements that seeks to establish the patriarchal origins of Tims Creek and to remind descendants of the ever-present threat posed by white outsiders to community unity and autonomy. This history, however, includes additional voices that challenge the centrality of Zeke's authoritative narrative, beginning with the frequent nagging interruptions of Jimmy's great-aunt Ruth, who was also present for the recording and who offers a dissenting perspective on Zeke's legend of patriarchal origins. Jimmy Green has provided elaborate annotation to the folktale, footnotes that trace elements in the narrative to their appearance in other oral and written histories. Jimmy has also included diary entries and a letter from two of the people mentioned in the footnotes, as well as his own autobiographical meditations on Zeke and Ruth. And, finally, the complete "Annotated Oral History," footnotes included, is edited, abridged, and introduced by Randall Garrett Kenan's pseudonym, Reginald Gregory Kain, a fictional scholar of anthropology and folklore at Sarah Lawrence (where Kenan taught during the composition of this "History"). Doris Betts further notes that the "History" is dedicated to Kenan's "real contemporaries," Nell Painter and Randy Page.[28] An extravagant mixture of history, folklore, natural science, and fiction, "Let the Dead Bury Their Dead" demonstrates the validity of the thoroughly postmodern approach to history that Kenan espouses in *Walking on Water*, where he remarks,

> Though I think history is far from a waste of time, I do believe it is never able to know the "truth." Which is not a question of history, in the end, but of the way we think of history. Regardless, we spill ink, and study documents, and uncover documents, and chase down clues, as if the past were a crime, and we, each and all, Nero Wolfes hell-bent on bringing the perpetrators to justice. It's a diverting game, often a tedious and boring game, but an instructive exercise, and historiography has this paradox at its center—when we write history, we are telling future readers more about ourselves than about the past. We are laying bare our own souls, in the

hope of illuminating the past, when what we are doing is merely adding another layer to the palimpsest of human records. (*Walking*, 337)

This perspective on historiography is not one shared by the Reverend Jimmy Green. Jimmy is obsessed with accurately fixing the truth of past events without recognizing how his annotated history blatantly exposes his own biases and interests. A deconstruction of Jimmy's history, however, requires a prior examination of the core narrative, Zeke's recitation, which itself dramatizes Kenan's principle of history as a "palimpsest" of individual revelations.

Zeke introduces his legend of Tims Creek's origins as an alternate history, boasting to his college-educated nephew that he won't find it "in none of them textbooks they give you up at that University" (283) (although, in fact, the numerous scholarly footnotes and other textual sources Jimmy has attached to Zeke's narrative account for more than half of the total text). Zeke begins in tall-tale mode, telling a seemingly aimless ghost story, full of slapstick humor, in which four grave robbers, one after the other, fall into the empty grave they have uncovered after being shocked by its newly risen former occupant. This resurrected ex-slave will later be revealed as the original patriarch and founder of the community; ironically named Pharaoh, this shaman led the first towns-people out of bondage and taught them self respect. Immediately following the desecration of Pharaoh's grave, the village becomes overwhelmed by the newly arisen dead.

Zeke—being an experienced storyteller—begins his tale in medias res, at the moment just before the climax, when "the Horror was let aloose" (319) and the dead of Snatchit returned from the grave to punish the living for falling away (in only one generation) from the teachings of Pharaoh, upon which the community was built. Like Twain's leisurely storytellers, Zeke takes his own good time to build to the final frenzy of blood-and-guts and fire from heaven. Having returned Pharaoh from the dead, Zeke then jumps back in time to speculate about Pharaoh's origins as an African shaman and to explain how Pharaoh originally founded the town of Snatchit (now Tims Creek). After raz-ing the plantation of Owen Cross—the white patriarch for whom Zeke and his family are named—Pharaoh led a group of slaves deep into the swamps to form a maroon society roughly near the present location of Tims Creek.[29]

So far, nothing in Zeke's tale appears incongruous with his position in the community as head deacon of the First Baptist Church: he emphasizes strong black male leadership, liberation from bondage, resistance to white oppression, and retribution against the oppressors. As he proceeds further, however, the tale introduces subversive content incongruous with Zeke's position as head deacon or his nephew's as minister. One year after Pharaoh's natural death, a honey-tongued tempter arrives in Snatchit, a "preacher-man" whom Zeke suggestively associates with white people by his light skin and eyes, his white Bible, and his insistence upon wearing only white suits, for which he offers scriptural support: "no impure raiments for the Servant of the Lord" (316). The following action combines a biblical parable of mankind's fall from grace with an Afrocentric criticism of Christianity, which reveals Zeke's buried ambivalences about his own participation in the promulgation of the "white man's religion."

In contrast to Pharaoh's pantheism, which emphasized unity and harmony—within the self, between the self and nature, among members of the community—the preacher-man sows division within the community by lording his leadership over everyone else, pitting neighbors against each other, and having the village's first church built—without windows "so they could concentrate on the Word of God" (315). In contrast to this preacher, who "knew the Bible backward, forward, and backward again" (314), Zeke explains that "Pharaoh hadn't been too big on the white man's God . . . told the people to love themselves and all things would follow, said God's in everything, everything, everywhere, in the trees, in dogs and cats and birds, even in them. Well that a lie, the Preacher say, God is high above and looking low, to believe otherwise, well, Preacher-man say, that's the sure way to hell and damnation" (315). With his fire-and-brimstone sermons, the preacher-man lures the community away from their own better natures (and yeoman self-sufficiency) to accept the creed of their oppressors.

The community's path of error culminates with the desecration of Pharaoh's grave, which they raid in search of a holy book that was buried with their leader. Just as the biblical Tree of Knowledge was forbidden Adam and Eve, access to this book was denied the legendary founders of Tims Creek. Sounding like Henry W. Grady and other apostles of northern capitalization of southern industry, the preacher-man tells the community that Pharaoh's book actually contains a treasure map that will lead them to "a great treasure more bountiful than that of the white men of the North" (319). By giving themselves over so completely to materialistic desire, the townspeople provoke their own apocalypse: the dead rise and are joined by a host of demons; together they lay waste to the town, killing, raping children and adults alike, taking vengeance on their enemies. Finally, all are consumed by fire that "rained down from the sky just like the Lord sent to the cities of Sodom and Gomorrah" (332). Zeke reports that "none of the wicked escaped" but for an old woman and a young boy by the name of Elihu McElwaine, who remained to rebuild the town from its ashes (332–33). This cleansing and rebirth is echoed by Pharaoh, who returns amid the flames, riding a bull; he lops the preacher-man's head off, takes a baby from his arms, and, before riding off again with the baby, declares,

"Damnation and ruin. What began as good has ended in evil. We are not ready" (332). This same sentiment—acceptance of past failure mixed with patient waiting for deliverance—appears throughout *Walking on Water*, as perhaps best demonstrated in the museum town of Allensworth, California, by Ed Pope's resurrection of Colonel Allensworth's dream of a yeoman utopia.

Kenan's work demonstrates a pastoral vision fundamentally different from that of most Euro-American literature. As compared with, for example, Fred Chappell's *Midquest* and his Kirkman quartet, which follow the models of classical and English pastoral poetry, Kenan invokes biblical pastoral, revisiting the past only to restore a proper vision of the future. In contrast to the ancient Greek vision of history as a series of progressively degraded ages—from gold to iron—biblical history records, within a linear narrative, cycles of disaster and renewal, each of which serves to prophesy a more glorious future. Having adopted this biblical sense of history for their own psychological and spiritual needs, African Americans have developed a version of pastoral that is less fully elegiac than that of classically influenced, Euro-American pastorals. Because the past contains the horrors of Middle Passage, slavery, and Jim Crow, African Americans cannot so fully seek refuge in the past, as Kenan aptly demonstrates with Zeke's tale.

Zeke Cross's tale is an organic part of the oral tradition from which it sprang, and, as such, with every performance it is constantly changing, revisiting the past, but open to new possibilities. Ruth's periodic interruptions, which challenge the details of Zeke's tale, signal that both she and he have heard numerous versions of the legend, demonstrating its importance and long history within the community. Also significant is the fact that Zeke first heard it from his grandfather, a point he reiterates on several occasions. In his concluding words, he emphasizes the authenticity of the tale: "All I know is what my granddaddy told me, and boy, that was like I told you, word for word, near bout. Near bout" (334). This deliciously comic "Near bout" of course suggests the extreme liberties Zeke has taken in his telling. In *Visitation*, Zeke fondly remembers his grandfather's extravagant imagination, and we can only assume that Zeke followed his model:

> Grandpap was a good tale-teller. He could put together the best lie I ever heard come out of a man's mouth, and not crack smile the first. He'd talk about sailing to Africa and Europe and all overseas, just as pretty, talking about them mountains and hills, so green, coconut trees against the shore and giraffe heads poking up over them, and wild cannibals with clothes made out of human hair, about sailing down the Mississippi, fighting wild Indians, about the time he went up to Canada tracking bear and

had to kill one with a fishing knife . . . and we sitting there, with our mouths gaped open, believing every word of it, knowing at the same time full well that Grandpap hadn't been no further south than Wilmington, not further west than Fayetteville, and no further north than Raleigh. (*Visitation*, 52)

The duality of Zeke's grandfather's tales—their simultaneous existence as "lies" and a miraculous alternate reality—recalls the similar duality of the legend Kenan records in *Walking on Water* of the saltwater Africans who refused slavery by either choosing suicide or by walking on water back to their homeland. In both cases, storytelling has provided communities a way of overcoming oppression by passing on to successive generations possibilities for freedom from the limiting circumstances of the past. In addition to providing an explanation of origins, the legend of Pharaoh and the Preacher-Man, like so many of Zeke's grandfather's tales, satisfies the important need of entertainment for children and thereby forges a bond between generations, a need it continues to serve as Zeke repeats it to his adult great-nephew, Jimmy.

Unfortunately, however, Jimmy is not capable of hearing this tale in the spirit that it is told. He takes it much too seriously. His personal involvement with Zeke's tale of community origins and patriarchs and matriarchs returning from the grave calls to mind his confession from the earlier novel: "I have never lost my fear of the dead. . . . In my dreams the dead rise, and they wear armor and are armed with bows and arrows and swords and guns and knives. Perhaps the war goes on. Perhaps the war will be won" (*Visitation*, 189). Jimmy might be described as Faulkner describes Quentin Compson: as "an empty hall echoing with sonorous defeated names; he was not a being, an entity, he was a commonwealth. He was a barracks filled with stubborn back-looking ghosts."[30] Rather than imaginatively engaging his community's oral history as a means of empowerment, Jimmy is overwhelmed by it. The war with the dead to which he alludes might be described in Freudian terms as a war between a repressed id and an overbearing superego. Whereas Zeke engages the tale libidinally, working through the sodomy and other assorted sex crimes of the reanimated dead with a gusto that provides a cleansing catharsis, Jimmy fears that catharsis. Significantly, just as Zeke's tale approaches its apocalyptic climax, just as the "Horror was let aloose" (319), Jimmy interposes a lengthy textual tangent that prolongs the revelation of that horror.

On the other hand, the content of the interposed text in question adds another invaluable layer to the palimpsest of this community's history, one that Jimmy has previously been complicit in silencing, one that points to Jimmy's secret personal interest in the saga. Zeke's narrative focuses on the supernatural events surrounding the early years in Snatchit, but much of Jimmy's annotation examines the Cross family's white ancestors and the subplot of life on the Owen Cross plantation, from which Pharaoh and his band of marooners escaped. Jimmy provides a lengthy excerpt from the diary of Owen's wife, Rebecca Cross, and the full text of a letter from his son, Phineas Cross, who became "one of the most eminent botanists of his day" and published several important works on carnivorous plants (320). This passionate love letter from Phineas to his gay lover at Oxford University was excluded from Phineas's published letters at the insistence of his family. It was recovered by Jimmy Green from the Phineas Cross Papers collected at the University of Texas at Austin (320). The letter contains a rhapsodic account (which reads like a gay parody of William Bartram) of Phineas's journey deep into the swamps of his homeland in search of the Venus's-flytrap. During this journey, Phineas comes across a group of escaped slaves, including Pharaoh, who months earlier had burned Phineas's father's home and killed Phineas's sadistic brother. Because Phineas is an abolitionist and sympathetic to Pharaoh's cause, the ex-slave spares his life, though he ensures Phineas's silence by "bewitching" him. Phineas recalls, "He merely raised his hand as if to silence me and I could not say one solitary word. It was perhaps the single most horrifying experience I have yet undergone. Paralysis it was" (325). Pharaoh further warns Phineas that if he ever speaks a word to anyone of this encounter, he "shall die in great agony" (325), a threat Phineas takes to heart, divulging the story only *in print* to his lover. To the general reader, Jimmy Green has ostensibly included this letter because of its significant references to Pharaoh, especially his magical powers, which play such an important part in the folklore about him, as represented in Zeke's tale. In light of Jimmy's personal history—as revealed in *A Visitation of Spirits*—however, the figure of Phineas Cross and his healthy acceptance of his own homosexuality are equally important.

The figure of Phineas becomes even more significant, uncannily so, when we recognize how his renown as a botanist and his studies of "Darwinian principles of adaptation" (320) mirror Horace Cross's amateur interests in botany and his high school science experiment, in which he studies tropism. Horace defines *tropism* for his class as an "orientation of an organism, usually by growth rather than by movement, in response to an external stimulus" (*Visitation*, 155), which might be interpreted as Kenan's theory of sexuality, or, to extend the metaphor further, his theory about healthy living, in general. Because Jimmy so thoroughly represses his own *tropism*, or *eros*, it should come as no surprise that he finally succumbs to his fear of the dead: in the introduction to Jimmy's "Oral History," his editor, Reginald Kain, relates that, returning from a ministers' conference in Atlanta, Jimmy suffered a fatal automobile accident just as he entered the town limits of Tims Creek (277). What desire might Jimmy have guiltily indulged while in the sin city, which prevents him from confronting his elders back home? He can almost be heard muttering to himself as he re-enters his hometown, "I don't hate it, I don't hate it."

To mirror the war between the dead and the living that culminates "Let the Dead Bury Their Dead," a textual "war" ensues within the "history" between the main narrative, told by Zeke, and the scholarly gloss provided by Jimmy. Just as Jimmy's interjection of textual sources both expands Zeke's narrative and impedes its developing momentum, Jimmy's gloss, in the form of frequent footnotes, authorizes the oral history, by authenticating it, and simultaneously removes authority from the oral history and places it within the scholarly, written history. Jimmy's gloss seeks to establish meaning along what Henry Louis Gates, Jr., refers to as the "semantic axis" of standard, white English, while Zeke's text creates meaning along the "rhetorical axis" of black vernacular.[31] Jimmy seeks to fix the signification of the story within a stable historical order that can be traced to written texts in libraries, whereas Zeke "Signifies" within a fluid, oral tradition. Gates refers to "Signifyin(g)" as "black double-voicedness; because it always entails formal revision and an intertextual relation."[32] Zeke's tale revises biblical myths, white histories of slavery, and most certainly his grandfather's version of the same narrative. Despite Jimmy's best scholarly efforts to control and limit Uncle Zeke's tale by framing it with a scholarly gloss, the oral narrative overwhelms and undercuts the authority of the framing narrator—as is the case in much southwestern humor and in Charles Chesnutt's *The Conjure Woman*, which Signifies on the tales of Thomas Nelson Page. Similarly, in "Let the Dead Bury Their Dead," the framing narrator's "book learning" serves to emphasize the vitality of the main narrative.

Jimmy's formal education as a biblical scholar (at the Southeastern Theological Seminary and Duke University), along with some studies in the graduate history program at the University of North Carolina (278–79) have trained him to locate truth as objectively as possible by contextualizing and intertextually triangulating any given data. This seems to be his method in annotating Zeke's oral history. He traces in the historical record the appearance of both major and incidental details from Zeke's story, thereby expanding, but also controlling and limiting, the significance of any detail and ultimately providing a critical reading that limits the meaning of Zeke's entire narrative. For example, the footnote Jimmy provides for Pharaoh's holy book discusses its possible real-world antecedents, including an Arabic version of the Koran, a book in Carthaginian "stolen from the library at Timbuktu," a book of Zoroastrian creation myths, a spell book, "the Book of Life, the Book of the Dead, a time-travel device," and finally a transliteration of the "traditional Yoruba libraries, somehow transcribed" (287). This footnote demonstrates the multiple purposes of Jimmy Green's footnotes: they seek to verify and extend a detail, leading the reader to other sources (often fictional, though often not) where the issue may be further explored, with the effect of expanding or even universalizing its significance— at the same time that such intertextuality distracts the reader's attention from the central narrative, thus diffusing its energy. Similar annotative discussions of other details from Zeke's story include, for example, Pharaoh's name and origins, slave uprisings and maroon societies in North Carolina and throughout the South, the history of the white Cross family, and speculations about the origins of a large mound in Tims Creek.

Unlike Jimmy's notes, which attempt positively to document the folklore of Zeke's tale in the scholarly record, Reginald Kain's several brief notes are more skeptical. As a more thoroughly disinterested scholar, he evidently views his role as a corrective one, checking Jimmy's oversights. His several notes all point to the lack of documentation for details from Zeke's narrative, with the overall effect of minimizing the significance of all scholarly efforts, including Jimmy's, to locate Zeke's tale in the written historical record, moving it farther into the realm of myth and folklore.

Two of Jimmy's more interesting notes take the form of botanical and anthropological discussions of the persimmon tree, which twice figures as a very minor detail in Zeke's story. Jimmy's botanical interests in the persimmon link him to Horace Cross and Phineas Cross, both persecuted because of their homosexuality. In an attempt at cultural recovery, he extensively explores the "dietary and medicinal" uses of the fruit and the special uses of the wood in a variety of specific cultures in America, Asia, Europe, and Africa so that the tree serves as a transcendental metaphor for the possibilities of global unity; simultaneously, the loss of this knowledge of the plant and its special, even "magical" (291), properties, suggests a pastoral lament of the fallenness of mankind, which, obviously, echoes the theme of the main narrative. These footnotes on the persimmon reveal how, in general, the notes interact with the main narrative: together the two take on a life of their own. Rather than achieving the ostensible purpose of anchoring the oral narrative in the "real world," thus defusing its anarchic energies, the footnotes are themselves pulled free from their purchase in the soil of reality and are swept along in the wake of the subconscious and symbolic energies of the oral narrative.

Although the main title Jimmy Green has given to his history—"Let the Dead Bury Their Dead"—suggests resignation on the part of the living, Jimmy is obviously anything but resigned. Together with A Visitation of Spirits, this novella offers its readers a cautionary tale of two young men who allow themselves to be overwhelmed by the mythologies of their insular community. Both

Jimmy and Horace are very widely read, but they are incapable of overcoming the ideologies rooted in the place and the people to which they were born. Their tragedy is exacerbated by the flight of their peers; Jimmy's brother is a lawyer in Washington, D.C., and his sister is pursuing a Ph.D. in architecture at Berkeley. In Tims Creek there is very little middle ground between flight from and foreclosure to the worldview of one's ancestors. This middle ground, a combination of new ideas with the old, is exactly the antidote Kenan proposes for a new generation of African Americans. While acknowledging a history of white oppression and celebrating the concomitant history of black resistance, he puts forth the need for a new vision of black life in America, one that is not fixated on the past, but that neither ignores it, one that embraces the yeoman values of independent, close-knit agrarian communities, such as Tims Creek (or Chinquapin), but finds the means of realistically incorporating those values into a new nonagrarian age. In *Walking on Water*, he writes that he has "come to the unshatterable conclusion that being black [is] indeed a willed affirmation" (627). He might make the same comment about being gay and black. In either case, Kenan serves as a Jeremiah figure—like generations of leaders before him—committed to leading his people out of bondage to false and defeating images of themselves, teaching them to fight for their own autonomy, and, like that mythical founder of Tims Creek, teaching them to love themselves.

CONCLUSION
The Yeoman's Legacy

In a 1991 essay on the future of southern literature, Doris Betts predicts that, because most new writers will live in urban rather than rural areas or small towns, their fictions will predominantly be set in such urban spaces.[1] So far, however, this has not much been the case in North Carolina. Contemporary writers, from Betts's generation to newcomers Randall Kenan and Charles Frazier, hail from rural or small town (or small city) backgrounds, and, though they may have moved to urban centers as adults, they rely most extensively upon childhood settings for their fictions. We have yet to see the great urban novel in North Carolina. In novels from North Carolina, the city is typically visited briefly or remembered and serves as an *other* space that casts in relief the primary setting of a rural area or small town. We are still waiting for someone to tell the story of North Carolina's metropolis, Charlotte, the way Tom Wolfe told the story of Atlanta in *A Man in Full* (1998). In the seventy years since the publication of *Look Homeward Angel* (1929), there is hardly anything more urban than Thomas Wolfe's early twentieth-century depiction of Asheville. The Asheville of Fred Chappell's *The Gaudy Place* (1973), for example, is no more cosmopolitan than the city Wolfe knew.

Despite all evidence to the contrary, Betts's prediction of a predominately urban southern literature is logically sound. It seems, indeed, inevitable that tomorrow's great writers will have to discover a subject matter radically differ-ent from their predecessors' pastoral response to change. As Frank Kermode observes, "Pastoral flourishes at a particular moment in the urban develop-ment, the phase in which the relationship of metropolis and country is still evident, and there are no children (as there are now) who have never seen a cow."[2] As the age approaches when the North Carolina writer's backward glance will fall not on the figure of the yeoman farmer but on a long-gone cul-de-sac, gilded by the misty recollections of suburban childhood, we will likely have a fundamentally new literature. The extent to which the values of the yeoman—prominent among them, egalitarianism, independence, interde-pendence, and a connection to nature—may transform themselves and survive within a new economy, of course, remains to be seen. In addition to the half

dozen writers who have been considered at length, a cursory study of nine additional writers provides further evidence of the yeoman ideal, even within
urban and suburban environments.

In both life and fiction, Allan Gurganus has found it necessary to leave the
state to find the urban experience. One of the state's most successful writers,
Gurganus pursued an education away from North Carolina in some of the
nation's most prestigious writing workshops. Born in 1947 in the eastern Piedmont city of Rocky Mount, Gurganus has studied and taught writing at the
Iowa Writers' Workshop, Stanford, Sarah Lawrence, and Duke. His first novel,
The Oldest Living Confederate Widow Tells All (1989), won the Sue Kaufman
Prize for First Fiction. Told in the voice of ninety-nine year old Lucy Marsden,
this novel chronicles the Civil War and its long aftermath. Gurganus's stories
have appeared in the *New Yorker*, the *Paris Review*, the *Atlantic Monthly*, and
Best American Short Stories. His story collection *White People* (1990) won the
1991 *Los Angeles Times* Book Prize for Fiction and the 1991 Southern Book
Award. He won the Lambda Literary Award and the National Magazine Prize
for *The Practical Heart* (2001), a collection of four novellas. *Plays Well with
Others* (1997) is set in New York City and chronicles the devastation of AIDS.
Gurganus remarks that *Confederate Widow* also resulted from his need to confront the AIDS crisis, noting that the novel is "very much about the grief of
young men burying other young men."[3] His fiction frequently champions outsiders, as do the several autobiographical stories in *White People*, which deal
with a precocious, artistic boy growing up in a conservative family and town.
As a gay writer, Gurganus often shares with women writers from North Carolina a critical vision of yeoman democracy as merely a conservative "savage
ideal." Having grown up in Rocky Mount, a town that he says was 60 percent
black during his childhood,[4] Gurganus shares with Reynolds Price an emphasis on the need for a critical understanding of the vital relations between blacks
and whites in his region, a theme that appears prominently in *Confederate
Widow* and in the novella "Blessed Assurance: A Moral Tale." For more than a
decade Gurganus has made his home in Hillsborough, North Carolina.

Born in 1960, Kaye Gibbons grew up seven miles south of Gurganus's Rocky
Mount, in the rural community of Bend of the River, located near the Tar
River.[5] Like Gurganus, Gibbons saw her first novel win the Sue Kaufman Prize
and later be adapted to television. Gibbons began writing *Ellen Foster* (1987)
while a student in Louis Rubin's southern literature class at the University of
North Carolina. She composed her first novel quickly, and it was published
with little revision by Rubin's then-young publishing company, Algonquin
Books of Chapel Hill.[6] A largely autobiographical novel, *Ellen Foster* recounts
a difficult passage in Ellen's childhood, chronicling life with an alcoholic father

following the death of the girl's mother. Gibbons's second novel, *A Virtuous Woman* (1989), also draws upon her memories of rural Nash County and comments on class differences she observed there. The novel's heroine, Ruby Pitt Woodrow, abandons her gentrified life first to marry a migrant farm laborer and then to marry an older tenant farmer named Jack Stokes. The novel is told in chapters that alternate between the perspectives of Ruby and Jack. Both of these early novels depict the struggles of strong young women to determine their own courses in life and, perhaps for that reason, were selected for Oprah Winfrey's Book Club.

Gibbons's third novel, *A Cure for Dreams* (1991), demonstrates a still greater willingness to experiment with point of view and a desire to explore hidden lives. In her research for the novel, Gibbons made use of the Federal Writers Project papers held in the Southern Historical Collection at the University of North Carolina at Chapel Hill; the novel's epigraph is a quote from W. T. Couch, regional director of the FWP: "With all our talk of democracy it seems not inappropriate to let the people speak for themselves." As in the fiction of Doris Betts and Lee Smith, Kaye Gibbons's novels enable the voices of women who have been silenced within the patriarchal societies in which they live. In *A Cure for Dreams*, the voices of three generations of women combine to tell their collective story; the novel's structure suggests both archival accuracy and the immediacy of oral history. Each chapter begins with a brief gloss from the compiler and presenter, Marjorie, while the body of narration is quoted from her deceased mother, Betty, but includes italicized passages that are remembered or reconstructed quotes from the grandmother, Lottie. This confluence of women's voices reinforces the solidarity of women against the impositions of men throughout the novel and, thus, offers a cure for their unfulfilled dreams of romantic love. In Gibbons's first three novels, Julian Mason finds frequent examples of "the strong, self-reliant individual coping with the quiet dramas and firm challenges of every day's journey and what that requires not only to survive but also to triumph."[7] Gibbons has since published five books in which she continues to depict strong female protagonists struggling for self-determination: *Charms for the Easy Life* (1993), *Sights Unseen* (1995), *On the Occasion of My Last Afternoon* (1998), *Divining Women* (2004), and *The Life All around Me by Ellen Foster* (2006).

Jill McCorkle's novels and short stories also deal with the struggles of women for self-determination. They are frequently set in small towns similar to her hometown of Lumberton, situated in southeastern North Carolina, next to Interstate 95. The interstate highway and the tacky businesses that proliferate around its exits find their way into the milieu of McCorkle's fiction, which might be described as minimalist; her characters are often so dependent upon the trappings of consumer culture that they find it difficult to construct an identity free of them. Such is the case, for example, in her short story "Gold Mine," in which hotel owners Ruthie and Jim Kates attempt to recover from the loss of tourist traffic along Highway 301 when I-95 is opened up to the west. Lynn Z. Bloom has called McCorkle's novels bildungsromans, observing how they tend to describe the education and growing self-awareness of adolescents, usually young women.[8] Self-awareness often comes when these young women gradually abandon the superficial perspectives of the consumer culture in which they live and begin to explore their own specific personal and familial histories. After completing a bachelor's degree at the University of North Carolina at Chapel Hill and an master's at Hollins College, McCorkle simultaneously published her first two novels, *The Cheerleader* and *July 7th* (1984) with Algonquin Books. Her other novels include *Tending to Virginia* (1987), *Ferris Beach* (1990), and *Carolina Moon* (1996). She has published three story collections: *Crash Diet* (1992), which won the 1993 New England Bookseller's Award, *Final Vinyl Days* (1998), and *Creatures of Habit* (2001). Her fiction has been selected four times by the *New York Times Book Review* for its Notable Books of the Year list, and her stories have twice been included in *The Best American Short Stories*. McCorkle has taught creative writing at Tufts University, North Carolina at Chapel Hill, Bennington College, Harvard University, and North Carolina State.

Thirty miles to the north of McCorkle's Lumberton, Tim McLaurin grew up in east Fayetteville, on the rough side of a rough town. Home to the sprawling U.S. Army base of Fort Bragg, Fayetteville is a city with more than its share of tattoo parlors, topless bars, and pool halls. The mean streets of Fayetteville provide the setting for McLaurin's first novel, *The Acorn Plan* (1988), which finds Billy Riley, recently returned from the Marine Corps, attempting to survive in a city where his employment opportunities are limited to mill work and the entertainment is typified by drinking and knife fighting. Like McLaurin, Billy Riley manages to escape this dangerous environment and becomes the first member of his family to go to college. McLaurin's autobiography, *Keeper of the Moon* (1991), his greatest achievement, also explores the author's ambivalence for the hardscrabble life of east Fayetteville and the surrounding rural areas, where common aspects of life include widespread alcoholism, violence, and backbreaking labor. In *Keeper*, McLaurin depicts cock fights and dog fights, and he tells of his own large collection of poisonous snakes that he exhibits in his traveling extravaganza, Wildman Mac and the Last Great Snakeshow. In more introspective passages, he examines his private struggle with bone cancer and his efforts to pursue a life of writing. Furthermore he examines a rural South quickly becoming overwhelmed by urbanization and overpopulation by northern immigrants and a new generation of southerners, who care little for the region's agrarian past. This theme of deracination appears in McLaurin's second novel, *Woodrow's Trumpet* (1989), and finds its most explicit expression in his book-length poem, *Lola* (1997), which relates the loss of a family farm and heritage that follows the death of John Wesley Stewart, whom McLaurin presents as one of the last of a dying breed of yeoman farmers. Again in the novels *Cured by Fire* (1995) and *The Last Great Snake Show* (1997), McLaurin relates tales of southerners dealing with change—both personal and cultural. The first episode of Gary Hawkins's public television documentary series *The Rough South* focuses on McLaurin and his hometown of east Fayetteville. Subsequent episodes deal with Harry Crews and Larry Brown,[9] whose "gritty" fiction about lower-class southerners McLaurin's writing resembles more than it does that of other, mostly middle-class, North Carolina writers. Until his death in 2002, McLaurin taught creative writing at North Carolina State University. A final novel, *Another Son of Man* (2004), was published posthumously.

Like McLaurin, Dale Ray Phillips writes gritty fiction, populated by what he describes as "lower class people, 'white trash,' people just struggling to get by, dealing with the world the only way they know how."[10] His stories honestly confront such matters as alcoholism, divorce, and dysfunctional families, but they do so with moving lyricism and with humor typical of the characters he chronicles. Extravagant images abound in his stories: a hand chopped off by a boat propeller, a newly divorced man wearing his ex-wife's skirt, a back yard filled with TVs showing the first moon landing. His characters are willing to take desperate measures to reinvent themselves, but their inevitable failures bring them back to a recognition of their own flawed though solid humanity; in quieter moments they rediscover a reconnection with family and sustaining cultural traditions, such as fishing, which figures prominently in several stories. Among other places, his stories have appeared in the *Atlantic, Harper's, GQ, Zoetrope,* and *Best American Short Stories.* His collection *My People's Waltz* (1999) might be described as a novel of stories, since it follows the life of a picaro named Richard, as he ages from young childhood to early middle age.

John Holman, an African American writer from the outskirts of Durham, now teaches at Georgia State University but continues to write about the community of his youth, which he describes in *Luminous Mysteries* (1998) as "a rural community tucked away from the city. A four-lane intersection with a stoplight protected their neighborhood's timeless character from the office buildings, fast-food restaurants, traffic, and white people."[11] *Luminous Mysteries,* a novel-in-stories that spans roughly thirty years from Grim Powers's childhood in the 1950s to his young adulthood, chronicles how this close-knit community loses its "timeless character," as the "liquor house" becomes a "drug house"

(2) and the community's boundaries become more porous in a post-integration era. Holman explores the difficulties of identity formation faced by black Americans whose communities are in a state of flux. Each of the novel's characters in some way struggles with identity: Lonnie, an ambitious local politician overcoming heroine addiction; his love interest, Butters, a black woman who bleaches her hair and wears green contact lenses but adamantly declares, "I'm a new stereotype, is what I am. I'm not a black woman trying to look white; I just look like one" (146); Grim Powers, who decides to become the first black cowboy from his town; and the ex-con, Belly-Man, who, in struggling to fashion a new identity for himself realizes that he "didn't expect to get back the person he had been, but he hadn't lost enough to be someone new" (49). Mayes, an academic, is another character caught between an old life and a new one, between the agrarian past of his grandparents and the artificiality and abstraction that characterize his day-to-day work in the academy. Mayes recalls the protagonist of "Squabble," the title story of Holman's 1990 collection—like Mayes, Aaron is a college professor, though recently unemployed, who experiences culture shock when he returns to his hometown and relearns the language of his people while taking a job as a bartender in a beer house on the edge of town. Holman's interest in the fragmentation of autonomous black communities resembles Randall Kenan's elegiac celebration of Tims Creek; however, in the semiurban black communities of Holman's fiction, a yeoman past appears even less available as a touchstone for blacks attempting to define themselves in a contemporary South.

As in the work of the six writers treated at length in this book, and in the several writers briefly discussed above, the challenge of adapting to rapidly changing landscapes—both literal and cultural—appears to be the most common theme among contemporary North Carolina writers. In the introduction to *This Is Where We Live: Short Stories by 25 Contemporary North Carolina Writers* (2000), Michael McFee observes that "Where we live now, in turn-of-the-century and turn-of-the-millennium North Carolina, is not where we lived before, as citizens or writers: it's a profoundly changed and profoundly changing world."[12] In some of the stories in McFee's anthology, such cultural fluidity serves as cause for celebration, as in Marianne Gingher's "Teen Angel" and P. B. Parris's "Carmen Miranda's Navel," in which the fluidity of urban popular culture serves as a means of feminist empowerment and identity formation. Other stories from the collection, such as Tony Earley's "The Prophet from Jupiter," offer a less sanguine view of urbanization and commercial culture. In Earley's story, a dam keeper for the Appalachian resort community of Lake Glen spends his days and nights regulating the lake's water level, fishing for a legendary man-sized catfish, and mourning both the failure of his marriage and the town's loss of autonomy to the horde of "Florida Yankees" who have over-run the community in a frenzy of land speculation. Like a biblical prophet, or like Oedipus or the Fisher King, this dam keeper meditates upon the fate of his fellow townspeople and patiently waits for enlightenment and delivery. The town's present cultural sterility mirrors his own actual sterility, and he traces both back to the building of the Lake Glen dam and the 1927 flood that cov-ered the original town of Uree, creating a tourist mecca around an artificial lake that would grow catfish to monstrous proportions and eventually divest the natives of their heritage.

"The Prophet from Jupiter" was anthologized in *Best American Short Stories* (1994), as was Earley's story "Charlotte" the previous year. Both stories also appear in Earley's collection *Here We Are in Paradise* (1994). "Charlotte" depicts North Carolina's metropolis as a city filled with transplants from vari-ous Piedmont mill towns who have come to the Queen City to forget their pasts over draft beer and frozen drinks that they enjoy in fern bars and massive sports arenas with other transplants who have similarly transformed themselves in gyms, tanning parlors, and hair salons liberal with peroxide. "Our lives are small and empty," the narrator laments, "and we thought they wouldn't be, once we moved to the city."[13] The story begins with a comic elegy for Char-lotte's mid-1980s loss of its sponsorship of professional wrestling to Ted Turner's cable TV network in Atlanta; ostensibly, Charlotteans are incapable of re-membering any event much farther in the past. The extent to which Earley himself is deeply interested in his region's agrarian past finds ample expression in his first novel, *Jim the Boy* (2000), set in the Appalachian foothills commu-nity of Aliceville during the Great Depression, a place that resembles Earley's hometown of Rutherfordton, North Carolina. Unlike the dark and satirical portraits of urbanization that appear in "Charlotte" and "The Prophet from Jupiter," the tone of Earley's novel is one of sublime innocence, creating a pas-toral mood that often resembles that of children's literature. Earley has also published a collection of essays, *Somehow Form a Family: Stories that are Mostly True* (2001). He teaches at Vanderbilt University and has been named by both *Granta* and the *New Yorker* as one of the twenty most promising young writers in America.

Like Tony Earley, other writers from western North Carolina have distin-guished themselves among the state's contemporary writers by very often look-ing back to the early twentieth century and late nineteenth century for their fictional settings. As Henderson County native Robert Morgan explains, such a remote past—in the form of language and folkways—has been generally better preserved in Appalachia, though the recent tourist boom is causing many Appalachian writers to feel a sense of urgency to glance backward and chronicle their region's past.[14] Although he has taught at Cornell for the past three decades, Morgan often remarks that he has "moved from Southern Appalachia to Northern Appalachia," noting that the "areas are similar in many ways, even in landscape."[15] Morgan's poetry and fiction are full of detailed information about the day-to-day lives of yeoman farmers from an earlier time. For example, his novel *Gap Creek* (1999) (an Oprah Winfrey Book Club selection) recounts the first year in the marriage of an Appalachian yeoman couple at the turn of the twentieth century and contains information from that era on many of the basic functions necessary to maintain a working farm, including hog butchering (down to the details of smoking the meat and rendering the lard), many other forms of food preparation and storage, hunting and gathering skills, planting and harvesting, bartering practices, traditional diagnoses and treatments for a variety of ailments, and even the most essential functions of birthing a child and preparing a corpse for burial. Morgan's short stories also often focus upon the specific labors of mountain yeomen and artisans; one of the best examples is found in "Poinsett's Bridge," which tells of a self-taught mason who progresses from building stone chimneys for family and friends to helping build the bridge that opens up his mountains to the eastern foothills and thus begins the accelerating process that will irreparably change his region.

Morgan's stories have been collected in *The Blue Valleys* (1989), *The Mountains Won't Remember Us* (1992), and *The Balm of Gilead Tree: New and Selected Stories* (1999). In addition to *Gap Creek*, he has published four other novels: *Brave Enemies* (2003), *This Rock* (2001), *The Hinterlands* (1994) and *The Truest Pleasure* (1995), listed by *Publishers Weekly* as one of the outstanding books of 1995 and first runner-up for the Southern Book Critics Circle Award. Like Fred Chappell's, Morgan's career has been divided between fiction and poetry; during the 1970s and 1980s he published a number of fine books of poetry, and 2000 saw his return to poetry with the publication of *Topsoil Road,* followed by *The Strange Attractor: New and Selected Poems* in 2004. As in his fiction, Morgan's poetry demonstrates a keen interest in preserving a way of life. With titles such as "Sharpening a Saw," "Mowing," "Squatting," "Family Bible," "Wind from a Waterfall," "Blowing Rock," and "Double Springs," Morgan's poems study the specific actions, artifacts, idioms, and landscapes of Appalachia, as he seeks simultaneously to evoke concrete experiences and recognize the cultural values and philosophical implications buried within them.

Charles Frazier's debut novel *Cold Mountain* (1997), won the prestigious National Book Award for Fiction (in a year when major publications by Don DeLillo and Thomas Pynchon made the competition especially fierce). Frazier's novel shares with Morgan's writing an interest in how a world of ideas is located within the artifacts and traditions of rural Appalachian culture. *Cold*

Mountain revisits the pivotal moment in southern history, the Civil War, from the perspective of a mountaineer soldier unambivalently unsympathetic to the Confederate cause; indeed, the novel levels equally harsh criticism at the Confederate military machine (including Robert E. Lee) and at the Union forces. This is not only the story of "rich man's battle, poor man's fight," but also that of the war between yeoman transcendentalism and modern materialism, a materialism which Frazier locates not in the urban North so much as in gentrified Charleston and the surrounding Tidewater culture. Born and reared in Andrews and Franklin, North Carolina, virtually under the shadow of the actual Cold Mountain, Charles Frazier grew up hearing family stories about his home. Frazier had published a nonfiction book on the Andes and a short story before deciding at age forty that he wanted to write a novel that would explicitly deal with Appalachian themes and culture. At the time, his recently retired father was at work on the family's history and told Frazier a story about a relative who had fought in some of the bloodiest battles in the Civil War and then, after being badly wounded, decided to leave the war and walk westward across the state toward home. This brief family anecdote provided the germ of *Cold Mountain*. Over the course of the following seven years, Frazier rigorously researched his topic, especially such areas as rural architecture, farming, and food preservation. He remarks that he "wanted to know what that world was like, the physical world of the nineteenth century, especially in the mountains. What were the processes of life, those basic things of food and shelter?"[16] During his research, Frazier relied heavily upon letters and journals from the period, in which he was "especially looking for interesting expressions, unusual words, any kind of thing that would let me, in language, alert the reader to the fact that this is another world. This is a world that occupies the same physical points of ours but was in many ways just unrecognizable to us."[17] *Cold Mountain* focuses on the schism between these two worlds created by the Civil War and thereby pursues its pastoral critique of the contemporary South, which is a world built by commercial capital and therefore antithetical to the yeoman way.

Frazier's second novel, *Thirteen Moons* (2006), is loosely based on the life of the "white chief" of the Cherokee, William Holland Thomas, fictionalized as the novel's erudite and aged narrator, Will Cooper. Cooper's rags-to-riches tale serves as an anti–Horatio Alger story. By surveying his own life, he likewise chronicles the tulmultuous changes wrought by capitalism, technology, and Manifest Destiny throughout the course of the nineteenth century. At the novel's beginning young Will, an orphan, is exiled from the home of his relatives and sent as a bound boy into the uncharted frontier of "Indian territory," which is nevertheless already becoming integrated into the world of market capital. The novel deals with the Cherokee removal under President

Andrew Jackson, and, although Frazier is careful to avoid sentimentalizing the Cherokee—in part by showing that they were represented, if nominally so, among Appalachian slaveowners—the novel elegizes the irrevocalbe loss of a way of life among the native inhabitants of western North Carolina, who emphasized subsistence and sustainability.

Like Frazier's two novels, so much of North Carolina's contemporary fiction is concerned with the state's rapidly changing culture, demographics, and economic base. This body of literature poses an unavoidable question: at what point does the state lose its regionally specific world view? In a state where yeoman farmers have been so thoroughly replaced by timber production and tourism in Appalachia, manufacturing, information technology, and service industries throughout the Piedmont, and agribusiness across the coastal plain, to what extent is a "yeoman ideal" likely to remain viable for successive generations of writers?

In 1961, the rural sociologist Samuel H. Hobbs, Jr., reported a fundamentally new trend in the state's agriculture, which he had observed in effect since the mid-1950s. For the first time since the Civil War the average farm size in the state began to increase. Other new trends were the rapid decrease in tenancy, a decrease in the number of farms, a large increase in the value of farm property, and the "rapid trends towards large-scale agriculture" that were made possible by "tremendous gains in mechanization and push-button farming." Hobbs concluded, "If these trends continue for another 15 or 20 years at the pace set in the last 5 or 10 years then agriculture in North Carolina and in the United States will bear little resemblance to agriculture as we have known it in the past."[18]

The rise of agribusiness in eastern North Carolina certainly proves the accuracy of Hobbs's predictions. Compared to the early decades of this century, when it was common even for the state's mill workers to raise and slaughter their own hogs, by the turn of the twenty-first century, North Carolina had become one of the nation's top pork producers, with seventy percent of hog production in the state controlled by Smithfield Foods and much of the remaining thirty percent controlled by corporations such as Premium Standard Farms, Prestage Farms, and Goldsboro Milling.[19]

Bob Geary reports that other crops "like potatoes and wheat, traditionally sold at market, are also going under contract to big agribusinesses and food companies in increasing numbers." Pittsboro-based advocacy group Rural Advancement Foundation International–USA (RAFI) observes that such contract farming, in which independent farmers are powerless in their negotiations with corporate buyers, "can make farmers feel like serfs on their own land." In the hog industry, corporate "integrators" earn ten times the profit made by the growers, while the growers (and the public) bear all of the financial risks of production and all legal responsibility for environmental damages caused by the farming—damages such as groundwater pollution and the massive fish kills in coastal waterways caused by pfiesteria blooms that have largely resulted from excess nutrients related to hog waste. Corporate integrators in the poultry industry operate with similar immunity. Even in the tobacco industry, with its long history of autumn tobacco barn auctions, contract farming has recently grown exponentially.[20] Finally Chris Burritt reports that the tobacco barns are closing because cigarette makers are buying eighty percent of their tobacco directly from producers through contract, thus avoiding the middle-man at auction and acquiring greater control over the production of the tobacco.[21] Based on recent trends, the future of farming in North Carolina will be dictated by corporate interests.

John Shelton Reed is prominent among South watchers who argue that the region's culture appears surprisingly resilient in the wake of large-scale changes in demographics, economics, education, and mass communication. In *The Enduring South*, Reed identifies persistent "localism" as one of the primary indicators of an enduring southern culture, noting that in 1983 southerners were roughly 20 percent more likely than northeasterners or midwesterners to prefer to remain in their own region.[22] One of the largest practical results of such a disparity in regional emigration is the continuing influx of northeasterners and midwesterners to the Sun Belt, possibly leading to ever greater dilution of its specific regional culture. On the other hand, such a cultural mixing might, in fact, call even greater attention to the pockets of traditional culture that remain relatively undiluted.

Among the writers included in McFee's 2000 anthology of North Carolina fiction, *This Is Where We Live*, half are nonnatives to North Carolina and their stories represent the distinctive geographies of their own respective pasts. Instead of describing a bland, monocultured melting pot, North Carolina's contemporary writers represent a diversity of backgrounds by which we are all potentially enriched. Furthermore most of these writers have served as teachers in the state's many thriving writing workshops, thereby helping to foster the literary renaissance of the past several decades. Whether the yeoman ideal will remain a dominant feature of the state's literature, or whether it will, rather, become only one of numerous perspectives in a more diverse literature, remains open for subsequent study.

NOTES

Introduction

1. William S. Powell, "Vale of Humility," e-mail to the author, October 7, 2002.

2. See Ritchie Devon Watson, Jr., *Yeoman versus Cavalier: The Old Southwest's Fictional Road to Rebellion* (Baton Rouge: Louisiana State University Press, 1993).

3. Bail J. Whiting, "GPF Reports on the Competition: North Carolina: The Research Triangle Park and 'Charlotte, USA,'" (Philadelphia: Greater Philadelphia First, 2002), www.gpf.biz.

4. James W. Clark, Jr., "North Carolina, Literature of," in *The Companion to Southern Literature*, eds. Joseph M. Flora and Lucinda H. MacKethan (Baton Rouge: Louisiana State University Press, 2001), 559.

5. Among the schools most noted for their creative writing programs are the University of North Carolina at Greensboro, University of North Carolina at Chapel Hill, North Carolina State, University of North Carolina at Wilmington, and Warren Wilson College. In addition to induction into the state's Literary Hall of Fame, annual literary prizes include the Sir Walter Raleigh Award and the North Carolina Award for Literature. WUNC-TV in Chapel Hill broadcasts a weekly program called *Book Watch* that features interviews with North Carolina writers. East Carolina University annually publishes the *North Carolina Literary Review*, which features critical articles on the state's literature. Currently the state boasts a number of fine literary journals that allow emerging writers from North Carolina to publish their work beside some of the best writers working throughout the nation; a short list of these publications includes the *Carolina Quarterly*, the *Greensboro Review*, the *Crescent Review*, the *Asheville Poetry Review*, *Pembroke Magazine*, *Cairn*, *Crucible*, the *Sandhills Review*, and the annual collection from Algonquin Books, *New Stories from the South*. North Carolina publishers of fiction and poetry include Banks Channel Books of Wilmington, Down Home Press of Asheboro, John F. Blair of Winston-Salem, and the national powerhouse Algonquin Books of Chapel Hill.

6. The conclusion briefly surveys the treatment of plain folk in the work of nine additional contemporary North Carolina writers: Tony Earley, Charles Frazier, Kaye Gibbons, Allan Gurganus, John Holman, Jill McCorkle, Tim McLaurin, Robert Morgan, and Dale Ray Phillips.

7. Frank L. Owsley, *Plain Folk of the Old South* (Baton Rouge: Louisiana State University Press, 1949), xi, 6–9, 13; Ritchie D. Watson, "Yeoman," in *Companion to Southern Literature*, 1009; and Paul D. Escott, introduction to *North Carolina Yeoman: The Diary of*

Basil Armstrong Thomasson, 1853–1862, ed. Paul D. Escott (Athens: University of Georgia Press, 1996), xi.

8. Watson, *Yeoman versus Cavalier*, 7.

9. Ibid., 8.

10. Watson, "Yeoman," 1009.

11. Paul D. Escott, *Many Excellent People: Power and Privilege in North Carolina, 1850–1900* (Chapel Hill: University of North Carolina Press, 1985), xvii.

12. Ibid., xviii–xix.

13. Bill Cecil-Fronsman, *Common Whites: Class and Culture in Antebellum North Carolina* (Lexington: University Press of Kentucky, 1992), 6.

14. Ibid., 1.

15. Harry L. Watson, "Conflict and Collaboration: Yeomen, Slaveholders, and Politics in the Antebellum South," *Social History* 10 (October 1985): 281; George M. Fredrickson, *The Black Image in the White Mind: The Debate on Afro-American Character and Destiny, 1817–1914* (New York: Harper and Row, 1971), xli–lxiii, 61–64; W. J. Cash, *The Mind of the South* (1941; New York: Vintage, 1991), 38–39, 66, 83–85; Escott, *Many Excellent People* 43, 114, 116, 135; and Michael Myerson, *Nothing Could Be Finer* (New York: International Publishers, 1978).

16. Herbert Aptheker, *American Negro Slave Revolts* (New York: International Publishers, 1943), 231–32, 243–44; Herbert Aptheker, *To Be Free* (New York: International Publishers, 1948), 18–19; William L. Andrews, introduction to *North Carolina Slave Narratives*, eds. William L. Andrews, et al. (Chapel Hill: University of North Carolina Press, 2003), 1–19; and Myerson, *Finer*, 15, 18–22.

17. John Hope Franklin, *The Free Negro in North Carolina, 1790–1860* (1943; Chapel Hill: University of North Carolina Press, 1995), 6–7.

18. Frenise A. Logan, *The Negro in North Carolina, 1876–1894* (Chapel Hill: University of North Carolina Press, 1964), 75–85; and Hugh Talmage Lefler and Albert Ray Newsome, *The History of North Carolina* (Chapel Hill: University of North Carolina Press, 1963), 491.

19. Robert Morgan, "O Lost, and Found," *Thomas Wolfe Review* 24.2 (Fall 2000): 6.

20. Louis D. Rubin, Jr., "Thomas Wolfe and the Place He Came From," in *A Gallery of Southerners* (Baton Rouge: Louisiana State University Press, 1982), 71.

21. Ibid., 72.

22. Ibid., 72.

23. Ibid., 72.

24. Frederick H. Koch, *Carolina Folk Plays* (New York: Henry Holt, 1922), xi.

25. Laurence G. Avery, *A Paul Green Reader* (Chapel Hill: University of North Carolina Press, 1998), 103.

26. Vincent S. Kenny, "Paul Green (1894–)," in *Southern Writers: A Biographical Dictionary*, eds. Robert Bain, Joseph M. Flora, and Louis D. Rubin (Baton Rouge: Louisiana State University Press, 1979), 193.

27. Thomas A. Underwood, *Allen Tate: Orphan of the South* (Princeton, N.J.: Princeton University Press, 2000), 281.

28. Ibid., 215.

29. Ibid., 281.

30. Julian Mason, "Charles Waddell Chesnutt (1858–1932)," in *Southern Writers: A Biographical Dictionary*, 77–79.

31. Andrews, introduction to *North Carolina Slave Narratives*, 2.

32. Fred Hobson, *Tell About the South: The Southern Rage to Explain* (1983; Baton Rouge: Louisiana State University Press, 1998), 62.

33. Ibid., 46.

34. Lovalerie King, "The Birth of A Nation," in *The Companion to Southern Literature*, 105.

35. Quoted in Fred Hobson, "Gerald White Johnson (1890–)" in *Southern Writers: A Biographical Dictionary*, 247.

36. William Faulkner, "Address upon Receiving the Nobel Prize for Literature: Stockholm, December 10, 1950," in *Essays, Speeches & Public Letters by William Faulkner*, ed. James B. Meriwether (New York: Random House, 1965), 120.

37. Hugh Talmage Lefler, *North Carolina Told by Contemporaries* (Chapel Hill: University of North Carolina Press, 1965), 420–21, 430–31.

38. Escott, introduction to *North Carolina Yeoman*, xi.

39. Owsley, *Plain Folk*, v–vi.

40. Several notable exceptions include Mary Weaks-Baxter, *Reclaiming the American Farmer: The Reinvention of a Regional Mythology in Twentieth-Century Southern Writing* (Baton Rouge: Louisiana State University Press, 2006); Ritchie D. Watson, Jr., "Frontier Yeoman versus Cavalier: The Dilemma of Antebellum Southern Fiction," in *The Frontier Experience and the American Dream: Essays on American Literature*, eds. David Mogen, Mark Busby, and Paul Bryant (College Station: Texas A&M University Press, 1989), 107–119; Cleanth Brooks, "The Plain People: Yeoman Farmers, Sharecroppers, and White Trash," in *William Faulkner: The Yoknapatawpha Country* (New Haven, Conn.: Yale University Press, 1963), 10–28; and Charmaine Allmon Mosby, "Gilmore Simms' Mississippi Yeomen," *McNeese Review* 30 (1983–1984): 3–11.

41. Frederick Law Olmstead, *A Journey in the Seaboard Slave States: With Remarks on Their Economy* (New York: Dix and Edwards, 1856), 366.

42. David Bertelson, *The Lazy South* (New York: Oxford University Press, 1967), 58.

43. William S. Powell, *North Carolina through Four Centuries* (Chapel Hill: University of North Carolina Press, 1989), 245–66.

44. Ibid., 315.

45. Ibid., 328.

46. John J. W. Rogers, "Piedmont," in *The Companion to Southern Literature*, 645.

47. John Hope Franklin argues that, although the total number of slaves in North Carolina continued to increase up until 1860, the "rate of increase had fallen off during the antebellum period, and the lack of profits, apparent even to the most rabid proslavery spokesman, heralded its demise as a constructive factor in the economic life of the State" (Franklin, *Free Negro*, 9). William C. Harris, by contrast, contends that during the 1850s slavery increased rapidly in North Carolina, especially in the Piedmont, because of that region's improvements in agriculture and transportation via rail. With rail extending as far west as Morganton in 1860, Harris speculates that slavery eventually would have even risen significantly throughout Appalachia. See William C. Harris, *North Carolina and the Coming of the Civil War* (Raleigh: Division of Archives and History, N.C. Department of Cultural Resources, 1988), 8.

48. W. C. Harris, *Civil War*, 43.

49. Ibid., 56.

50. Eugene D. Genovese, "Yeoman Farmers in a Slaveholders' Democracy," in *Fruits of Merchant Capital: Slavery and Bourgeois Property in the Rise and Expansion of Capitalism*, eds. Eugene D. Genovese and Elizabeth Fox-Genovese (New York: Oxford University Press, 1983), 255.

51. Owsley, *Plain Folk*, 135; Escott, introduction to *North Carolina Yeoman*, xlviii.

52. H. Watson, "Conflict and Collaboration," 277.

53. Ibid., 280.

54. Ibid., 287.

55. Stephanie McCurry, "Producing Dependence: Women, Work, and Yeoman Households in Low-Country South Carolina," in *Neither Lady nor Slave: Working Women of the Old South*, eds. Susanna Delfino and Michele Gillespie (Chapel Hill: University of North Carolina Press, 2002), 59.

56. For case studies of the barter system in yeoman communities, see Arthur C. Menius, III, "James Bennitt: Portrait of an Antebellum Yeoman," *North Carolina Historical Review*, 8 (1981): 305–26; and John T. Schlotterbeck, "The 'Social Economy' of an Upper South Community: Orange and Greene Counties, Virginia, 1815–1860," in *Class Conflict, and Consensus: Antebellum Southern Community Studies*, eds. Orville Vernon Burton and Robert C. McMath, Jr. (Westport, Conn.: Greenwood, 1982).

57. Owsley, *Plain Folk*, 115.

58. Escott, introduction to *North Carolina Yeoman*, xlvii.

59. Ibid., xix.

60. Owsley, *Plain Folk*, 95.

61. Thomas Jefferson, *Notes on the State of Virginia*, ed. William Peden (1787; Chapel Hill: University of North Carolina Press, 1955), 165.

62. Ibid., 164–65.

63. J. Hector St. John de Crèvecoeur, *Letters from an American Farmer* (1782; London: J. M. Dent and Sons, 1912), 55.

64. Rex Burns, *Success in America: The Yeoman Dream and the Industrial Revolution* (Amherst: University of Massachusetts Press, 1976), viii.

65. Ibid., 1.

66. Escott, introduction to *North Carolina Yeoman*, xlv–xlvi.

67. Owsley, *Plain Folk*, 134.

68. Ibid., v.

69. Doris Betts, "We Were the Snopeses: A Writer and Her Piedmont," *Southern Cultures* (Summer 1999): 9.

70. Quoted in Susan Ketchin, *The Christ-Haunted Landscape: Faith and Doubt in Southern Fiction* (Jackson: University Press of Mississippi, 1994), 254.

71. In *Many Excellent People*, Escott argues against designation of small slaveholders as yeomen, citing the greater cultivation of cash crops among farmers who owned even several slaves. Studies that include small slaveowners among the yeomanry include Cecil-Fronsman's *Common Whites* and James Oakes's *The Ruling Race: A History of American Slaveholders* (New York: Knopf, 1982). In *Kinship and Neighborhood in a Southern Community* (Knoxville: University of Tennessee Press, 1987), Robert Kenzer demonstrates the extensive intermarriage between small slaveholders and nonslaveholders in antebellum Orange County, North Carolina, which suggests the extent to which both groups were integrated into the same community. David Golightly Harris's journals also suggest the extent to which this small slaveholder from the South Carolina upcountry intermingled

with his nonslaveholding neighbors. See David Golightly Harris, *Piedmont Farmer: The Journals of David Golightly Harris, 1855–1870*, ed. Philip N. Racine (Knoxville: University of Tennessee Press, 1990).

72. See Steven Hahn, "Class and State in Postemancipation Societies: Southern Planters in Comparative Perspective," *American Historical Review* 95 (1990): 83–98; and Powell, *North Carolina*, 417.

73. In *Slavery in the American Mountain South* (New York: Cambridge University Press, 2003), Wilma Dunaway has recently demonstrated that small plantations appeared in nearly every region of southern Appalachia. Nevertheless, her data shows that only about 10 percent of households owned slaves in western North Carolina—and even fewer in the more mountainous regions (25, 32), with large plantations being uncommon. Although Appalachian writers, such as John Ehle, Wilma Dykeman, and Thomas Wolfe, have addressed racial injustice, race is less of an issue for most contemporary writers from western North Carolina.

74. Michael McFee, introduction to *This Is Where We Live: Stories by 25 Contemporary North Carolina Writers*, ed. Michael McFee (Chapel Hill: University of North Carolina Press, 2000), xiv.

Doris Betts

1. Lefler, *North Carolina Told by Contemporaries*, 450–51.

2. Dorothy Scura, "Doris Betts (1932–)," in *Fifty Southern Writers after 1900: A Bio-Bibliographical Sourcebook*, eds. Joseph M. Flora and Robert Bain (New York: Greenwood, 1987), 55.

3. Dorothy Scura, "Doris Betts at Mid-Career: Her Voice and Her Art," in *Southern Women Writers: The New Generation*, ed. Tonette Bond Inge (Tuscaloosa: University of Alabama Press, 1990), 164.

4. Betts, "Snopeses," 15.

5. Jacquelyn Dowd Hall, James Leloudis, Robert Korstad, Mary Murphy, Lu Ann Jones, and Chris Daly, eds., *Like a Family: The Making of a Southern Cotton Mill World* (Chapel Hill: University of North Carolina Press, 1987), 6.

6. Ibid., 6. For an excellent overview of the rise of commercial agriculture and the textile industry throughout Piedmont North Carolina, see Hall et al., *Like a Family*. Also helpful are I. A. Newby, *Plain Folk in the New South: Social Change and Cultural Persistence 1880–1915* (Baton Rouge: Louisiana State University Press, 1989); Wayne K. Durrill, "Producing Poverty: Local Government and Economic Development in a New South County, 1874–1884," *Journal of American History* 71 (March 1985): 764–81; Genovese, "Yeoman Farmers," 249–64; H. Watson, "Conflict and Collaboration," 273–98; and C. Vann Woodward, *Origins of the New South, 1877–1913* (Baton Rouge: Louisiana State University Press, 1951). Samuel Hobbs's *North Carolina Economic and Social* (Chapel Hill: University of North Carolina Press, 1930) provides helpful graphs that chart economic and demographic statistics for 1910–1927, showing the concomitant increase of manufacturing and decrease of tenant farming in Piedmont counties (94, 123, and 138).

7. Powell, *North Carolina*, 417.

8. Newby, *Plain Folk*, 58.

9. Ibid., 59–60.

10. Lefler, *North Carolina Told by Contemporaries*, 424.

11. Ibid., 522–28.

12. *Mill News*, October 14, 1920, High Shoals Cotton Mill Company, High Shoals, North Carolina, 24.

13. Betts, "Snopeses," 15.

14. Ibid., 6.

15. Scura, "Doris Betts," 54.

16. Doris Betts, *The Gentle Insurrection and Other Stories* (New York: Putnam's, 1954), 228. Further references noted parenthetically are to this edition.

17. John A. Salmond, *Gastonia 1929: The Story of the Loray Mill Strike* (Chapel Hill: University of North Carolina Press, 1995), 4.

18. Newby, *Plain Folk*, 26.

19. Escott, *Many Excellent People*, 9.

20. Ibid., 10.

21. Salmond, *Gastonia*, 2–13.

22. Betts, "Mark of Distinction," in *Gentle Insurrection*, 31.

23. Newby, *Plain Folk*, 12.

24. For a thorough listing of salaries for a wide range of textile jobs during the early twentieth century, see Hall et al., *Like a Family*, 79–80.

25. Doris Betts, "Faith and Intellect: Remarks Made by Doris Betts at the Billy Graham 'Reason to Live' Lecture Series," Carmichael Auditorium, University of North Carolina at Chapel Hill, September 28, 1982, 1.

26. Scura, "Doris Betts," 54.

27. Scura, "Doris Betts," 55; and W. Dale Brown, "Interview with Doris Betts," *Southern Quarterly* 34.2 (Winter 1996): 94.

28. Brown, "Interview," 94.

29. Ibid., 103.

30. Ibid., 103.

31. David Marion Holman, "Faith and the Unanswerable Questions: The Fiction of Doris Betts," *Southern Literary Journal* 15.1 (Fall 1982): 19.

32. Ibid., 22.

33. Ketchin, *Christ-Haunted Landscape*, 248.

34. Ibid., 244.

35. Brown, "Interview," 101.

36. Ibid., 101.

37. Ketchin, *Christ-Haunted Landscape*, 249.

38. Brown, "Interview," 95.

39. Betts, "Faith and Intellect," 1–3.

40. Marti Greene, "A Conversation with Doris Betts," *Carolina Quarterly* 52.2 (Spring 2000): 65.

41. Ibid., 65.

42. Christie Anne Farnham, ed. *Women of the American South: A Multicultural Reader* (New York: New York University Press, 1997), 74–75.

43. Cecil-Fronsman, *Common Whites*, 8.

44. Brown, "Interview," 102.

45. Doris Betts, "Opening Statement: The Arts, the Humanities, the University and Public Culture," Institute for the Arts and Humanities, University of North Carolina at Chapel Hill, Autumn Sunday Symposium, October 10, 1993, 7.

46. Cash, *Mind of the South*, 200–201.

47. Ibid., 192.
48. Ibid., 192.
49. Betts, "Snopeses," 9.
50. Ibid., 9.
51. Cash, *Mind of the South*, 215.
52. Ibid., 196.
53. Ibid., 164.
54. Betts, "Snopeses," 13.
55. Ibid., 9.
56. Ibid., 6.
57. Doris Betts, *The River to Pickle Beach* (New York: Harper and Row, 1972), 122. Further references noted parenthetically are to this edition.
58. Farnham, *Women of the American South*, 74.
59. Ibid., 74–75.
60. Escott, *Many Excellent People*, 26.
61. Farnham, *Women of the American South*, 75.
62. Cash, *Mind of the South*, 89–90.
63. Ketchin, *Christ-Haunted Landscape*, 246.
64. Escott, *Many Excellent People*, 26.
65. Ibid., 27.
66. Ibid., 27.
67. Ketchin, *Christ-Haunted Landscape*, 254.
68. Ibid., 254–55.
69. Fred Chappell, *Plow Naked: Selected Writings on Poetry* (Ann Arbor: University of Michigan Press, 1993), 77.
70. Cash, *Mind of the South*, 45.
71. Ibid., 44.
72. Ibid., 45.
73. Myerson, *Finer*, 34.
74. See Cecil-Fronsman, *Common Whites*, 16–18; Escott, *Many Excellent People*, 5–9.
75. Escott, *Many Excellent People*, 4.
76. Ibid., 7–9.
77. Hinton Rowan Helper, *The Impending Crisis of the South: How to Meet It*, ed. George M. Fredrickson (1857; Cambridge, Mass.: Harvard University Press, 1968), 331.
78. Ibid., 348.
79. George M. Fredrickson, introduction to *The Impending Crisis of the South*, xxxix.
80. Ibid., xli.
81. Doris Betts, "Many Souths and Broadening Scale: A Changing Southern Literature," in *The Future South: A Historical Perspective for the Twenty-first Century*, eds. Joe P. Dunn and Howard L. Preston (Chicago: University of Illinois Press, 1991), 177.
82. Doris Betts, *Beasts of the Southern Wild and Other Stories* (1973; New York: Scribner, 1998), 98. Further references noted parenthetically are to this edition.
83. Cecil-Fronsman, *Common Whites*, 145.
84. Ibid., 145.
85. Hall et al., *Like a Family*, 18.
86. McCurry, "Producing Dependence," 66.
87. Ibid., 55.

88. Ibid., 58.

89. Doris Betts, *Souls Raised From the Dead* (New York: Knopf, 1994), 193. Further references noted parenthetically are to this edition.

90. Ketchin, *Christ-Haunted Landscape*, 240.

91. Ibid., 243.

92. Ibid., 258.

93. Ibid., 244–45.

94. Ibid., 244.

95. Betts, "Many Souths," 178.

96. Ibid., 181.

97. Greene, "Conversation," 72.

98. John Crowe Ransom et al., introduction to *I'll Take My Stand: The South and the Agrarian Tradition* (1930; Baton Rouge: Louisiana State University Press, 1977), xxxviii.

99. Ibid., xxxviii.

100. Ibid., xlii.

101. Ketchin, *Christ-Haunted Landscape*, 258.

Chapter 2: Reynolds Price

1. Reynolds Price, *The Promise of Rest* (New York: Scribner, 1995), 15. Further references noted parenthetically are to this edition.

2. Betts, "Many Souths," 178.

3. S. D. Williams, "Reynolds Price on the South, Literature, and Himself," in *Conversations with Reynolds Price*, ed. Jefferson Humphries (1987; Jackson: University Press of Mississippi, 1991), 280.

4. Ibid., 278.

5. Daphne Athas, "Reynolds Price," in *Conversations with Reynolds Price*, 273.

6. Lefler and Newsome, *History*, 119.

7. Athas, "Reynolds Price," 273–74.

8. Robert Lockhart, Steve Haughney, and David Olson, "Interview," in *Conversations with Reynolds Price*, 47.

9. Dannye Romine Powell, "Interview with Reynolds Price," 1988, in *Parting the Curtains: Interviews by Dannye Romine Powell* (New York: Anchor, 1994), 356.

10. Anne Hobson Freeman, "Penetrating a Small Patch of the Surface of the Earth," *Virginia Quarterly Review* 51.4 (Autumn 1975): 638.

11. D. R. Powell, "Interview," 356.

12. Powell, *North Carolina*, 407.

13. Steven Hahn points out that despite the South's prominence in national politics during the antebellum period, when the region "dominated the presidency, the Supreme Court, the speakership of the House of Representatives, and the diplomatic corps," between 1865 and 1912 they claimed just 7 of 31 seats on the Supreme Court, 2 of 12 House speakerships, 14 of 133 cabinet appointments, and except for the "unusual case of Andrew Johnson," not even a single *nomination* for the presidency or vice-presidency. (See Hahn, "Class and State," 94–95.) Wesley Allen Riddle reports, for example, that among southern planters who "persisted," "personal wealth probably diminished by 70 to 80 percent" and that "the national political power of the planter class was gone forever, and local political hegemony of planters was severely altered" (see Wesley Allen Riddle, "The Origins of Black Sharecropping," *Mississippi Quarterly* 49.1 [Winter 1995–96]: 57).

See also Edward L. Ayers, *The Promise of the New South: Life after Reconstruction* (Oxford: Oxford University Press, 1992), 24–25.

14. Powell, *North Carolina*, 415.

15. D. R. Powell, "Interview," 356.

16. Chappell, *Plow Naked*, 20–21.

17. Ibid., 24.

18. James A. Schiff, *Understanding Reynolds Price* (Columbia: University of South Carolina Press, 1996), 118.

19. John Wain, "Mantle of Faulkner?" *New Republic* (May 14, 1966): 32.

20. Benjamin DeMott, "A Minor Faulkner" *Saturday Review* 8.4 (April 1981): 72.

21. Athas, "Reynolds Price," 273.

22. Faulkner, "Nobel Address," 119.

23. Rubin, "Thomas Wolfe," 72–73.

24. Williams, "Reynolds Price," 279.

25. Ibid., 279.

26. Lockhart et al., "Interview," 47.

27. Ibid., 47.

28. Reynolds Price, "An Awful Gift and a Blindness," *Southern Review* (Spring 2000): 388.

29. Edgar Allan Poe, "The Poetic Principle," in *Edgar Allan Poe: Selected Prose, Poetry, and Eureka* (New York: Rinehart, 1950), 417.

30. Reynolds Price, *Clear Pictures* (New York: Atheneum, 1989), 172. Further references noted parenthetically are to this edition.

31. Reynolds Price, "A Chain of Love," in *The Collected Stories* (New York: Atheneum, 1993), 499. Further references noted parenthetically are to this edition.

32. Reynolds Price, *A Long and Happy Life* (New York: Atheneum, 1962), 3. Further references noted parenthetically are to this edition.

33. Wallace Kaufman, "Portrait of the Artist as a Young Voyeur," in *Reynolds Price: From A Long and Happy Life to Good Hearts, with a Bibliography: Proceedings of the Seventh Annual Southern Writers' Symposium, Methodist College, April 15–16, 1988*, eds. Sue Laslie Kimball and Lynn Veach Sadler (Fayetteville, N.C.: Methodist College Press, 1989), 8.

34. Fred Chappell, *Midquest: A Poem* (Baton Rouge: Louisiana State University Press, 1981), 136. Further references noted parenthetically are to this edition.

35. Schiff, *Understanding*, 34.

36. Constance Rooke, *Reynolds Price* (Boston: Twayne, 1983), 17.

37. Schiff, *Understanding*, 35.

38. William Alexander Percy, *Lanterns on the Levee: Recollections of a Planter's Son* (1941; Baton Rouge: Louisiana State University Press, 1993), 19.

39. Ayers, *Promise*, 24–25.

40. Chappell, *Plow Naked*, 73.

41. D. R. Powell, "Interview," 356.

42. In *Common Whites*, Bill Cecil-Fronsman identifies small slaveowners as yeomen, as does James Oakes in *The Ruling Race*. In *Plain Folk of the Old South* Frank Owsley argues that there was extensive "intermingling" of nonslaveowners and even large planters in church, schools, and family relations (134). Owsley's portrait of a harmonious southern society free of intense class tensions contradicts the views of most recent scholars,

including Harry Watson, Wilma Dunaway, and Paul Escott, who identify the planters' domination of the market economy as deleterious to the viability of the yeoman's pursuit of a competency. In "Yeoman Farmers in a Slaveholders' Democracy," Eugene Genovese makes a useful distinction regarding the attitudes toward planters expressed by yeomen living in regions heavily populated by planters (such as Price's Warren County during the antebellum period) and yeomen of the upland South, where wealthy planters were less prevalent. Appalachian yeomen, for example, tended to be more antagonistic to the aristocracy than did yeomen living in closer proximity to them, who, according to Genovese, benefited from various forms of assistance from planters.

43. Kenzer, Kinship, 41–46.

44. Laban Miles Hoffman, Our Kin (1915; Baltimore: Gateway Press, 1980), 151; Adam Cloninger, Will and Estate Records, Lincoln County Archives, Lincolnton, N.C.

45. Harris, Piedmont Farmer, 1.

46. Ibid., 13–18.

47. Ibid., 18.

48. Ibid., 4.

49. Ibid., 17.

50. Ibid., 9.

51. Thomasson, North Carolina Yeoman, 290.

52. Kenzer, Kinship, 42.

53. Ibid., 42–46.

54. Powell, North Carolina, 417.

55. Ibid., 417.

56. Ibid., 422.

57. Lefler and Newsome, History, 491.

58. Linda Flowers, Thrown Away: Failures of Progress in Eastern North Carolina (Knoxville: University of Tennessee Press, 1990), 1–6.

59. Hobbs, Economic and Social, 76.

60. Escott, Many Excellent People, 178.

61. Reynolds Price, Kate Vaiden (New York: Atheneum, 1986), 38. Further references noted parenthetically are to this edition.

62. Fred Chappell, Brighten the Corner Where You Are (New York: St. Martin's, 1989), 9–28. Further references noted parenthetically are to this edition.

63. Price, "Awful Gift," 387.

64. Ketchin, Christ-Haunted Landscape, 258.

65. D. R. Powell, "Interview," 358.

66. Betts, "Many Souths," 170.

67. Reynolds Price, The Surface of Earth (New York: Atheneum: 1975), 398. Further references noted parenthetically are to this edition.

68. Price, "Awful Gift," 393.

69. Ibid., 393–94.

70. Ibid., 386.

71. Frye Gaillard, "Black Politics in the 1980s," in Becoming Truly Free: 300 Years of Black History in the Carolinas, ed. Frye Gaillard (Charlotte: Charlotte Observer, 1985), 57.

72. Richard Maschal, "1965–1980: A Transformation," in Becoming Truly Free: 300 Years of Black History in the Carolinas, 42–54.

73. Hobbs's *North Carolina Economic and Social* provides graphs that vividly depict the rise of industry and the related decrease of tenant farming in the Piedmont throughout the early decades of the twentieth century.

74. Logan, *Negro*, 82–83.

75. Maschal, "1965–1980," 51.

76. Schiff, *Understanding*, 66–67.

77. D. R. Powell, "Interview," 374.

78. Richard Gilman, "A Mastadon of a Novel, by Reynolds Price," in *Critical Essays on Reynolds Price*, ed. James Schiff (1975; New York: G. K. Hall, 1998), 68.

Chapter 3: Fred Chappell's Prison/Arcadia

1. George Hovis, "An Interview with Fred Chappell," *Carolina Quarterly* 52.1 (Fall/Winter 1999): 72.

2. Ronald Eller, *Miners, Millhands, and Mountaineers: Industrialization of the Appalachian South, 1880–1930* (Knoxville: University of Tennessee Press, 1982), 99–111.

3. Ibid., 108.

4. Carl Alwin Schenck, *The Birth of Forestry in America: Biltmore Forest School, 1898–1913* (Santa Cruz, Calif.: Forest History Society, 1974), 148.

5. Eller, *Miners*, 109.

6. Ibid., xix-xx.

7. See Paul Salstrom, *Appalachia's Path to Dependency: Rethinking a Region's Economic History, 1730–1940* (Lexington: University Press of Kentucky, 1994), xx–xxi.

8. Lucinda Hardwick MacKethan, *The Dream of Arcady: Place and Time in Southern Literature* (Baton Rouge: Louisiana State University Press, 1980), 16.

9. George Garrett, foreword to *Dream Garden: The Poetic Vision of Fred Chappell*, ed. Patrick Baser (Baton Rouge: Louisiana State University Press, 1997), xiii.

10. Ibid., xiv.

11. Lee Smith, critical blurb, dust jacket to Fred Chappell, *I Am One of You Forever* (Baton Rouge: Louisiana State University Press, 1985).

12. Michael McFee, "The Epigrammatical Fred Chappell," *Southern Literary Journal* 31.2 (1999): 96.

13. Eller, *Miners*, 25–26.

14. Ibid., 28–29.

15. Hovis, "Interview," 71.

16. Fred Chappell, "A Pact With Faustus," *Mississippi Quarterly* 37 (1984). Rpt. in *The Fred Chappell Reader*, ed. Dabney Stuart (New York: St. Martin's, 1987), 481.

17. Chappell, *Plow Naked*, 20.

18. Ibid., 14.

19. Ibid., 6.

20. Chappell, "Pact," 480.

21. Chappell, "Pact," 481.

22. Ibid., 481.

23. Chappell, *Plow Naked*, 12.

24. Ibid., 9.

25. Letter to the author, March 22, 2002.

26. Fred Chappell, *The Gaudy Place* (New York: Harcourt Brace, 1973), 65. Further references noted parenthetically are to this edition.

27. Hovis, "Interview," 75.

28. Chappell acknowledges the important influence of Faulkner and Camus on his first novel in "An Interview with Fred Chappell" (Hovis, 71). Also, in "A Pact With Faustus" he lists *The Sound and The Fury* among the five novels he has most often read, the others being *Doctor Faustus*, *Don Quixote*, *Adventures of Huckleberry Finn*, and *The Sun Also Rises* (479).

29. Fred Chappell, *It is Time, Lord* (New York: Atheneum, 1963), 34–35. Further references noted parenthetically are to this edition.

30. Fred Chappell, *Look Back All the Green Valley* (New York: Picador, 1999), 183. Further references noted parenthetically are to this edition.

31. Hovis, "Interview," 71.

32. Fred Chappell, *Dagon*, in *The Fred Chappell Reader*, 53. Further references noted parenthetically are to this edition.

33. While I do not discuss *The Inkling* here, it very much fits the pattern found in both *It Is Time, Lord* and *Dagon*. The boy protagonist, Jan, and his sister, Timmie, both spiral into states of increasing dementia, which their dysfunctional home life only serves to exacerbate. David Paul Ragan notes that the relationship between Jan and Timmie "almost seems an extension of the childhood relationship between James Christopher and his sister" in *It Is Time, Lord*, and that "the relationship between Laura and Jan at the end of *The Inkling* seems to prefigure the relationship between Peter Leland and Mina" in *Dagon*. David Paul Ragan, "Flying by Night: An Early Interview with Fred Chappell," *North Carolina Literary Review* 7 (1998): 111.

34. In an early interview, Chappell actually used Poe's language in describing his own goal to write novels that were capable of being read in "one sitting." See John Sopko and John Carr, "Dealing with the Grotesque: Fred Chappell," in *Kite Flying and Other Irrational Acts: Conversations with Twelve Southern Writers*, ed. John Carr (Baton Rouge: Louisiana State University Press, 1972), 225.

35. W. H. Auden, introduction to *Edgar Allan Poe: Selected Prose, Poetry, and Eureka*, ed. W. H. Auden (New York: Hold, Rinehart, 1950), vi.

36. Hovis, "Interview," 71.

37. David Paul Ragan, "Fred Chappell (1936–)," in *Contemporary Poets, Dramatists, Essayists, and Novelists of the South: A Bio-Bibliographical Sourcebook*, eds. Robert Bain and Joseph M. Flora (Westport, Conn.: Greenwood, 1994), 93.

38. Fred Chappell, personal interview, September 12, 1999. Chapel Hill, N.C. Note that each of the other citations of this interview refer to the version published in the *Carolina Quarterly* 52.1.

39. Frank Kermode, *English Pastoral Poetry: From the Beginnings to Marvell* (New York: Barnes and Noble, 1952), 15.

40. Wilma Dunaway, *The First American Frontier: Transition to Capitalism in Southern Appalachia, 1700–1860* (Chapel Hill: University of North Carolina Press, 1996).

41. Salstrom, *Appalachia's Path*, xxiii.

42. See, for example, Dunaway's *The First American Frontier*.

43. Eller, *Miners*, 9–12.

44. Salstrom, *Appalachia's Path*, xv.

45. Dunaway, *Slavery*, 25.

46. Ibid., 32.

47. Ibid., 34–35.

48. Ibid., 35.

49. Ibid., 37–38.

50. Salstrom, *Appalachia's Path*, xiii–xxiii.

51. Chappell, *Plow Naked*, 73.

52. Ibid., 73.

53. Kermode, *English Pastoral Poetry*, 15.

54. Ibid., 14.

55. Chappell, "Pact," 489.

56. Kermode, *English Pastoral Poetry*, 15.

57. While a student at Duke, Chappell was heavily influenced by Eliot and labored upon a "longish, heavily Eliotic" poem through as many as forty drafts. See Chappell, *Plow Naked*, 23.

58. T. S. Eliot, *The Waste Land and Other Poems* (New York: Harvest, 1934), 42.

59. Kermode, *English Pastoral Poetry*, 43.

60. J. E. Congleton, *Theories of Pastoral Poetry in England, 1684–1798* (Gainesville: University of Florida Press, 1952), 4.

61. Quoted in Kenneth S. Lynn, *Mark Twain and Southwestern Humor* (Westport, Conn.: Greenwood, 1972), 27.

62. Houston A. Baker, Jr., *Modernism and the Harlem Renaissance* (Chicago: University of Chicago Press, 1987).

63. MacKethan, *Dream of Arcady*, 6.

64. Chappell, *Plow Naked*, 76.

65. Ibid., 77.

66. Hovis, "Interview," 78.

67. Fred Chappell, *I Am One of You Forever* (Baton Rouge: Louisiana State University Press, 1985), 51. Further references noted parenthetically are to this edition.

68. Carol Mitchell, "Some Differences in Male and Female Joke-Telling," in *Women's Folklore, Women's Culture* (Philadelphia: University of Pennsylvania Press, 1985), 167.

69. Ibid., 169–70.

70. Ibid., 170.

71. Ibid., 169.

72. Hovis, "Interview," 71.

73. Fred Chappell, *Look Back All the Green Valley* (New York: Picador, 1999), 183. Further references noted parenthetically are to this edition.

74. Fred Chappell, letter to the author, March 4, 2000.

75. Kermode, *English Pastoral Poetry*, 40.

76. Ralph Waldo Emerson, "The American Scholar," in *Selected Writings of Emerson*, ed. Donald McQuade (New York: Modern Library, 1981), 46.

77. Ralph Waldo Emerson, "The Poet," in *Selected Writings of Emerson*, ed. Donald McQuade (New York: Modern Library, 1981), 304.

Chapter 4: Lee Smith

1. For a more complete listing of Smith's awards and chronology of her personal and professional life to 1991, see Dorothy Combs Hill, *Lee Smith* (New York: Twayne, 1992), xiii–xv.

2. Elizabeth Pell Broadwell, "Lee Smith (1944–)," in *Contemporary Fiction Writers of the South*, 420–21; and Nancy C. Parish, *Lee Smith, Annie Dillard, and the Hollins Group: A Genesis of Writers* (Baton Rouge: Louisiana State University Press, 1998), 170–71.

3. Virginia A. Smith, "On Regionalism, Women's Writing, and Writing as a Woman: A Conversation with Lee Smith," *Southern Review* 26 (1990): 791.

4. Parish, *Lee Smith*, 166.

5. Lee Smith, *The Last Girls* (Chapel Hill: Algonquin, 2002), 109. Further references noted parenthetically are to this edition.

6. Lee Smith, *Family Linen* (New York: Putnam's, 1985), 47. Further references noted parenthetically are to this edition.

7. V. A. Smith, "On Regionalism," 791.

8. Lee Smith, *Me and My Baby View the Eclipse* (New York: Putnam's, 1990), 79.

9. Fred Hobson, *The Southern Writer in the Postmodern World* (Athens: University of Georgia Press, 1991), 31–32.

10. Parish, *Lee Smith*, 167.

11. Ibid., 166.

12. Anne Goodwyn Jones, "The World of Lee Smith," *Southern Quarterly* 22.1 (1983): 119–20.

13. Lee Smith, *Oral History* (New York: Putnam's, 1983), 151. Further references noted parenthetically are to this edition.

14. Julius Rowan Raper, "Inventing Modern Southern Fiction: A Postmodern View," *Southern Literary Journal* 22 (Spring 1990): 9–10.

15. Lee Smith, *The Devil's Dream* (New York: Putnam's, 1992), 67. Further references noted parenthetically are to this edition.

16. McCurry, "Producing Dependence," 55.

17. Jones, "World," 119.

18. Ibid., 119.

19. Hobson, *Southern Writer*, 28.

20. Raper, "Inventing," 11.

21. Ibid., 10.

22. Ben Jennings, "Language and Reality in Lee Smith's *Oral History*," *Iron Mountain Review* 3.1 (1986): 10.

23. Nonstandard spellings in Ivy's narration will remain unacknowledged.

24. Lee Smith, *Fair and Tender Ladies* (New York: Putnam's, 1988), 35–36. Further references noted parenthetically are to this edition.

25. Eudora Welty, "Place in Fiction," in *A Modern Southern Reader*, eds. Ben Forkner and Patrick Samway (Atlanta: Peachtree, 1986), 546.

Chapter 5: Clyde Edgerton

1. Of his home town, Edgerton recalls, "The only people I knew who were black, I would see at a little community store." He also recalls how his father once refused to allow one of Clyde's black friends to play at their house simply because of his race (Sara Elliot, "Interview with Clyde Edgerton: Conducted by students in English 110: Experience of Fiction at Northern Illinois University," April 13, 1995).

2. Sterling Hennis, "Clyde Edgerton (1944–)," in *Contemporary Fiction Writers of the South*, 114.

3. Clyde Edgerton, *Clyde Edgerton Papers (1918–1992)*, No. 4616 Series 4.2, Box 23, Folder 134, Southern Historical Collection at the University of North Carolina at Chapel Hill. For a study of this period in Edgerton's life and work, see George Hovis, "The *Raney* Controversy: Clyde Edgerton's Battle with Campbell University over Creative Freedom," *Southern Cultures* (Summer 2001): 60–83.

4. Clyde Edgerton, "On R. W. Emerson," in David Perkins, *Books of Passage: 27 North Carolina Writers on Books that Changed Their Lives*, ed. David Perkins (Asheboro, N.C.: Down Home, 1997), 65.

5. Ibid., 66.

6. Ibid., 66.

7. Ibid., 67.

8. Clyde Edgerton, "Head Stung, Heart Stung," in *Eudora Welty: Writers' Reflections upon First Reading Welty*, ed. Pearl Amelia McHaney (Athens, Ga.: Hill Street Press, 1999), 23–26.

9. Joseph M. Flora, "A Suitable Villain: Mormonism in Clyde Edgerton's *Redeye: A Western*," *Southern Quarterly* 38.1 (Fall 1999): 159.

10. Scott Romine, *The Narrative Forms of Southern Community* (Baton Rouge: Louisiana State University Press, 1999), 206.

11. M. Thomas Inge, *Faulkner, Sut, and Other Southerners* (West Cornwall, Conn.: Locust Hill, 1992), 3.

12. Tony Earley, "Letter from Sister: What We Learned at the P. O.," *Oxford American* 25 (1999): 15.

13. Ketchin, *Christ-Haunted Landscape*, 364.

14. Louis D. Rubin, personal interview, April 18, 1995.

15. *Where Trouble Sleeps* began as a memoir, before Edgerton decided to adapt these materials to fiction. Clyde Edgerton, personal interview, November 12, 1996.

16. Clyde Edgerton, *Raney* (Chapel Hill: Algonquin, 1985), 119–20. Further references noted parenthetically are to this edition.

17. Clyde Edgerton, *Killer Diller* (Chapel Hill: Algonquin, 1991), 8. Further references noted parenthetically are to this edition.

18. Ketchin, *Christ-Haunted Landscape*, 364.

19. Ibid., 364.

20. Price, "Awful Gift," 386.

21. Orville Hicks, "Jack and the Heifer's Hide," in *Jack Tales for Children of All Ages* [audio recording] (Whitesburg, Ky.: June Appal Recordings, 1990).

22. Lillian Smith, *Killers of the Dream* (New York: Norton, 1949), 78.

23. Frederick Engels, *The Origin of the Family, Private Property, and the State* (1884; New York: International Publishers, 1942).

24. Nancy Chodorow, *The Reproduction of Mothering: Psychoanalysis and the Sociology of Gender* (Berkeley: University of California Press, 1978), 31.

25. Ibid., 10.

26. Ibid., 169.

27. Kenn Robbins, "A Conversation with Clyde Edgerton," *Southern Quarterly* 30.1 (1991), 60–61.

28. Chodorow, *Reproduction*, 31.

29. Sally G. McMillen, "Southern Women and the Sunday School Movement,

1865–1915," in *Plain Folk of the South Revisited*, ed. Samuel C. Hyde, Jr. (Baton Rouge: Louisiana State University Press, 1997), 132–133.

30. Ibid., 134.

31. Ibid., 149.

32. Ibid., 149–50.

33. Ibid., 129–33.

34. Ibid., 158.

35. Clyde Edgerton, personal interview, April 26, 1994.

36. Clyde Edgerton, *In Memory of Junior* (Chapel Hill: Algonquin, 1992), 17. Further references noted parenthetically are to this edition.

37. Henry Adams, *The Education of Henry Adams: An Autobiography* (1918; Boston: Houghton Mifflin, 1971), 57.

38. Sigmund Freud, *Three Contributions to the Theory of Sex*, in *The Basic Writings of Sigmund Freud*, ed. and trans. A. A. Brill (1905; New York: Random House, 1938), 617–18.

39. Clyde Edgerton, *The Floatplane Notebooks* (Chapel Hill: Algonquin, 1988), 241–42. Further references noted parenthetically are to this edition.

40. Owsley, *Plain Folk*, 24–25.

41. Ibid., 28.

42. Ibid., 34.

43. William H. Sparks, *The Memories of Fifty Years* (Philadelphia: Claxton, Remsen, and Haffelinger, 1870), 331.

44. Elizabeth Jane Harrison, *Female Pastoral: Women Writers Re-Visioning the American South* (Knoxville: University of Tennessee Press, 1991), 3.

45. Ibid., 3.

46. Baldwin Longstreet, "The Fight," in *Georgia Scenes, Characters, Incidents, &c., in the First Half Century of the Republic* (1935; Savannah, Ga.: Beehive Press, 1992), 59.

47. Ketchin, *Christ-Haunted Landscape*, 361.

48. Edgerton, personal interview, April 26, 1994.

49. Ibid.

50. This pastoral device of recurring rituals associated with specific dates appears in Reynolds Price's *A Long and Happy Life* in the context of the family's church; that no such pastoral treatment of a religious calendar of events appears anywhere in Edgerton's oeuvre reinforces his typically ambivalent depiction of religion in community life.

51. Escott, introduction to *North Carolina Yeoman*, xlvii.

52. Ralph Waldo Emerson, "Divinity School Address," in *Selected Writings of Emerson*, ed. Donald McQuade (New York: Modern Library, 1981), 68.

53. Robert Penn Warren, "The Use of the Past," in *New and Selected Essays* (New York: Random House, 1989), 51.

54. Walter Sullivan, "The New Faustus: The Southern Renascence and the Joycean Aesthetic," in *Southern Fiction Today: Renascence and Beyond*, ed. George Core (Athens: University of Georgia Press, 1969), 10.

55. Ibid., 13–14.

56. Chappell, *Plow Naked*, 77.

57. See Edgerton, "On Emerson."

58. Elliot, "Interview with Clyde Edgerton."

Chapter 6: Randall Kenan

1. Olmstead, *Journey*, 367.

2. The narratives of Moses Roper, Lunsford Lane, Moses Grandy, and Thomas H. Jones have been reissued together in *North Carolina Slave Narratives*, ed. William L. Andrews et al.

3. Lefler, *North Carolina Told by Contemporaries*, 263–64.

4. Ibid., 263–64, 269–70, 274–75; Powell, *North Carolina*, 328; Logan, *Negro*, 5–7; Franklin, *Free Negro*, 6–7; and Myerson, *Finer*, 15.

5. Logan, *Negro*, 7, 84; Lefler, *North Carolina Told by Contemporaries*, 403–04; Myerson, *Finer*, 72–73.

6. Myerson, *Finer*, 74–75.

7. Michael Myerson's *Nothing Could Be Finer* provides a compelling account of the Wilmington Ten case and its cultural context. See especially 76–79. See also Wayne King, "The Case against the Wilmington Ten," *New York Times Magazine*, December 3, 1978; and Larry Reni Thomas, *The True Story behind the Wilmington Ten* (Hampton, Va.: U.B. and U.S. Communication Systems, 1993).

8. Randall Kenan, "My Chapter on Randall Kenan," e-mail to the author, February 8, 2006.

9. Ibid.

10. Logan, *Negro*, Chapter Eight, "Your Work Is the Tilling of the Ground," 75–85; Flowers, *Throwed Away*, 4–5; and Lefler and Newsome, *History*, 491.

11. *Let the Dead Bury Their Dead* also won the Lambda Book Award, was named a *New York Times* Notable Book for 1992, and was a finalist for the *Los Angeles Times* Book Prize for fiction. Kenan's other honors include the Mary Francis Hobson Medal for Arts and Letters, a Whiting Writer's Award, the Sherwood Anderson Award, a Guggenheim Fellowship, and the American Academy of Arts and Letters' Prix de Rome.

12. Randall Kenan, *A Visitation of Spirits* (New York: Grove, 1989), 188. Further references noted parenthetically are to this edition.

13. Randall Kenan, *Walking on Water* (New York: Knopf, 1999), xii. Further references noted parenthetically are to this edition.

14. Hobson, *Southern Writer*, 101.

15. Ibid., 101.

16. Robert B. Stepto, *From Behind the Veil: A Study of Afro-American Narrative*, 2nd ed. (Chicago: University of Illinois Press, 1991).

17. Henry Louis Gates, Jr., introduction to *Bearing Witness: Selections from African-American Autobiography in the Twentieth Century*, ed. Henry Louis Gates, Jr. (New York: Pantheon, 1991), 5.

18. Doris Betts, "Randall Garrett Kenan: Myth and Reality in Tims Creek," in *Southern Writers at Century's End*, eds. Jeffrey J. Folks and James A. Perkins (Lexington: University Press of Kentucky, 1997), 9–10.

19. Trudier Harris, *The Power of the Porch: The Storyteller's Craft in Zora Neale Hurston, Gloria Naylor, and Randall Kenan* (Athens: University of Georgia Press, 1996), 108.

20. Randall Kenan, *Let the Dead Bury Their Dead* (New York: Harcourt Brace, 1992), 333. Further references noted parenthetically are to this edition.

21. Randall Kenan, "'If I Could Tell You, I Would Let You Know': Author Perspective/Reader Perception of Gay Characters in Literature," panel at the Tennessee Williams/New Orleans Literary Festival, March 31, 1996, panel moderator, Mark Zumpe.

22. Frederick Douglass, *Narrative of the Life of Frederick Douglass, an American Slave. Written By Himself*, in *The Classic Slave Narratives*, ed. Henry Louis Gates, Jr. (1845; New York: Mentor, 1987), 294.

23. Charles I. Nero, "Toward a Black Gay Aesthetic: Signifying in Contemporary Black Gay Literature," *African American Literary Theory: A Reader*, ed. Winston Napier (1991; New York: New York University Press, 2000), 410.

24. Cheryl Clarke, "The Failure to Transform: Homophobia in the Black Community," in *Home Girls: A Black Feminist Anthology*, ed. Barbara Smith (New York: Kitchen Table: Women of Color Press, 1983), 206.

25. Marlon B. Ross, "Some Glances at the Black Fag: Race, Same-Sex Desire, and Cultural Belonging," in *African American Literary Theory: A Reader*, ed. Winston Napier (1994; New York: New York University Press, 2000), 504.

26. Robert McRuer, "A Visitation of Difference: Randall Kenan and Black Queer Theory," in *Critical Essays: Gay and Lesbian Writers of Color*, ed. Emmanuel S. Nelson (New York: Haworth, 1993), 230.

27. Ibid., 230.

28. Betts, "Randall Garrett Kenan," 16.

29. Around the turn of the nineteenth century, slave rebellions and maroon society activity were frequent in the counties surrounding Kenan's Duplin County. Near Wilmington, runaway slaves followed a leader called the "General of the Swamps." In 1804 slave uprisings in Johnston, Sampson, and Wayne counties resulted in the arrest and severe punishment of roughly twenty slaves. In 1821, maroon groups in Bladen, Onslow, and Carteret counties followed a leader called Isam, who went by the alias of "General Jackson." See Myerson, *Finer*, 15; Aptheker, *American Negro*, 231–32, 243–44; Aptheker, *To Be Free*, 18–19.

30. William Faulkner, *Absalom, Absalom!* (1936; New York: Vintage, 1990), 7.

31. Henry Louis Gates, Jr., *The Signifying Monkey: A Theory of African-American Literary Criticism* (New York: Oxford University Press, 1988), 44–51.

32. Ibid., 51.

Conclusion

1. Betts, "Many Souths."

2. Kermode, *English Pastoral Poetry*, 15

3. Taylor Sisk, "Do, Tell: Allan Gurganus, Genial Troublemaker, On Living and Imagining the Local Life," *Independent Weekly*, September 8, 1999, 13.

4. Ibid., 10.

5. Julian Mason, "Kaye Gibbons (1960–)," in *Contemporary Fiction Writers of the South*, 156.

6. Ibid., 157.

7. Ibid., 159.

8. Lynn Z. Bloom, "Jill McCorkle (1958–)," in *Contemporary Fiction Writers of the South*, 297–301.

9. Jerry Leath Mills, "Tim McLaurin (1953–)," in *Contemporary Fiction Writers of the South*, 303.

10. George Hovis and Timothy Williams, "Old Times on the Haw: An Interview with Dale Ray Phillips," *Carolina Quarterly* 55.3 (Summer 2003): 65.

11. John Holman, *Luminous Mysteries* (New York: Harcourt Brace, 1998), 1. Further references noted parenthetically are to this edition.

12. McFee, introduction to *This Is Where We Live*, xiv.

13. Tony Earley, "Charlotte," in *Here We Are in Paradise* (New York: Little Brown, 1994), 35.

14. Robert Morgan, Public Reading of *Gap Creek*, Association of Graduate English Students, Creative Speakers Series, University of North Carolina at Chapel Hill, November 8, 1999.

15. Robert West, "The Art of Far and Near: An Interview with Robert Morgan," *Carolina Quarterly* 49.3 (1997): 57.

16. "*Cold Mountain* by Charles Frazier," *Storylines Southeast* radio broadcast, cohosts Doris Betts and Darrell Stover, sponsored by the American Library Association and the National Endowment for the Humanities, WUNC-FM, Chapel Hill, North Carolina, November 14, 1999.

17. Ibid.

18. Lefler, *North Carolina Told by Contemporaries*, 520.

19. See *Mill News*, October 14, 1920, and George Hovis, "Industry Meets Agriculture: The Emergence of the Farmer/Peddler in the Carolina Piedmont," *North Carolina Folklore Journal* 41.1 (1994): 31–32). See also Bob Geary, "Growing Pains: A Farmer's Bill of Rights Would Protect Small Growers Against Big Corporations. Does It Have a Chance in North Carolina?" *Independent Weekly*, February 7, 2001: 13–14.

20. Geary, "Growing Pains," 13–14.

21. Chris Burritt, "Direct Sales Threatening Tobacco Auction houses: Many Could Close Across the Southeast," *Atlanta Journal-Constitution*, February 16, 2001: B-1.

22. John Shelton Reed, *The Enduring South: Subcultural Persistence in Mass Society* (Chapel Hill: University of North Carolina Press, 1986), 96.

BIBLIOGRAPHY

Adams, Henry. *The Education of Henry Adams: An Autobiography.* 1918. Boston: Houghton Mifflin, 1971.

Alexander, Charles. *Battles and Victories of Allen Allensworth, A.M., Ph.D. Lieutenant-Colonel, Retired, U.S. Army.* Boston: Sherman, French & Co., 1914.

Andrews, William L., ed. *North Carolina Slave Narratives: The Lives of Moses Roper, Lunsford Lane, Moses Grandy, & Thomas H. Jones.* Chapel Hill: University of North Carolina Press, 2003.

———, Minrose C. Gwin, Trudier Harris, and Fred Hobson, eds. *The Literature of the American South: A Norton Anthology.* New York: Norton, 1998.

Applewhite, James. "Southern Writing and the Problem of the Father." *Southern Literature and Literary Theory.* Ed. Jefferson Humphries. Athens: University of Georgia Press, 1990.

Aptheker, Herbert. *American Negro Slave Revolts.* New York: International Publishers, 1943.

———. *To Be Free.* New York: International Publishers, 1948.

Athas, Daphne. "Reynolds Price." *Conversations with Reynolds Price.* Ed. Jefferson Humphries. 1987. Jackson: University Press of Mississippi, 1991. 272–76.

———. "Why There Are No Southern Writers." *Women Writers of the Contemporary South.* Ed. Peggy Whitman Prenshaw. Jackson: University Press of Mississippi, 1984. 295–306.

Auden, W. H. Introduction. *Edgar Allan Poe: Selected Prose, Poetry, and Eureka.* Ed. W. H. Auden. New York: Hold, Rinehart, 1950.

Avery, Laurence G. *A Paul Green Reader.* Chapel Hill: University of North Carolina Press, 1998.

Ayers, Edward L. *The Promise of the New South: Life after Reconstruction.* New York: Oxford University Press, 1992.

Bain, Robert, Joseph M. Flora, and Louis D. Rubin, Jr., eds. *Southern Writers: A Biographical Dictionary.* Baton Rouge: Louisiana State University Press, 1979.

Baker, Houston A., Jr. *Modernism and the Harlem Renaissance.* 1987. Chicago: University of Chicago Press, 1989.

Bertelson, David. *The Lazy South.* New York: Oxford University Press, 1967.

Betts, Doris. *Beasts of the Southern Wild and Other Stories.* 1973. New York: Scribner, 1998.

———. "Faith and Intellect: Remarks made by Doris Betts at the Billy Graham 'Reason to Live' Lecture Series," Carmichael Auditorium, University of North Carolina at Chapel Hill, September 28, 1982. North Carolina Collection, Wilson Library, University of North Carolina at Chapel Hill.

————. *The Gentle Insurrection and Other Stories*. New York: Putnam's, 1954.

————. *Heading West*. New York: Knopf, 1981.

————. "Many Souths and Broadening Scale: A Changing Southern Literature." *The Future South: A Historical Perspective for the Twenty-first Century*. Ed. Joe P. Dunn and Howard L. Preston. Chicago: University of Illinois Press, 1991. 158–87.

————. "Opening Statement: The Arts, the Humanities, the University and Public Culture." Institute for the Arts and Humanities, University of North Carolina at Chapel Hill, Autumn Sunday Symposium, October 10, 1993. North Carolina Collection, Wilson Library, University of North Carolina at Chapel Hill.

————. "Randall Garrett Kenan: Myth and Reality in Tims Creek." *Southern Writers at Century's End*. Eds. Jeffrey J. Folks and James A Perkins. Lexington: University Press of Kentucky, 1997. 9–20.

————. *The River to Pickle Beach*. New York: Harper & Row, 1972.

————. *The Scarlet Thread*. New York: Harper & Row, 1964.

————. *The Sharp Teeth of Love*. New York: Knopf, 1997.

————. *Souls Raised from the Dead*. New York: Knopf, 1994.

————. "We Were the Snopeses: A Writer and Her Piedmont." *Southern Cultures* (Summer 1999): 5–19.

Bloom, Lynn Z. "Jill McCorkle (1958–)." *Contemporary Fiction Writers of the South: A Bio-Bibliographical Sourcebook*. Eds. Joseph M. Flora and Robert Bain. Westport, Conn.: Greenwood, 1993. 295–302.

Boles, John B. "Foreword: Revisiting the Plain Folk of the South." *Plain Folk of the South Revisited*. Ed. Samuel C. Hyde, Jr. Baton Rouge: Louisiana State University Press, 1997. ix–xix.

Broadwell, Elizabeth Pell. "Lee Smith (1944–)." *Contemporary Fiction Writers of the South: A Bio-Bibliographical Sourcebook*. Eds. Joseph M. Flora and Robert Bain. Westport, Conn.: Greenwood, 1993. 420–31.

Brooks, Cleanth. "The Plain People: Yeoman Farmers, Sharecroppers, and White Trash." *William Faulkner: The Yoknapatawpha Country*. New Haven, Conn.: Yale University Press, 1963. 10–28.

Brown, W. Dale. "Dusty's Flying Taxi." Interview with Clyde Edgerton. *Carolina Quarterly* 46.2 (1994): 38–59.

————. "Interview with Doris Betts." *Southern Quarterly* 34.2 (Winter 1996): 91–104.

Burns, Rex. *Success in America: The Yeoman Dream and the Industrial Revolution*. Amherst: University of Massachusetts Press, 1976.

Burritt, Chris. "Direct Sales Threatening Tobacco Auction Houses: Many Could Close across the Southeast." *Atlanta Journal-Constitution*. February 16, 2001, B-1.

Byrd, William. *Prose Works: Narratives of a Colonial Virginian*. 1841. Ed. Louis B. Wright. Cambridge, Mass.: Belknap Press of Harvard University Press, 1966.

Cash, W. J. *The Mind of the South*. 1941. New York: Vintage, 1991.

Cecil-Fronsman, Bill. *Common Whites: Class and Culture in Antebellum North Carolina*. Lexington: University Press of Kentucky, 1992.

Chappell, Fred. *Brighten the Corner Where You Are*. New York: St. Martin's, 1989.

————. *Dagon*. 1968. *The Fred Chappell Reader*. Ed. Dabney Stuart. New York: St. Martin's, 1987. 47–163.

————. *Farewell, I'm Bound to Leave You*. New York: Picador, 1996.

————. *The Gaudy Place*. New York: Harcourt Brace, 1973.

————. *I Am One of You Forever*. Baton Rouge: Louisiana State University Press, 1985.

————. *It Is Time, Lord*. New York: Atheneum, 1963.

————. *Look Back All the Green Valley*. New York: Picador, 1999.

————. *Midquest: A Poem*. Baton Rouge: Louisiana State University Press, 1981.

————. *Moments of Light*. Los Angeles: New South, 1980.

————. *More Shapes Than One*. New York: St. Martin's, 1991.

————. "A Pact with Faustus." *Mississippi Quarterly* 37 (1984). Rpt. in *The Fred Chappell Reader*. Ed. Dabney Stuart. New York: St. Martin's, 1987.

————. *Plow Naked: Selected Writings on Poetry*. Ann Arbor: University of Michigan Press, 1993.

————. "The Surface of Earth." Review of *The Surface of Earth*, by Reynolds Price. *Duke Alumni Register* 62.1 (October 1975): 6.

Chodorow, Nancy. *The Reproduction of Mothering: Psychoanalysis and the Sociology of Gender*. Berkeley: University of California Press, 1978.

Clark, James W., Jr. "North Carolina, Literature of." *The Companion to Southern Literature: Themes, Genres, Places, People, Movements, and Motifs*. Eds. Joseph M. Flora and Lucinda H. MacKethan. Baton Rouge: Louisiana State University Press, 2002. 557–66.

Clarke, Cheryl. "The Failure to Transform: Homophobia in the Black Community." *Home Girls: A Black Feminist Anthology*. Ed. Barbara Smith. New York: Kitchen Table: Women of Color Press, 1983. 197–208.

Cloninger, Adam. Will and Estate Sale Records. Lincoln County Archives, Lincolnton, N.C.

"*Cold Mountain* by Charles Frazier." *Storylines Southeast* radio broadcast. Co-hosts Doris Betts and Darrell Stover. Sponsored by American Library Association and the National Endowment for the Humanities. WUNC-FM, Chapel Hill. November 14, 1999.

Congleton, J. E. *Theories of Pastoral Poetry in England, 1684–1798*. Gainesville: University of Florida Press, 1952.

de Crèvecoeur, J. Hector St. John. *Letters from an American Farmer*. 1782; London: J. M. Dent & Sons, 1912.

DeMott, Benjamin. "A Minor Faulkner." Review of *The Source of Light*, by Reynolds Price. *Saturday Review* 8.4 (April 1981): 72.

Donovan, Josephine. *Feminist Theory: The Intellectual Traditions of American Feminism*. New York: Ungar, 1985.

Douglass, Frederick. *Narrative of the Life of Frederick Douglass, an American Slave. Written by Himself*. 1845. *The Classic Slave Narratives*. Ed., Henry Louis Gates, Jr. New York: Mentor, 1987. 243–331.

Dunaway, Wilma A. *The First American Frontier: Transition to Capitalism in Southern Appalachia, 1700–1860*. Chapel Hill: University of North Carolina Press, 1996.

————. *Slavery in the American Mountain South*. Cambridge: Cambridge University Press, 2003.

Durrill, Wayne K. "Producing Poverty: Local Government and Economic Development in a New South County, 1874–1884," *Journal of American History* 71 (March 1985): 764–81.

Dvorak, Angeline Godwin. "Cooking as Mission and Ministry in Southern Culture: The Nurturers of Clyde Edgerton's *Walking across Egypt*, Fannie Flagg's *Fried Green Tomatoes at the Whistle Stop Café*, and Anne Tyler's *Dinner at the Homesick Restaurant*." *Southern Quarterly* 30.2–3 (119): 90–97.

Earley, Tony. "Charlotte." *Here We Are in Paradise*. New York: Little Brown, 1994. 33–55.
———. *Jim the Boy*. New York: Little, Brown, 2000.
———. "Letter from Sister: What We Learned at the P.O." *Oxford American* 25 (1999): 14–16.
———. "The Prophet from Jupiter." *Here We Are in Paradise*. New York: Little Brown, 1994. 3–32.
Edgerton, Clyde. *Clyde Edgerton Papers (1918–1992)*. No. 4616 Series 4.2, Box 23, Folder 134. In the Southern Historical Collection, Wilson Library, University of North Carolina at Chapel Hill.
———. *The Floatplane Notebooks*. Chapel Hill: Algonquin, 1988.
———. "Head Stung, Heart Stung." *Eudora Welty: Writers' Reflections upon First Reading Welty*. Ed. Pearl Amelia McHaney. Athens: Hill Street Press, 1999. 23–27.
———. *In Memory of Junior*. Chapel Hill: Algonquin, 1992.
———. *Killer Diller*. Chapel Hill: Algonquin, 1991.
———. *Lunch at the Piccadilly*. Chapel Hill: Algonquin, 2003
———. "On Ralph Waldo Emerson." *Books of Passage: 27 North Carolina Writers on the Books that Changed Their Lives*. Ed. David Perkins. Asheboro, N.C.: Down Home, 1997. 63–68.
———. *Raney*. Chapel Hill: Algonquin, 1985.
———. *Solo: My Adventures in the Air*. Chapel Hill: Algonquin, 2005.
———. *Walking across Egypt*. Chapel Hill: Algonquin, 1987.
———. *Where Trouble Sleeps*. Chapel Hill: Algonquin, 1997.
Eliot, T. S. *The Waste Land and Other Poems*. New York: Harvest, 1934.
Eller, Ronald D. *Miners, Millhands, and Mountaineers: Industrialization of the Appalachian South, 1880–1930*. Knoxville: University of Tennessee Press, 1982.
Elliot, Sara. "Interview with Clyde Edgerton: Conducted by students in English 110: Experience of Fiction at Northern Illinois University." April 13, 1995.
Emerson, Ralph Waldo. *Selected Writings of Emerson*. Ed. Donald McQuade. New York: Modern Library, 1981.
Engels, Frederick. *The Origin of the Family, Private Property, and the State*. 1884; New York: International, 1942.
Escott, Paul D. Introduction. *North Carolina Yeoman: The Diary of Basil Armstrong Thomasson, 1853–1826*, by Basil Armstrong Thomasson. Ed. Paul D. Escott. Athens: University of Georgia Press, 1996. xi–lxvi.
———. *Many Excellent People: Power and Privilege in North Carolina, 1850–1900*. Chapel Hill: University of North Carolina Press, 1985.
———. "Yeoman Independence and the Market: Social Status and Economic Development in Antebellum North Carolina," *North Carolina Historical Review* 66.3 (July 1989): 275–300.
Evans, Elizabeth. *Doris Betts*. New York: Twayne, 1997.
Farnham, Christie Anne, ed. *Women of the American South: A Multicultural Reader*. New York: New York University Press, 1997.
Faulkner, William. *Absalom, Absalom!* 1936; New York: Vintage, 1990.
———. "Address upon Receiving the Nobel Prize for Literature: Stockholm, December 10, 1950." *Essays, Speeches & Public Letters by William Faulkner*. Ed., James B. Meriwether. New York: Random House, 1965. 119–21.

Flora, Joseph M. "A Suitable Villain: Mormonism in Clyde Edgerton's *Redeye: A West-ern*." *Southern Quarterly* 38.1 (Fall 1999): 159–63.

Flora, Joseph M., and Robert Bain, eds. *Contemporary Fiction Writers of the South: A Bio-Bibliographical Sourcebook*. Westport, Conn.: Greenwood, 1993.

Flora, Joseph M., and Lucinda H. MacKethan. *The Companion to Southern Literature: Themes, Genres, Places, People, Movements, and Motifs*. Baton Rouge: Louisiana State University Press, 2002.

Flowers, Linda. *Throwed Away: Failures of Progress in Eastern North Carolina*. Knoxville: University of Tennessee Press, 1990.

Franklin, John Hope. *The Free Negro in North Carolina, 1790–1860*. 1943. Chapel Hill: University of North Carolina Press, 1995.

Frazier, Charles. *Cold Mountain*. New York: Atlantic Monthly Press, 1997.

Fredrickson, George M. *The Black Image in the White Mind: The Debate on Afro-American Character and Destiny, 1817–1914*. New York: Harper & Row, 1971.

———. Introduction. *The Impending Crisis of the South: How to Meet It*, by Hinton Rowan Helper. Ed. George M. Fredrickson. 1857; Cambridge, Mass.: Harvard University Press, 1968. ix–lxiii.

Freeman, Anne Hobson. "Penetrating a Small Patch of the Surface of Earth." *Virginia Quarterly Review* 51.4 (Autumn 1975): 637–41.

Freud, Sigmund. *Three Contributions to the Theory of Sex: The Basic Writings of Sigmund Freud*. Tr. and ed. A. A. Brill. 1905; New York: Random, 1938. 553–629.

Gaillard, Frye. "Black Politics in the 1980s." *Becoming Truly Free: 300 Years of Black History in the Carolinas*. Ed. Frye Gaillard. Charlotte: Charlotte Observer, 1985.

Garrett, George. Foreword. *Dream Garden*. Ed. Patrick Bizzaro. Baton Rouge: Louisiana State University Press, 1997. xiii–xv.

Gates, Henry Louis, Jr. Introduction. *Bearing Witness: Selections from African-American Autobiography in the Twentieth Century*. New York: Pantheon, 1991.

———. *The Signifying Monkey: A Theory of African-American Literary Criticism*. New York: Oxford University Press, 1988.

Geary, Bob. "Growing Pains: A Farmer's Bill of Rights Would Protect Small Growers Against Big Corporations. Does It Have a Chance in North Carolina?" *Independent Weekly*. February 7, 2001, 13–14.

Genovese, Eugene D. "Yeoman Farmers in a Slavehoders' Democracy," *Fruits of Merchant Capital: Slavery and Bourgeois Property in the Rise and Expansion of Capitalism*. Eds. Eugene D. Genovese and Elizabeth Fox-Genovese. New York: Oxford University Press, 1983. 249–64.

Gibbons, Kaye. *A Cure for Dreams*. Chapel Hill: Algonquin, 1991.

———. *Ellen Foster*. Chapel Hill: Algonquin, 1987.

———. *A Virtuous Woman*. Chapel Hill: Algonquin, 1989.

Gilman, Richard. "A Mastodon of a Novel, by Reynolds Price." 1975. *Critical Essays on Reynolds Price*. Ed. James Schiff. New York: G. K. Hall, 1998. 68–71.

Greene, Marti. "A Conversation with Doris Betts." *Carolina Quarterly* 52.2 (Spring 2000): 59–73.

Gurganus, Allan. *Oldest Living Confederate Widow Tells All*. New York: Knopf, 1989.

———. *Plays Well With Others*. New York: Knopf, 1997.

———. *White People*. New York: Knopf, 1991.

Hahn, Steven. "Class and State in Postemancipation Societies: Southern Planters in Comparative Perspective." *American Historical Review* 95 (1990): 83–98.

Hall, Jacquelyn Dowd, James Leloudis, Robert Korstad, Mary Murphy, Lu Ann Jones, and Christopher B. Daly. *Like a Family: The Making of a Southern Cotton Mill World,* Chapel Hill: University of North Carolina Press, 1987; New York: Norton, 1989.

Harris, David Golightly. *Piedmont Farmer: The Journals of David Golightly Harris, 1855–1870.* Ed. Philip N. Racine. Knoxville: University of Tennessee Press, 1990.

Harris, Trudier. *The Power of the Porch: The Storyteller's Craft in Zora Neale Hurston, Gloria Naylor, and Randall Kenan.* Athens: University of Georgia Press, 1996.

Harris, William C. *North Carolina and the Coming of the Civil War.* Raleigh: Division of Archives and History, North Carolina Department of Cultural Resources, 1988.

Harrison, Elizabeth Jane. *Female Pastoral: Women Writers Re-Visioning the American South.* Knoxville: University Tennessee Press, 1991.

Helper, Hinton Rowan. *The Impending Crisis of the South: How to Meet It.* 1857. Ed. George M. Fredrickson. Cambridge, Mass.: Harvard University Press, 1968.

Hennis, Sterling. "Clyde Edgerton (1944–)." *Contemporary Fiction Writers of the South: A Bio-Bibliographical Sourcebook.* Eds. Joseph M. Flora and Robert Bain. Westport, Conn.: Greenwood, 1993. 112–22.

Hicks, Orville. "Jack and the Heifer's Hide." *Jack Tales for Children of All Ages* [audio recording]. Whitesburg, Ky.: June Appal Recordings, 1990.

Hill, Dorothy Combs. *Lee Smith.* New York: Twayne, 1992.

Hobbs, Samuel Huntington, Jr. *North Carolina Economic and Social.* Chapel Hill: University of North Carolina Press, 1930.

Hobson, Fred. "Gerald White Johnson (1890–)." *Southern Writers: A Biographical Dictionary.* Eds. Robert Bain, Joseph M. Flora, and Louis D. Rubin, Jr. Baton Rouge: Louisiana State University Press, 1979. 247–49.

———. *The Southern Writer in the Postmodern World.* Athens: University of Georgia Press, 1991.

———. *Tell about the South: The Southern Rage to Explain.* 1983. Baton Rouge: Louisiana State University Press, 1998.

———. "Wilbur Joseph Cash (1900–1941)." *Southern Writers: A Biographical Dictionary.* Eds. Robert Bain, Joseph M. Flora, and Louis D. Rubin, Jr. Baton Rouge: Louisiana State University Press, 1979. 71–72.

Hoffman, Laban Miles. *Our Kin.* 1915; Baltimore: Gateway Press, 1980.

Holman, David Marion. "Faith and the Unanswerable Questions: The Fiction of Doris Betts." *Southern Literary Journal* 15.1 (Fall 1982): 15–22.

Holman, John. *Luminous Mysteries.* New York: Harcourt Brace, 1998.

———. *Squabble and Other Stories.* New York: Ticknor and Fields, 1990.

Hovis, George. "Assuming the Mantle of Storyteller: Fred Chappell and Frontier Humor." *The Enduring Legacy of Old Southwest Humor.* Ed. Ed Piacentino. Baton Rouge: Louisiana State University Press, 2006. 156–73.

———. "Darker Vices and Nearly Incomprehensible Sins: The Fate of Poe in Fred Chappell's Early Novels." *More Lights Than One: On The Fiction of Fred Chappell.* Ed. Patrick Bizzaro. Louisiana State University Press, 2004. 28–50.

———. "'I Contain Multitudes': Randall Kenan's *Walking on Water* as Collective Autobiography." *Southern Literary Journal* 36.2 (Spring 2004): 100–125.

———. "Industry Meets Agriculture: The Emergence of the Farmer/Peddler in the Carolina Piedmont." *North Carolina Folklore Journal* 41.1 (1994): 24–34.

———. "An Interview with Fred Chappell." *Carolina Quarterly* 52.1 (Fall/Winter 1999): 67–79.

———. "The Legacy of Thomas Wolfe in Contemporary North Carolina Fiction." *Thomas Wolfe Review* 29.1 and 2 (2005): 76–90.

———. "The *Raney* Controversy: Clyde Edgerton's Battle with Campbell University over Creative Freedom." *Southern Cultures* (Summer 2001): 60–83.

———. "'When You Got True Dirt, You Got Everything You Need': Forging an Appalachian Arcadia in Fred Chappell's *Midquest*." *Mississippi Quarterly* 53.3 (Summer 2000): 389–414.

Hovis, George, and Timothy Williams. "Old Times on the Haw: An Interview with Dale Ray Phillips." *Carolina Quarterly* 55.3 (Summer 2003): 63–73.

Hyde, Samuel C., Jr., ed. *Plain Folk of the South Revisited*. Baton Rouge: Louisiana State University Press, 1997.

Inge, M. Thomas. *Faulkner, Sut, and Other Southerners*. West Cornwall, Conn.: Locust Hill, 1992.

Iser, Wolfgang. *Spenser's Arcadia: The Interrelation of Fiction and History*. Protocol of the Thirty-Eighth Colloquy: April 13, 1980. The Center for Hermeneutical Studies in Hellenistic and Modern Culture. The Graduate Theological Union and the University of California. Berkeley, Calif.: 1980.

Jefferson, Thomas. *Notes on the State of Virginia*. 1787. Ed. William Peden. Chapel Hill: University of North Carolina Press, 1955.

Jennings, Ben. "Language and Reality in Lee Smith's *Oral History*." *Iron Mountain Review* 3.1 (1986): 10–14.

Jones, Anne Goodwyn. "The World of Lee Smith." *Southern Quarterly* 22.1 (1983): 115–39.

Jones, Rev. Thomas H. "The Experience of Rev. Thomas H. Jones, Who Was a Slave for Forty-Three Years." *North Carolina Slave Narratives: The Lives of Moses Roper, Lunsford Lane, Moses Grandy, & Thomas H. Jones*. Ed. William L. Andrews. 1885. Chapel Hill: University of North Carolina Press, 2003. 203–79.

Kaufman, Wallace. "Portrait of the Artist as a Young Voyeur." *Reynolds Price: From A Long and Happy Life to Good Hearts, With a Bibliography*. Proceedings of the Seventh Annual Southern Writers' Symposium, Methodist College, April 15–16, 1988. Eds. Sue Laslie Kimball and Lynn Veach Sadler. Fayetteville, North Carolina: Methodist College Press, 1989. 7–13.

Kenan, Randall. "'If I Could Tell You, I Would Let You Know': Author Perspective/Reader Perception of Gay Characters in Literature." Panel at the Tennessee Williams/New Orleans Literary Festival, March 31, 1996. Panel Moderator, Mark Zumpe.

———. *Let the Dead Bury Their Dead*. New York: Harcourt Brace, 1992.

———. *A Visitation of Spirits*. New York: Grove, 1989.

———. *Walking on Water: Black American Lives at the Turn of the Twenty-First Century*. New York: Knopf, 1999.

Kenny, Vincent S. "Paul Green (1894–)." *Southern Writers: A Biographical Dictionary*. Eds. Robert Bain, Joseph M. Flora, and Louis D. Rubin, Jr. Baton Rouge: Louisiana State University Press, 1979. 193–94.

Kenzer, Robert C. *Enterprising Southerners: Black Economic Success in North Carolina, 1865–1915*. Charlottesville: University Press of Virginia, 1997.

———. *Kinship and Neighborhood in a Southern Community: Orange County, North Carolina, 1849–1881*. Knoxville: University of Tennessee Press, 1987.

Kermode, Frank. *English Pastoral Poetry: From the Beginnings to Marvell*. New York: Barnes & Noble, 1952.

Ketchin, Susan. *The Christ-Haunted Landscape: Faith and Doubt in Southern Fiction*. Jackson: University Press of Mississippi, 1994.

King, Lovalerie. "The Birth of a Nation." *The Companion to Southern Literature: Themes, Genres, Places, People, Movements, and Motifs*. Eds. Joseph M. Flora and Lucinda H. MacKethan. Baton Rouge: Louisiana State University Press, 2002. 104–5.

King, Wayne. "The Case against the Wilmington Ten." *New York Times Magazine*. December 3, 1978.

Koch, Frederick H., ed. *Carolina Folk Plays*. New York: Henry Holt, 1922.

Kreyling, Michael. *Inventing Southern Literature*. Jackson: University Press of Mississippi, 1998.

———. "Reynolds Price." *The History of Southern Literature*. Ed. Louis D. Rubin, Jr., Blyden Jackson, Rayburn S. Moore, Lewis P. Simpson, and Thomas Daniel Young. Baton Rouge: Louisiana State University Press, 1985. 518–22.

Lane, Lunsford. "The Narrative of Lunsford Lane, formerly of Raleigh, N.C." *North Carolina Slave Narratives: The Lives of Moses Roper, Lunsford Lane, Moses Grandy, & Thomas H. Jones*. Ed. William L. Andrews. 1842. Chapel Hill: University of North Carolina Press, 2003. 93–130.

Lang, John. "Points of Kinship: Community and Allusion in Fred Chappell's *Midquest*." *Dream Garden*. Ed. Patrick Bizzaro. Baton Rouge: Louisiana State University Press, 1997. 97–117.

———. *Understanding Fred Chappell*. Columbia: University of South Carolina Press, 2000.

———. "Windies and Rusties: Fred Chappell as Humorist." *More Lights Than One: The Fiction of Fred Chappell*. Ed., Patrick Bizzaro. Baton Rouge: Louisiana State University Press, 2004.

Lefler, Hugh Talmage. *North Carolina Told by Contemporaries*. Chapel Hill: University of North Carolina Press, 1965.

Lefler, Hugh Talmage, and Albert Ray Newsome. *The History of North Carolina*. Chapel Hill: University of North Carolina Press, 1963.

Lockhart, Robert, Steve Haughney, and David Olson. "Interview with Reynolds Price." (*Ariel*, 1972). *Conversations with Reynolds Price*. Ed. Jefferson Humphries. Jackson: University Press of Mississippi, 1991. 36–49.

Logan, Frenise A. *The Negro in North Carolina, 1876–1894*. Chapel Hill: University of North Carolina Press, 1964.

Longstreet, Augustus Baldwin. "The Fight." *Georgia Scenes, Characters, Incidents, &c., in the First Half Century of the Republic*. 1935; Savannah, Georgia: Beehive Press, 1992.

Lynn, Kenneth S. *Mark Twain and Southwestern Humor*. Westport, Conn.: Greenwood, 1972.

MacKethan, Lucinda Hardwick. *The Dream of Arcady: Place and Time in Southern Literature*. Baton Rouge: Louisiana State University Press, 1980.

Marshall, Paule. *Praisesong for the Widow*. 1929. New York: Putnam's, 1983.

Maschal, Richard. "1965–1980: A Transformation." *Becoming Truly Free: 300 Years of Black History in the Carolinas*. Ed. Frye Gaillard. Charlotte: Charlotte Observer, 1985.

Mason, Julian. "Charles Waddell Chesnutt (1858–1932)." *Southern Writers: A Biographical Dictionary*. Eds. Robert Bain, Joseph M. Flora, and Louis D. Rubin, Jr. Baton Rouge: Louisiana State University Press, 1979. 77–79.

———. "Kaye Gibbons (1960–)." *Contemporary Fiction Writers of the South: A Bio-Bibliographical Sourcebook*. Eds. Joseph M. Flora and Robert Bain. Westport, Conn.: Greenwood, 1993. 156–68.

McCorkle, Jill. "Gold Mine." *Crash Diet*. Chapel Hill: Algonquin, 1992.

McCurry, Stephanie. "Producing Dependence: Women, Work, and Yeoman Households in Low-Country South Carolina." *Neither Lady nor Slave: Working Women of the Old South*. Eds. Susanna Delfino and Michele Gillespie. Chapel Hill: University of North Carolina Press, 2002. 55–71.

McFee, Michael. "The Epigrammatical Fred Chappell." *Southern Literary Journal* 31.2 (1999): 95–108.

———. Introduction. *This Is Where We Live: Short Stories by 25 Contemporary North Carolina Writers*. Ed. Michael McFee. Chapel Hill: University of North Carolina Press, 2000.

McLaurin, Tim. *The Acorn Plan*. New York: Norton, 1988.

———. *Keeper of the Moon*. New York: Norton, 1991.

———. *Lola*. Asheboro, N.C.: Down Home Press, 1997.

McMillen, Sally G. "Southern Women and the Sunday-School Movement, 1865–1915." Hyde, *Plain Folk of the South Revisited* 129–60.

McRuer, Robert. "A Visitation of Difference: Randall Kenan and Black Queer Theory." *Critical Essays: Gay and Lesbian Writers of Color*. Ed. Emmanuel S. Nelson. New York: Haworth, 1993. 221–32.

Menius, Arthur C., III. "James Bennitt: Portrait of an Antebellum Yeoman." *North Carolina Historical Review* 8 (1981): 305–26.

Mill News. High Shoals Cotton Mill Company, High Shoals, N.C., October 14, 1920.

Mills, Jerry Leath. "Tim McLaurin (1953–)." *Contemporary Fiction Writers of the South: A Bio-Bibliographical Sourcebook*. Eds. Joseph M. Flora and Robert Bain. Westport, Conn.: Greenwood, 1993. 303–10.

Mitchell, Carol. "Some Differences in Male and Female Joke-Telling." In *Women's Folklore, Women's Culture*. Eds. Rosan A. Jordan and Susan J. Kalcik. Philadelphia: University of Pennsylvania Press, 1985. 163–86.

Morgan, Robert. *Gap Creek*. Chapel Hill: Algonquin, 1999.

———. "O Lost, and Found." *Thomas Wolfe Review* 24.2 (Fall 2000): 3–9.

———. "Poinsett's Bridge." *The Mountains Won't Remember Us and Other Stories*. Atlanta: Peachtree, 1992. 1–22.

———. *Topsoil Road*. Baton Rouge: Louisiana State University Press, 2000.

Mosby, Charmaine Allmon. "Gilmore Simms' Mississippi Yeomen." *McNeese Review* 30 (1983–1984): 3–11.

Murphy, Bruce, ed. *Benét's Reader's Encyclopedia*. 4th ed. New York: HarperCollins, 1996.

Myerson, Michael. *Nothing Could Be Finer*. New York: International Publishers, 1978.

Nero, Charles I. "Toward a Black Gay Aesthetic: Signifying in Contemporary Black Gay Literature." 1991. *African American Literary Theory: A Reader*. Ed. Winston Napier. New York: New York University Press, 2000. 399–420.

Newby, I. A. *Plain Folk in the New South: Social Change and Cultural Persistence, 1880–1915*. Baton Rouge: Louisiana State University Press, 1989.

Oakes, James. *The Ruling Race: A History of American Slaveholders*. New York: Knopf, 1982.

Olmsted, Frederick Law. *A Journey in the Seaboard Slave States; With Remarks on Their Economy*. New York: Dix and Edwards, 1856.

Owsley, Frank L. *Plain Folk of the Old South*. Baton Rouge: Louisiana State University Press, 1949.

Parish, Nancy C. *Lee Smith, Annie Dillard, and the Hollins Group: A Genesis of Writers*. Baton Rouge: Louisiana State University Press, 1998.

Percy, William Alexander. *Lanterns on the Levee: Recollections of a Planter's Son*. 1941; Louisiana State University Press, 1993.

Phillips, Dale Ray. *My People's Waltz*. New York: Norton, 1999.

Poe, Edgar Allan. "The Poetic Principle." *Edgar Allan Poe: Selected Prose, Poetry, and Eureka*. New York: Rinehart, 1950.

Powell, Dannye Romine. "Interview with Reynolds Price." 1988. *Parting the Curtains: Interviews by Dannye Romine Powell*. New York: Anchor, 1994.

Powell, William S. *North Carolina through Four Centuries*. Chapel Hill: University of North Carolina Press, 1989.

Price, Reynolds. "An Awful Gift and a Blindness." *Southern Review* (Spring 2000): 385–394.

———. "A Chain of Love." *The Collected Stories*. New York: Atheneum, 1993.

———. *Clear Pictures*. New York: Atheneum, 1989.

———. *Kate Vaiden*. New York: Atheneum, 1986.

———. *A Long and Happy Life*. New York: Atheneum, 1962.

———. *The Promise of Rest*. New York: Scribner, 1995.

———. *The Surface of Earth*. New York: Atheneum, 1975.

———. *The Tongues of Angels*. New York: Atheneum, 1990.

Raban, Jonathan. "In the Cool, Green Archipelago of Seattle, Seclusion Reigns and Every Home Is an Island: America's Most Private City." *Travel Holiday*, November 1991, 60.

Racine, Philip N. Introduction. David Golightly Harris. *Piedmont Farmer: The Journals of David Golightly Harris, 1855–1870*. Ed. Philip N. Racine. Knoxville: University of Tennessee Press, 1990. 1–26.

Ragan, David Paul. "Flying by Night: An Early Interview with Fred Chappell" *North Carolina Literary Review* 7 (1998): 111.

———. "Fred Chappell (1936–)." *Contemporary Poets, Dramatists, Essayists, and Novelists of the South: A Bio-Bibliographical Sourcebook*, eds. Robert Bain and Joseph M. Flora (Westport, Conn.: Greenwood, 1994). 91–103.

Ransom, John Crowe, et al. Introduction. *I'll Take My Stand: The South and the Agrarian Tradition*. 1930; Baton Rouge: Louisiana State University Press, 1977.

Raper, Julius. "Inventing Modern Southern Fiction: A Postmodern View." *Southern Literary Journal* 22 (Spring 1990): 3–18.

Reed, John Shelton. *The Enduring South: Subcultural Persistence in Mass Society*. Chapel Hill: University of North Carolina Press, 1986.

Riddle, Wesley Allen. "The Origins of Black Sharecropping." *Mississippi Quarterly* 49.1 (Winter 1995–96): 53–71.

Robbins, Kenn. "A Conversation with Clyde Edgerton." *Southern Quarterly* 30.1 (1991): 59–65.

Rogers, John J. W. "Piedmont." *The Companion to Southern Literature: Themes, Genres, Places, People, Movements, and Motifs.* Eds. Joseph M. Flora and Lucinda H. MacKethan. Baton Rouge: Louisiana State University Press, 2002. 645–46.

Romine, Scott. *The Narrative Forms of Southern Community.* Baton Rouge: Louisiana State University Press, 1999.

Rooke, Constance. *Reynolds Price.* Boston: Twayne, 1983.

Ross, Marlon B. "Some Glances at the Black Fag: Race, Same-Sex Desire, and Cultural Belonging." 1994. *African American Literary Theory: A Reader.* Ed. Winston Napier. New York: New York University Press, 2000. 498–522.

Rubin, Louis D., Jr. "Thomas Wolfe and the Place He Came From." *A Gallery of Southerners.* Baton Rouge: Louisiana State University Press, 1982. 67–84.

Sadler, Lynn Veach. "The 'Mystical Grotesque' in the Life and Works of Reynolds Price." *Southern Literary Journal* 21.2 (Spring 1989): 27–40.

Salmond, John A. *Gastonia 1929: The Story of the Loray Mill Strike.* Chapel Hill: University of North Carolina Press, 1995.

Salstrom, Paul. *Appalachia's Path to Dependency: Rethinking a Region's Economic History, 1730–1940.* Lexington: University Press of Kentucky, 1994.

Sanders, Lynn Moss. "'The People Who Seem to Matter Most to Me': Folklore as an Agent of Social Change in the Work of Howard W. Odum and Paul Green." *Southern Literary Journal* 24 (Spring 1992): 62–75.

Schenck, Carl Alwin. *The Birth of Forestry in America: Biltmore Forest School, 1898–1913.* Santa Cruz, Calif.: Forest History Society, 1974.

Schiff, James A. *Understanding Reynolds Price.* Columbia: University of South Carolina Press, 1996.

Schlotterbeck, John T. "The 'Social Economy' of an Upper South Community: Orange and Greene Counties, Virginia, 1815–1860." *Class, Conflict, and Consensus: Antebellum Southern Community Studies.* Eds. Orville Vernon Burton and Robert C. McMath, Jr. Westport, Conn.: Greenwood, 1982.

Scura, Dorothy. "Doris Betts (1932–)." *Fifty Southern Writers After 1900: A Bio-Bibliographical Sourcebook.* Ed. Joseph M. Flora and Robert Bain. New York: Greenwood, 1987. 161–79.

———. "Doris Betts at Mid-Career: Her Voice and Her Art." *Southern Women Writers: The New Generation.* Ed. Tonette Bond Inge. Tuscaloosa: University of Alabama Press, 1990. 161–79.

Sisk, Taylor. "Do, Tell: Allan Gurganus, Genial Troublemaker, On Living and Imagining the Local Life." *Independent Weekly,* September 8, 1999, 10+.

Smith, Lee. *The Devil's Dream.* New York: Putnam's, 1992.

———. *Fair and Tender Ladies.* New York: Putnam's, 1988.

———. *Family Linen.* New York: Putnam's, 1985.

———. *The Last Day the Dogbushes Bloomed.* New York: Harper and Row, 1968.

———. *The Last Girls.* Chapel Hill: Algonquin, 2002.

———. "News of the Spirit." *News of the Spirit: Stories.* New York: Putnam's, 1997. 203–67.

———. *Oral History.* New York: Putnam's, 1983.

———. *Saving Grace.* New York: Putnam's, 1995.

————. "Tongues of Fire." *Me and My Baby View the Eclipse: Stories*. New York: Putnam's, 1990. 71–116.

Smith, Lillian. *Killers of the Dream*. New York: Norton, 1949.

Smith, Virginia A. "On Regionalism, Women's Writing, and Writing as a Woman: A Conversation with Lee Smith." *Southern Review* 26 (1990): 784–95.

Sopko, John, and John Carr. "Dealing with the Grotesque: Fred Chappell." In *Kite Flying and Other Irrational Acts: Conversations with Twelve Southern Writers*. Ed. John Carr. Baton Rouge: Louisiana State University Press, 1972.

Sparks, William H. *The Memories of Fifty Years*. Philadelphia: Claxton, Remsen & Haffelinger, 1870.

Stepto, Robert B. *From Behind the Veil: A Study of Afro-American Narrative*. 2nd ed. Chicago: University of Illinois Press, 1991.

Stewart, Dabney. Introduction. *The Fred Chappell Reader*. Ed. Dabney Stuart. New York: St. Martin's, 1987.

Sullivan, Walter. "The New Faustus: The Southern Renascence and the Joycean Aesthetic." *Southern Fiction Today: Renascence and Beyond*. Ed. George Core. Athens: University Georgia Press, 1969. 1–15.

Thomas, Larry Reni. *The True Story Behind the Wilmington Ten*. Hampton, Va.: U.B. and U.S. Communications Systems, 1993.

Thomasson, Basil Armstrong. *North Carolina Yeoman: The Diary of Basil Armstrong Thomasson, 1853–1826*. Ed. Paul D. Escott. Athens: University of Georgia Press, 1996.

Turkle, Sherry. *Life on the Screen: Identity in the Age of the Internet*. New York: Simon & Schuster, 1995.

Underwood, Thomas A. *Allen Tate: Orphan of the South*. Princeton, N.J.: Princeton University Press, 2000.

Wain, John. "Mantle of Faulkner?" *New Republic*, May 14, 1966, 31–33.

Warren, Robert Penn. "The Use of the Past." *New and Selected Essays*. New York: Random House, 1989. 29–55.

Watson, Harry L. "Conflict and Collaboration: Yeomen, Slaveholders, and Politics in the Antebellum South." *Social History* 10 (October 1985): 273–98.

Watson, Ritchie Devon, Jr. "Frontier Yeoman Versus Cavalier: The Dilemma of Antebellum Southern Fiction." *The Frontier Experience and the American Dream: Essays on American Literature*. Eds. David Mogen, Mark Busby, and Paul Bryant. College Station: Texas A&M University Press, 1989. 107–19.

————. "Yeoman." *The Companion to Southern Literature: Themes, Genres, Places, People, Movements, and Motifs*. Eds. Joseph M. Flora and Lucinda H. MacKethan. Baton Rouge: Louisiana State University Press, 2002. 1008–11.

————. *Yeoman Versus Cavalier: The Old Southwest's Fictional Road to Rebellion*. Baton Rouge: Louisiana State University Press, 1993.

Weaks-Baxter, Mary. *Reclaiming the American Farmer: The Reinvention of a Regional Mythology in Twentieth-Century Southern Writing*. Baton Rouge: Louisiana State University Press, 2006.

Welty, Eudora. "Place in Fiction." *A Modern Southern Reader*. Eds. Ben Forkner and Patrick Samway. Atlanta: Peachtree, 1986.

West, Robert. "The Art of Far and Near: An Interview with Robert Morgan." *Carolina Quarterly* 49.3 (1997): 46–68.

Whiting, Bail J., Senior Advisor. "GPF Reports on the Competition: North Carolina: The Research Triangle Park and 'Charlotte, USA.'" Philadelphia: Greater Philadelphia First, 2002. www.gpf.biz.

Williams, S. D. "Reynolds Price on the South, Literature, and Himself." *Conversations with Reynolds Price*, ed. Jefferson Humphries. 1987. Jackson: University Press of Mississippi, 1991. 277–83.

Woodward, C. Vann. *Origins of the New South, 1877–1913*. Baton Rouge: Louisiana State University Press, 1951.

Wyatt-Brown, Bertram. *Southern Honor: Ethics and Behavior in the Old South*. New York: Oxford University Press, 1982.

INDEX

318 INDEX

Edgerton, Clyde, (*continued*)
183, 186, 195, 211; Durham County,
N.C., 18; feminism, 204; *The Floatplane
Notebooks*, 180–83, 189, 204, 211,
212–25; frontier humor, 185, 210; gender roles, 186–201, 205–6; humor, 185,
220; *Killer Diller*, 181, 183, 189; *Lunch
at the Piccadilly*, 183, 211; masculinity,
20, 181, 192, 194, 198, 201–2, 205–6,
208–9, 212, 223–25; matriarchy, 20,
180, 182, 187, 191–93, 196, 198–201,
212; *In Memory of Junior*, 180–81, 183,
202–12, 213, 225, 252; modernity,
181–82, 202, 208, 210, 213, 215; music,
181; pastoral, 215; Piedmont, 20, 180,
219; race relations, 17–18, 20, 22, 23,
59, 82, 188–91, 201, 221–23, 294n1;
Raney, 17, 82, 180–85, 186–201, 202,
203–5, 208, 212–13, 221, 225, 249,
252, 256; *Redeye*, 181, 183, 189; religion, 20, 181, 183, 185, 189, 191–92,
195–96, 212, 217, 219; satire, 184; sexuality, 182, 197; social class, 203–4,
206–7; *Solo*, 183; transcendentalism,
183, 224–25; Vietnam War, 216–17,
219, 221; *Walking Across Egypt*, 181,
183; *Where Trouble Sleeps*, 180, 183,
186–87, 188, 197, 212, 225
egalitarianism, 16–18, 27, 29, 47, 48, 52,
97, 134, 234, 270
Eliot, T. S., 102, 119
Eller, Ronald D., 98
Ellison, Ralph, 246
Emerson, Ralph Waldo, 135, 183, 217, 224
Engels, Frederick, 192
Episcopal church, 32, 71, 94
Escott, Paul D., 4, 5, 11, 14, 16, 27, 39,
40, 43, 214
evangelicalism, 39, 40, 141
Evans, Walker, 65, 145
evil, 33, 49, 50, 65, 165, 186, 188, 216,
237, 245, 264

faculty, 23, 134
faith, 31–33, 50–52, 124, 129, 224
family; history, 17, 97, 162, 195, 218; saga,
4, 138, 141–42, 184
farm, 2, 11, 12, 14, 18, 23, 25, 27–29,
75–79, 98, 99, 100, 112, 114–18,

144–48, 151–54, 173, 180, 202–4,
206–8; ownership, 2, 78, 79, 113 (*see
also* farmland; farmer, landless; tenant
farmers); women, 49, 148. *See also* agriculture; life, 20, 26, 117–18, 173, 180,
206–7
farmer father, 118, 128
farmers, 4, 11, 12, 14, 15, 22, 24–28, 31,
32, 47, 48, 59, 73–78, 98–100, 105,
112, 135–37, 180–81, 207–8; black, 6,
20, 227, 229, 240; landless, 1, 5, 27,
111, 113, 134 (*see also* farm ownership;
farmland; land; tenant farmers); small,
13, 14, 24, 44, 59, 76–78
Farmers' Alliance, 227
farming, 2, 58, 117, 121, 124, 135, 164,
241, 278, 280; cattle, 25; community,
58, 68, 124, 126, 130, 135, 202, 229,
248; families, 14, 25, 28, 66, 83, 124;
history, 202; hog, 25 (*see also* hog
killing; industry, hog); poultry, 25, 280
(*see also* industry, poultry)
farmland, 99, 181, 208, 213. *See also* farm
ownership; farmer, landless; land
Farnham, Christie Anne, 39
Faulkner, William, 5, 6, 7, 11, 58, 61, 63,
64, 84, 86–88, 99, 102, 106, 115, 143,
157, 163, 184–85, 225, 252–54, 261,
267
Fayetteville, North Carolina, 8, 265,
273–74
fighting, 273; dog, 273. *See also* cockfighting
fish kill, 280
fishing, 183, 206, 208, 211, 274–75
Flora, Joseph M., 184
Florida, 161, 211–14, 220, 250
flying, plane, 200, 206, 214, 220
folklore, 8, 118, 146, 167, 170, 190, 259,
261, 266, 268
football, 117, 200, 214, 221. *See also*
sports
Fort Bragg, North Carolina, 273
Franklin, Benjamin, 111, 132, 134, 136
Franklin, John Hope, 6, 248
Franklin, North Carolina, 278
Frazier, Charles, 100, 138, 270, 277–79
Frederickson, George M., 13, 44
Freeman, Mary Wilkins, 108

See also farm ownership; farmer, land-
less; farmland
Lane, Lunsford, 9, 226–27
Lanier, Sidney, 99
Las Vegas, Nevada, 232, 242–43
Lee, Howard, 85
Lightner, Clarence, 85
Live-at-Home movement, 11
Logan, Frenise A., 85
Longstreet, Augustus Baldwin, 209
Los Angeles, California, 93, 235, 242,
244–45
Louisiana, 232
Louisiana State University Press, 100
lower-class community members, 71
Lower South. See Deep South
lumber. See industry, extractive; timber
lynching, 81, 221–22
Lynn, Kenneth, 122
Lytle, Andrew, 8

MacKethan, Lucinda H., 99
Macon, North Carolina, 74
Madison, Wisconsin, 236
Maidstone, Saskatchewan, 240
Malcolm X, 245
management, 27, 28, 30, 36
market economy, 11, 13, 14, 17, 24, 43,
44, 48, 75, 111, 116
Marquez, Gabriel García, 143
marriage, 53, 54, 86, 90, 91, 140–41, 143,
161, 172, 182, 189, 193, 201–2, 219,
227, 275, 277
Marshall, Paule, 247
Maschal, Richard, 85
Mason, Bobbie Ann, 201
mass communication, 280
McCorkle, Jill, 3, 185, 272–73
McCullers, Carson, 201
McCurry, Stephanie, 14, 48, 147
McFee, Michael, 3, 21, 102, 275
McLaurin, Tim, 72, 273–74
McMillen, Sally G., 195–96
McRuer, Robert, 260
Mecklenburg Historical Society, 1
Mencken, H. L., 10, 52
Methodist church, 39, 114, 141, 157. See
also Protestant church
Micheaux, Oscar, 239

Midwest, 57, 232, 240, 280
military, 53, 60, 217, 228, 258
mill town, 22, 23, 25–30, 36, 37, 49
Millennial Gathering of Southern Writers,
84
mills, paper, 99, 100, 118, 136. See also
Chappell, Fred; Champion Paper Company; timber
mills, textile. See industry, textile;
textiles
Milosz, Czeslaw, 50
Milton, John, 64, 86, 169, 176, 213
mining, coal, 98, 138–39, 164, 171, 175
minister, 106, 187, 192, 196, 254–55, 262,
266. See also preacher
Minneapolis, Minnesota, 243–44
minstrelcy, 123, 185
miscegenation, 86, 87, 188, 203, 253
Mississippi, 3, 6, 49, 72, 122, 253, 264
money, 14, 27, 48, 78, 86, 111–12, 114,
134, 158–59, 250
moonshine, 114, 123, 210–11
Morgan, Robert, 3, 6, 100, 138, 276–77
mountaineer, 19, 61, 84, 98, 101, 103,
109, 113, 121, 131, 134, 138–39, 146,
148, 189; women, 128, 138
mountains, 1, 2, 19, 97, 98, 103–4,
107–8, 110–11, 142, 145–48, 150–52,
155–58, 162–64, 167–72, 174–75,
177–78, 277–78. See also Appalachia
mule, 25, 112, 123, 152, 154, 234
music, 199, 204; baroque, 64; fiddle, 151;
gospel, 244; pop, 176; traditional bluegrass, 43
musical instruments, 76

Nabokov, Vladimir, 261
narrators, 129–30, 151, 157, 184, 216,
219, 259
Nash County, N.C., 272
Nashville Agrarians, 8, 31, 55, 65
nation, 9, 10, 93, 98, 215, 228, 233, 235,
241, 247, 271, 279
Navy, U.S., 68. See also military
Nero, Charles I., 255
New Bern, North Carolina, 59
New South, 10, 31, 36, 44
New York, New York, 235
Nietzsche, Friedrich, 32